THE FAMILY ALBUM OF
FAVORITE POEMS

THE FAMILY ALBUM OF

FAVORITE POEMS

EDITED BY

P. EDWARD ERNEST

ILLUSTRATED BY

LEONARD VOSBURGH

GROSSET & DUNLAP *Publishers* NEW YORK

PRINTED IN THE UNITED STATES OF AMERICA

ACKNOWLEDGMENTS

THE Editor and Grosset & Dunlap, Inc. gratefully acknowledge the permission granted by the following authors, publishers, and authors' representatives to reprint selections from their publications. Recognition is also made of indebtedness, even when unspecified, to poets and original publishers for the use of many poems which are now in the public domain.

J. ALBERT & SON PTY. LTD. for "Heaven Will Protect the Working Girl" by Edgar Smith. Used by permission of the publishers as Owners of the Copyright for Australia and New Zealand.

YOUNG E. ALLISON III for "Derelict" by Young E. Allison.

LOUISE ANDREWS for "The Purple Cow" from *The Burgess Nonsense Book* by Gelett Burgess.

EDWARD ARNOLD (PUBLISHERS) LTD. for "Tenderheartedness," "Misfortunes Never Come Singly," "Mr. Jones," and "Aunt Eliza" by Harry Graham. Reprinted by permission of the publishers.

THE ATLANTA CONSTITUTION for "Tollable Well" by Frank L. Stanton.

FRANCIS H. BANGS for " 'Don't Care' and 'Never Mind' " by John Kendrick Bangs.

ERNEST BENN LIMITED for "The Spell of the Yukon," "The Shooting of Dan McGrew," and "The Cremation of Sam McGee" by Robert Service from *The Collected Poems of Robert Service.*

MARTHA T. BENNETT for "The Flag Goes By" by Henry Holcomb Bennett.

WILLIAM BLACKWOOD & SONS LTD. for "The Highwayman" from *Collected Poems, Volume I* by Alfred Noyes.

THE BOBBS-MERRILL COMPANY, INC. for "When the Frost Is on the Punkin" and "The Old Swimmin'-Hole" from *Neghborly Poems,* "A Barefoot Boy" from *Armazindy,* "Out to Old Aunt Mary's" from *Afterwhiles,* "Little Orphant Annie" from *Rhymes of Childhood,* and "The Old Times Were the Best" from *The Complete Works of James Whitcomb Riley,* all by James Whitcomb Riley; "Keep a-Goin' " and "Sweetes' L'i'l' Feller" from *Songs from Dixie Land* by Frank L. Stanton.

BERTON BRALEY for his poem "Do It Now."

BRANDT & BRANDT for "Music I Heard" from *Collected Poems* by Conrad Aiken.

JONATHAN CAPE LIMITED for "Leisure" by W. H. Davies from *The Collected Poems of W. H. Davies,* and used also by permission of Mrs. H. M. Davies.

CHATTO & WINDUS, LTD. for "The Groundhog" from *Selected Poems* by Richard Eberhart; "Greater Love," "Arms and the Boy," and "Anthem for Doomed Youth" by Wilfred Owen from *Poems of Wilfred Owen.*

CLARKE & WAY, INC. for "Spring Air" and "Elegy on Gordon Barber" by Gene Derwood from *The Poems of Gene Derwood,* published by Clarke & Way, Inc.

v

CONSOLIDATED MUSIC PUBLISHERS, INC. for "Silver Threads Among the Gold" by Eben E. Rexford.

CRITERION BOOKS, INC. for "Sonnet to My Mother." Reprinted from George Barker: Collected Poems, 1930–1955, Copyright © 1957 by George Granville Barker. By permission of the publishers, Criterion Books, Inc.

E. E. CUMMINGS for his poem "what if a much of a which of a wind," copyright, 1944, by E. E. Cummings. Reprinted by permission from Poems 1923–1954 (Harcourt, Brace and Company).

CURTIS BROWN LTD. for "The Sea-Gull," "The Turtle," "Reflections on Ice-Breaking," and "Portrait of the Artist as a Prematurely Old Man" from Many Long Years Ago by Ogden Nash.

J. CURWEN & SONS LTD. for "Onward Christian Soldiers" by Sabine Baring-Gould. Reprinted by permission.

THE JOHN DAY COMPANY, INC. for "Fife Tune" from Selected Verse by John Manifold. Copyright 1946 by The John Day Company. Used also by permission of Messrs. Dennis Dobson, Ltd.

J. M. DENT & SONS, LTD. for "Do Not Go Gentle Into That Good Night" and "A Refusal to Mourn the Death, by Fire, of a Child in London" by Dylan Thomas.

DODD, MEAD & COMPANY, INC. for "The Soldier" and "The Great Lover" by Rupert Brooke, reprinted from The Collected Poems of Rupert Brooke. Copyright 1915 by Dodd, Mead & Company, Copyright 1941 by Edward Marsh; "Kashmiri Song," reprinted from India's Love Lyrics by Laurence Hope. Copyright 1906 by Dodd, Mead & Company; "The Spell of the Yukon," "The Shooting of Dan McGrew," and "The Cremation of Sam McGee" by Robert Service, reprinted from The Collected Poems of Robert Service. Copyright 1907, 1912, 1916, 1921 by Dodd, Mead & Company; "How to Tell the Wild Animals" from Baubles by Carolyn Wells. Copyright 1917 by Dodd, Mead & Company; "Cynara" by Ernest Dowson, reprinted from The Poems of Ernest Dowson. All copyright selections used by permission of Dodd, Mead & Company.

DOUBLEDAY & COMPANY, INC. for "Baseball's Sad Lexicon" from In Other Words by Franklin P. Adams. Copyright 1912 by Franklin P. Adams. Reprinted by permission of Doubleday & Co., Inc.; "If" from Rewards and Fairies. Copyright 1910 by Rudyard Kipling, "Gunga Din" from Departmental Ditties and Ballads & Barrack-Room Ballads, "Recessional" from The Five Nations, "L'Envoi" from The Seven Seas, and "Mother O' Mine" from The Light That Failed, all by Rudyard Kipling. Rudyard Kipling selections reprinted by permission of Mrs. George Bambridge and Doubleday & Co., Inc.; "A Hub for the Universe," "Good-bye My Fancy!" "Animals," "Song of the Open Road," "O Captain, My Captain," and "I Hear America Singing" by Walt Whitman.

E. P. DUTTON & CO., INC. for "America the Beautiful" from the book Poems by Katharine Lee Bates; "O Little Town of Bethlehem" and "Christmas Everywhere" from the book Christmas Songs and Easter Carols by Phillips Brooks. Copyright, 1903, by E. P. Dutton & Co., Inc.; "Where Did You Come From?" from the book At the Back of the North Wind by George MacDonald; "The Spires of Oxford" from the book The Spires of Oxford and Other Poems by Winifred M. Letts. Copyright, 1917, by E. P. Dutton & Co., Inc. Renewal, 1945, by Winifred M. Letts; "A Christmas Carol" from the book The Wild Knight and Other Poems by G. K. Chesterton. All copyright selections reprinted by permission of the publishers, E. P. Dutton & Co., Inc.

PAUL ELDER'S, BOOKS for "Be Strong" by Maltbie Davenport Babcock.

NORMA MILLAY ELLIS for "Renascence," "Recuerdo," "Euclid Alone," and "First Fig" from Collected Poems by Edna St. Vincent Millay, Harper & Brothers, Copyright 1912, 1918, 1919, 1920, 1940, 1946, 1947, 1948 by Edna St. Vincent Millay. Reprinted by permission of Norma Millay Ellis.

FABER AND FABER LIMITED for "Journey of the Magi" by T. S. Eliot; "In Memory of W. B. Yeats" and "Musée des Beaux Arts" by W. H. Auden; "Ultima Ratio Regum" by Stephen Spender; "Sonnet to My Mother" by George Barker; and "The Road" by Edwin Muir.

B. FELDMAN AND CO. LTD. for "Heaven Will Protect the Working Girl" by Edgar Smith. Used by permission of the publishers.

GROVE PRESS, INC. for "The Road" from *Collected Poems 1921–1951* by Edwin Muir. Used by permission of the publishers.

HARCOURT, BRACE AND COMPANY, INC. for "Journey of the Magi" from *Collected Poems 1909–1935* by T. S. Eliot, copyright, 1936, by Harcourt, Brace and Company, Inc.

HARPER & BROTHERS for "If I Were King" by Justin Huntly McCarthy; "The Sycophantic Fox and the Gullible Raven" by Guy Wetmore Carryl; "Over the Hill to the Poor-House" by Will Carleton; "Tenderheartedness," "Misfortunes Never Come Singly," "Mr. Jones," and "Aunt Eliza" by Harry Graham.

CHAS. K. HARRIS MUSIC PUBLISHING COMPANY, INC. for "Heaven Will Protect the Working Girl" by Edgar Smith. Copyright Renewed 1937 by Chas. K. Harris Music Publishing Co., Inc. Used By Permission.

WILLIAM HEINEMANN, LTD. for "Kashmiri Song" from *India's Love Lyrics* by Laurence Hope.

HENRY HOLT AND COMPANY, INC. for "Fire and Ice," "The Road Not Taken," "The Hardship of Accounting," "Stopping by Woods on a Snowy Evening," and "Mending Wall" by Robert Frost from *Complete Poems of Robert Frost.* Copyright, 1930, 1949, by Henry Holt and Company, Inc. Used also by permission of Messrs. Jonathan Cape, Ltd.; "Reveille," "When I Was One-and-Twenty," "Loveliest of Trees," and "With Rue My Heart Is Laden" from *A Shropshire Lad* by A. E. Housman; "Fog" from *Chicago Poems* by Carl Sandburg. Copyright, 1916, by Henry Holt and Company, Inc. Copyright, 1944, by Carl Sandburg; "The Golf Links" from *Portraits in Protest* by Sarah N. Cleghorn. Copyright, 1917, by Henry Holt and Company, Inc. All selections used by permission of the publishers, Henry Holt and Company, Inc.

HOUGHTON MIFFLIN COMPANY for "Grieve Not Ladies" from *Shoes That Danced* by Anna Hempstead Branch; "Out Where the West Begins" from *Out Where the West Begins* by Arthur Chapman; "Patterns" by Amy Lowell from *Complete Poetical Works of Amy Lowell;* "Nearer Home" by Phoebe Cary; "Duty," "Give All to Love," "Concord Hymn," "Good-Bye," "The Rhodora," and "Fable" by Ralph Waldo Emerson; "The Captain's Daughter" by James T. Fields; "Jim Bludso" by John Hay; "Old Ironsides," "The Height of the Ridiculous," "God Save the Flag," "The Ballad of the Oysterman," "The Deacon's Masterpiece or, The Wonderful 'One-Hoss Shay,'" and "The Chambered Nautilus" by Oliver Wendell Holmes; "The Battle Hymn of the Republic" by Julia Ward Howe; "A Psalm of Life," "The Builders," "The Arrow and the Song," "My Lost Youth," "The Tide Rises, the Tide Falls," "The Village Blacksmith," "O Ship of State," "Charlemagne," "Paul Revere's Ride," "The Wreck of the Hesperus," "The Children's Hour," "The Day Is Done," "There Was a Little Girl," and "Christmas Bells" by Henry Wadsworth Longfellow; "What Is So Rare as a Day in June" and "Not Only Around Our Infancy" by James Russell Lowell; "Woman's Will" by John G. Saxe; and "Barbara Frietchie" by John Greenleaf Whittier.

BRUCE HUMPHRIES, INC. for "Money" from *Yours for the Asking* by Richard Armour, Copyright 1942 by Bruce Humphries, Inc.

ETHEL JACOBSON for her poem "Atomic Courtesy."

ELISABETH LAMBERT for her poem "Brave Old World." By permission of the author. © 1957 by Oscar Williams, from *The Silver Treasury of Light Verse,* a Mentor Book.

JOHN LANE THE BODLEY HEAD LTD. for "Thirty Bob a Week" by John Davidson.

ALAN JAY LERNER for his lyric "With a Little Bit of Luck" from the musical play *My Fair Lady* by Alan Jay Lerner with music by Frederick Loewe. Copyright © 1956 by Alan Jay Lerner and Frederick Loewe. Chappell & Co., Inc., New York, N. Y. Publisher and Owner of allied rights throughout the world.

D. B. WYNDHAM LEWIS for his poem "A Shot at Random."

J. B. LIPPINCOTT COMPANY for "Nursery Rhyme for the Tender-Hearted" from *Hide and Seek* by Christopher Morley. Copyright 1920, 1947 by Christopher Morley; "The Highwayman" from *Collected Poems, Volume I* by Alfred Noyes. Copyright 1913, 1941 by Alfred Noyes; and "Sheridan's Ride" by Thomas Buchanan Read from *Complete Poetical Works of Thomas Buchanan Read;* all published by J. B. Lippincott Company.

LITTLE, BROWN & COMPANY for "The Sea-Gull," "The Turtle," "Reflections on Ice-Breaking," and "Portrait of the Artist as a Prematurely Old Man" from *Many Long Years Ago* by Ogden Nash. Copyright 1931, 1935 and 1940 by Ogden Nash. Used by permission of Little, Brown & Co.; "The Night Has a Thousand Eyes" by Francis William Bourdillon; "I Never Saw a Moor," "I Died for Beauty," and "A Narrow Fellow in the Grass" by Emily Dickinson; and "Look Up" by Edward Everett Hale.

LOTHROP, LEE AND SHEPARD CO. for "The House by the Side of the Road" from *Dreams in Homespun* by Sam Walter Foss, by permission of Lothrop, Lee & Shepard Co., Inc.

ROBERT M. MCBRIDE COMPANY for "The Moo-Cow-Moo" by Edmund Vance Cooke.

MCCLELLAND & STEWART LIMITED for "The Soldier" and "The Great Lover" by Rupert Brooke from *The Collected Poems of Rupert Brooke.*

THE MACMILLAN COMPANY, New York, for "The Man He Killed" and "The Darkling Thrush" from *Collected Poems* by Thomas Hardy, Copyright by The Macmillan Company; "Abraham Lincoln Walks at Midnight," "The Congo," "The Moon's the North Wind's Cooky," and "Factory Windows Are Always Broken" from *Collected Poems* by Vachel Lindsay, Copyright by The Macmillan Company; "On Growing Old," "The West Wind," and "Laugh and Be Merry" from *Poems* by John Masefield, Copyright by John Masefield; "When You Are Old," "For Anne Gregory," "The Lake Isle of Innisfree," and "Sailing to Byzantium" from *Collected Poems* by William Butler Yeats, Copyright by The Macmillan Company; "A Song for Our Flag" from *Little Book of Homespun Verse* by Margaret E. Sangster, Copyright by The Macmillan Company; "The Dark Hills" and "Mr. Flood's Party" from *Collected Poems* by Edwin Arlington Robinson, Copyright by The Macmillan Company; "Locksley Hall," "Choric Song of the Lotos-Eaters," "Tears, Idle Tears," "The Charge of the Light Brigade," "Flower in the Crannied Wall," "Blow, Bugle, Blow," "The Brook's Song," "The Lady of Shalott," "Crossing the Bar," and "Ring Out, Wild Bells" by Alfred, Lord Tennyson. Copyright selections used by permission of The Macmillan Company.

MACMILLAN & Co. LTD., London, for "The Yarn of the 'Nancy Bell'" from *The Bab Ballads* and "Ko-Ko's Song" from *The Mikado* by Sir W. S. Gilbert. Used by permission of the author's representatives and Macmillan & Co. Ltd.; "The Man He Killed" and "The Darkling Thrush" by Thomas Hardy, taken from *The Collected Poems of Thomas Hardy,* by permission of the Trustees of the Hardy Estate, Macmillan & Co. Ltd. and The Macmillan Company of Canada Limited; "If" from *Rewards and Fairies* and "Mother O' Mine" from *The Light That Failed* by Rudyard Kipling.

MRS. JOHN G. MAGEE, the author's mother, for "High Flight" by John Gillespie Magee, Jr. Reprinted by permission.

VIRGIL MARKHAM for "The Man with the Hoe," "Preparedness," and "A Creed" by Edwin Markham. Reprinted by permission of Virgil Markham.

ELLEN C. MASTERS (Mrs. Edgar Lee Masters) for "Anne Rutledge," from *Spoon River Anthology,* by Edgar Lee Masters, published by The Macmillan Company.

HUGHES MEARNS for his poem "The Little Man Who Wasn't There."

METHUEN & CO. LTD. for "Recessional" from *The Five Nations,* "L'Envoi" from *The Seven Seas* and "Gunga Din" from *Barrack Room Ballads* by Rudyard Kipling.

JUANITA J. MILLER for "Columbus" by Joaquin Miller from *The Poetical Works of Joaquin Miller.* Copyright Renewed 1951 by Juanita J. Miller.

ALIDA MONRO (Mrs. Harold Monro) for "Milk for the Cat" by Harold Monro.

JOHN MURRAY (PUBLISHERS) LTD. for "The Spires of Oxford" from *The Spires of Oxford and Other Poems* by Winifred M. Letts.

NEW DIRECTIONS for "Do Not Go Gentle Into That Good Night" and "A Refusal to Mourn the Death, by Fire, of a Child in London" by Dylan Thomas from *The Collected Poems of Dylan Thomas.* Copyright 1952, 1953 by Dylan Thomas; "Greater Love," "Arms and the Boy," and "Anthem for Doomed Youth" by Wilfred Owen from *Poems of Wilfred Owen.* All Rights Reserved. All selections reprinted by permission of New Directions.

HAROLD OBER ASSOCIATES for "Song of a Mischievous Dog" by Dylan Thomas. Copyright © 1925 by Dylan Thomas. Reprinted by permission of Harold Ober Associates Inc.

OXFORD UNIVERSITY PRESS, INC., New York, for "Music I Heard" from *Collected Poems* by Conrad Aiken. Copyright 1953 by Conrad Aiken; "The Groundhog" from *Selected Poems* by Richard Eberhart, 1951. Both reprinted by permission of Oxford University Press, Inc.

OXFORD UNIVERSITY PRESS, London, for "The Leaden Echo and the Golden Echo," "Pied Beauty," and "God's Grandeur" by Gerard Manley Hopkins from *Poems of Gerard Manley Hopkins,* edited by W. H. Gardner.

PUNCH for "In Flanders Fields" by Captain John D. McCrae and "Genius" by R. J. P. Hewison, Copyright, *Punch.* Used also by permission of The Ben Roth Agency.

RAND MCNALLY & COMPANY, Conkey Division, for "Solitude" by Ella Wheeler Wilcox.

RANDOM HOUSE, INC. for "Musée des Beaux Arts" and "In Memory of W. B. Yeats" by W. H. Auden from *The Collected Poetry of W. H. Auden.* Copyright 1940 by W. H. Auden; "Ultima Ratio Regum" from *Collected Poems 1928–1953* by Stephen Spender. Copyright 1942 by Stephen Spender; "The Yarn of the 'Nancy Bell'" and "Ko-Ko's Song" by Sir W. S. Gilbert from the Modern Library edition, *The Complete Plays of Gilbert and Sullivan.* All copyright selections reprinted by permission of Random House, Inc.

THE REILLY & LEE CO. for "It Couldn't Be Done," "Stick to It," and "Just Folks" from the book, *Collected Verse,* by Edgar A. Guest, copyright 1934 by The Reilly & Lee Co., Chicago.

THE RYERSON PRESS, Toronto, Canadian publishers, for "The Spell of the Yukon," "The Shooting of Dan McGrew," and "The Cremation of Sam McGee" by Robert Service from *The Collected Poems of Robert Service.*

THE SAN FRANCISCO EXAMINER for "Casey at the Bat" by Ernest Lawrence Thayer.

G. SCHIRMER, INC. for "Oh Promise Me" by Clement Scott.

CHARLES SCRIBNER'S SONS for "Miniver Cheevy," reprinted from *The Town Down the River* by Edwin Arlington Robinson. Copyright 1901 Charles Scribner's Sons; renewal copyright 1938 Ruth Nivison; "A Minuet on Reaching the Age of Fifty," reprinted from *Poems* by George Santayana. Copyright 1923 Charles Scribner's Sons; renewal copyright 1951 George Santayana; "I Have a Rendezvous with Death," reprinted from *Poems* by Alan Seeger. Copyright 1916 Charles Scribner's Sons; renewal copyright 1944 Elsie Adams Seeger; "Reliance," reprinted from *Music and Other Poems* by Henry van Dyke. Copyright 1904 Charles Scribner's Sons; renewal copyright 1932 Henry van Dyke; "America for Me" by Henry van Dyke, reprinted from *The Poems of Henry van Dyke.* Copyright 1911 Charles Scribner's Sons; renewal copyright 1939 Tertius van Dyke; "Richard Cory" from *The Children of the Night* by Edwin Arlington Robinson; "Invictus" from *Poems* by William Ernest Henley; "The Hound of Heaven" from *Poems* by Francis Thompson; "The Sugar Plum Tree," "Wynken, Blynken and Nod," "Little Boy Blue," "The Duel," and "Jest 'Fore Christmas" from *Poems of Childhood* by Eugene Field; "The Land of Counterpane," "Good and Bad Children," "The Swing," and "The Lamplighter" from *A Child's Garden of Verses* by Robert Louis Stevenson. All copyright selections used with permission of Charles Scribner's Sons.

SIDGWICK & JACKSON LTD. for "The Soldiers" and "The Great Lover" by Rupert Brooke from *The Collected Poems of Rupert Brooke*. Reprinted also by permission of the Author's Representatives.

THE SOCIETY OF AUTHORS for "Reveille," "When I Was One-and-Twenty," "Loveliest of Trees," "With Rue My Heart Is Laden," and "Infant Innocence" by A. E. Housman. Permission granted by The Society of Authors as the literary representative of the Trustees of the Estate of the late A. E. Housman, and Messrs. Jonathan Cape, Ltd., publishers of A. E. Housman's *Collected Poems;* "The Listeners" by Walter de la Mare. Permission granted by The Literary Trustees of Walter de la Mare and The Society of Authors as their representative; "On Growing Old," "The West Wind," and "Laugh and Be Merry" by John Masefield. Permission granted by The Society of Authors and Dr. John Masefield, O.M.

THE SPECTATOR for "A Prayer for a Little Home."

JERRY VOGEL MUSIC COMPANY, INC. for "Trees" by Joyce Kilmer. Used by special permission of copyright owner, Jerry Vogel Music Company, Inc., New York 36, N. Y.

KENNETH WARD for his poem "Investor's Soliloquy."

A. P. WATT & SON for "If" from *Rewards and Fairies,* "Recessional" from *The Five Nations,* "Mother O' Mine" from *The Light That Failed,* "L'Envoi" from *The Seven Seas,* and "Gunga Din" from *Barrack Room Ballads,* all by Rudyard Kipling, and reprinted by permission of Mrs. George Bambridge and The Macmillan Company of Canada Ltd.; "A Christmas Carol" from *The Wild Knight* by G. K. Chesterton, reprinted by permission of Miss D. E. Collins, and by Messrs. J. M. Dent & Sons Ltd.; "When You Are Old," "The Lake Isle of Innisfree," "For Anne Gregory," and "Sailing to Byzantium" by W. B. Yeats from *Collected Poems of W. B. Yeats,* reprinted by permission of Mrs. W. B. Yeats and The Macmillan Company of Canada Ltd.; "It Pays" by Arnold Bennett, reprinted by permission of The Owner of the Copyright; "Warning to Children" from *Collected Poems* by Robert Graves, published by Doubleday & Co., Inc. and Cassell & Co. Ltd., reprinted by permission of the author; "If I Were King" by Justin Huntly McCarthy, reprinted by permission of the author's executrix.

LIVINGSTON WELCH for his poem "Bang Street."

OSCAR WILLIAMS for his poems "The Last Supper" and "The Praying Mantis Visits a Pent House" from *Selected Poems* (Charles Scribner's Sons), copyright, 1947, by Oscar Williams; for "One Morning the World Woke Up" from *That's All That Matters* (Creative Age Press), copyright, 1945, by Oscar Williams; all by permission of the author; "Song: I Can't Be Talkin' of Love, Dear" by Esther Mathews from *Poetry* (and *A Little Treasury of Modern Poetry*), copyright, 1938, by Modern Poetry Association, by permission of Oscar Williams.

FREDERICKA WRIGHT for "Letter to the City Clerk" by Frederick A. Wright.

A careful effort has been made to trace the ownership of poems included in this anthology in order to secure permission to reprint copyright material and to make full acknowledgment of their use. If any error of omission has occurred, it is purely inadvertent, and will be corrected in subsequent editions, provided written notification is made to the publisher, Grosset & Dunlap, Inc., 1107 Broadway, New York 10, New York.

TO MY FAMILY

CONTENTS

BOOK I

LIFE IS REAL, LIFE IS EARNEST

SOLITUDE

Laugh, and the world laughs with
   you;
  Weep, and you weep alone,
For the sad old earth must
   borrow its mirth,
  But has trouble enough of its
   own.
Sing, and the hills will answer;
  Sigh, it is lost on the air,
The echoes bound to a joyful
   sound,
  But shrink from voicing care.

Rejoice, and men will seek you;
  Grieve, and they turn and go.
They want full measure of all
   your pleasure,
  But they do not need your woe.

Be glad, and your friends are many;
  Be sad, and you lose them all,—
There are none to decline your
   nectared wine,
  But alone you must drink life's
   gall.

Feast, and your halls are crowded;
  Fast, and the world goes by.
Succeed and give, and it helps
   you live,
  But no man can help you die.
There is room in the halls of
   pleasure
  For a long and lordly train,
But one by one we must all file on
  Through the narrow aisles of
   pain.

ELLA WHEELER WILCOX

3

GRADATIM

Heaven is not reached at a single
  bound;
    But we build the ladder by
    which we rise
    From the lowly earth to the
    vaulted skies,
And we mount to its summit
  round by round.

I count this thing to be grandly
  true,
    That a noble deed is a step
    toward God,
    Lifting the soul from the
    common sod
To a purer air and a broader
  view.

We rise by things that are 'neath
  our feet;
    By what we have mastered of
    good and gain,
    By the pride deposed and the
    passion slain,
And the vanquished ills that we
  hourly meet.

We hope, we aspire, we resolve,
  we trust,
    When the morning calls us to
    life and light;
    But our hearts grow weary,
    and ere the night,
Our lives are trailing the sordid
  dust.

We hope, we resolve, we aspire,
  we pray,
    And we think that we mount
    the air on wings
    Beyond the recall of sensual
    things,
While our feet still cling to the
  heavy clay.

Wings for angels, but feet for
  men!
    We may borrow the wings to
    find the way;
    We may hope, and resolve, and
    aspire, and pray;
But our feet must rise, or we fall
  again.

Only in dreams is a ladder thrown
    From the weary earth to the
    sapphire walls,
    But the dreams depart, and the
    vision falls,
And the sleeper wakes on his
  pillow of stone.

Heaven is not reached at a single
  bound;
    But we build the ladder by
    which we rise
    From the lowly earth to the
    vaulted skies,
And we mount to its summit
  round by round.

JOSIAH GILBERT HOLLAND

IF

If you can keep your head when all about you
    Are losing theirs and blaming it on you;
If you can trust yourself when all men doubt you,
    But make allowance for their doubting too:
If you can wait and not be tired by waiting,
    Or, being lied about, don't deal in lies,
Or being hated don't give way to hating,
    And yet don't look too good, nor talk too wise;

If you can dream—and not make dreams your master;
    If you can think—and not make thoughts your aim,
If you can meet with Triumph and Disaster
    And treat those two impostors just the same:
If you can bear to hear the truth you've spoken
    Twisted by knaves to make a trap for fools,
Or watch the things you gave your life to, broken,
    And stoop and build 'em up with worn-out tools;

If you can make one heap of all your winnings
    And risk it on one turn of pitch-and-toss,
And lose, and start again at your beginnings,
    And never breathe a word about your loss:
If you can force your heart and nerve and sinew
    To serve your turn long after they are gone,
And so hold on when there is nothing in you
    Except the Will which says to them: "Hold on!"

If you can talk with crowds and keep your virtue,
    Or walk with Kings—nor lose the common touch,
If neither foes nor loving friends can hurt you,
    If all men count with you, but none too much:
If you can fill the unforgiving minute
    With sixty seconds' worth of distance run,
Yours is the Earth and everything that's in it,
    And—which is more—you'll be a Man, my son!

RUDYARD KIPLING

OPPORTUNITY

Master of human destinies am I.
Fame, love, and fortune on my footsteps wait,
Cities and fields I walk; I penetrate
Deserts and seas remote, and, passing by
Hovel, and mart, and palace, soon or late
I knock unbidden, once at every gate!
If sleeping, wake—if feasting, rise before
I turn away. It is the hour of fate,
And they who follow me reach every state
Mortals desire, and conquer every foe
Save death; but those who doubt or hesitate,
Condemned to failure, penury and woe,
Seek me in vain and uselessly implore—
I answer not, and I return no more.

JOHN JAMES INGALLS

ABOU BEN ADHEM

Abou Ben Adhem (may his tribe increase!)
Awoke one night from a deep dream of peace,
And saw, within the moonlight in his room,
Making it rich, and like a lily in bloom,
An Angel writing in a book of gold:

Exceeding peace had made Ben Adhem bold,
And to the Presence in the room he said,
"What writest thou?" The Vision raised its head,
And with a look made of all sweet accord
Answered, "The names of those who love the Lord."

"And is mine one?" said Abou. "Nay, not so,"
Replied the Angel. Abou spoke more low,
But cheerly still; and said, "I pray thee, then,
Write me as one that loves his fellow-men."

The Angel wrote, and vanished. The next night
It came again with a great wakening light,
And showed the names whom love of God had blessed,
And, lo! Ben Adhem's name led all the rest!

LEIGH HUNT

IT COULDN'T BE DONE

Somebody said that it couldn't be done,
   But he with a chuckle replied
That "maybe it couldn't," but he would be one
   Who wouldn't say so till he'd tried.
So he buckled right in with the trace of a grin
   On his face. If he worried he hid it.
He started to sing as he tackled the thing
   That couldn't be done, and he did it.

Somebody scoffed: "Oh, you'll never do that;
   At least no one ever has done it";
But he took off his coat and he took off his hat,
   And the first thing we knew he'd begun it.
With a lift of his chin and a bit of a grin,
   Without any doubting or quiddit,
He started to sing as he tackled the thing
   That couldn't be done, and he did it.

There are thousands to tell you it cannot be done,
   There are thousands to prophesy failure;
There are thousands to point out to you, one by one,
   The dangers that wait to assail you.
But just buckle in with a bit of a grin,
   Just take off your coat and go to it;
Just start to sing as you tackle the thing
   That "cannot be done," and you'll do it.

EDGAR A. GUEST

THE BUILDERS

All are architects of Fate,
   Working in these walls of Time;
Some with massive deeds and great,
   Some with ornaments of rhyme.

Nothing useless is, or low;
   Each thing in its place is best;
And what seems but idle show
   Strengthens and supports the rest.

For the structure that we raise,
   Time is with materials filled;
Our to-days and yesterdays
   Are the blocks with which we
      build.

Truly shape and fashion these;
   Leave no yawning gaps
      between;
Think not, because no man sees,
   Such things will remain unseen.

In the elder days of Art,
   Builders wrought with greatest
      care

Each minute and unseen part;
   For the Gods see everywhere.

Let us do our work as well,
   Both the unseen and the seen;
Make the house, where Gods may
      dwell,
   Beautiful, entire, and clean.

Else our lives are incomplete,
   Standing in these walls of
      Time,
Broken stairways, where the feet
   Stumble as they seek to climb.

Build to-day, then, strong and sure,
   With a firm and ample base;
And ascending and secure
   Shall to-morrow find its place.

Thus alone can we attain
   To those turrets, where the eye
Sees the world as one vast plain,
   And one boundless reach of sky.

HENRY WADSWORTH LONGFELLOW

DON'T GIVE UP

'Twixt failure and success the point's so fine
Men sometimes know not when they touch the line,
Just when the pearl was waiting one more plunge,
How many a struggler has thrown up the sponge!
Then take this honey from the bitterest cup:
"There is no failure save in giving up!"

ANONYMOUS

BETTER THAN GOLD

Better than grandeur, better than gold,
Than rank and titles a thousandfold,
Is a healthy body and a mind at ease,
And simple pleasures that always please.
A heart that can feel for another's woe,
And share his joys with a genial glow;
With sympathies large enough to enfold
All men as brothers, is better than gold.

Better than gold is a conscience clear,
Though toiling for bread in an humble sphere,
Doubly blessed with content and health,
Untried by the lusts and cares of wealth,
Lowly living and lofty thought
Adorn and ennoble a poor man's cot;
For mind and morals in nature's plan
Are the genuine tests of an earnest man.

Better than gold is a peaceful home
Where all the fireside characters come,
The shrine of love, the heaven of life,
Hallowed by mother, or sister, or wife.
However humble the home may be,
Or tried with sorrow by heaven's decree,
The blessings that never were bought or sold,
And center there, are better than gold.

Abram Joseph Ryan

MY CREED

I would be true, for there are those who trust me;
I would be pure, for there are those who care;
I would be strong, for there is much to suffer;
I would be brave, for there is much to dare.
I would be friend of all—the poor—the friendless;
I would be giving and forget the gift;
I would be humble, for I know my weakness;
I would look up—and laugh—and love—and lift.

Howard Arnold Walter

L'ENVOI

When earth's last picture is painted, and the tubes are twisted and dried,
When the oldest colors have faded, and the youngest critic has died,
We shall rest, and, faith, we shall need it—lie down for an æon or two,
Till the Master of All Good Workmen shall set us to work anew!

And those that were good will be happy: they shall sit in a golden chair;
They shall splash at a ten-league canvas with brushes of comets' hair;
They shall find real saints to draw from—Magdalene, Peter, and Paul;
They shall work for an age at a sitting and never be tired at all!

And only the Master shall praise us, and only the Master shall blame;
And no one shall work for money, and no one shall work for fame;
But each for the joy of the working, and each, in his separate star,
Shall draw the Thing as he sees It for the God of Things as They Are!

RUDYARD KIPLING

I SHALL NOT PASS THIS WAY AGAIN

A Symphony

I shall not pass this way again—
　Although it bordered be with
　　flowers,
　Although I rest in fragrant
　　bowers,
　　And hear the singing
　　Of song-birds winging
To highest heaven their gladsome
　　flight;
Though moons are full and stars
　are bright,
And winds and waves are softly
　sighing,
While leafy trees make low
　replying;
Though voices clear in joyous
　strain
Repeat a jubilant refrain;
Though rising suns their radiance
　throw
On summer's green and winter's
　snow,
In such rare splendor that my heart
Would ache from scenes like these
　to part;
　Though beauties heighten,
　And life-lights brighten,
And joys proceed from every
　pain,—
I shall not pass this way again.

Then let me pluck the flowers
    that blow,
And let me listen as I go
    To music rare
    That fills the air;
    And let hereafter
    Songs and laughter
Fill every pause along the way;
And to my spirit let me say:
"O soul, be happy; soon 'tis trod,
The path made thus for thee by
    God.
Be happy, thou, and bless His
    name
By whom such marvellous beauty
    came."
And let no chance by me be lost
To kindness show at any cost.
I shall not pass this way again;
Then let me now relieve some
    pain,
Remove some barrier from the
    road,
Or brighten some one's heavy load;
A helping hand to this one lend,
Then turn some other to befriend.

    O God, forgive
    That now I live
As if I might, sometime, return
To bless the weary ones that yearn

For help and comfort every day,—
For there be such along the way.
O God, forgive that I have seen
The beauty only, have not been
Awake to sorrow such as this;
That I have drunk the cup of
    bliss
Remembering not that those there
    be
Who drink the dregs of misery.

I love the beauty of the scene,
Would roam again o'er fields so
    green;
But since I may not, let me spend
My strength for others to the
    end,—
For those who tread on rock and
    stone,
And bear their burdens all alone,
Who loiter not in leafy bowers,
Nor hear the birds nor pluck the
    flowers.
A larger kindness give to me,
A deeper love and sympathy;
    Then, O, one day
    May someone say—
Remembering a lessened pain—
"Would she could pass this way
    again."

                EVA ROSE YORK

DO IT NOW

If with pleasure you are viewing
    any work a man is doing,
  If you like him or you love him,
    tell him now;
Don't withhold your approbation
    till the parson makes oration
And he lies with snowy lilies on
    his brow;
No matter how you shout it he
    won't really care about it;
  He won't know how many tear-
    drops you have shed;
If you think some praise is due him
    now's the time to slip it to him,
For he cannot read his tomb-
    stone when he's dead.

More than fame and more than
    money is the comment kind
  and sunny
And the hearty, warm approval
    of a friend.
For it gives to life a savor, and it
    makes you stronger, braver,
And it gives you heart and spirit
    to the end;
If he earns your praise—bestow it;
    if you like him let him know it;
  Let the words of true encourage-
    ment be said;
Do not wait till life is over and he's
    underneath the clover,
  For he cannot read his tombstone
    when he's dead.

BERTON BRALEY

IT'S A GAY OLD WORLD

It's a gay old world when you're gay,
And a glad old world when
    you're glad;
  But whether you play
  Or go toiling away
It's a sad old world when you're sad.

It's a grand old world if you're great,
And a mean old world if you're small;

It's a world full of hate
For the foolish who prate
Of the uselessness of it all.

It's a beautiful world to see
Or it's dismal in every zone;
  The thing it must be
  In its gloom or its glee
Depends on yourself alone.

ANONYMOUS

TRY SMILING

When the weather suits you not,
    Try smiling;
When your coffee isn't hot,
    Try smiling.
When your neighbors don't do
  right,
Or your relatives all fight,
Sure 'tis hard, but then you
  might—
    Try smiling.

Doesn't change the things, of
  course—
    Just smiling;
But it cannot make them worse,
    Just smiling.
And it seems to help your case,
Brightens up a gloomy place;
Then, it sort o' rests your face—
    Just smiling.
        ANONYMOUS

EVOLUTION

When you were a tadpole and I
  was a fish
In the Paleozoic time,
And side by side, on the ebbing tide,
We sprawled through the ooze
  and slime,
Or skittered with many a caudal
  flip
Through the depths of the
  Cambrian fen,
My heart was rife with the joy of
  life,
For I loved you even then.

Mindless we lived and mindless
  we loved,
And mindless at last we died;
And deep in a rift of the Caradoc
  drift,
We slumbered side by side.

The world turned on in the
  lathe of Time,
The hot lands heaved amain,
Till we caught our breath from
  the womb of death,
And crept into light again.

We were Amphibians, scaled and
  tailed,
And drab as a dead man's hand:
We coiled at ease 'neath the
  dripping trees,
Or trailed through the mud and
  sand,
Croaking and blind, with our
  three-clawed feet,
Writing a language dumb,
With never a spark in the
  empty dark
To hint at a life to come.

Yet happy we lived and happy we
loved,
And happy we died once more:
Our forms were rolled in the
clinging mold
Of a Neocomian shore.
The æons came and the æons fled,
And the sleep that wrapped us fast
Was riven away in a newer day,
And the night of death was past.

Then light and swift through the
jungle trees
We swung in our airy flights;
Or breathed in the balms of the
fronded palms,
In the hush of the moonless nights.
And oh, what beautiful years were
these,
When our hearts clung each to
each;
When life was filled, and our
senses thrilled
In the first faint dawn of speech!

Thus life by life, and love by love,
We passed through the cycles
strange;
And breath by breath, and death
by death,
We followed the chain of change;
Till there came a time in the law
of life
When over the nursing sod
The shadows broke, and the soul
awoke
In a strange, dim dream of God.
I was thewed like an Aurochs bull,
And tusked like the great Cave
Bear;
And you, my sweet, from head to
feet,

Were gowned in your glorious
hair.
Deep in the gloom of a fireless
cave,
When the nights fell o'er the
plain,
And the moon hung red o'er the
river bed,
We mumbled the bones of the
slain.

I flaked a flint to a cutting edge,
And shaped it with brutish craft:
I broke a shank from the
woodland dank,
And fitted it, head to haft.
Then I hid me close to the reedy
tarn,
Where the Mammoth came to
drink:
Through brawn and bone I drave
the stone,
And slew him upon the brink.

Loud I howled through the
moonless wastes,
Loud answered our kith and kin:
From west and east to the
crimson feast
The clan came trooping in.
O'er joint and gristle and padded
hoof,
We fought and clawed and tore,
And cheek by jowl, with many a
growl,
We talked the marvel o'er.
I carved that fight on a reindeer
bone,
With rude and hairy hand:
I pictured his fall on the cavern
wall,

That men might understand.
For we lived by blood, and the
  right of might,
Ere human laws were drawn,
And the Age of Sin did not begin
Till our brutal tusks were gone.

And that was a million years ago,
In a time that no man knows;
Yet here tonight, in the mellow
  light,
We sit at Delmonico's.
Your eyes are deep as the Devon
  springs,
Your hair as dark as jet:
Your years are few, your life is
  new,
Your soul untried, and yet—

Our trail is on the Kimmeridge
  clay,
And the scarp of the Purbeck
  flags:
We have left our bones in the
  Bagshot stones,
And deep in the Coralline crags.
Our love is old, our lives are old,
And death shall come amain:
Should it come today, what man
  may say
We shall not live again?

God wrought our souls from the
  Tremadoc beds,
And furnished them wings to fly:
He sowed our spawn in the
  world's dim dawn,
And I know that it shall not die;
Though cities have sprung above
  the graves
Where the crook-boned men made
  war,
And the ox-wain creeks o'er the
  buried caves,
Where the mummied Mammoths
  are.

For we know that the clod, by the
  grace of God,
Will quicken with voice and
  breath;
And we know that Love, with
  gentle hand,
Will beckon from death to death.
And so, as we linger at luncheon
  here,
Over many a dainty dish,
Let us drink anew to the time
  when you
Were a tadpole and I was a fish.

          LANGDON SMITH

THE ARROW AND THE SONG

I shot an arrow into the air,
It fell to earth, I knew not where;
For, so swiftly it flew, the sight
Could not follow it in its flight.

I breathed a song into the air,
It fell to earth, I knew not where;
For who has sight so keen and strong,
That it can follow the flight of song?

Long, long, afterward, in an oak
I found the arrow, still unbroke;
And the song, from beginning to end,
I found again in the heart of a friend.

HENRY WADSWORTH LONGFELLOW

"DON'T CARE" AND "NEVER MIND"

"Don't care" is no friend of mine.
  I "don't care" for him.
When he comes it is a sign
  Sense is growing dim.
He is not the thing of pride
  Some folks seem to think.
Folly is his constant guide,
  Bread and meat and drink.

Not to care when things go
    wrong,
  Not to care when ill
Rises up to check your song,
  And your heart to chill—
That were foolishness indeed
  Of an arrant sort.
Nothing is too slight to heed
  On the way to port.

But the sunny "Never Mind,"
  He's a different wight.
Helps us when the day's inclined
  Not to treat us right;
Softens every bitter blast,
  Warms us when we're cold;
When the sky is overcast,
  Keeps us blithe and bold.

Bids all sorrow go its way.
  Helps us stay our tears,
And when life seems drear and
    gray,
  Quiets all our fears.
When it comes to share and share,
  I shall be resigned
If some other gets "Don't Care"—
  I'll take "Never Mind!"

JOHN KENDRICK BANGS

OH PROMISE ME

Oh promise me, that some day
  you and I
Will take our love together to
  some sky
Where we can be alone and faith
  renew,
And find the hollows where
  those flowers grew,
Those first sweet violets of early
  Spring,
Which come in whispers, thrill us
  both and sing
Of love unspeakable that is to be;
Oh promise me! Oh promise me!

Oh promise me, that you will
  take my hand,
The most unworthy in this lonely
  land,
And let me sit beside you, in your
  eyes
Seeing the vision of our paradise,
Hearing God's message while the
  organ rolls
Its mighty music to our very souls;
No love less perfect than a life
  with thee;
Oh promise me! Oh promise me!

CLEMENT SCOTT

SUCCESS

Success is speaking words of praise,
In cheering other people's ways,
In doing just the best you can,
With every task and every plan,
It's silence when your speech would hurt,
Politeness when your neighbor's curt,
It's deafness when the scandal flows,
And sympathy with others' woes,
It's loyalty when duty calls,
It's courage when disaster falls,
It's patience when the hours are long,
It's found in laughter and in song,
It's in the silent time of prayer,
In happiness and in despair,
In all of life and nothing less,
We find the thing we call success.

ANONYMOUS

THE HOUSE BY THE SIDE OF THE ROAD

There are hermit souls that live withdrawn
In the place of their self-content;
There are souls like stars, that dwell apart,
In a fellowless firmament;
There are pioneer souls that blaze their paths
Where highways never ran—
But let me live by the side of the road
And be a friend to man.

Let me live in a house by the side of the road,
Where the race of men go by—
The men who are good and the men who are bad,
As good and as bad as I.
I would not sit in the scorner's seat,
Or hurl the cynic's ban—
Let me live in a house by the side of the road
And be a friend to man.

I see from my house by the side of the road,
By the side of the highway of life,
The men who press with the ardor of hope,
The men who are faint with the strife.
But I turn not away from their smiles nor their tears,
Both parts of an infinite plan—
Let me live in a house by the side of the road
And be a friend to man.

I know there are brook-gladdened meadows ahead,
And mountains of wearisome height;
That the road passes on through the long afternoon
And stretches away to the night.
But still I rejoice when the travelers rejoice,
And weep with the strangers that moan,
Nor live in my house by the side of the road
Like a man who dwells alone.

Let me live in my house by the side of the road,
It's here the race of men go by—
They are good, they are bad, they are weak, they are strong,
Wise, foolish—so am I;
Then why should I sit in the scorner's seat,
Or hurl the cynic's ban?
Let me live in my house by the side of the road
And be a friend to man.

SAM WALTER FOSS

KEEP A STIFF UPPER LIP

There has something gone wrong,
  My brave boy, it appears,
For I see your proud struggle
  To keep back the tears.
That is right; when you cannot
  Give trouble the slip,
Then bear it, still keeping
  A stiff upper lip!

Though you cannot escape
  Disappointment and care,
There's one thing you can do,—
  It is, learn how to bear.
If when for life's prizes
  You're running, you trip,
Get up, start again,
  Keep a stiff upper lip!

Let your hands and your conscience
  Be honest and clean;
Scorn to touch or to think
  Of the thing that is mean;
But hold on to the pure
  And the right with firm grip;
And though hard be the task,
  Keep a stiff upper lip!

Through childhood, through
    manhood,
  Through life to the end,
Struggle bravely and stand
  By your colors, my friend;
Only yield when you must,
  Never give up the ship,
But fight on to the last
  With a stiff upper lip.

PHOEBE CARY

I NEVER SAW A MOOR

I never saw a moor,
I never saw the sea;
Yet know I how the heather looks,
And what a wave must be.

I never spoke with God,
Nor visited in heaven;
Yet certain am I of the spot
As if the chart were given.

EMILY DICKINSON

PIPPA'S SONG

The year's at the spring,
And day's at the morn;
Morning's at seven;
The hill-side's dew-pearl'd;

The lark's on the wing;
The snail's on the thorn;
God's in His heaven—
All's right with the world!

ROBERT BROWNING

REVEILLE

Wake: the silver dusk returning
    Up the beach of darkness brims,
And the ship of sunrise burning
    Strands upon the eastern rims.

Wake: the vaulted shadow shatters,
    Trampled to the floor it spanned,
And the tent of night in tatters
    Straws the sky-pavilioned land.

Up, lad, up, 'tis late for lying:
    Hear the drums of morning play;
Hark, the empty highways crying
    'Who'll beyond the hills away?'

Towns and countries woo together,
    Forelands beacon, belfries call;
Never lad that trod on leather
    Lived to feast his heart with all.

Up, lad: thews that lie and cumber
    Sunlit pallets never thrive;
Morns abed and daylight slumber
    Were not meant for man alive.

Clay lies still, but blood's a rover;
    Breath's a ware that will not keep.
Up, lad: when the journey's over
    There'll be time enough to sleep.

A. E. HOUSMAN

LAUGH AND BE MERRY

Laugh and be merry, remember, better the world with a song,
Better the world with a blow in the teeth of a wrong.
Laugh, for the time is brief, a thread the length of a span.
Laugh and be proud to belong to the old proud pageant of man.

Laugh and be merry: remember, in olden time,
God made Heaven and Earth for joy He took in a rime,
Made them, and filled them full with the strong red wine of His mirth,
The splendid joy of the stars: the joy of the earth.

So we must laugh and drink from the deep blue cup of the sky,
Join the jubilant song of the great stars sweeping by,
Laugh, and battle, and work, and drink of the wine outpoured
In the dear green earth, the sign of the joy of the Lord.

Laugh and be merry together, like brothers akin,
Guesting awhile in the rooms of a beautiful inn,
Glad till the dancing stops, and the lilt of the music ends.
Laugh till the game is played; and be you merry, my friends.

JOHN MASEFIELD

PRESS ONWARD

Keep a brave spirit, and never despair;
Hope brings you messages through the keen air—
Good is victorious—God everywhere.

Grand are the battles which you have to fight,
Be not downhearted, but valiant for right;
Hope, and press forward, your face to the light.

ANONYMOUS

TALL OAKS FROM LITTLE ACORNS GROW

You'd scarce expect one of my age
To speak in public on the stage,
And if I chance to fall below
Demosthenes or Cicero,
Don't view me with a critic's eye,
But pass my imperfections by.
Large streams from little
    fountains flow,
Tall oaks from little acorns grow;
And though now I am small and
    young,
Of judgment weak and feeble
    tongue,
Yet all great, learned men, like me
Once learned to read their ABC.
But why may not Columbia's soil
Rear men as great as Britain's
    Isle,
Exceed what Greece and Rome
    have done
Or any land beneath the sun?
Mayn't Massachusetts boast as
    great
As any other sister state?
Or where's the town, go far or
    near,
That does not find a rival here?
Or where's the boy but three feet
    high
Who's made improvement more
    than I?
These thoughts inspire my
    youthful mind
To be the greatest of mankind:
Great, not like Caesar, stained
    with blood,
But only great as I am good.

DAVID EVERETT

"TOLLABLE WELL!"

Spite o' the tempests a-blowin',
    Still had one story to tell:
Bright, sunny weather, or snowin',
    Allus felt "tollable well."

Half o' the settlement sighin'—
    Things gone to ruin, pell-mell!
Never did hear him a-cryin'—
    Allus felt "tollable well!"

'Course he had trouble an' sorrow
    (Come to us all fer a spell),
But, seein' a brighter to-morrow,
    He allus felt "tollable well."

FRANK L. STANTON

STICK TO IT

Stick to it, boy,
  Through the thick and the thin
    of it!
Work for the joy
  That is born of the din of it.
But don't let them fret you;
Dangers are lurking,
But just keep on working.
If it's worth while and you're
    sure of the right of it,
Stick to it, boy, and make a real
    fight of it.

Stick to it, lad,
  Be not frail and afraid of it;
Stand to the gad
  For the man to be made of it.
Deaf to the sneering
And blind to the jeering,

Willing to master
The present disaster,
Stick to it, lad, through the trial
    and test of it,
Patience and courage will give
    you the best of it.

Stick to it, youth,
  Be not sudden to fly from it;
This is the truth,
  Triumph may not far lie from it
Dark is the morning
Before the sun's dawning,
Battered and sore of it
Bear a bit more of it,
Stick to it, even though blacker
    than ink it is,
Victory's nearer, perhaps, than
    you think it is!

EDGAR A. GUEST

BE STRONG

Be strong!
We are not here to play, to
  dream, to drift;
We have hard work to do, and
  loads to lift;
Shun not the struggle—face it;
  'tis God's gift.

Be strong!
Say not, "The days are evil.
  Who's to blame?"
And fold the hands and acquiesce
  —oh shame!

Stand up, speak out, and bravely,
  in God's name.

Be strong!
It matters not how deep
  intrenched the wrong,
How hard the battle goes, the day
  how long;
Faint not—fight on! To-morrow
  comes the song.

MALTBIE DAVENPORT BABCOCK

THE LIFE THAT COUNTS

The life that counts must toil and
  fight;
Must hate the wrong and love
  the right;
Must stand for truth, by day, by
  night—
  This is the life that counts.

The life that counts must hopeful be;
In darkest night make melody;
Must wait the dawn on bended
  knee—
  This is the life that counts.

The life that counts must aim to
  rise
Above the earth to sunlit skies;
Must fix its gaze on Paradise—
  This is the life that counts.

The life that counts must helpful
  be;
The cares and needs of others see;
Must seek the slaves of sin to
  free—
  This is the life that counts.

The life that counts is linked
  with God;
And turns not from the cross—
  the rod;
But walks with joy where Jesus
  trod—
  This is the life that counts.

ANONYMOUS

DO IT NOW!

If you've got a job to do,
          Do it now!
If it's one you wish were through
          Do it now!
If you're sure the job's your own,
Don't hem and haw and groan—
          Do it now!
Don't put off a bit of work,
          Do it now!
It doesn't pay to shirk,
          Do it now!

If you want to fill a place
And be useful to the race,
Just get up and take a brace—
          Do it now!
Don't linger by the way,
          Do it now!
You'll lose if you delay,
          Do it now!
If the other fellows wait,
Or postpone until it's late,
You hit up a faster gait—
          Do it now!

ANONYMOUS

PADDLE YOUR OWN CANOE

Voyager upon life's sea,
  To yourself be true;
And where'er your lot may be,
  Paddle your own canoe.
Never, though the winds may
    rave,
  Falter nor look back,
But upon the darkest wave
  Leave a shining track.

Nobly dare the wildest storm,
  Stem the hardest gale,
Brave of heart and strong of arm,
  You will never fail.
When the world is cold and dark,
  Keep an end in view,
And toward the beacon mark
  Paddle your own canoe.

Every wave that bears you on
  To the silent shore,
From its sunny source has gone
  To return no more:
Then let not an hour's delay
  Cheat you of your due;
But while it is called to-day,
  Paddle your own canoe.

If your birth denied you wealth,
  Lofty state, and power,
Honest fame and hardy health
  Are a better dower;

But if these will not suffice,
  Golden gain pursue,
And to win the glittering prize,
  Paddle your own canoe.

Would you wrest the wreath of
    fame
  From the hand of Fate?
Would you write a deathless name
  With the good and great?
Would you bless your fellowmen?
  Heart and soul imbue
With the holy task, and then
  Paddle your own canoe.

Would you crush the tyrant
    Wrong,
  In the world's fierce fight?
With a spirit brave and strong,
  Battle for the Right;
And to break the chains that bind
  The many to the few—
To enfranchise slavish mind,
  Paddle your own canoe.

Nothing great is lightly won,
  Nothing won is lost—
Every good deed nobly done,
  Will repay the cost;
Leave to Heaven, in humble trust,
  All you will to do;
But if you succeed, you must
  Paddle your own canoe.
                    SARAH K. BOLTON

WHERE THERE'S A WILL THERE'S A WAY

We have faith in old proverbs full
    surely,
    For Wisdom has traced what
    they tell,
And Truth may be drawn up as
    purely
    From them, as it may from "a well."
Let us question the thinkers and doers,
    And hear what they honestly say;
And you'll find they believe, like
    bold wooers,
    In "Where there's a will there's
    a way."

The hills have been high for
    man's mounting,
    The woods have been dense
    for his axe,
The stars have been thick for
    his counting,
    The sands have been wide for
    his tracks,
The sea has been deep for his diving,
    The poles have been broad for
    his sway,
But bravely he's proved in his
    striving,
    That "Where there's a will
    there's a way."

Have ye vices that ask a destroyer?
    Or passions that need your control?
Let Reason become your
    employer,
    And your body be ruled by
    your soul.

Fight on, though ye bleed in the
    trial,
    Resist with all strength that ye
    may;
Ye may conquer Sin's host by
    denial;
    For "Where there's a will
    there's a way."

Have ye Poverty's pinching to
    cope with?
    Does Suffering weigh down
    your might?
Only call up a spirit to hope with,
    And dawn may come out of
    the night.
Oh! much may be done by defying
    The ghosts of Despair and Dismay;
And much may be gained by relying
    On "Where there's a will there's
    a way."

Should ye see, afar off, that worth
    winning,
    Set out on the journey with trust;
And ne'er heed if your path at
    beginning
    Should be among brambles and
    dust.
Though it is but by footsteps ye do it,
    And hardships may hinder and
    stay;
Walk with faith, and be sure
    you'll get through it;
    For "Where there's a will
    there's a way."

ELIZA COOK

KEEP A-GOIN'

If you strike a thorn or rose,
    Keep a-goin'!
If it hails or if it snows,
    Keep a-goin'!
'Taint no use to sit an' whine
When the fish ain't on your line;
Bait your hook an' keep a-tryin'—
    Keep a-goin'!

When the weather kills your crop,
    Keep a-goin'!
Though 'tis work to reach the
      top,
    Keep a-goin'!

S'pose you're out o' ev'ry dime,
Gittin' broke ain't any crime;
Tell the world you're feelin'
    prime—
    Keep a-goin'!

When it looks like all is up,
    Keep a-goin'!
Drain the sweetness from the cup,
    Keep a-goin'!
See the wild birds on the wing,
Hear the bells that sweetly ring,
When you feel like singin', sing—
    Keep a-goin'!

FRANK L. STANTON

TRY, TRY AGAIN

'Tis a lesson you should heed,
    Try, try again;
If at first you don't succeed,
    Try, try again;
Then your courage should appear,
For, if you will persevere,
You will conquer, never fear;
    Try, try again.

Once or twice though you should
      fail,
    Try, try again;
If you would at last prevail,
    Try, try again;

If we strive, 'tis no disgrace
Though we do not win the race;
What should you do in the case?
    Try, try again.

Time will bring you your reward,
    Try, try again.
All that other folks can do,
Why, with patience, should not
    you?
Only keep this rule in view;
    Try, try again.

ANONYMOUS

IF YOU HAVE A FRIEND

If you have a friend worth loving,
  Love him! Yes, and let him
    know
That you love him, ere life's
    evening
  Tinge his brow with sunset
    glow.
Why should good words ne'er be
    said
Of a friend—till he is dead?

If you hear a song that thrills you,
  Sung by any child of song,
Praise it! Do not let the singer
  Wait deserved praises long.
Why should one who thrills your
    heart
Lack the joy you may impart?

If you hear a prayer that moves
    you
  By its humble, pleading tone,
Join it! Do not let the seeker
  Bow before its God alone.
Why should not your brother share
The strength of "two or three" in
    prayer?

If you see the hot tears falling
  From a brother's weeping eyes,
Share them! And by kindly sharing

Own our kinship in the skies.
Why should anyone be glad
When a brother's heart is sad?

If a silvery laugh goes rippling
  Through the sunshine on his
    face,
Share it! 'Tis the wise man's
    saying—
  For both grief and joy a place.
There's health and goodness in
    the mirth
In which an honest laugh has
    birth.

If your work is made more easy
  By a friendly, helping hand,
Say so! Speak out brave and truly
  Ere the darkness veil the land.
Should a brother workman dear
Falter for a word of cheer?

Scatter thus your seeds of kindness
  All enriching as you go—
Leave them! Trust the Harvest-
    Giver;
  He will make each seed to
    grow.
So, until the happy end,
Your life shall never lack a friend.

ANONYMOUS

RELIANCE

Not to the swift, the race:
Not to the strong, the fight:
Not to the righteous, perfect grace:
Not to the wise, the light.

But often faltering feet
Come surest to the goal;
And they who walk in darkness meet
The sunrise of the soul.

A thousand times by night
The Syrian hosts have died;

A thousand times the vanquished
right
Hath risen, glorified.

The truth the wise men sought
Was spoken by a child;
The alabaster box was brought
In trembling hands defiled.

Not from my torch, the gleam,
But from the stars above:
Not from my heart, life's crystal
stream,
But from the depths of Love.

HENRY VAN DYKE

PREPAREDNESS

For all your days prepare,
And meet them ever alike:
When you are the anvil, bear—
When you are the hammer,
strike.

EDWIN MARKHAM

DUTY

So nigh is grandeur to our dust,
So near is God to man,
When Duty whispers low, "Thou
must,"
The youth replies, "I can."

RALPH WALDO EMERSON

LOOK UP!

Look up! and not down;
Out! and not in;
Forward! and not back;
And lend a hand.

EDWARD EVERETT HALE

A RULE

Do all the good you can,
By all the means you can,
In all the ways you can,
In all the places you can,
At all the times you can,
To all the people you can,
As long as ever you can.

JOHN WESLEY

WHEN MY SHIP COMES IN

Somewhere, out on the blue seas
    sailing,
  Where the winds dance and
    spin;
Beyond the reach of my eager
    hailing,
  Over the breakers' din;
Out where the dark storm-clouds
    are lifting,
Out where the blinding fog is
    drifting,
Out where the treacherous sand is
    shifting,
  My ship is coming in.

Oh, I have watched till my eyes
    were aching,
  Day after weary day;
Or, I have hoped till my heart
    was breaking,
  While the long nights ebbed
    away;
Could I but know where the
    waves had tossed her,
Could I but know what storms
    had crossed her,
Could I but know where the
    winds had lost her,
  Out in the twilight gray!

But though the storms her course
    have altered,
  Surely the port she'll win;
Never my faith in my ship has
    faltered,
  I know she is coming in.

For through the restless ways of
    her roaming,
Through the mad rush of the
    wild waves foaming,
Through the wild crest of the
    billows combing,
  My ship is coming in.

Breasting the tides where the
    gulls are flying,
  Swiftly she's coming in;
Shallows and deeps and rocks
    defying,
  Bravely she's coming in;
Precious the love she will bring to
    bless me,
Snowy the arms she will bring to
    caress me,
In the proud purple of kings she
    will dress me,
  My ship that is coming in.

White in the sunshine her sails
    will be gleaming,
  See, where my ship comes in;
At mast-head and peak her colors
    streaming,
  Proudly she's sailing in;
Love, hope, and joy on her decks
    are cheering,
Music will welcome her glad
    appearing,
And her heart will sing at her
    stately nearing,
  When my ship comes in.

ROBERT J. BURDETT

SOMEBODY

Somebody did a golden deed;
Somebody proved a friend in need;
Somebody sang a beautiful song;
Somebody smiled the whole day long;
Somebody thought " 'Tis sweet to live";

Somebody said "I'm glad to give"
Somebody fought a valiant fight;
Somebody lived to shield the
   right;
  Was that "somebody" you?

ANONYMOUS

ON HIS BLINDNESS

When I consider how my light is spent
Ere half my days, in this dark world and wide,
And that one talent which is death to hide
Lodged with me useless, though my soul more bent

To serve therewith my Maker, and present
My true account, lest he returning chide,—
Doth God exact day-labor, light denied?
I fondly ask:—But Patience, to prevent

That murmur, soon replies; God doth not need
Either man's work, or his own gifts: who best
Bear his mild yoke, they serve him best: His state

Is kingly; thousands at his bidding speed
And post o'er land and ocean without rest:—
They also scrvc who only stand and wait.

JOHN MILTON

A PSALM OF LIFE

Tell me not, in mournful numbers,
Life is but an empty dream!—
For the soul is dead that slumbers,
And things are not what they seem.

Life is real! Life is earnest!
And the grave is not its goal;
Dust thou art, to dust returnest,
Was not spoken of the soul.

Not enjoyment, and not sorrow
Is our destined end or way;
But to act, that each tomorrow
Find us farther than today.

Art is long, and Time is fleeting,
And our hearts, though stout and
    brave,
Still, like muffled drums, are beat-
    ing
Funeral marches to the grave.

In the world's broad field of battle,
In the bivouac of life,

Be not like dumb, driven cattle!
Be a hero in the strife!

Trust no Future, howe'er pleasant!
Let the dead Past bury its dead!
Act,—act in the living Present!
Heart within, and God o'erhead!

Lives of great men all remind us
We can make our lives sublime,
And, departing, leave behind us
Footprints on the sand of time—

Footprints, that perhaps another,
Sailing o'er life's solemn main,
A forlorn and shipwrecked brother,
Seeing, shall take heart again.

Let us, then, be up and doing,
With a heart for any fate;
Still achieving, still pursuing,
Learn to labor and to wait.
HENRY WADSWORTH LONGFELLOW

BOOK II

THE HUMAN SPIRIT

"OH, WHY SHOULD THE SPIRIT OF MORTAL BE PROUD?"

Oh, why should the spirit of mortal be proud?
Like a swift-flitting meteor, a fast-flying cloud,
A flash of the lightning, a break of the wave,
He passeth from life to his rest in the grave.

The leaves of the oak and the willow shall fade,
Be scattered around, and together be laid;
As the young and the old, the low and the high,
Shall crumble to dust and together shall lie.

The child that a mother attended and loved,
The mother that infant's affection who proved,
The husband that mother and infant who blessed,—
Each, all, are away to their dwellings of rest.

The maid on whose brow, on whose cheek, in whose eye,
Shone beauty and pleasure,—her triumphs are by;
And alike from the minds of the living erased
Are the memories of mortals who loved her and praised.

The hand of the king, that the scepter hath borne;
The brow of the priest, that the mitre hath worn;
The eyes of the sage, and the heart of the brave,—
Are hidden and lost in the depths of the grave.

The peasant, whose lot was to sow and to reap;
The herdsman, who climbed with his goats up the steep;
The beggar, who wandered in search of his bread,—
Have faded away like the grass that we tread.

The saint who enjoyed the communion of heaven,
The sinner who dared to remain unforgiven,
The wise and the foolish, the guilty and just,
Have quietly mingled their bones in the dust.

So the multitude goes, like the flower or weed,
That withers away to let others succeed;
So the multitude comes, even those we behold,
To repeat every tale that has often been told.

For we are the same things our fathers have been;
We see the same sights our fathers have seen;
We drink the same stream, we feel the same sun,
And run the same course our fathers have run.

The thoughts we are thinking our fathers do think;
From the death we are shrinking our fathers did shrink;
To the life we are clinging our fathers did cling,
But it speeds from us all like the bird on the wing.

They loved,—but the story we cannot unfold;
They scorned,—but the heart of the haughty is cold;
They grieved,—but no wail from their slumbers will come;
They joyed,—but the tongue of their gladness is dumb.

They died,—ah! they died;—we, things that are now,
That walk on the turf that lies over their brow,
And make in their dwellings a transient abode,
Meet the changes they met on their pilgrimage road.

Yea, hope and despondency, pleasure and pain,
Are mingled together in sunshine and rain:
And the smile and the tear, the song and the dirge,
Still follow each other like surge upon surge.

'Tis the wink of an eye; 'tis the draught of a breath
From the blossom of health to the paleness of death,
From the gilded saloon to the bier and the shroud;
Oh, why should the spirit of mortal be proud?

                                        WILLIAM KNOX

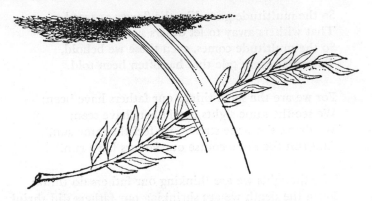

DEATH BE NOT PROUD

Death be not proud, though some have called thee
Mighty and dreadfull, for thou art not soe,
For those whom thou think'st thou dost overthrow
Die not, poore death, nor yet canst thou kill mee.
From rest and sleepe, which but thy pictures bee,
Much pleasure, then from thee, much more must flow,
And soonest our best men with thee doe goe,
Rest of their bones, and soules deliverie.
Thou art slave to Fate, Chance, kings, and desperate men,
And dost with poyson, warre, and sicknesse dwell,
And poppie, or charmes can make us sleepe as well,
And better than thy stroake; why swell'st thou then?
One short sleepe past, wee wake eternally,
And death shall be no more; death, thou shalt die.

JOHN DONNE

L'ALLEGRO

Hence loathed Melancholy
  Of *Cerberus,* and blackest
  midnight born,
In *Stygian* Cave forlorn
  'Mongst horrid shapes, and
  shreiks, and sights unholy,
Find out som uncouth cell,
  Where brooding darknes
  spreads his jealous wings,
And the night-Raven sings;
  There under *Ebon* shades, and
  low-brow'd Rocks,
As ragged as thy Locks,
  In dark *Cimmerian* desert ever
  dwell.
But com thou Goddes fair and
  free,
In Heav'n yclep'd *Euphrosyne,*
And by men, heart-easing Mirth,
Whom lovely *Venus* at a birth
With two sister Graces more
To ivy-crowned *Bacchus* bore;
Or whether (as som Sager sing)
The frolick Wind that breathes
  the Spring,
Zephir with *Aurora* playing,
As he met her once a Maying,
There on Beds of Violets blew,
And fresh blown Roses washt in
  dew,
Fill'd her with thee a daughter
  fair,
So bucksom, blith, and debonair.
Haste thee nymph, and bring
  with thee
Jest and youthful Jollity,

Quips and Cranks, and wanton
  Wiles,
Nods, and Becks, and Wreathed
  Smiles,
Such as hang on *Hebe's* cheek,
And love to live in dimple sleek;
Sport that wrincled Care derides,
And Laughter holding both his
  sides.
Com, and trip it as ye go
On the light fantastick toe,
And in thy right hand lead with
  thee,
The Mountain Nymph, sweet
  Liberty;
And if I give thee honour due,
Mirth, admit me of thy crue
To live with her, and live with
  thee,
In unreproved pleasures free;
To hear the Lark begin his flight,
And singing startle the dull night,
From his watch-towre in the skies,
Till the dappled dawn doth rise;
Then to com in spight of sorrow,
And at my window bid good
  morrow,
Through the Sweet-Briar, or the
  Vine,
Or the twisted Eglantine.
While the Cock with lively din,
Scatters the rear of darknes thin,
And to the stack, or the Barn dore,
Stoutly struts his Dames before,
Oft list'ning how the Hounds and
  horn

Chearly rouse the slumbring morn,
From the side of som Hoar Hill,
Through the high wood echoing
    shrill.
Som time walking not unseen
By Hedge-row Elms, on Hillocks
    green,
Right against the Eastern gate,
Wher the great Sun begins his
    state,
Rob'd in flames, and Amber light,
The clouds in thousand Liveries
    dight.
While the Plowman neer at hand,
Whistles ore the Furrow'd Land,
And the Milkmaid singeth blithe,
And the Mower whets his sithe,
And every Shepherd tells his tale
Under the Hawthorn in the dale.
Streit mine eye hath caught new
    pleasures
Whilst the Lantskip round it
    measures,
Russet Lawns, and Fallows Gray,
Where the nibbling flocks do
    stray,
Mountains on whose barren brest
The labouring clouds do often
    rest:
Meadows trim with Daisies pide,
Shallow Brooks, and Rivers wide.
Towers, and Battlements it sees
Boosom'd high in tufted Trees,
Wher perhaps som beauty lies,
The Cynosure of neighbouring
    eyes.
Hard by, a Cottage chimney
    smokes,
From betwixt two aged Okes,
Where *Corydon* and *Thyrsis* met,

Are at their savory dinner set
Of Hearbs, and other Country
    Messes,
Which the neat-handed *Phillis*
    dresses;
And then in haste her Bowre she
    leaves,
With *Thestylis* to bind the
    Sheaves;
Or if the earlier season lead
To the tann'd Haycock in the
    Mead,
Som times with secure delight
The up-land Hamlets will invite,
When the merry Bells ring round,
And the jocond rebecks sound
To many a youth, and many a
    maid,
Dancing in the Chequer'd shade;
And young and old com forth to
    play
On a Sunshine Holyday,
Till the live-long day-light fail,
Then to the Spicy Nut-brown Ale,
With stories told of many a feat,
How *Faery Mab* the junkets eat,
She was pincht, and pull'd she
    sed,
And he by Friars Lanthorn led
Tells how the drudging *Goblin*
    swet,
To ern his Cream-bowle duly set,
When in one night, ere glimps of
    morn,
His shadowy Flale hath thresh'd
    the Corn
That ten day-labourers could not
    end,
Then lies him down the Lubbar
    Fend.

And stretch'd out all the
    Chimney's length,
Basks at the fire his hairy
    strength;
And Crop-full out of dores he
    flings,
Ere the first Cock his Mattin rings.
Thus don the Tales, to bed they
    creep,
By whispering Windes soon lull'd
    asleep.
Towred Cities please us then,
And the busie humm of men,
Where throngs of Knights and
    Barons bold,
In weeds of Peace high triumphs
    hold,
With store of Ladies, whose bright
    eies
Rain influence, and judge the prise
Of Wit, or Arms, while both
    contend
To win her Grace, whom all
    commend.
There let *Hymen* oft appear
In Saffron robe, with Taper clear,
And pomp, and feast, and revelry,
With mask, and antique
    Pageantry,
Such sights as youthful Poets dream
On Summer eeves by haunted stream.

Then to the well-trod stage anon,
If *Jonsons* learned Sock be on,
Or sweetest *Shakespear* fancies
    childe,
Warble his native Wood-notes
    wilde,
And ever against eating Cares,
Lap me in soft *Lydian* Aires,
Married to immortal verse
Such as the meeting soul may
    pierce
In notes, with many a winding
    bout
Of lincked sweetnes long drawn
    out,
With wanton heed, and giddy
    cunning,
The melting voice through mazes
    running;
Untwisting all the chains that ty
The hidden soul of harmony.
That *Orpheus* self may heave his
    head
From golden slumber on a bed
Of heapt *Elysian* flowres, and hear
Such streins as would have won
    the ear
Of *Pluto,* to have quite set free
His half regain'd *Eurydice.*
These delights, if thou canst give,
Mirth with thee, I mean to live.

JOHN MILTON

DO NOT GO GENTLE INTO THAT GOOD NIGHT

Do not go gentle into that good
night,
Old age should burn and rave at
close of day;
Rage, rage against the dying of
the light.

Though wise men at their end
know dark is right,
Because their words had forked no
lightning they
Do not go gentle into that good
night.

Good men, the last wave by,
crying how bright
Their frail deeds might have
danced in a green bay,
Rage, rage against the dying of
the light.

Wild men who caught and sang
the sun in flight,
And learn, too late, they grieved
it on its way,
Do not go gentle into that good
night.

Grave men, near death, who see
with blinding sight
Blind eyes could blaze like
meteors and be gay,
Rage, rage against the dying of
the light.

And you, my father, there on the
sad height,
Curse, bless, me now with your
fierce tears, I pray.
Do not go gentle into that good night.
Rage, rage against the dying of the light.

DYLAN THOMAS

IN MEMORY OF W. B. YEATS

I

He disappeared in the dead of winter:
The brooks were frozen, the air-ports almost deserted,
And snow disfigured the public statues;
The mercury sank in the mouth of the dying day.
O all the instruments agree
The day of his death was a dark cold day.

Far from his illness
The wolves ran on through the evergreen forests,
The peasant river was untempted by the fashionable quays;
By mourning tongues
The death of the poet was kept from his poems.

But for him it was his last afternoon as himself,
An afternoon of nurses and rumours;
The provinces of his body revolted,
The squares of his mind were empty,
Silence invaded the suburbs,
The current of his feeling failed: he became his admirers.

Now he is scattered among a hundred cities
And wholly given over to unfamiliar affections;
To find his happiness in another kind of wood
And be punished under a foreign code of conscience.
The words of a dead man
Are modified in the guts of the living.

But in the importance and noise of to-morrow
When the brokers are roaring like beasts on the floor of the Bourse,
And the poor have the sufferings to which they are fairly accustomed,
And each in the cell of himself is almost convinced of his freedom;
A few thousand will think of this day
As one thinks of a day when one did something slightly unusual.

O all the instruments agree
The day of his death was a dark cold day.

II

You were silly like us: your gift survived it all;
The parish of rich women, physical decay,
Yourself; mad Ireland hurt you into poetry.
Now Ireland has her madness and her weather still,
For poetry makes nothing happen: it survives
In the valley of its saying where executives
Would never want to tamper; it flows south
From ranches of isolation and the busy griefs,
Raw towns that we believe and die in; it survives,
A way of happening, a mouth.

III

Earth, receive an honoured guest;
William Yeats is laid to rest:
Let the Irish vessel lie
Emptied of its poetry.

Time that is intolerant
Of the brave and innocent,
And indifferent in a week
To a beautiful physique,

Worships language and forgives
Everyone by whom it lives;
Pardons cowardice, conceit,
Lays its honours at their feet.

Time that with this strange excuse
Pardoned Kipling and his views,
And will pardon Paul Claudel,
Pardons him for writing well.

In the nightmare of the dark
All the dogs of Europe bark,

And the living nations wait,
Each sequestered in its hate;

Intellectual disgrace
Stares from every human face,
And the seas of pity lie
Locked and frozen in each eye.

Follow, poet, follow right
To the bottom of the night,
With your unconstraining voice
Still persuade us to rejoice;

With the farming of a verse
Make a vineyard of the curse,
Sing of human unsuccess
In a rapture of distress;

In the deserts of the heart
Let the healing fountain start,
In the prison of his days
Teach the free man how to praise.

W. H. AUDEN

RUBÁIYÁT OF OMAR KHAYYÁM
OF NAISHÁPÚR

Wake! For the Sun who scattered into flight
The Stars before him from the Field of Night,
  Drives Night along with them from Heav'n, and strikes
The Sultán's Turret with a Shaft of Light.

Before the phantom of False morning died,
Methought a Voice within the Tavern cried,
  "When all the Temple is prepared within,
Why nods the drowsy Worshipper outside?"

And, as the Cock crew, those who stood before
The Tavern shouted—"Open then the door!
  You know how little while we have to stay,
And, once departed, may return no more."

Now the New Year reviving old Desires,
The thoughtful Soul to Solitude retires,
  Where the WHITE HAND OF MOSES on the Bough
Puts out, and Jesus from the Ground suspires.

Iram indeed is gone with all his Rose,
And Jamshyd's Sev'n-ringed Cup where no one knows;
  But still a Ruby kindles in the Vine,
And many a Garden by the Water blows.

And David's lips are lockt; but in divine
High-piping Pehleví, with "Wine! Wine! Wine!
    Red Wine!"—the Nightingale cries to the Rose
That sallow cheek of hers to incarnadine.

Come, fill the Cup, and in the fire of Spring
Your Winter-garment of Repentance fling:
    The Bird of Time has but a little way
To flutter—and the Bird is on the Wing.

Whether at Naishápúr or Babylon,
Whether the Cup with sweet or bitter run,
    The Wine of Life keeps oozing drop by drop,
The Leaves of Life keep falling one by one.

Each Morn a thousand Roses brings, you say;
Yes, but where leaves the Rose of Yesterday?
    And this first Summer month that brings the Rose
Shall take Jamshyd and Kaikobád away.

Well, let it take them. What have we to do
With Kaikobád the Great, or Kaikhosrú?
    Let Zál and Rustum bluster as they will,
Or Hátim call to Supper—heed not you.

With me along the strip of Herbage strown
That just divides the desert from the sown,
    Where name of Slave and Sultán is forgot—
And Peace to Mahmúd on his golden Throne!

A Book of Verses underneath the Bough,
A Jug of Wine, a Loaf of Bread—and Thou
    Beside me singing in the Wilderness—
Oh, Wilderness were Paradise enow!

Some for the Glories of This World; and some
Sigh for the Prophet's Paradise to come;
    Ah, take the Cash, and let the Credit go,
Nor heed the rumble of a distant Drum!

Look to the blowing Rose about us—"Lo,
Laughing," she says, "into the world I blow,
    At once the silken tassel of my Purse
Tear, and its Treasure on the Garden throw."

And those who husbanded the Golden grain,
And those who flung it to the winds like Rain,
    Alike to no such aureate Earth are turned
As, buried once, Men want dug up again.

The Worldly Hope men set their Hearts upon
Turns Ashes—or it prospers; and anon,
    Like Snow upon the Desert's dusty Face,
Lighting a little hour or two—is gone.

Think, in this battered Caravanserai
Whose Portals are alternate Night and Day,
    How Sultán after Sultán with his Pomp
Abode his destined Hour, and went his way.

They say the Lion and the Lizard keep
The Courts where Jamshyd gloried and drank deep:
    And Bahrám, that great Hunter—the Wild Ass
Stamps o'er his Head, but cannot break his Sleep.

I sometimes think that never blows so red
The Rose as where some buried Cæsar bled;
    That every Hyacinth the Garden wears
Dropt in her Lap from some once lovely Head.

And this reviving Herb whose tender Green
Fledges the River-Lip on which we lean—
    Ah, lean upon it lightly! for who knows
From what once lovely Lip it springs unseen!

Ah, my Belovéd, fill the cup that clears
To-DAY of past regrets and future Fears:
    To-morrow!—Why, To-morrow I may be
Myself with Yesterday's Sev'n thousand Years.

For some we loved, the loveliest and the best
That from his Vintage rolling Time hath prest,
   Have drunk their Cup a Round or two before,
And one by one crept silently to rest.

And we, that now make merry in the Room
They left, and Summer dresses in new bloom,
   Ourselves must we beneath the Couch of Earth
Descend—ourselves to make a Couch—for whom?

Ah, make the most of what we yet may spend,
Before we too into the Dust descend;
   Dust into Dust, and under Dust, to lie,
Sans Wine, sans Song, sans Singer, and—sans End!

Alike for those who for TO-DAY prepare,
And those that after some TO-MORROW stare,
   A Muezzín from the Tower of Darkness cries,
"Fools! Your reward is neither Here nor There."

Why, all the Saints and Sages who discussed
Of the Two Worlds so wisely—they are thrust
   Like foolish Prophets forth; their Words to Scorn
Are scatter'd, and their Mouths are stopt with Dust.

Myself when young did eagerly frequent
Doctor and Saint, and heard great argument
   About it and about: but evermore
Came out by the same door where in I went.

With them the seed of Wisdom did I sow,
And with mine own hand wrought to make it grow;
   And this was all the Harvest that I reap'd—
"I came like Water, and like Wind I go."

Into this Universe, and *Why* not knowing,
Nor *Whence*, like Water willy-nilly flowing;
   And out of it, as Wind along the Waste,
I know not *Whither*, willy-nilly blowing.

What, without asking, hither hurried *Whence?*
And, without asking, *Whither* hurried hence!
   Oh, many a Cup of this forbidden Wine
Must drown the memory of that insolence!

Up from Earth's Centre through the Seventh Gate
I rose, and on the Throne of Saturn sate;
   And many a Knot unravel'd by the Road;
But not the Master-knot of Human Fate.

There was the Door to which I found no Key;
There was the Veil through which I might not see:
   Some little talk awhile of ME AND THEE
There was—and then no more of THEE AND ME.

Earth could not answer; nor the Seas that mourn
In flowing Purple, of their Lord forlorn;
   Nor rolling Heaven, with all his Signs revealed
And hidden by the sleeve of Night and Morn.

Then of the THEE IN ME who works behind
The Veil, I lifted up my hands to find
   A Lamp amid the Darkness; and I heard,
As from Without—"THE ME WITHIN THEE BLIND!"

Then to the Lip of this poor earthen Urn
I lean'd, the Secret of my Life to learn:
   And Lip to Lip it murmur'd—"While you live,
Drink!—for, once dead, you never shall return."

I think the Vessel, that with fugitive
Articulation, answer'd, once did live,
   And drink; and Ah! the passive Lip I kiss'd,
How many Kisses might it take—and give!

For I remember stopping by the way
To watch a Potter thumping his wet Clay:
   And with its all-obliterated Tongue
It murmured—"Gently, Brother, gently, pray!"

And has not such a Story from of Old
Down Man's successive generations roll'd,
   Of such a clod of saturated Earth
Cast by the Maker into Human mould?

And not a drop that from our Cups we throw
For Earth to drink of, but may steal below
   To quench the fire of Anguish in some Eye
There hidden—far beneath, and long ago.

As then the Tulip from her morning sup
Of Heav'nly Vintage from the soil looks up,
   Do you devoutly do the like, till Heav'n
To Earth invert you—like an empty Cup.

Perplext no more with Human or Divine,
To-morrow's tangle to the winds resign,
   And lose your fingers in the tresses of
The Cypress-slender Minister of Wine.

And if the Wine you drink, the Lip you press,
End in what All begins and ends in—Yes;
   Think then you are TO-DAY what YESTERDAY
You were—TO-MORROW you shall not be less.

So when the Angel of the darker Drink
At last shall find you by the river-brink,
   And, offering his Cup, invite your Soul
Forth to your Lips to quaff—you shall not shrink.

Why, if the Soul can fling the Dust aside,
And naked on the Air of Heaven ride,
   Were't not a Shame—were't not a Shame for him
In this clay carcase crippled to abide?

'Tis but a Tent where takes his one-day's rest
A Sultán to the realm of Death addrest;
   The Sultán rises, and the dark Ferrásh
Strikes, and prepares it for another Guest.

And fear not lest Existence closing your
Account, and mine, should know the like no more;
    The Eternal Sákí from that Bowl has pour'd
Millions of Bubbles like us, and will pour.

When you and I behind the Veil are past,
Oh, but the long, long while the World shall last,
    Which of our Coming and Departure heeds
As the SEA's SELF should heed a pebble-cast.

A Moment's Halt—a momentary taste
Of BEING from the Well amid the Waste—
    And Lo!—the phantom Caravan has reach'd
The NOTHING it set out from—Oh, make haste!

Would you that spangle of Existence spend
About THE SECRET—quick about it, Friend!
    A Hair perhaps divides the False and True—
And upon what, prithee, may Life depend?

A Hair perhaps divides the False and True;
Yes; and a single Alif were the clue—
    Could you but find it—to the Treasure-house,
And peradventure to THE MASTER too;

Whose secret Presence, through Creation's veins
Running Quicksilver-like eludes your pains;
    Taking all shapes from Máh to Máhi; and
They change and perish all—but He remains;

A moment guess'd—then back behind the Fold
Immerst of Darkness round the Drama roll'd
    Which, for the Pastime of Eternity,
He does Himself contrive, enact, behold.

But if in vain, down on the stubborn floor
Of Earth, and up to Heav'n's unopening door,
    You gaze TO-DAY, while You are You—how then
TO-MORROW, You when shall be You no more?

Waste not your Hour, nor in the vain pursuit
Of This and That endeavour and dispute;
   Better be jocund with the fruitful Grape
Than sadden after none, or bitter, Fruit.

You know, my Friends, with what a brave Carouse
I made a Second Marriage in my house;
   Divorced old barren Reason from my Bed,
And took the Daughter of the Vine to Spouse.

For "IS" and "IS-NOT" though with Rule and Line,
And "UP-AND-DOWN" by Logic I define,
   Of all that one should care to fathom, I
Was never deep in anything but—Wine.

Ah, but my Computations, People say,
Reduced the Year to better reckoning?—Nay,
   'Twas only striking from the Calendar
Unborn To-morrow, and dead Yesterday.

And lately, by the Tavern Door agape,
Came shining through the Dusk an Angel Shape
   Bearing a Vessel on his Shoulder; and
He bid me taste of it; and 'twas—the Grape!

The Grape that can with Logic absolute
The Two-and-Seventy jarring Sects confute:
   The sovereign Alchemist that in a trice
Life's leaden metal into Gold transmute:

The mighty Mahmúd, Allah-breathing Lord,
That all the misbelieving and black Horde
   Of Fears and Sorrows that infest the Soul
Scatters before him with his whirlwind Sword.

Why, be this Juice the growth of God, who dare
Blaspheme the twisted tendril as a Snare?
   A Blessing, we should use it, should we not?
And if a Curse—why, then, Who set it there?

I must abjure the Balm of Life, I must,
Scared by some After-reckoning ta'en on trust,
   Or lured with Hope of some Diviner Drink,
To fill the Cup—when crumbled into Dust!

O threats of Hell and Hopes of Paradise!
One thing at least is certain,—*This* Life flies;
   One thing is certain and the rest is Lies;
The Flower that once has blown for ever dies.

Strange, is it not? that of the myriads who
Before us passed the door of Darkness through
   Not one returns to tell us of the Road
Which to discover we must travel too.

The Revelations of Devout and Learn'd
Who rose before us, and as Prophets burn'd,
   Are all but Stories, which, awoke from Sleep
They told their fellows, and to Sleep return'd.

I sent my Soul through the Invisible,
Some letter of that After-life to spell:
   And by and by my Soul return'd to me,
And answered "I Myself am Heav'n and Hell":

Heav'n but the Vision of fulfill'd Desire,
And Hell the Shadow from a Soul on fire,
   Cast on the Darkness into which Ourselves,
So late emerged from, shall so soon expire.

We are no other than a moving row
Of Magic Shadow-shapes that come and go
   Round with this Sun-illumined Lantern held
In Midnight by the Master of the Show;

But helpless Pieces of the Game He plays
Upon this Chequer-board of Nights and Days;
   Hither and thither moves, and checks, and slays,
And one by one back in the Closet lays.

The Ball no question makes of Ayes and Noes,
But Here or There as strikes the Player goes;
  And He that tossed you down into the Field,
He knows about it all—HE knows—HE knows!

The Moving Finger writes; and, having writ,
Moves on: nor all your Piety nor Wit
  Shall lure it back to cancel half a Line,
Nor all your Tears wash out a Word of it.

And that inverted Bowl they call the Sky,
Whereunder crawling coop'd we live and die,
  Lift not your hands to *It* for help—for It
As impotently rolls as you or I.

With Earth's first Clay They did the Last Man knead,
And there of the Last Harvest sowed the Seed:
  And the first Morning of Creation wrote
What the Last Dawn of Reckoning shall read.

YESTERDAY *This* Day's Madness did prepare;
TO-MORROW's Silence, Triumph, or Despair:
  Drink! for you know not whence you came, nor why:
Drink! for you know not why you go, nor where.

I tell you this—When, started from the Goal,
Over the flaming shoulders of the Foal
  Of Heav'n Parwín and Mushtarí they flung,
In my predestined Plot of Dust and Soul

The Vine had struck a fibre: which about
It clings my Being—let the Dervish flout;
  Of my Base metal may be filed a Key,
That shall unlock the Door he howls without.

And this I know: whether the one True Light
Kindle to Love, or Wrath-consume me quite,
  One Flash of It within the Tavern caught
Better than in the Temple lost outright.

What! out of senseless Nothing to provoke
A conscious Something to resent the yoke
   Of unpermitted Pleasure, under pain
Of Everlasting Penalties, if broke!

What! from his helpless Creature he repaid
Pure Gold for what he lent him dross-allayed—
   Sue for a Debt we never did contract,
And cannot answer—Oh, the sorry trade!

Oh Thou, who didst with pitfall and with gin
Beset the Road I was to wander in,
   Thou wilt not with Predestined Evil round
Enmesh, and then impute my Fall to Sin!

Oh Thou, who Man of baser Earth didst make
And ev'n with Paradise devise the Snake:
   For all the Sin wherewith the Face of Man
Is blacken'd—Man's Forgiveness give—and take!

   .   .   .   .   .

As under cover of departing Day
Slunk hunger-stricken Ramazán away,
   Once more within the Potter's house alone
I stood, surrounded by the Shapes of Clay.

Shapes of all Sorts and Sizes, great and small,
That stood along the floor and by the wall;
   And some loquacious Vessels were; and some
Listen'd perhaps, but never talk'd at all.

Said one among them—"Surely not in vain
My substance of the common Earth was ta'em
   And to this Figure moulded, to be broke,
Or trampled back to shapeless Earth again."

Then said a Second—"Ne'er a peevish Boy
Would break the Bowl from which he drank in joy;
   And He that with his hand the Vessel made
Will surely not in after Wrath destroy."

After a momentary silence spake
Some Vessel of a more ungainly Make;
　　"They sneer at me for leaning all awry:
What! did the Hand then of the Potter shake?"

Whereat some one of the loquacious Lot—
I think a Súfi pipkin—waxing hot—
　　"All this of Pot and Potter—Tell me, then,
Who is the Potter, pray, and who the Pot?"

"Why," said another, "Some there are who tell
Of one who threatens he will toss to Hell
　　The luckless Pots he marr'd in making—Pish!
He's a Good Fellow, and 'twill all be well."

"Well," murmur'd one, "Let whoso make or buy,
My Clay with long Oblivion is gone dry:
　　But fill me with the old familiar Juice,
Methinks I might recover by and by."

So while the Vessels one by one were speaking,
The little Moon look'd in that all were seeking:
　　And then they jogg'd each other, "Brother! Brother!
Now for the Porter's shoulder-knot a-creaking!"

　　　　.　　.　　.　　.　　.

Ah, with the Grape my fading Life provide,
And wash the Body whence the Life has died,
　　And lay me, shrouded in the living Leaf,
By some not unfrequented Garden-side.

That ev'n my buried Ashes such a snare
Of Vintage shall fling up into the Air
　　As not a True-believer passing by
But shall be overtaken unaware.

Indeed the Idols I have loved so long
Have done my credit in this World much wrong:
　　Have drown'd my Glory in a shallow Cup,
And sold my Reputation for a Song.

Indeed, indeed, Repentance oft before
I swore—but was I sober when I swore?
   And then and then came Spring, and Rose-in-hand
My thread-bare Penitence apieces tore.

And much as Wine has play'd the Infidel,
And robb'd me of my Robe of Honour—Well,
   I wonder often what the Vintners buy
One half so precious as the stuff they sell.

Yet Ah, that Spring should vanish with the Rose!
That Youth's sweet-scented manuscript should close!
   The Nightingale that in the branches sang,
Ah whence, and whither flown again, who knows!

Would but the Desert of the Fountain yield
One glimpse—if dimly, yet indeed, reveal'd,
   To which the fainting Traveller might spring,
As springs the trampled herbage of the field!

Would but some wingèd Angel ere too late
Arrest the yet unfolded Roll of Fate,
   And make the stern Recorder otherwise
Enregister, or quite obliterate!

Ah Love! could you and I with Him conspire
To grasp this sorry Scheme of Things entire,
   Would not we shatter it to bits—and then
Re-mould it nearer to the Heart's Desire!

     .   .   .   .   .

Yon rising Moon that looks for us again—
How oft hereafter will she wax and wane;
   How oft hereafter rising look for us
Through this same Garden—and for *one* in vain!

And when like her, oh Sákí, you shall pass
Among the Guests Star-scatter'd on the Grass,
   And in your joyous errand reach the spot
Where I made One—turn down an empty Glass!

              TAMÁM

                EDWARD FITZGERALD

LOCKSLEY HALL

Comrades, leave me here a little, while as yet 'tis early morn:
Leave me here, and when you want me, sound upon the bugle-horn.
'Tis the place, and all around it, as of old, the curlews call,
Dreary gleams about the moorland flying over Locksley Hall;
Locksley Hall, that in the distance overlooks the sandy tracts,
And the hollow ocean-ridges roaring into cataracts.

Many a night from yonder ivied casement, ere I went to rest,
Did I look on great Orion sloping slowly to the West.
Many a night I saw the Pleiads, rising thro' the mellow shade,
Glitter like a swarm of fire-flies tangled in a silver braid.
Here about the beach I wander'd, nourishing a youth sublime
With the fairy tales of science, and the long result of Time;
When the centuries behind me like a fruitful land reposed;
When I clung to all the present for the promise that it closed:
When I dipt into the future far as human eye could see;
Saw the Vision of the world, and all the wonder that would be.—

In the Spring a fuller crimson comes upon the robin's breast;
In the Spring the wanton lapwing gets himself another crest;
In the Spring a livelier iris changes on the burnish'd dove;
In the Spring a young man's fancy lightly turns to thoughts of love.

Then her cheek was pale and thinner than should be for one so young,
And her eyes on all my motions with a mute observance hung.
And I said, "My cousin Amy, speak, and speak the truth to me,
Trust me, cousin, all the current of my being sets to thee."
On her pallid cheek and forehead came a colour and a light,
As I have seen the rosy red flushing in the northern night.
And she turn'd—her bosom shaken with a sudden storm of sighs—
All the spirit deeply dawning in the dark of hazel eyes—

Saying, "I have hid my feelings, fearing they should do me wrong;"
Saying, "Dost thou love me, cousin?" weeping, "I have loved thee long."

Love took up the glass of Time, and turn'd it in his glowing hands;
Every moment, lightly shaken, ran itself in golden sands.
Love took up the harp of Life, and smote on all the chords with might;
Smote the chord of Self, that, trembling, pass'd in music out of sight.
Many a morning on the moorland did we hear the copses ring,
And her whisper throng'd my pulses with the fullness of the Spring.
Many an evening by the waters did we watch the stately ships,
And our spirits rush'd together at the touching of the lips.

O my cousin, shallow-hearted! O my Amy, mine no more!
O the dreary, dreary moorland! O the barren, barren shore!
Falser than all fancy fathoms, falser than all songs have sung,
Puppet to a father's threat, and servile to a shrewish tongue!
Is it well to wish thee happy?—having known me—to decline
On a range of lower feelings and a narrower heart than mine!
Yet it shall be: thou shalt lower to his level day by day,
What is fine within thee growing coarse to sympathize with clay.

As the husband is, the wife is: thou art mated with a clown,
And the grossness of his nature will have weight to drag thee down.
He will hold thee, when his passion shall have spent its novel force,
Something better than his dog, a little dearer than his horse.
What is this? his eyes are heavy: think not they are glazed with wine.
Go to him: it is thy duty: kiss him: take his hand in thine.
It may be my lord is weary, that his brain is over-wrought:
Soothe him with thy finer fancies, touch him with thy lighter thought.

He will answer to the purpose, easy things to understand—
Better thou wert dead before me, tho' I slew thee with my hand!
Better thou and I were lying, hidden from the heart's disgrace,
Roll'd in one another's arms, and silent in a last embrace.
Cursed be the social wants that sin against the strength of youth!
Cursed be the social lies that warp us from the living truth!
Cursed be the sickly forms that err from honest Nature's rule!
Cursed be the gold that gilds the straiten'd forehead of the fool!

Well—'tis well that I should bluster!—Hadst thou less unworthy proved—
Would to God—for I had loved thee more than ever wife was loved.
Am I mad, that I should cherish that which bears but bitter fruit?
I will pluck it from my bosom, tho' my heart be at the root.

Never, tho' my mortal summers to such length of years should come
As the many-winter'd crow that leads the clanging rookery home.
Where is comfort? in division of the records of the mind?
Can I part her from herself, and love her, as I knew her, kind?

I remember one that perish'd: sweetly did she speak and move:
Such a one do I remember, whom to look at was to love.
Can I think of her as dead, and love her for the love she bore?
No—she never loved me truly: love is love for evermore.
Comfort? comfort scorn'd of devils! this is truth the poet sings,
That a sorrow's crown of sorrow is remembering happier things.

Drug thy memories, lest thou learn it, lest thy heart be put to proof,
In the dead unhappy night, and when the rain is on the roof.
Like a dog, he hunts in dreams, and thou art staring at the wall,
Where the dying night-lamp flickers, and the shadows rise and fall.
Then a hand shall pass before thee, pointing to his drunken sleep,
To thy widow'd marriage-pillows, to the tears that thou wilt weep.
Thou shalt hear the "Never, never," whisper'd by the phantom years,
And a song from out the distance in the ringing of thine ears;
And an eye shall vex thee, looking ancient kindness on thy pain.
Turn thee, turn thee on thy pillow: get thee to thy rest again.

Nay, but Nature brings thee solace; for a tender voice will cry.
'Tis a purer life than thine; a lip to drain thy trouble dry.
Baby lips will laugh me down: my latest rival brings thee rest.
Baby fingers, waxen touches, press me from the mother's breast.
O, the child too clothes the father with a dearness not his due.
Half is thine and half is his: it will be worthy of the two.

O, I see thee old and formal, fitted to thy petty part,
With a little hoard of maxims preaching down a daughter's heart.
"They were dangerous guides the feelings—she herself was not exempt—
Truly, she herself had suffer'd"—Perish in thy self-contempt!
Overlive it—lower yet—be happy! wherefore should I care?
I myself must mix with action, lest I wither by despair.
What is that which I should turn to, lighting upon days like these?
Every door is barr'd with gold, and opens but to golden keys.
Every gate is throng'd with suitors, all the markets overflow.
I have but an angry fancy: what is that which I should do?

I had been content to perish, falling on the foeman's ground,
When the ranks are roll'd in vapour, and the winds are laid with sound.

But the jingling of the guinea helps the hurt that Honour feels,
And the nations do but murmur, snarling at each other's heels.
Can I but relive in sadness? I will turn that earlier page.
Hide me from my deep emotion, O thou wondrous Mother-Age!

Make me feel the wild pulsation that I felt before the strife,
When I heard my days before me, and the tumult of my life;
Yearning for the large excitement that the coming years would yield,
Eager-hearted as a boy when first he leaves his father's field,
And at night along the dusky highway near and nearer drawn,
Sees in heaven the light of London flaring like a dreary dawn;
And his spirit leaps within him to be gone before him then,
Underneath the light he looks at, in among the throngs of men;
Men, my brothers, men the workers, ever reaping something new:
That which they have done but earnest of the things that they shall do:
For I dipt into the future, far as human eye could see,
Saw the Vision of the world, and all the wonder that would be;
Saw the heavens fill with commerce, argosies of magic sails,
Pilots of the purple twilight, dropping down with costly bales;
Heard the heavens fill with shouting, and there rain'd a ghastly dew
From the nations' airy navies grappling in the central blue;
Far along the world-wide whisper of the south-wind rushing warm,
With the standards of the peoples plunging thro' the thunder storm;
Till the war-drum throbb'd no longer, and the battle flags were furl'd
In the Parliament of man, the Federation of the world.
There the common sense of most shall hold a fretful realm in awe,
And the kindly earth shall slumber, lapt in universal law.

So I triumphed, ere my passion sweeping thro' me left me dry,
Left me with the palsied heart, and left me with the jaundiced eye;
Eye, to which all order festers, all things here are out of joint,
Science moves, but slowly slowly, creeping on from point to point:
Slowly comes a hungry people, as a lion, creeping nigher,
Glares at one that nods and winks behind a slowly-dying fire.
Yet I doubt not thro' the ages one increasing purpose runs,
And the thoughts of men are widen'd with the process of the suns.

What is that to him that reaps not harvest of his youthful joys,
Tho' the deep heart of existence beat for ever like a boy's?
Knowledge comes, but wisdom lingers, and I linger on the shore,
And the individual withers, and the world is more and more.
Knowledge comes, but wisdom lingers, and he bears a laden breast,
Full of sad experience, moving toward the stillness of his rest.

Hark, my merry comrades call me, sounding on the bugle-horn,
They to whom my foolish passion were a target for their scorn:
Shall it not be scorn to me to harp on such a moulder'd string?
I am shamed thro' all my nature to have loved so slight a thing.
Weakness to be wroth with weakness! woman's pleasure, woman's
    pain—
Nature made them blinder motions bounded in a shallower brain:
Woman is the lesser man, and all thy passions, match'd with mine,
Are as moonlight unto sunlight, and as water unto wine—

Here at least, where nature sickens, nothing. Ah, for some retreat
Deep in yonder shining Orient, where my life began to beat;
Where in wild Mahratta-battle fell my father evil-starr'd;—
I was left a trampled orphan, and a selfish uncle's ward.
Or to burst all links of habit—there to wander far away,
On from island unto island at the gateways of the day.
Larger constellations burning, mellow moons and happy skies,
Breadths of tropic shade and palms in cluster, knots of Paradise.
Never comes the trader, never floats an European flag,
Slides the bird o'er lustrous woodland, swings the trailer from the crag;
Droops the heavy-blossom'd bower, hangs the heavy-fruited tree—
Summer isles of Eden lying in dark-purple spheres of sea.

There methinks would be enjoyment more than in this march of mind,
In the steamship, in the railway, in the thoughts that shake mankind.
There the passions cramp'd no longer shall have scope and breathing-
    space;
I will take some savage woman, she shall rear my dusky race.
Iron-jointed, supple-sinew'd, they shall dive, and they shall run,
Catch the wild goat by the hair, and hurl their lances in the sun;
Whistle back the parrot's call, and leap the rainbows of the brooks,
Not with blinded eyesight poring over miserable books—

Fool, again the dream, the fancy! but I *know* my words are wild,
But I count the gray barbarian lower than the Christian child.
I, to herd with narrow foreheads, vacant of our glorious gains,
Like a beast with lower pleasures, like a beast with lower pains!
Mated with a squalid savage—what to me were sun or clime?
I the heir of all the ages, in the foremost files of time—
I that rather held it better men should perish one by one,
Than that earth should stand at gaze like Joshua's moon in Ajalon!

Not in vain the distance beacons. Forward, forward let us range.
Let the great world spin for ever down the ringing grooves of change.
Thro' the shadow of the globe we swept into the younger day:
Better fifty years of Europe than a cycle of Cathay.
Mother-Age (for mine I knew not) help me as when life begun:
Rift the hills, and roll the waters, flash the lightnings, weigh the Sun—
O, I see the crescent promise of my spirit hath not set.
Ancient founts of inspiration well thro' all my fancy yet.

Howsoever these things be, a long farewell to Locksley Hall!
Now for me the woods may wither, now for me the rooftree fall.
Comes a vapour from the margin, blackening over heath and holt,
Cramming all the blast before it, in its breast a thunderbolt.
Let it fall on Locksley Hall, with rain or hail, or fire or snow;
For the mighty wind arises, roaring seaward, and I go.

ALFRED, LORD TENNYSON

ANNABEL LEE

It was many and many a year ago,
  In a kingdom by the sea,
That a maiden there lived whom you may know
  By the name of Annabel Lee;—
And this maiden she lived with no other thought
  Than to love and be loved by me.

I was a child and *she* was a child,
  In this kingdom by the sea,
But we loved with a love that was more than love—
  I and my Annabel Lee—
With a love that the wingèd seraphs in Heaven
  Coveted her and me.

And this was the reason that, long ago,
  In this kingdom by the sea,
A wind blew out of a cloud, chilling
  My beautiful Annabel Lee;
So that her high-born kinsmen came
  And bore her away from me,
To shut her up in a sepulcher
  In this kingdom by the sea.

The angels, not half so happy in Heaven,
   Went envying her and me:—
Yes!—that was the reason (as all men know,
   In this kingdom by the sea)
That the wind came out of the cloud, by night,
   Chilling and killing my Annabel Lee.

But our love it was stronger by far than the love
   Of those who were older than we—
   Of many far wiser than we—
And neither the angels in Heaven above,
   Nor the demons down under the sea,
Can ever dissever my soul from the soul
   Of the beautiful Annabel Lee:—

For the moon never beams without bringing me dreams
   Of the beautiful Annabel Lee;
And the stars never rise but I feel the bright eyes
   Of the beautiful Annabel Lee;
And so, all the night-tide, I lie down by the side
Of my darling,—my darling,—my life and my bride,
   In her sepulcher there by the sea—
   In her tomb by the sounding sea.

                    EDGAR ALLAN POE

THE GROUNDHOG

In June, amid the golden fields,
I saw a groundhog lying dead.
Dead lay he; my senses shook,
And mind outshot our naked
  frailty.
There lowly in the vigorous
  summer
His form began its senseless change,
And made my senses waver dim
Seeing nature ferocious in him.
Inspecting close his maggots' might

And seething cauldron of his being,
Half with loathing, half with a
  strange love,
I poked him with an angry stick.
The fever arose, became a flame
And Vigour circumscribed the skies,
Immense energy in the sun,
And through my frame a sunless
  trembling.
My stick had done nor good nor
  harm.

Then stood I silent in the day
Watching the object, as before;
And kept my reverence for
  knowledge
Trying for control, to be still,
To quell the passion of the blood;
Until I had bent down on my
  knees
Praying for joy in the sight of
  decay.
And so I left; and I returned
In Autumn strict of eye, to see
The sap gone out of the
  groundhog,
But the bony sodden hulk
  remained.
But the year had lost its meaning,
And in intellectual chains
I lost both love and loathing,
Mured up in the wall of wisdom.
Another summer took the fields
  again
Massive and burning, full of life,

But when I chanced upon the
  spot
There was only a little hair left,
And bones bleaching in the
  sunlight
Beautiful as architecture;
I watched them like a geometer,
And cut a walking stick from a
  birch.
It has been three years, now.
There is no sign of the
  groundhog.
I stood there in the whirling
  summer,
My hand capped a withered heart,
And thought of China and of
  Greece,
Of Alexander in his tent;
Of Montaigne in his tower,
Of Saint Theresa in her wild
  lament.

RICHARD EBERHART

THE NOBLEST ROMAN

This was the noblest Roman of
  them all:
All the conspirators, save only he,
Did that they did in envy of great
  Caesar;
He only, in a general honest thought
And common good to all, made
  one of them.

His life was gentle, and the
  elements
So mix'd in him that Nature
  might stand up
And say to all the world "This
  was a man!"

WILLIAM SHAKESPEARE

MUSÉE DES BEAUX ARTS

About suffering they were never wrong,
The Old Masters: how well they understood
Its human position; how it takes place
While someone else is eating or opening a window or just walking
    dully along;
How, when the aged are reverently, passionately waiting
For the miraculous birth, there always must be
Children who did not specially want it to happen, skating
On a pond at the edge of the wood:
They never forgot
That even the dreadful martyrdom must run its course
Anyhow in a corner, some untidy spot
Where the dogs go on with their doggy life and the torturer's horse
Scratches its innocent behind on a tree.

In Brueghel's *Icarus,* for instance: how everything turns away
Quite leisurely from the disaster; the ploughman may
Have heard the splash, the forsaken cry,
But for him it was not an important failure; the sun shone
As it had to on the white legs disappearing into the green
Water; and the expensive delicate ship that must have seen
Something amazing, a boy falling out of the sky,
Had somewhere to get to and sailed calmly on.

W. H. AUDEN

A POISON TREE

I was angry with my friend:
I told my wrath, my wrath did end.
I was angry with my foe:
I told it not, my wrath did grow.

And I watered it in fears,
Night and morning with my tears;
And I sunnèd it with smiles,
And with soft deceitful wiles.

And it grew both day and night,
Till it bore an apple bright;
And my foe beheld it shine,
And he knew that it was mine,

And into my garden stole,
When the night had veiled the pole:
In the morning glad I see
My foe outstretched beneath the tree.

WILLIAM BLAKE

PATTERNS

I walk down the garden paths,
And all the daffodils
Are blowing, and the bright blue
    squills.

I walk down the patterned garden
    paths
In my stiff, brocaded gown.
With my powdered hair and
    jeweled fan
I too am a rare
Pattern. As I wander down
The garden paths.

My dress is richly figured,
And the train
Makes a pink and silver stain
On the gravel, and the thrift
Of the borders.
Just a plate of current fashion,
Tripping by in high-heeled,
    ribboned shoes
Not a softness anywhere about
    me,
Only whale-bone and brocade.
And I sink on a seat in the shade
Of a lime tree. For my passion
Wars against the stiff brocade.
The daffodils and squills
Flutter in the breeze
As they please.
And I weep;
For the lime tree is in blossom
And one small flower has dropped
    upon my bosom.

And the plashing of waterdrops
In the marble fountain
Comes down the garden paths.
The dripping never stops.
Underneath my stiffened gown
Is the softness of a woman bathing
    in a marble basin,
A basin in the midst of hedges
    grown
So thick, she cannot see her lover
    hiding,
But she guesses he is near,
And the sliding of the water
Seems the stroking of a dear
Hand upon her.
What is Summer in a fine
    brocaded gown!
I should like to see it lying in a
    heap upon the ground,
All the pink and silver crumpled
    up on the ground.

I would be the pink and silver as
    I ran along the paths,
And he would stumble after,
Bewildered by my laughter.
I should see the sun flashing from
    his sword hilt and the buckles
    on his shoes.
I would choose
To lead him in a maze along the
    patterned paths,
A bright and laughing maze for
    my heavy-booted lover,
Till he caught me in the shade,

And the buttons of his waistcoat
  bruised my body as he clasped
  me,
Aching, melting, unafraid.
With the shadows of the leaves
  and the sundrops,
And the plopping of the
  waterdrops,
All about us in the open
  afternoon—
I am very like to swoon
With the weight of this brocade,
For the sun sifts through the
  shade.

Underneath the fallen blossom
In my bosom,
Is a letter I have hid.
It was brought to me this morning
  by a rider from the Duke.
"Madam, we regret to inform you
  that Lord Hartwell
Died in action Thursday se'nnight."
As I read it in the white, morning
  sunlight,
The letters squirmed like snakes.
"Any answer, Madam," said my
  footman.
"No," I told him.
"See that the messenger takes
  some refreshment.
No, no answer."
And I walked into the garden,
Up and down the patterned paths,
In my stiff, correct brocade.
The blue and yellow flowers stood
  up proudly in the sun,
Each one.
I stood upright too,
Held rigid to the pattern

By the stiffness of my gown.
Up and down I walked,
Up and down.

In a month he would have been
  my husband.
In a month, here, underneath this
  lime,
He would have broken the
  pattern;
He for me, and I for him,
He as Colonel, I as Lady,
On this shady seat.
He had a whim
That sunlight carried blessing.
And I answered, "It shall be as
  you have said."
Now he is dead.
In Summer and in Winter I shall
  walk
Up and down
The patterned garden paths
In my stiff, brocaded gown.
The squills and daffodils
Will give place to pillared roses,
  and to asters, and to snow.
I shall go
Up and down,
In my gown.
Gorgeously arrayed,
Boned and stayed.
And the softness of my body will
  be guarded from embrace
By each button, hook and lace.
For the man who should loose me
  is dead,
Fighting with the Duke in
  Flanders,
In a pattern called a war.
Christ! What are patterns for?

          AMY LOWELL

THANATOPSIS

To him who in the love of Nature holds
Communion with her visible forms, she speaks
A various language; for his gayer hours
She has a voice of gladness, and a smile
And eloquence of beauty, and she glides
Into his darker musings, with a mild
And healing sympathy, that steals away
Their sharpness, ere he is aware. When thoughts
Of the last bitter hour come like a blight
Over thy spirit, and sad images
Of the stern agony, and shroud, and pall,
And breathless darkness, and the narrow house,
Make thee to shudder and grow sick at heart;—
Go forth, under the open sky, and list
To Nature's teachings, while from all around—
Earth and her waters, and the depths of air—
Comes a still voice:—

              Yet a few days, and thee
The all-beholding sun shall see no more
In all his course; nor yet in the cold ground,
Where thy pale form was laid with many tears,
Nor in the embrace of ocean, shall exist
Thy image. Earth, that nourished thee, shall claim
Thy growth, to be resolved to earth again,
And, lost each human trace, surrendering up
Thine individual being, shalt thou go
To mix forever with the elements,
To be a brother to the insensible rock
And to the sluggish clod, which the rude swain
Turns with his share, and treads upon. The oak
Shall send his roots abroad, and pierce thy mould.

Yet not to thine eternal resting-place
Shalt thou retire alone, nor couldst thou wish
Couch more magnificent. Thou shalt lie down
With patriarchs of the infant world—with kings,
The powerful of the earth—the wise, the good,
Fair forms, and hoary seers of ages past,
All in one mighty sepulchre. The hills
Rock-ribbed and ancient as the sun,—the vales
Stretching in pensive quietness between;
The venerable woods—rivers that move
In majesty, and the complaining brooks
That make the meadows green; and, poured round all,
Old Ocean's gray and melancholy waste,—
Are but the solemn decorations all
Of the great tomb of man. The golden sun,
The planets, all the infinite host of heaven,
Are shining on the sad abodes of death
Through the still lapse of ages. All that tread
The globe are but a handful to the tribes
That slumber in its bosom.— Take the wings
Of morning, pierce the Barcan wilderness,
Or lose thyself in the continuous woods
Where rolls the Oregon, and hears no sound,
Save his own dashings—yet the dead are there;
And millions in those solitudes, since first
The flight of years began, have laid them down
In their last sleep—the dead reign there alone.
So shalt thou rest, and what if thou withdraw
In silence from the living, and no friend
Take note of thy departure? All that breathe
Will share thy destiny. The gay will laugh
When thou art gone, the solemn brood of care
Plod on, and each one as before will chase
His favorite phantom; yet all these shall leave
Their mirth and their employments, and shall come
And make their bed with thee. As the long train
Of ages glides away, the sons of men—
The youth in life's fresh spring, and he who goes
In the full strength of years, matron and maid,
The speechless babe, and the gray-headed man—
Shall one by one be gathered to thy side,
By those, who in their turn shall follow them.

So live, that when thy summons comes to join
The innumerable caravan, which moves
To that mysterious realm, where each shall take
His chamber in the silent halls of death,
Thou go not, like the quarry-slave at night,
Scourged to his dungeon, but, sustained and soothed
By an unfaltering trust, approach thy grave
Like one who wraps the drapery of his couch
About him, and lies down to pleasant dreams.

WILLIAM CULLEN BRYANT

AUGURIES OF INNOCENCE

To see a World in a grain of sand,
And a Heaven in a wild flower,
Hold Infinity in the palm of your
   hand,
And Eternity in an hour.
A robin redbreast in a cage
Puts all Heaven in a rage.
A dove-house fill'd with doves and
   pigeons
Shudders Hell thro' all its regions.
A dog starv'd at his master's gate
Predicts the ruin of the State.
A horse misus'd upon the road
Calls to Heaven for human blood.
Each outcry of the hunted hare
A fibre from the brain does tear.
A skylark wounded in the wing,
A cherubim does cease to sing.

The game-cock clipt and arm'd
   for fight
Does the rising sun affright.
Every wolf's and lion's howl
Raises from Hell a Human soul.
The wild deer, wandering here
   and there,
Keeps the Human soul from care.
The lamb misus'd breeds public
   strife,
And yet forgives the butcher's
   knife.
The bat that flits at close of eve
Has left the brain that won't believe.
The owl that calls upon the night
Speaks the unbeliever's fright.
He who shall hurt the little wren
Shall never be belov'd by men.

He who the ox to wrath has mov'd
Shall never be by woman lov'd.
The wanton boy that kills the fly
Shall feel the spider's enmity.
He who torments the chafer's sprite
Weaves a bower in endless night.
The caterpillar on the leaf
Repeats to thee thy mother's grief.
Kill not the moth nor butterfly,
For the Last Judgment draweth
   nigh.
He who shall train the horse to
   war
Shall never pass the polar bar.
The beggar's dog and widow's cat,
Feed them, and thou wilt grow fat.
The gnat that sings his summer's
   song
Poison gets from Slander's tongue.
The poison of the snake and newt
Is the sweat of Envy's foot.
The poison of the honey-bee
Is the artist's jealousy.
The prince's robes and beggar's rags
Are toadstools on the miser's bags.
A truth that's told with bad intent
Beats all the lies you can invent.
It is right it should be so;
Man was made for joy and woe;
And when this we rightly know,
Thro' the world we safely go.
Joy and woe are woven fine,
A clothing for the soul divine;
Under every grief and pine
Runs a joy with silken twine.
The babe is more than swaddling-
   bands;
Throughout all these human lands
Tools were made, and born were
   hands,
Every farmer understands.

Every tear from every eye
Becomes a babe in Eternity;
This is caught by Females bright,
And return'd to its own delight.
The bleat, the bark, bellow, and
   roar
Are waves that beat on Heaven's
   shore.
The babe that weeps the rod
   beneath
Writes revenge in realms of death.
The beggar's rags, fluttering in air,
Does to rags the heavens tear.
The soldier, arm'd with sword
   and gun,
Palsied strikes the summer's sun.
The poor man's farthing is worth
   more
Than all the gold on Afric's shore.
One mite wrung from the
   labourer's hands
Shall buy and sell the miser's lands:
Or, if protected from on high,
Does that whole nation sell and buy.
He who mocks the infant's faith
Shall be mock'd in Age and Death.
He who shall teach the child to
   doubt
The rotting grave shall ne'er get out.
He who respects the infant's faith
Triumphs over Hell and Death.
The child's toys and the old man's
   reasons
Are the fruits of the two seasons.
The questioner, who sits so sly,
Shall never know how to reply.
He who replies to words of Doubt
Doth put the light of knowledge
   out.
The strongest poison ever known
Came from Caesar's laurel crown.

Nought can deform the human race
Like to the armour's iron brace.
When gold and gems adorn the
plough
To peaceful arts shall Envy bow.
A riddle, or the cricket's cry,
Is to Doubt a fit reply.
The emmet's inch and eagle's mile
Make lame Philosophy to smile.
He who doubts from what he sees
Will ne'er believe, do what you
please.
If the Sun and Moon should doubt,
They'd immediately go out.
To be in a passion you good may do,
But no good if a passion is in you.
The whore and gambler, by the state
Licensed, build that nation's fate.
The harlot's cry from street to
street
Shall weave Old England's
winding-sheet.

The winner's shout, the loser's
curse,
Dance before dead England's
hearse.
Every night and every morn
Some to misery are born.
Every morn and every night
Some are born to sweet delight.
Some are born to sweet delight,
Some are born to endless night.
We are led to believe a lie
When we see not thro' the eye,
Which was born in a night, to
perish in a night,
When the Soul slept in beams of
light.
God appears, and God is Light,
To those poor souls who dwell in
Night;
But does a Human Form display
To those who dwell in realms of
Day.

WILLIAM BLAKE

TO A LOUSE, ON SEEING ONE ON A LADY'S BONNET AT CHURCH

Ha! whare ye gaun, ye crowlan
ferlie!
Your impudence protects you
sairly:
I canna say but ye strunt rarely,
Owre gawze and lace;
Tho' faith, I fear ye dine but
sparely,
On sic a place.

Ye ugly, creepan, blastet
wonner,
Detested, shunn'd, by saunt an'
sinner,
How daur ye set your fit upon her,
Sae fine a Lady!
Gae somewhere else and seek your
dinner,
On some poor body.

Swith, in some beggar's haffet
    squattle;
There ye may creep, and sprawl,
    and sprattle,
Wi' ither kindred, jumping cattle,
    In shoals and nations;
Whare horn nor bane ne'er daur
    unsettle
        Your thick plantations.

Now haud you there, ye're out
    o' sight,
Below the fatt'rels, snug and tight,
Na faith ye yet, ye'll no be right,
    Till ye've got on it,
The vera tapmost, towrin height
    O' Miss's bonnet.

My sooth! right bauld ye set
    your nose out,
As plump an' gray as onie grozet:
O for some rank, mercurial rozet,
    Of fell, red smeddum,
I'd gie you sic a hearty dose o't,
    Wad dress your droddum!

I wad na been surpriz'd to spy
You on an auld wife's flainen toy;
Or aiblins some bit duddie boy,
    On's wylecoat;
But Miss's fine Lunardi, fye!
    How daur ye do't?

O Jenny dinna toss your head,
An' set your beauties a' abroad!
Ye little ken what cursed speed
    The beastie's makin!
Thae winks and finger-ends, I
    dread,
        Are notice takin!

O wad some Pow'r the giftie gie
    us
To see oursels as ithers see us!
It wad frae monie a blunder free
    us
        An' foolish notion:
What airs in dress an' gait wad
    lea'e us,
        And ev'n Devotion!
                ROBERT BURNS

Droddum: breech	Flainen: flannel	Rozet: rosin
Fatt'rels: folderols	Grozet: gooseberry	Smeddum: powder
Ferlie: wonder	Haffet: temple	Toy: old-fashioned
		headdress

THE GREAT LOVER

I have been so great a lover: filled
   my days
So proudly with the splendour of
   Love's praise,
The pain, the calm, and the
   astonishment,
Desire illimitable, and still
   content,
And all dear names men use, to
   cheat despair,
For the perplexed and viewless
   streams that bear
Our hearts at random down the
   dark of life.
Now, ere the unthinking silence
   on that strife
Steals down, I would cheat drowsy
   Death so far,
My night shall be remembered
   for a star
That outshone all the suns of all
   men's days.
Shall I not crown them with
   immortal praise
Whom I have loved, who have
   given me, dared with me
High secrets, and in darkness
   knelt to see
The inenarrable godhead of
   delight?
Love is a flame;—we have
   beaconed the world's night.
A city:—and we have built it,
   these and I.
An emperor:—we have taught the
   world to die.

So, for their sakes I loved, ere I
   go hence,
And the high cause of Love's
   magnificence,
And to keep loyalties young, I'll
   write those names
Golden for ever, eagles, crying
   flames,
And set them as a banner, that
   men may know,
To dare the generations, burn,
   and blow
Out on the wind of Time, shining
   and streaming. . . .

These I have loved:
   White plates and cups, clean-
   gleaming,
Ringed with blue lines; and
   feathery, faery dust;
Wet roofs, beneath the lamp-light;
   the strong crust
Of friendly bread; and many-
   tasting food;
Rainbows; and the blue bitter
   smoke of wood;
And radiant raindrops couching
   in cool flowers;
And flowers themselves, that sway
   through sunny hours,
Dreaming of moths that drink
   them under the moon;
Then, the cool kindliness of
   sheets, that soon
Smooth away trouble; and the
   rough male kiss

Of blankets; grainy wood; live
    hair that is
Shining and free; blue-massing
    clouds; the keen
Unpassioned beauty of a great
    machine;
The benison of hot water; furs to
    touch;
The good smell of old clothes;
    and other such—
The comfortable smell of friendly
    fingers,
Hair's fragrance, and the musty
    reek that lingers
About dead leaves and last year's
    ferns. . . .
                Dear names,
And thousand others throng to
    me! Royal flames;
Sweet water's dimpling laugh
    from tap or spring;
Holes in the ground; and voices
    that do sing:
Voices in laughter, too; and body's
    pain,
Soon turned to peace; and the
    deep-panting train;
Firm sands; the little dulling edge
    of foam
That browns and dwindles as the
    wave goes home;
And washen stones, gay for an
    hour; the cold
Graveness of iron; moist black
    earthen mould;
Sleep; and high places; footprints
    in the dew;
And oaks; and brown horse-
    chestnuts, glossy-new;

And new-peeled sticks; and
    shining pools on grass;—
All these have been my loves. And
    these shall pass.
Whatever passes not, in the great
    hour,
Nor all my passion, all my
    prayers, have power
To hold them with me through
    the gate of Death.
They'll play deserter, turn with
    traitor breath,
Break the high bond we made,
    and sell Love's trust
And sacramental covenant to the
    dust.

—Oh, never a doubt but,
    somewhere, I shall wake,
And give what's left of love again,
    and make
New friends, now strangers. . .
           But the best I've known,
Stays here, and changes, breaks,
    grows old, is blown
About the winds of the world, and
    fades from brains
Of living men, and dies.
           Nothing remains.

O dear my loves, O faithless, once
    again
This one last gift I give: that after
    men
Shall know, and later lovers, far-
    removed
Praise you, "All these were
    lovely"; say, "He loved."
                RUPERT BROOKE

ON FIRST LOOKING INTO CHAPMAN'S HOMER

Much have I travelled in the realms of gold,
   And many goodly states and kingdoms seen;
   Round many western islands have I been
Which bards in fealty to Apollo hold.
Oft of one wide expanse had I been told
   That deep-browed Homer ruled as his demesne:
   Yet did I never breathe its pure serene
Till I heard Chapman speak out loud and bold:
Then felt I like some watcher of the skies
   When a new planet swims into his ken;
Or like stout Cortez, when with eagle eyes
   He stared at the Pacific—and all his men
Looked at each other with a wild surmise—
   Silent, upon a peak in Darien.

                JOHN KEATS

A GOOD NAME

Iago. Good name in man and
   woman, dear my lord,
Is the immediate jewel of their souls:
Who steals my purse steals trash;
   'tis something, nothing;
'Twas mine, 'tis his, and has been
   slave to thousands.

But he that filches from me my
   good name
Robs me of that which not
   enriches him
And makes me poor indeed.

      WILLIAM SHAKESPEARE

CHORIC SONG OF THE LOTOS-EATERS

There is sweet music here that softer falls
Than petals from blown roses on the grass,
Or night-dews on still waters between walls
Of shadowy granite, in a gleaming pass;
Music that gentlier on the spirit lies,
Than tired eyelids upon tired eyes;
Music that brings sweet sleep down from the blissful skies.
Here are cool mosses deep,
And through the moss the ivies creep,
And in the stream the long-leaved flowers weep,
And from the craggy ledge the poppy hangs in sleep.
Why are we weighed upon with heaviness,
And utterly consumed with sharp distress,
While all things else have rest from weariness?
All things have rest; why should we toil alone,
We only toil, who are the first of things,
And make perpetual moan,
Still from one sorrow to another thrown;
Nor ever fold our wings,
And cease from wanderings,
Nor steep our brows in slumber's holy balm;
Nor harken what the inner spirit sings,
"There is no joy but calm!"—
Why should we only toil, the roof and crown of things?

Lo! in the middle of the wood,
The folded leaf is wooed from out the bud
With winds upon the branch, and there
Grows green and broad, and takes no care,
Sun-steeped at noon, and in the moon
Nightly dew-fed; and turning yellow
Falls, and floats adown the air.
Lo! sweetened with the summer light,
The full-juiced apple, waxing over-mellow,
Drops in a silent autumn night.

All its allotted length of days
The flower ripens in its place,
Ripens and fades, and falls, and hath no toil,
Fast-rooted in the fruitful soil.

Hateful is the dark-blue sky,
Vaulted o'er the dark-blue sea.
Death is the end of life; ah, why
Should life all labour be?
Let us alone. Time driveth onward fast,
And in a little while our lips are dumb.
Let us alone. What is it that will last?
All things are taken from us, and become
Portions and parcels of the dreadful past.
Let us alone. What pleasure can we have
To war with evil? Is there any peace
In ever climbing up the climbing wave?
All things have rest, and ripen toward the grave
In silence—ripen, fall, and cease;
Give us long rest or death, dark death, or dreamful ease.

How sweet it were, hearing the downward stream
With half-shut eyes ever to seem
Falling asleep in a half-dream!
To dream and dream, like yonder amber light,
Which will not leave the myrrh-bush on the height;
To hear each other's whispered speech;
Eating the Lotos day by day,
To watch the crisping ripples on the beach,
And tender curving lines of creamy spray;
To lend our hearts and spirits wholly
To the influence of mild-minded melancholy;
To muse and brood and live again in memory,
With those old faces of our infancy
Heaped over with a mound of grass,
Two handfuls of white dust, shut in an urn of brass!

Dear is the memory of our wedded lives,
And dear the last embraces of our wives
And their warm tears; but all hath suffered change;
For surely now our household hearths are cold,
Our sons inherit us, our looks are strange,

And we should come like ghosts to trouble joy.
Or else the island princes over-bold
Have eat our substance, and the minstrel sings
Before them of the ten years' war in Troy,
And our great deeds, as half-forgotten things.
Is there confusion in the little isle?
Let what is broken so remain.
The gods are hard to reconcile;
'Tis hard to settle order once again.
There *is* confusion worse than death,
Trouble on trouble, pain on pain,
Long labour unto aged breath,
Sore tasks to hearts worn out by many wars
And eyes grown dim with gazing on the pilot-stars.
But, propped on beds of amaranth and moly,
How sweet—while warm airs lull us, blowing lowly—
With half-dropped eyelid still,
Beneath a heaven dark and holy,
To watch the long bright river drawing slowly
His waters from the purple hill—
To hear the dewy echoes calling
From cave to cave through the thick-twined vine—
To watch the emerald-coloured water falling
Through many a woven acanthus-wreath divine!
Only to hear and see the far-off sparkling brine,
Only to hear were sweet, stretched out beneath the pine.

The Lotos blooms below the barren peak,
The Lotos blows by every winding creek;
All day the wind breathes low with mellower tone;
Through every hollow cave and alley lone
Round and round the spicy downs the yellow Lotos-dust is blown.
We have had enough of action, and of motion we,
Rolled to starboard, rolled to larboard, when the surge
    was seething free,
Where the wallowing monster spouted his foam-fountains in the sea.
Let us swear an oath, and keep it with an equal mind,
In the hollow Lotos-land to live and lie reclined
On the hills like gods together, careless of mankind.
For they lie beside their nectar, and the bolts are hurled
Far below them in the valleys, and the clouds are lightly curled
Round their golden houses, girdled with the gleaming world;

Where they smile in secret, looking over wasted lands,
Blight and famine, plague and earthquake, roaring deeps and fiery sands,
Clanging fights, and flaming towns, and sinking ships, and praying
    hands.
But they smile, they find a music centered in a doleful song
Steaming up, a lamentation and an ancient tale of wrong,
Like a tale of little meaning though the words are strong;
Chanted from an ill-used race of men that cleave the soil,
Sow the seed, and reap the harvest with enduring toil,
Storing yearly little dues of wheat, and wine and oil;
Till they perish and they suffer—some, 'tis whispered—down in hell
Suffer endless anguish, others in Elysian valleys dwell,
Resting weary limbs at last on beds of asphodel.
Surely, surely, slumber is more sweet than toil, the shore
Than labour in the deep mid-ocean, wind and wave and oar;
O rest ye, brother mariners, we will not wander more.

ALFRED, LORD TENNYSON

ODE ON A GRECIAN URN

Thou still unravished bride of quietness,
    Thou foster child of Silence and slow Time,
Sylvan historian, who canst thus express
    A flowery tale more sweetly than our rhyme:
What leaf-fring'd legend haunts about thy shape
    Of deities or mortals, or of both,
        In Tempe or the dales of Arcady?
What men or gods are these? What maidens loath?
    What mad pursuit? What struggle to escape?
        What pipes and timbrels? What wild ecstasy?

Heard melodies are sweet, but those unheard
    Are sweeter; therefore, ye soft pipes, play on;
Not to the sensual ear, but, more endeared,
    Pipe to the spirit ditties of no tone;
Fair youth, beneath the trees, thou canst not leave
    Thy song, nor ever can those trees be bare;
        Bold Lover, never, never canst thou kiss,
Though winning near the goal—yet, do not grieve;
    She cannot fade, though thou hast not thy bliss,
        For ever wilt thou love, and she be fair!

Ah, happy, happy boughs! that cannot shed
    Your leaves, nor ever bid the Spring adieu;
And, happy melodist, unwearièd,
    For ever piping songs for ever new;
More happy love! more happy, happy love!
    For ever warm and still to be enjoy'd,
        For ever panting, and for ever young;
All breathing human passion far above,
    That leaves a heart high-sorrowful and cloy'd,
        A burning forehead, and a parching tongue.

Who are these coming to the sacrifice?
    To what green altar, O mysterious priest,
Lead'st thou that heifer lowing at the skies,
    And all her silken flanks with garlands drest?

What little town by river or seashore,
    Or mountain-built with peaceful citadel,
        Is emptied of this folk, this pious morn?
And, little town, thy streets for evermore
    Will silent be; and not a soul to tell
        Why thou art desolate, can e'er return.

O Attic shape! Fair attitude! with brede
    Of marble men and maidens overwrought,
With forest branches and the trodden weed;
    Thou, silent form, dost tease us out of thought
As doth eternity: Cold Pastoral!
    When old age shall this generation waste,
        Thou shalt remain, in midst of other woe
Than ours, a friend to man, to whom thou say'st,
    "Beauty is truth, truth beauty,"—that is all
        Ye know on earth, and all ye need to know.

JOHN KEATS

LIFE

Life! I know not what thou art,
But know that thou and I must
    part;
And when, or how, or where we
    met,
I own to me's a secret yet.
But this I know, when thou art
    fled,
Where'er they lay these limbs, this
    head,
No clouds so valueless shall be
As all that then remains of me.

Life! we've been long together,
Through pleasant and through
    cloudy weather;
  'Tis hard to part when friends
    are dear;
  Perhaps 'twill cost a sigh, a tear;—
Then steal away, give little
    warning,
  Choose thine own time;
Say not Good-night, but in some
    brighter clime
  Bid me Good-morning!

ANNA LETITIA BARBAULD

ATALANTA IN CALYDON

Chorus

Before the beginning of years
  There came to the making of
    man
Time, with a gift of tears;
  Grief, with a glass that ran;
Pleasure, with pain for leaven;
  Summer, with flowers that fell;
Remembrance fallen from heaven,
  And madness risen from hell;
Strength without hands to smite;
  Love that endures for a breath;
Night, the shadow of light,
  And life, the shadow of death.

And the high gods took in hand
  Fire, and the falling of tears,
And a measure of sliding sand
  From under the feet of the years;
And froth and drift of the sea;
  And dust of the labouring earth;
And bodies of things to be
  In the houses of death and of
    birth;
And wrought with weeping and
    laughter,
  And fashion'd with loathing
    and love,
With life before and after
  And death beneath and above,
For a day and a night and a
    morrow,

That his strength might endure
    for a span
With travail and heavy sorrow,
  The holy spirit of man.

From the winds of the north and
    the south
  They gather'd as unto strife;
They breathed upon his mouth,
  They filled his body with life;
Eyesight and speech they wrought
  For the veils of the soul therein,
A time for labour and thought,
  A time to serve and to sin;
They gave him light in his ways,
  And love, and a space for
    delight,
And beauty and length of days,
  And night, and sleep in the
    night.
His speech is a burning fire;
  With his lips he travaileth;
In his heart is a blind desire,
  In his eyes foreknowledge of
    death;
He weaves, and is clothed with
    derision;
  Sows, and he shall not reap;
His life is a watch or a vision
  Between a sleep and a sleep.

ALGERNON CHARLES SWINBURNE

I DIED FOR BEAUTY

I died for beauty, but was scarce
Adjusted in the tomb,
When one who died for truth was
   lain
In an adjoining room.

He questioned softly why I failed?
"For beauty," I replied.
"And I for truth,—the two are
   one;
We brethren are," he said.

And so, as kinsmen met a night,
We talked between the rooms,
Until the moss had reached our lips,
And covered up our names.

EMILY DICKINSON

OZYMANDIAS

I met a traveler from an antique land
Who said: Two vast and trunkless legs of stone
Stand in the desert. Near them, on the sand,
Half sunk, a shattered visage lies, whose frown,
And wrinkled lip, and sneer of cold command,
Tell that its sculptor well those passions read
Which yet survive, stamped on these lifeless things,
The hand that mocked them and the heart that fed;
And on the pedestal these words appear:
"My name is Ozymandias, king of kings:
Look on my works, ye Mighty, and despair!"
Nothing beside remains. Round the decay
Of that colossal wreck, boundless and bare
The lone and level sands stretch far away.

PERCY BYSSHE SHELLEY

SONG

When I am dead, my dearest,
  Sing no sad songs for me;
Plant thou no roses at my head,
  Nor shady cypress-tree:
Be the green grass above me
  With showers and dewdrops
    wet;
And if thou wilt, remember,
  And if thou wilt, forget.

I shall not see the shadows,
  I shall not feel the rain;
I shall not hear the nightingale
  Sing on, as if in pain:
And dreaming through the
    twilight
  That doth not rise nor set,
Haply I may remember
  And haply may forget.

CHRISTINA ROSSETTI

TO THINE OWN SELF BE TRUE

There, my blessings with thee!
And these few precepts in thy memory
Look thou character. Give thy thoughts no tongue,
Nor any unproportioned thought his act.
Be thou familiar, but by no means vulgar;
The friends thou hast, and their adoption tried,
Grapple them to thy soul with hoops of steel;
But do not dull thy palm with entertainment
Of each new-hatched, unfledged comrade. Beware
Of entrance to a quarrel, but, being in,
Bear 't that the opposèd may beware of thee.
Give every man thine ear, but few thy voice;
Take each man's censure, but reserve thy judgement.
Costly thy habit as thy purse can buy,
But not expressed in fancy; rich, not gaudy;
For the apparel oft proclaims the man,
And they in France of the best rank and station
Are most select and generous, chief in that.
Neither a borrower, nor a lender be;
For loan oft loses both itself and friend,
And borrowing dulls the edge of husbandry.
This above all: to thine own self be true,
And it must follow, as the night the day,
Thou canst not then be false to any man.

WILLIAM SHAKESPEARE

CHARACTER OF THE HAPPY WARRIOR

Who is the happy Warrior? Who is he
That every man in arms should wish to be?
—It is the generous Spirit, who, when brought
Among the tasks of real life, hath wrought
Upon the plan that pleased his boyish thought:
Whose high endeavours are an inward light
That makes the path before him always bright:
Who, with a natural instinct to discern
What knowledge can perform, is diligent to learn;
Abides by this resolve, and stops not there,
But makes his moral being his prime care;
Who, doomed to go in company with Pain,
And Fear, and Bloodshed, miserable train!
Turns his necessity to glorious gain;
In face of these doth exercise a power
Which is our human nature's highest dower;
Controls them and subdues, transmutes, bereaves
Of their bad influence, and their good receives:
By objects, which might force the soul to abate
Her feeling, rendered more compassionate;
Is placable—because occasions rise
So often that demand such sacrifice;
More skilful in self-knowledge, even more pure,
As tempted more; more able to endure,
As more exposed to suffering and distress;
Thence, also, more alive to tenderness.
—'Tis he whose law is reason; who depends
Upon that law as on the best of friends;
Whence, in a stage where men are tempted still
To evil for a guard against worse ill,
And what in quality or act is best
Doth seldom on a right foundation rest,
He labours good on good to fix, and owes
To virtue every triumph that he knows:
—Who, if he rises to station of command,

Rises by open means; and there will stand
On honourable terms, or else retire,
And in himself possess his own desire;
Who comprehends his trust, and to the same
Keeps faithful with a singleness of aim;
And therefore does not stoop, nor lie in wait
For wealth, or honours, or for worldly state;
Whom they must follow, on whose head must fall,
Like showers of manna, if they come at all:
Whose powers shed round him in the common strife,
Or mild concerns of ordinary life,
A constant influence, a peculiar grace;
But who, if he be called upon to face
Some awful moment to which Heaven has joined
Great issues, good or bad for human kind,
Is happy as a Lover; and attired
With sudden brightness, like a Man inspired;
And through the heat of conflict, keeps the law
In calmness made, and sees what he foresaw;
Or if an unexpected call succeed,
Come when it will, is equal to the need:
—He who, though thus endued as with a sense
And faculty for storm and turbulence,
Is yet a Soul whose master-bias leans
To homefelt pleasures and to gentle scenes;
Sweet images! which, wheresoe'er he be,
Are at his heart; and such fidelity
It is his darling passion to approve;
More brave for this, that he hath much to love:—
'Tis finally, the Man, who, lifted high,
Conspicuous object in a Nation's eye,
Or left unthought-of in obscurity,—
Who, with a toward or untoward lot,
Prosperous or adverse, to his wish or not—
Plays in the many games of life, that one
Where what he most doth value must be won:
Whom neither shape of danger can dismay,
Nor thought of tender happiness betray;
Who, not content that former worth stand fast,
Looks forward, persevering to the last,
From well to better, daily self-surpast:

Who, whether praise of him must walk the earth
For ever, and to noble deeds give birth,
Or he must fall, to sleep without his fame,
And leave a dead unprofitable name—
Finds comfort in himself and in his cause;
And, while the mortal mist is gathering, draws
His breath in confidence of Heaven's applause:
This is the happy Warrior; this is He
That every Man in arms should wish to be

WILLIAM WORDSWORTH

A HUB FOR THE UNIVERSE

I have said that the soul is not more than the body,
And I have said that the body is not more than the soul,
And nothing, not God, is greater to one than one's self is,
And whoever walks a furlong without sympathy walks to his own
    funeral drest in his shroud,
And I or you pocketless of a dime may purchase the pick of the earth,
And to glance with an eye or show a bean in its pod confounds the
    learning of all times,
And there is no trade or employment but the young man following it
    may become a hero,
And there is no object so soft but it makes a hub for the wheeled
    universe.

WALT WHITMAN

IN READING GAOL BY READING TOWN

In Reading gaol by Reading town
    There is a pit of shame,
And in it lies a wretched man
    Eaten by teeth of flame,
In a burning winding-sheet he lies,
    And his grave has got no name.

And there, till Christ call forth
        the dead,
    In silence let him lie:
No need to waste the foolish tear,

Or heave the windy sigh:
The man had killed the thing he loved,
    And so he had to die.

And all men kill the thing they
        love,
    By all let this be heard,
Some do it with a bitter look,
    Some with a flattering word,
The coward does it with a kiss,
    The brave man with a sword!

OSCAR WILDE

WITH RUE MY HEART IS LADEN

With rue my heart is laden
  For golden friends I had,
For many a rose-lipt maiden
  And many a lightfoot lad.

By brooks too broad for leaping
  The lightfoot boys are laid;
The rose-lipt girls are sleeping
  In fields where roses fade.

A. E. HOUSMAN

FIRE AND ICE

Some say the world will end in fire,
Some say in ice.
From what I've tasted of desire
I hold with those who favor fire.
But if it had to perish twice,

I think I know enough of hate
To say that for destruction ice
Is also great
And would suffice.

ROBERT FROST

EUCLID ALONE

Euclid alone has looked on Beauty bare.
Let all who prate of Beauty hold their peace,
And lay them prone upon the earth and cease
To ponder on themselves, the while they stare
At nothing, intricately drawn nowhere
In shapes of shifting lineage; let geese
Gabble and hiss, but heroes seek release
From dusty bondage into luminous air.
O blinding hour, O holy, terrible day,
When first the shaft into his vision shone
Of light anatomized! Euclid alone
Has looked on Beauty bare. Fortunate they
Who, though once only and then but far away,
Have heard her massive sandal set on stone.

EDNA ST. VINCENT MILLAY

ODE TO A NIGHTINGALE

My heart aches, and a drowsy
    numbness pains
  My sense, as though of hemlock
    I had drunk,
Or emptied some dull opiate to
    the drains
  One minute past, and Lethe-
    wards had sunk:
'Tis not through envy of thy
    happy lot,
  But being too happy in thine
    happiness—
      That thou, light-wingèd
      Dryad of the trees,
      In some melodious plot
Of beechen green, and shadows
    numberless,
  Singest of summer in full-
    throated ease.

O for a draught of vintage! that
    hath been
  Cooled a long age in the deep-
    delvèd earth,

Tasting of Flora and the country
    green,
  Dance, and Provençal song, and
    sunburnt mirth!
O for a beaker full of the warm
    South,
  Full of the true, the blushful
    Hippocrene,
      With beaded bubbles winking
      at the brim,
      And purple-stainèd mouth;
That I might drink, and leave
    the world unseen,
  And with thee fade away into
    the forest dim:

Fade away, dissolve, and quite
    forget
  What thou among the leaves
    hast never known,
The weariness, the fever, and the
    fret
  Here, where men sit and hear
    each other groan;

Where palsy shakes a few, sad, last
    gray hairs,
  Where youth grows pale, and
    specter-thin, and dies;
    Where but to think is to be
     full of sorrow
     And leaden-eyed despairs,
  Where Beauty cannot keep her
    lustrous eyes,
    Or new Love pine at them
    beyond to-morrow.

Away! away! for I will fly to thee,
  Not charioted by Bacchus and
    his pards,
But on the viewless wings of Poesy,
  Though the dull brain
    perplexes and retards:
Already with thee! tender is the
    night,
  And haply the Queen-Moon is
    on her throne,
    Clustered around by all her
     starry Fays;
    But here there is no light,
  Save what from heaven is with
    the breezes blown
    Through verdurous glooms
    and winding mossy ways.

I cannot see what flowers are at
    my feet,
  Nor what soft incense hangs
    upon the boughs,
But, in embalmèd darkness, guess
    each sweet
  Wherewith the seasonable
    month endows
The grass, the thicket, and the
    fruit-tree wild;
  White hawthorn, and the
    pastoral eglantine;

Fast-fading violets covered up
    in leaves;
    And mid-May's eldest child,
The coming musk-rose, full of
    dewy wine,
    The murmurous haunt of
    flies on summer eves.

Darkling I listen; and for many a
    time
  I have been half in love with
    easeful Death,
Called him soft names in many a
    musèd rhyme,
  To take into the air my quiet
    breath;
Now more than ever seems it rich
    to die,
  To cease upon the midnight
    with no pain,
    While thou art pouring forth
    thy soul abroad
    In such an ecstasy!
  Still wouldst thou sing, and I
    have ears in vain—
    To thy high requiem become
    a sod.

Thou wast not born for death,
    immortal Bird!
  No hungry generations tread
    thee down;
The voice I hear this passing
    night was heard
  In ancient days by emperor and
    clown:
Perhaps the self-same song that
    found a path
  Through the sad heart of Ruth,
    when, sick for home,
    She stood in tears amid the
    alien corn;

The same that oft-times hath
Charmed magic casements,
    opening on the foam
Of perilous seas, in faery
    lands forlorn.

Forlorn! the very word is like a bell
  To toll me back from thee to
    my sole self!
Adieu! the fancy cannot cheat so well
  As she is famed to do, deceiving elf.

Adieu! adieu! thy plaintive
    anthem fades
Past the near meadows, over the
    still stream,
  Up the hill-side; and now 'tis
    buried deep
  In the next valley-glades:
Was it a vision, or a waking
    dream?
Fled is that music:—Do I
    wake or sleep?

JOHN KEATS

THE ROAD

There is a road that turning
  always
Cuts off the country of Again.
Archers stand there on every side
  And as it runs Time's deer is
    slain,
  And lies where it has lain.

That busy clock shows never an
  hour.
  All flies and all in flight must
    tarry.
The hunter shoots the empty air
  Far on before the quarry,
  Which falls though nothing's
    there to parry.

The lion couching in the centre
  With mountain head and
    sunset brow
Rolls down the everlasting slope
  Bones picked an age ago,
  And the bones rise up and go.

There the beginning finds the end
  Before beginning ever can be,
And the great runner never leaves

The starting and the finishing tree,
The budding and the fading tree.

There the ship sailing safe in
  harbour
  Long since in many a sea was
    drowned.
The treasure burning in her hold
  So near will never be found,
  Sunk past all sound.

There a man on a summer
    evening
  Reclines at ease upon his tomb
And is his mortal effigy.
  And there within the womb,
  The cell of doom,

The ancestral deed is thought and
    done,
  And in a million Edens fall
A million Adams drowned in
    darkness
  For small is great and great is
    small,
  And a blind seed all.

EDWIN MUIR

TOMORROW AND TOMORROW AND TOMORROW

To-morrow, and to-morrow, and
to-morrow,
Creeps in this petty pace from day
to day,
To the last syllable of recorded
time;
And all our yesterdays have
lighted fools
The way to dusty death. Out, out,
brief candle!

Life's but a walking shadow, a
poor player
That struts and frets his hour
upon the stage,
And then is heard no more; it is
a tale
Told by an idiot, full of sound
and fury,
Signifying nothing.

WILLIAM SHAKESPEARE

THE QUALITY OF MERCY IS NOT STRAIN'D

The quality of mercy is not
strain'd,
It droppeth as the gentle rain
from heaven
Upon the place beneath: it is
twice bless'd;
It blesseth him that gives and him
that takes:
'Tis mightiest in the mightiest; it
becomes
The throned monarch better than
his crown;
His sceptre shows the force of
temporal power,

The attribute to awe and majesty,
Wherein doth sit the dread and
fear of kings;
But mercy is above this sceptred
sway,
It is enthroned in the hearts of
kings,
It is an attribute to God himself,
And earthly power doth then
show likest God's
When mercy seasons justice.

WILLIAM SHAKESPEARE

TO BE OR NOT TO BE

To be, or not to be: that is the question:
Whether 'tis nobler in the mind to suffer
The slings and arrows of outrageous fortune,
Or to take arms against a sea of troubles,
And by opposing end them? To die: to sleep;
No more; and, by a sleep to say we end
The heart-ache and the thousand natural shocks
That flesh is heir to, 'tis a consummation
Devoutly to be wish'd. To die, to sleep;
To sleep: perchance to dream: ay, there's the rub;
For in that sleep of death what dreams may come
When we have shuffled off this mortal coil,
Must give us pause. There's the respect
That makes calamity of so long life;
For who would bear the whips and scorns of time,
The oppressor's wrong, the proud man's contumely,
The pangs of dispriz'd love, the law's delay,
The insolence of office, and the spurns
That patient merit of the unworthy takes,
When he himself might his quietus make
With a bare bodkin? who would fardels bear,
To grunt and sweat under a weary life,
But that the dread of something after death,
The undiscover'd country from whose bourn
No traveller returns, puzzles the will,
And makes us rather bear those ills we have
Than fly to others that we know not of?
Thus conscience does make cowards of us all;
And thus the native hue of resolution
Is sicklied o'er with the pale cast of thought,
And enterprises of great pith and moment
With this regard their currents turn awry,
And lose the name of action.
WILLIAM SHAKESPEARE

WHAT IF A MUCH OF A WHICH OF A WIND

what if a much of a which of a
    wind
gives the truth to summer's lie;
bloodies with dizzying leaves the
    sun
and yanks immortal stars awry?
Blow king to beggar and queen to
    seem
(blow friend to fiend: blow space
    to time)
—when skies are hanged and
    oceans drowned,
the single secret will still be man

what if a keen of a lean wind flays
screaming hills with sleet and snow:
strangles valleys by ropes of thing
and stifles forests in white ago?
Blow hope to terror; blow seeing
    to blind
(blow pity to envy and soul to mind)

—whose hearts are mountains,
    roots are trees,
it's they shall cry hello to the
    spring

what if a dawn of a doom of a
    dream
bites this universe in two,
peels forever out of his grave
and sprinkles nowhere with me
    and you?
Blow soon to never and never to
    twice
(blow life to isn't: blow death to
    was)
—all nothing's only our hugest
    home;
the most who die, the more we
    live

                    E. E. CUMMINGS

A CREED

There is a destiny that makes us
    brothers;
  None goes his way alone:
All that we send into the lives of
    others
  Comes back into our own.

I care not what his temples or his
    creeds,
  One thing holds firm and fast—
That into his fateful heap of days
    and deeds
  The soul of man is cast.

                    EDWIN MARKHAM

RENASCENCE

All I could see from where I stood
Was three long mountains and a
 wood;
I turned and looked another way,
And saw three islands in a bay.
So with my eyes I traced the line
Of the horizon, thin and fine,
Straight around till I was come
Back to where I'd started from;
And all I saw from where I stood
Was three long mountains and a
 wood.

Over these things I could not see:
These were the things that
 bounded me.
And I could touch them with my
 hand,
Almost, I thought, from where I
 stand!
And all at once things seemed so
 small
My breath came short, and scarce
 at all.
But, sure, the sky is big, I said:
Miles and miles above my head.
So here upon my back I'll lie
And look my fill into the sky.
And so I looked, and after all,
The sky was not so very tall.

The sky, I said, must somewhere
 stop . . .
And—sure enough!—I see the top!
The sky, I thought, is not so grand;
I 'most could touch it with my
 hand!
And reaching up my hand to try,
I screamed, to feel it touch the sky.
I screamed, and—lo!—Infinity
Came down and settled over me;
Forced back my scream into my
 chest;
Bent back my arm upon my
 breast;
And, pressing of the Undefined
The definition on my mind,
Held up before my eyes a glass
Through which my shrinking
 sight did pass
Until it seemed I must behold
Immensity made manifold;
Whispered to me a word whose
 sound
Deafened the air for worlds
 around,
And brought unmuffled to my
 ears
The gossiping of friendly spheres,
The creaking of the tented sky,
The ticking of Eternity.

I saw and heard, and knew at last
The How and Why of all things,
    past,
And present, and forevermore.
The Universe, cleft to the core,
Lay open to my probing sense,
That, sickening, I would fain
    pluck thence
But could not,—nay! but needs
    must suck
At the great wound, and could
    not pluck
My lips away till I had drawn
All venom out.—Ah, fearful pawn:
For my omniscience paid I toll
In infinite remorse of soul.
All sin was of my sinning, all
Atoning mine, and mine the gall
Of all regret. Mine was the weight
Of every brooded wrong, the hate
That stood behind each envious
    thrust,
Mine every greed, mine every lust.

And all the while, for every grief,
Each suffering, I craved relief
With individual desire;
Craved all in vain! And felt fierce
    fire
About a thousand people crawl;
Perished with each,—then
    mourned for all!

A man was starving in Capri;
He moved his eyes and looked at
    me;
I felt his gaze, I heard his moan,
And knew his hunger as my own.
I saw at sea a great fog bank
Between two ships that struck and
    sank;

A thousand screams the heavens
    smote;
And every scream tore through
    my throat.

No hurt I did not feel, no death
That was not mine; mine each
    last breath
That, crying, met an answering
    cry
From the compassion that was I.
All suffering mine, and mine its
    rod;
Mine, pity like the pity of God.
Ah, awful weight! Infinity
Pressed down upon the finite Me!
My anguished spirit, like a bird,
Beating against my lips I heard;
Yet lay the weight so close about
There was no room for it without.
And so beneath the weight lay I
And suffered death, but could not
    die.

Long had I lain thus, craving
    death,
When quietly the earth beneath
Gave way, and inch by inch, so
    great
At last had grown the crushing
    weight,
Into the earth I sank till I
Full six feet under ground did lie,
And sank no more,—there is no
    weight
Can follow here, however great.
From off my breast I felt it roll,
And as it went my tortured soul
Burst forth and fled in such a gust
That all about me swirled the
    dust.

Deep in the earth I rested now.
Cool is its hand upon the brow
And soft its breast beneath the
    head
Of one who is so gladly dead.
And all at once, and over all
The pitying rain began to fall;
I lay and heard each pattering
    hoof
Upon my lowly, thatchèd roof,
And seemed to love the sound far
    more
Than ever I had done before.
For rain it hath a friendly sound
To one who's six feet under
    ground;
And scarce the friendly voice or
    face,
A grave is such a quiet place.

The rain, I said, is kind to come
And speak to me in my new
    home.
I would I were alive again
To kiss the fingers of the rain,
To drink into my eyes the shine
Of every slanting silver line,
To catch the freshened, fragrant
    breeze
From drenched and dripping
    apple-trees.
For soon the shower will be done,
And then the broad face of the sun
Will laugh above the rain-soaked
    earth
Until the world with answering
    mirth
Shakes joyously, and each round
    drop
Rolls, twinkling, from its grass-
    blade top.

How can I bear it, buried here,
While overhead the sky grows
    clear
And blue again after the storm?
O, multi-coloured, multi-form,
Belovèd beauty over me,
That I shall never, never see
Again! Spring-silver, autumn-gold,
That I shall never more behold!—
Sleeping your myriad magics
    through,
Close-sepulchred away from you!
O God, I cried, give me new birth,
And put me back upon the earth!
Upset each cloud's gigantic gourd
And let the heavy rain, down-
    poured
In one big torrent, set me free,
Washing my grave away from me!

I ceased; and through the breath-
    less hush
That answered me, the far-off rush
Of herald wings came whispering
Like music down the vibrant string
Of my ascending prayer, and—
    crash!
Before the wild wind's whistling
    lash
The startled storm-clouds reared
    on high
And plunged in terror down the
    sky!
And the big rain in one black wave
Fell from the sky and struck my
    grave.

I know not how such things can be;
I only know there came to me
A fragrance such as never clings
To aught save happy living things;

A sound as of some joyous elf
Singing sweet songs to please him-
    self,
And, through and over everything,
A sense of glad awakening.
The grass, a-tiptoe at my ear,
Whispering to me I could hear;
I felt the rain's cool finger-tips
Brushed tenderly across my lips,
Laid gently on my sealèd sight,
And all at once the heavy night
Fell from my eyes and I could
    see!—
A drenched and dripping apple-
    tree,
A last long line of silver rain,
A sky grown clear and blue again.
And as I looked a quickening
    gust
Of wind blew up to me and thrust
Into my face a miracle
Of orchard-breath, and with the
    smell,—
I know not how such things can
    be!—
I breathed my soul back into me.

Ah! Up then from the ground
    sprang I
And hailed the earth with such a
    cry
As is not heard save from a man
Who has been dead, and lives again.
About the trees my arms I wound;
Like one gone mad I hugged the
    ground;
I raised my quivering arms on
    high;

I laughed and laughed into the sky;
Till at my throat a strangling sob
Caught fiercely, and a great heart-
    throb
Sent instant tears into my eyes:
O God, I cried, no dark disguise
Can e'er hereafter hide from me
Thy radiant identity!
Thou canst not move across the
    grass
But my quick eyes will see Thee
    pass,
Nor speak, however silently,
But my hushed voice will answer
    Thee.
I know the path that tells Thy way
Through the cool eve of every day;
God, I can push the grass apart
And lay my finger on Thy heart!

The world stands out on either
    side
No wider than the heart is wide;
Above the world is stretched the
    sky,—
No higher than the soul is high.
The heart can push the sea and
    land
Farther away on either hand;
The soul can split the sky in two,
And let the face of God shine
    through.
But East and West will pinch the
    heart
That can not keep them pushed
    apart;
And he whose soul is flat—the sky
Will cave in on him by and by.

EDNA ST. VINCENT MILLAY

RIDDLE OF THE WORLD

Know then thyself, presume not God to scan,
The proper study of Mankind is Man.
Plac'd on this isthmus of a middle state,
A Being darkly wise, and rudely great:
With too much knowledge for the Sceptic side,
With too much weakness for the Stoic's pride,
He hangs between; in doubt to act, or rest;
In doubt to deem himself a God, or Beast;
In doubt his Mind or Body to prefer;
Born but to die, and reas'ning but to err;
Alike in ignorance, his reason such,
Whether he thinks too little, or too much:
Chaos of Thought and Passion, all confus'd;
Still by himself abus'd, or disabus'd;
Created half to rise, and half to fall;
Great Lord of all things, yet a prey to all;
Sole judge of truth, in endless error hurl'd:
The glory, jest, and riddle of the world!

ALEXANDER POPE

ALPS ON ALPS

A little learning is a dang'rous thing;
Drink deep, or taste not the Pierian spring:
There shallow draughts intoxicate the brain,
And drinking largely sobers us again.
Fir'd at first sight with what the Muse imparts,
In fearless youth we tempt the heights of Arts,
While from the bounded level of our mind,
Short views we take, nor see the lengths behind;
But more advanc'd, behold with strange surprise
New distant scenes of endless science rise!
So pleas'd at first the tow'ring Alps we try,
Mount o'er the vales, and seem to tread the sky,

Th' eternal snows appear already past,
And the first clouds and mountains seem the last:
But, those attain'd, we tremble to survey
The growing labours of the lengthen'd way,
Th' increasing prospect tires our wand'ring eyes,
Hills peep o'er hills, and Alps on Alps arise!

ALEXANDER POPE

BOOK III

A GARLAND OF LOVE POEMS

A RED, RED ROSE

O, my luve is like a red, red rose,
 That's newly sprung in June.
O my luve is like the melodie
 That's sweetly played in tune.

As fair art thou, my bonnie lass,
 So deep in luve am I,
And I will luve thee still, my
 dear,
 Till a' the seas gang dry.

Till a' the seas gang dry, my dear,
 And the rocks melt wi' the sun!
And I will luve thee still, my dear,
 While the sands o' life shall run.

And fare thee weel, my only luve,
 And fare thee weel awhile!
And I will come again, my luve,
 Though it were ten thousand
 mile!

ROBERT BURNS

LOVE NOT ME

Love not me for comely grace,
For my pleasing eye or face,
Nor for any outward part:
No, nor for a constant heart!
For these may fail or turn to ill:
 So thou and I shall sever.

Keep therefore a true woman's
 eye,
And love me still, but know not
 why!
So hast thou the same reason still
 To doat upon me ever.

ANONYMOUS

THERE IS A LADY SWEET AND KIND

There is a Lady sweet and kind,
Was never face so pleased my
 mind;
I did but see her passing by,
And yet I love her till I die.

Her gesture, motion, and her
 smiles,
Her wit, her voice my heart
 beguiles,

Beguiles my heart, I know not why,
And yet I love her till I die.

Cupid is wingèd and doth range,
Her country so my love doth
 change:
But change she earth, or change
 she sky,
Yet will I love her till I die.

ANONYMOUS

BELIEVE ME, IF ALL THOSE ENDEARING YOUNG CHARMS

Believe me, if all those endearing
   young charms,
  Which I gaze on so fondly
   today,
Were to change by tomorrow,
   and fleet in my arms,
  Like fairy-gifts fading away,
Thou wouldst still be adored, as
   this moment thou art,
  Let thy loveliness fade as it will,
And around the dear ruin each
   wish of my heart
  Would entwine itself verdantly
   still.

It is not while beauty and youth
   are thine own,
  And thy cheeks unprofaned by a tear,
That the fervour and faith of a
   soul can be known,
  To which time will but make
   thee more dear;
No, the heart that has truly loved
   never forgets,
  But as truly loves on to the close,
As the sunflower turns on her
   god, when he sets,
  The same look which she
   turned when he rose.

THOMAS MOORE

FOR ANNE GREGORY

"Never shall a young man,
Thrown into despair
By those great honey-colored
Ramparts at your ear,
Love you for yourself alone
And not your yellow hair."

"But I can get a hair-dye
And set such color there,
Brown, or black, or carrot,

That young men in despair
May love me for myself alone
And not my yellow hair."

"I heard an old religious man
But yesternight declare
That he had found a text to prove
That only God, my dear,
Could love you for yourself alone
And not your yellow hair."

WILLIAM BUTLER YEATS

THE NIGHT HAS A THOUSAND EYES

The night has a thousand eyes,
　And the day but one;
Yet the light of the bright world
　　dies
　With the dying sun.

The mind has a thousand eyes,
　And the heart but one;
Yet the light of a whole life dies
　When love is done.

FRANCIS WILLIAM BOURDILLON

JENNY KISS'D ME

Jenny kiss'd me when we met,
　Jumping from the chair she
　　sat in;
Time, you thief, who love to get
　Sweets into your list, put
　　　that in!

Say I'm weary, say I'm sad,
　Say that health and wealth
　　have miss'd me,
Say I'm growing old, but add,
　Jenny kiss'd me.

LEIGH HUNT

TO THE VIRGINS

Gather ye rosebuds while ye may,
　Old Time is still a-flying;
And this same flower that smiles
　　today,
　Tomorrow will be dying.

The glorious lamp of heaven, the
　　sun,
　The higher he's a-getting,
The sooner will his race be run,
　And nearer he's to setting.

That age is best which is the first,
　When youth and blood are
　　warmer;
But being spent, the worse and worst
　Times still succeed the former.

Then be not coy, but use your time,
　And while ye may, go marry;
For, having lost but once your
　　prime,
　You may forever tarry.

ROBERT HERRICK

SHE WALKS IN BEAUTY

She walks in beauty, like the night
  Of cloudless climes and starry
    skies;
And all that's best of dark and
    bright
  Meet in her aspect and her
    eyes:
Thus mellowed to that tender
    light
  Which heaven to gaudy day
    denies.

One shade the more, one ray the
    less,
  Had half impaired the
    nameless grace

Which waves in every raven tress,
  Or softly lightens o'er her face;
Where thoughts serenely sweet
    express
  How pure, how dear their
    dwelling-place.

And on that cheek, and o'er that
    brow,
  So soft, so calm, yet eloquent,
The smiles that win, the tints that
    glow,
  But tell of days in goodness
    spent,
A mind at peace with all below,
  A heart whose love is innocent!

GEORGE GORDON, LORD BYRON

SO, WE'LL GO NO MORE A-ROVING

So, we'll go no more a-roving
  So late into the night,
Though the heart be still as
    loving,
  And the moon be still as bright.

For the sword outwears its sheath,
  And the soul wears out the
    breast,

And the heart must pause to
    breathe,
  And Love itself have rest.

Though the night was made for
    loving,
  And the day returns too soon,
Yet we'll go no more a-roving
  By the light of the moon.

GEORGE GORDON, LORD BYRON

HELEN

Was this the face that launched a
thousand ships,
And burned the topless towers of
Ilium?—
Sweet Helen, make me immortal
with a kiss!—
Her lips suck forth my soul: see
where it flees!—
Come, Helen, come, give me my
soul again.
Here will I dwell, for heaven is
in these lips,
And all is dross that is not
Helena.
I will be Paris, and for love of
thee,
Instead of Troy, shall Wittenberg
be sacked,
And I will combat with weak
Menelaus,
And wear thy colours on my
plumèd crest;
Yes, I will wound Achilles in the
heel,
And then return to Helen for a
kiss.
Oh, thou art fairer than the
evening air
Clad in the beauty of a thousand
stars;
Brighter art thou than flaming
Jupiter
When he appeared to hapless
Semele;
More lovely than the monarch of
the sky
In wanton Arethusa's azured
arms;
And none but thou shalt be my
paramour!

CHRISTOPHER MARLOWE

WHO EVER LOVED, THAT LOVED NOT
AT FIRST SIGHT?

It lies not in our power to love or
hate,
For will in us is overruled by fate.
When two are stripped, long ere
the course begin,
We wish that one should lose, the
other win;
And one especially do we affect
Of two gold ingots, like in each
respect:
The reason no man knows; let it
suffice
What we behold is censured by
our eyes.
Where both deliberate, the love
is slight:
Who ever loved, that loved not at
first sight?

CHRISTOPHER MARLOWE

HARK, HARK! THE LARK

Hark, hark! the lark at heaven's
    gate sings,
  And Phoebus 'gins arise,
His steeds to water at those
    springs
  On chaliced flowers that lies;

And winking Mary-buds begin
  To ope their golden eyes;
With every thing that pretty is,
  My lady sweet, arise:
    Arise, arise!
    WILLIAM SHAKESPEARE

SONG

Ask me no more where Jove
  bestows,
When June is past, the fading rose;
For in your beauty's orient deep
These flowers, as in their causes, sleep.

Ask me no more whither do stray
The golden atoms of the day;
For, in pure love, heaven did
  prepare
Those powders to enrich your hair.

Ask me no more whither doth haste
The nightingale, when May is past;

For in your sweet dividing throat
She winters, and keeps warm her
  note.

Ask me no more where those stars
  light
That downwards fall in dead of
  night;
For in your eyes they sit, and there
Fixèd become, as in their sphere.

Ask me no more if east or west
The Phœnix builds her spicy nest;
For unto you at last she flies,
And in your fragrant bosom dies.
    THOMAS CAREW

IF I WERE KING

If I were king—ah, love, if I were king—
What tributary nations would I bring
To stoop before your sceptre and to swear
Allegiance to your lips and eyes and hair;
Beneath your feet what treasures I would fling:—
The stars should be your pearls upon a string,
The world a ruby for your finger ring,
And you should have the sun and moon to wear,
        If I were king.
Let these wild dreams and wilder words take wing,
Deep in the woods I hear a shepherd sing
A simple ballad, to a sylvan air,
Of love that ever finds your face more fair;
I could not give you any goodlier thing
        If I were king.
        JUSTIN HUNTLY McCARTHY

MUSIC I HEARD

Music I heard with you was more than music,
And bread I broke with you was more than bread;
Now that I am without you, all is desolate;
All that was once so beautiful is dead.

Your hands once touched this table and this silver,
And I have seen your fingers hold this glass.
These things do not remember you, beloved,
And yet your touch upon them will not pass.

For it was in my heart you moved among them,
And blessed them with your hands and with your eyes;
And in my heart they will remember always,—
They knew you once, O beautiful and wise.
        CONRAD AIKEN

SHE WAS A PHANTOM OF DELIGHT

She was a phantom of delight
When first she gleamed upon my
    sight;
A lovely apparition, sent
To be a moment's ornament;
Her eyes as stars of twilight fair;
Like twilight's, too, her dusky
    hair;
But all things else about her
    drawn
From May-time and the cheerful
    dawn;
A dancing shape, an image gay,
To haunt, to startle, and waylay.

I saw her upon nearer view,
A spirit, yet a woman too!
Her household motions light and
    free,
And steps of virgin liberty;
A countenance in which did meet
Sweet records, promises as sweet;

A creature not too bright or good
For human nature's daily food,
For transient sorrows, simple
    wiles,
Praise, blame, love, kisses, tears,
    and smiles.

And now I see with eye serene
The very pulse of the machine;
A being breathing thoughtful
    breath,
A traveler between life and death;
The reason firm, the temperate
    will,
Endurance, foresight, strength,
    and skill;
A perfect woman, nobly planned
To warn, to comfort, and
    command;
And yet a spirit still, and bright
With something of angelic light.

WILLIAM WORDSWORTH

SONG

I can't be talkin' of love, dear,
I can't be talkin' of love.
If there be one thing I can't talk of
That one thing do be love.

But that's not sayin' that I'm not
    lovin'—
Still water, you know, runs deep,

An' I do be lovin' so deep, dear,
I be lovin' you in my sleep.

But I can't be talkin' of love, dear,
I can't be talkin' of love,
If there be one thing I can't talk of
That one thing do be love.

ESTHER MATHEWS

RECUERDO

We were very tired, we were very merry—
We had gone back and forth all night on the ferry.
It was bare and bright, and smelled like a stable—
But we looked into a fire, we leaned across a table,
We lay on a hill-top underneath the moon;
And the whistles kept blowing, and the dawn came soon.

We were very tired, we were very merry—
We had gone back and forth all night on the ferry;
And you ate an apple, and I ate a pear,
From a dozen of each we had bought somewhere;
And the sky went wan, and the wind came cold,
And the sun rose dripping, a bucketful of gold.

We were very tired, we were very merry,
We had gone back and forth all night on the ferry.
We hailed, "Good morrow, mother!" to a shawl-covered head,
And bought a morning paper, which neither of us read;
And she wept, "God bless you!" for the apples and pears,
And we gave her all our money but our subway fares.

EDNA ST. VINCENT MILLAY

THE CONSTANT LOVER

Out upon it, I have loved
  Three whole days together!
And am like to love three more,
  If it prove fair weather.

Time shall moult away his wings
  Ere he shall discover
In the whole wide world again
  Such a constant lover.

But the spite on't is, no praise
  Is due at all to me:
Love with me had made no stays,
  Had it any been but she.

Had it any been but she,
  And that very face,
There had been at least ere this
  A dozen dozen in her place.

SIR JOHN SUCKLING

CAKES AND ALE

I gave her Cakes and I gave her
    Ale,
  I gave her Sack and Sherry;
I kissed her once and I kissed her
    twice,
  And we were wondrous merry.

I gave her Beads and Bracelets
    fine,
  I gave her Gold down derry.

I thought she was afeard till she
    stroked my Beard,
  And we were wondrous merry.

Merry my Hearts, merry my
    Cocks, merry my Sprights.
Merry merry merry my hey
    down derry.
I kissed her once and I kissed her
    twice,
  And we were wondrous merry.

          ANONYMOUS

MAID OF ATHENS, ERE WE PART

Maid of Athens, ere we part,
Give, oh give me back my heart!
Or, since that has left my breast,
Keep it now, and take the rest!
Hear my vow before I go,
Ζώη μοῦ, σάζ ἀγαπῶ.

By those tresses unconfined,
Woo'd by each Ægean wind;
By those lids whose jetty fringe
Kiss thy soft cheeks' blooming
    tinge;
By those wild eyes like the roe,
Ζώη μοῦ, σάζ ἀγαπῶ.

By that lip I long to taste;
By that zone-encircled waist;
By all the token-flowers that tell
What words can never speak so
    well;
By love's alternate joy and woe,
Ζώη μοῦ, σάζ ἀγαπῶ.

Maid of Athens! I am gone;
Think of me, sweet! when alone.
Though I fly to Istambol,
Athens holds my heart and soul:
Can I cease to love thee? No!
Ζώη μοῦ, σάζ ἀγαπῶ.
GEORGE GORDON, LORD BYRON

COMIN' THRO' THE RYE

Gin a body meet a body
Comin' thro' the rye,
Gin a body kiss a body,
Need a body cry?
Every lassie has her laddie—
Ne'er a ane hae I;
Yet a' the lads they smile at me
When comin' thro' the rye.
Amang the train there is a swain
I dearly lo'e mysel';
But whaur his hame, or what his
     name,
I dinna care to tell.

Gin a body meet a body
Comin' frae the town,
Gin a body greet a body,
Need a body frown?
Every lassie has her laddie—
Ne'er a ane hae I;
Yet a' the lads they smile at me
When comin' thro' the rye.
Amang the train there is a swain
I dearly lo'e mysel';
But whaur his hame, or what his
     name,
I dinna care to tell.

ROBERT BURNS

UPON JULIA'S CLOTHES

Whenas in silks my Julia goes,
Then, then, methinks, how
     sweetly flows
The liquefaction of her clothes.

Next, when I cast mine eyes, and see
That brave vibration, each way
     free,
O, how that glittering taketh me!

ROBERT HERRICK

LOVE ME LITTLE, LOVE ME LONG

Love me little, love me long,
Is the burden of my song:
Love that is too hot and strong
     Burneth soon to waste.
I am with little well content,
And a little from thee sent
Is enough, with true intent,
     To be steadfast friend.
Love me little, love me long,
Is the burden of my song.

Say thou lov'st me while thou live,
I to thee my love will give,
Never dreaming to deceive
     While that life endures:
Nay, and after death in sooth,
I to thee will keep my truth,
As now when in my May of youth,
     This my love assures.
Love me little, love me long,
Is the burden of my song.

Constant love is moderate ever,
And it will through life persever,
Give to me that with true
    endeavor
  I will it restore:
A suit of durance let it be,

For all weathers, that for me,
For the land or for the sea,
  Lasting evermore.
Love me little, love me long,
Is the burden of my song.
                          ANONYMOUS

SPRING AIR

In blows the loitering air of
    spring,
Scarcely a-blow, a-blow, a lively
    gas.
It makes the secret life-cells ring
And quicken, while the blood-
    waves pass.
Floss nothingness, we feel it cling,
Resile,—silent as space, unseen as
    glass
Unlustred, softer than the weakest
    thing.
Such air can enter nostrils,
    sudden as light
The eye, fair words the ear, or
    flight
The nerve-knot, or your
    unexpected love
My startled heart. Down from
    above,
Or from the south, or flowered
    west,
Or from the oceaned east, or here
Blown first by spring, this air
    possessed
By spring is Ah! so lithe this year.
The curtain flies before this
    wonder.
Talk fast. Speak swift before the
    heart's asunder.

And for this guile . . . no cold-
    ice gates?
Nothing to hold it quietly down,
    a-down,
The while the senses sleep? Full
    spates
Of air enter this room in town.
Such air draws creatures to their
    mates
And, wild, peels off the winter's
    brown
From tree; ruffles the bird and
    motivates
The northern winging to the
    utmost nest;
Breaks out the bud's first scent
    and, lest
Two living things escape and
    keep hearts steady,
Beguiles us at this window; heady
And rich, murmurs; touches like flesh
Of loving fingers, timorous but sure.
Intoxicant is this mild, fresh
Warm breath of spring, all mad
    and pure.
Is this my hand in yours? Am I
So close? Wait till the insinuant
    wind's gone by . . .
                          GENE DERWOOD

IF THOU MUST LOVE ME

If thou must love me, let it be for naught
Except for love's sake only. Do not say,
"I love her for her smile—her look—her way
Of speaking gently,—for a trick of thought
That falls in well with mine, and certes brought
A sense of pleasant ease on such a day"—
For these things in themselves, Belovèd, may
Be changed, or change for thee—and love, so wrought,
May be unwrought so. Neither love me for
Thine own dear pity's wiping my cheeks dry:
A creature might forget to weep, who bore
Thy comfort long, and lose thy love thereby!
But love me for love's sake, that evermore
Thou mayst love on, through love's eternity.

ELIZABETH BARRETT BROWNING

HOW DO I LOVE THEE?

How do I love thee? Let me count the ways.
I love thee to the depth and breadth and height
My soul can reach, when feeling out of sight
For the ends of Being and ideal Grace.
I love thee to the level of everyday's
Most quiet need, by sun and candle-light.
I love thee freely, as men strive for Right;
I love thee purely, as they turn from Praise.
I love thee with the passion put to use
In my old griefs, and with my childhood's faith.
I love thee with a love I seemed to lose
With my lost saints,—I love thee with the breath,
Smiles, tears, of all my life!—and, if God choose,
I shall but love thee better after death.

ELIZABETH BARRETT BROWNING

ENCOURAGEMENTS TO A LOVER

Why so pale and wan, fond lover?
   Prythee, why so pale?
Will, when looking well can't
     move her,
   Looking ill prevail?
   Prythee, why so pale?

Why so dull and mute, young
     sinner?
   Prythee, why so mute?

Will, when speaking well can't win her,
   Saying nothing do't?
   Prythee, why so mute?

Quit, quit, for shame! this will
     not move,
   This cannot take her;
If of herself she will not love,
   Nothing can make her:
   The devil take her!

SIR JOHN SUCKLING

ROSE AYLMER

Ah, what avails the sceptred race,
   Ah, what the form divine!
What every virtue, every grace!
   Rose Aylmer, all were thine.

Rose Aylmer, whom these
   wakeful eyes
   May weep, but never see,
A night of memories and of sighs
   I consecrate to thee.

WALTER SAVAGE LANDOR

TO AURORA

O if thou knew'st how thou thyself dost harm,
And dost prejudge thy bliss, and spoil my rest;
Then thou would'st melt the ice out of thy breast
And thy relenting heart would kindly warm.
O if thy pride did not our joys controul,
What world of loving wonders should'st thou see!
For if I saw thee once transform'd in me,
Then in thy bosom I would pour my soul;
Then all my thoughts should in thy visage shine,
And if that aught mischanced thou should'st not moan
Nor bear the burthen of thy griefs alone;
No, I would have my share in what were thine:
And whilst we thus should make our sorrows one,
This happy harmony would make them none.

WILLIAM ALEXANDER, EARL OF STERLINE

A BIRTHDAY

My heart is like a singing bird
　　Whose nest is in a watered
　　　shoot;
My heart is like an apple-tree
　　Whose boughs are bent with
　　　thick-set fruit;
My heart is like a rainbow shell
　　That paddles in a halcyon sea;
My heart is gladder than all these,
　　Because my love is come to me.

Raise me a dais of silk and down;
　　Hang it with vair and purple
　　　dyes;
Carve it in doves and
　　　pomegranates,
　　And peacocks with a hundred eyes;
Work it in gold and silver grapes,
　　In leaves and silver fleurs-de-lys;
Because the birthday of my life
　　Is come, my love is come to me.

CHRISTINA ROSSETTI

TO LUCASTA, ON GOING TO THE WARS

Tell me not, sweet, I am unkind,
　　That from the nunnery
Of thy chaste breast and quiet mind
　　To war and arms I fly.

True, a new mistress now I chase,
　　The first foe in the field;

And with a stronger faith embrace
　　A sword, a horse, a shield.

Yet this inconstancy is such
　　As thou too shalt adore;
I could not love thee, dear, so much,
　　Loved I not honor more.

RICHARD LOVELACE

LOVE'S SECRET

Never seek to tell thy love,
　　Love that never told can be;
For the gentle wind doth move
　　Silently, invisibly.

I told my love, I told my love,
　　I told her all my heart,
Trembling, cold, in ghastly fears,
　　Ah! she did depart!

Soon after she was gone from me,
　　A traveller came by,
Silently, invisibly:
　　He took her with a sigh.

WILLIAM BLAKE

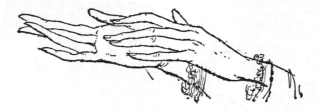

KASHMIRI SONG

Pale hands I love beside the Shalimar,
  Where are you now? Who lies beneath your spell?
Whom do you lead on Rapture's Roadway, far,
  Before you agonize them in farewell?

Or, pale dispensers of my Joys and Pains,
  Holding the doors of Heaven and of Hell,
How the hot blood rushed wildly through the veins
  Beneath your touch, until you waved farewell.

Pale hands, pink-tipped, like Lotus buds that float
  On those cool waters where we used to dwell,
I would have rather felt you round my throat
  Crushing out life than waving me farewell!

LAURENCE HOPE

WHAT IS YOUR SUBSTANCE

What is your substance, whereof are you made,
That millions of strange shadows on you tend?
Since every one hath, every one, one shade,
And you, but one, can every shadow lend.
Describe Adonis, and the counterfeit
Is poorly imitated after you;
On Helen's cheek all art of beauty set,
And you in Grecian tires are painted new:

Speak of the spring and plenty of the year,
The one doth shadow of your beauty show,
The other as your bounty doth appear;
And you in every blessèd shape we know.
In all external grace you have some part,
But you like none, none you, for constant heart.

WILLIAM SHAKESPEARE

A WOMAN'S LAST WORD

Let's contend no more, Love,
  Strive nor weep:
All be as before, Love,
  —Only sleep!

What so wild as words are?
  I and thou
In debate, as birds are,
  Hawk on bough!

See the creature stalking
  While we speak!
Hush and hide the talking,
  Cheek on cheek!

What so false as truth is,
  False to thee?
Where the serpent's tooth is,
  Shun the tree—

Where the apple reddens
  Never pry—
Lest we lose our Edens,
  Eve and I.

Be a God and hold me
  With a charm!
Be a man and fold me
  With thine arm!

Teach me, only teach, Love!
  As I ought
I will speak thy speech, Love,
  Think thy thought—

Meet, if thou require it,
  Both demands,
Laying flesh and spirit
  In thy hands.

That shall be tomorrow,
  Not tonight:
I must bury sorrow
  Out of sight:

—Must a little weep, Love,
  (Foolish me!)
And so fall asleep, Love,
  Loved by thee.

ROBERT BROWNING

NOT MARBLE, NOR THE GILDED MONUMENTS

Not marble, nor the gilded monuments
Of princes, shall outlive this powerful rhyme;
But you shall shine more bright in these contents
Than unswept stone besmear'd with sluttish time.
When wasteful war shall statues overturn,
And broils root out the work of masonry,
Nor Mars his sword nor war's quick fire shall burn
The living record of your memory.

'Gainst death and all-oblivious enmity
Shall you pace forth; your praise shall still find room
Even in the eyes of all posterity
That wears this world out to the ending doom.
So, till the judgment that yourself arise,
You live in this, and dwell in lovers' eyes.

WILLIAM SHAKESPEARE

SINCE BRASS, NOR STONE, NOR EARTH

Since brass, nor stone, nor earth, nor boundless sea,
But sad mortality o'er-sways their power,
How with this rage shall beauty hold a plea,
Whose action is no stronger than a flower?
O, how shall summer's honey breath hold out
Against the wrackful siege of battering days,
When rocks impregnable are not so stout,
Nor gates of steel so strong, but Time decays?

O fearful meditation! where, alack,
Shall Time's best jewel from Time's chest lie hid?
Or what strong hand can hold his swift foot back?
Or who his spoil of beauty can forbid?
O, none, unless this miracle have might,
That in black ink my love may still shine bright.

WILLIAM SHAKESPEARE

TIRED WITH ALL THESE

Tired with all these, for restful
  death I cry,—
As, to behold desert a beggar born,
And needy nothing trimm'd in
  jollity,
And purest faith unhappily
  forsworn,
And gilded honour shamefully
  misplaced,
And maiden virtue rudely
  strumpeted,
And right perfection wrongfully
  disgraced,
And strength by limping sway
  disablèd,

And art made tongue-tied by
  authority,
And folly doctor-like controlling
  skill,
And simple truth miscall'd
  simplicity,
And captive good attending
  captain ill:
Tired with all these, from these
  would I be gone,
Save that, to die, I leave my love
  alone.

WILLIAM SHAKESPEARE

THE GREAT ADVENTURER

Over the mountains
  And over the waves,
Under the fountains
  And under the graves;
Under floods that are deepest,
  Which Neptune obey;
Over rocks that are steepest
  Love will find out the way.

Where there is no place
  For the glow-worm to lie;
Where there is no space
  For receipt of a fly;

Where the midge dares not venture
  Lest herself fast she lay;
If love come, he will enter
  And soon find out his way.

You may esteem him
  A child for his might;
Or you may deem him
  A coward from his flight;
But if she whom love doth honour
  Be conceal'd from the day,
Set a thousand guards upon her,
  Love will find out the way.

Some think to lose him
    By having him confined;
And some do suppose him,
    Poor thing, to be blind;
But if ne'er so close ye wall him,
    Do the best that you may,
Blind love, if so ye call him,
    Will find out his way.

You may train the eagle
    To stoop to your fist;
Or you may inveigle
    The phoenix of the east;
The lioness, ye may move her
    To give o'er her prey;
But you'll ne'er stop a lover:
    He will find out his way.

ANONYMOUS

GIVE ALL TO LOVE

Give all to love;
Obey thy heart;
Friends, kindred, days,
Estate, good-fame,
Plans, credit, and the Muse,—
Nothing refuse.

'Tis a brave master;
Let it have scope:
Follow it utterly,
Hope beyond hope:
High and more high
It dives into noon,
With wing unspent,
Untold intent;
But it is a god,
Knows its own path,
And the outlets of the sky.

It was never for the mean;
It requireth courage stout,
Souls above doubt,
Valor unbending;
It will reward,—
They shall return
More than they were,
And ever ascending.

Leave all for love;
Yet, hear me, yet,

One word more thy heart
    behoved,
One pulse more of firm
    endeavor,—
Keep thee to-day
To-morrow, forever,
Free as an Arab
Of thy beloved.

Cling with life to the maid;
But when the surprise,
First vague shadow of surmise
Flits across her bosom young
Of a joy apart from thee,
Free be she, fancy-free;
Nor thou detain her vesture's
    hem,
Nor the palest rose she flung
From her summer diadem.

Though thou loved her as
    thyself,
As a self of purer clay,
Though her parting dims
    the day,
Stealing grace from all alive;
Heartily know,
When half-gods go,
The gods arrive.

RALPH WALDO EMERSON

FAREWELL TO NANCY

Ae fond kiss, and then we sever!
Ae fareweel, alas, for ever!
Deep in heart-wrung tears I'll
  pledge thee,
Warring sighs and groans I'll
  wage thee.
Who shall say that fortune grieves
  him
While the star of hope she leaves
  him?
Me, nae cheerfu' twinkle
  lights me,
Dark despair around benights me.

I'll ne'er blame my partial fancy,
Naething could resist my Nancy;
But to see her, was to love her;
Love but her, and love for ever.

Had we never lov'd sae kindly,
Had we never lov'd sae blindly,
Never met—or never parted,
We had ne'er been broken hearted.

Fare thee weel, thou first and
  fairest!
Fare thee weel, thou best and
  dearest!
Thine be ilka joy and treasure,
Peace, enjoyment, love, and
  pleasure.
Ae fond kiss, and then we sever;
Ae farewell, alas, for ever!
Deep in heart-wrung tears I
  pledge thee,
Warring sighs and groans I'll
  wage thee.

ROBERT BURNS

THE PASSIONATE SHEPHERD TO HIS LOVE

Come live with me and be my Love,
And we will all the pleasures prove
That valleys, groves, hills and fields,
Woods or steepy mountain yields.

And we will sit upon the rocks
Seeing the shepherds feed their
  flocks.
By shallow rivers, to whose falls
Melodious birds sing madrigals.

And I will make thee beds of roses
And a thousand fragrant posies,
A cap of flowers, and a kirtle
Embroidered all with leaves of
  myrtle.

A gown made of the finest wool,
Which from our pretty lambs we
  pull,
Fair linèd slippers for the cold,
With buckles of the purest gold.

A belt of straw and ivy buds,
With coral clasps and amber studs:
And if these pleasures may thee
   move,
Come live with me and by my
   Love.

The shepherd swains shall dance
   and sing
For thy delight each May-morning:
If these delights thy mind may
   move,
Then live with me and be my Love.

CHRISTOPHER MARLOWE

TO HELEN

Helen, thy beauty is to me
   Like those Nicèan barks of yore
That gently, o'er a perfumed sea,
   The weary way-worn wanderer
     bore
   To his own native shore.

On desperate seas long wont to
   roam,
   Thy hyacinth hair, thy classic
     face,

Thy Naiad airs have brought me
   home
   To the glory that was Greece,
And the grandeur that was Rome.

Lo, in yon brilliant window-niche
   How statue-like I see thee stand,
   The agate lamp within thy hand,
Ah! Psyche, from the regions which
   Are holy land!

EDGAR ALLAN POE

TO HIS COY MISTRESS

Had we but world enough, and
   time,
This coyness, lady, were no crime.
We would sit down, and think
   which way
To walk, and pass our long love's
   day.
Thou by the Indian Ganges' side
Should'st rubies find: I by the
   tide

Of Humber would complain. I
   would
Love you ten years before the
   Flood,
And you should, if you please,
   refuse
Till the conversion of the Jews.
My vegetable love should grow
Vaster than empires, and more
   slow.

An hundred years should go to
　　praise
Thine eyes, and on they forehead
　　gaze:
Two hundred to adore each
　　breast:
But thirty thousand to the rest;
An age at least to every part,
And the last age should show
　　your heart.
For, lady, you deserve this state,
Nor would I love at lower rate.
　　But at my back I always hear
Time's wingèd chariot hurrying
　　near:
And yonder all before us lie
Deserts of vast eternity.
Thy beauty shall no more be
　　found;
Nor, in thy marble vault, shall
　　sound
My echoing song: then worms
　　shall try
That long-preserved virginity,
And your quaint honour turn to
　　dust,
And into ashes all my lust.

The grave's a fine and private
　　place,
But none, I think, do there em-
　　brace.
　　Now, therefore, while the
　　youthful hue
Sits on thy skin like morning dew,
And while thy willing soul trans-
　　pires
At every pore with instant fires,
Now let us sport us while we may;
And now, like amorous birds of
　　prey,
Rather at once our Time devour,
Than languish in his slow-chapt
　　power.
Let us roll all our strength and all
Our sweetness up into one ball,
And tear our pleasures with
　　rough strife
Thorough the iron gates of life.
Thus, though we cannot make
　　our sun
Stand still, yet we will make him
　　run.

ANDREW MARVELL

SALLY IN OUR ALLEY

Of all the girls that are so smart
  There's none like pretty Sally;
She is the darling of my heart,
  And she lives in our alley.
There is no lady in the land
  Is half so sweet as Sally;
She is the darling of my heart,
  And she lives in our alley.

Her father he makes cabbage nets,
  And through the streets does
    cry 'em;
Her mother she sells laces long
  To such as please to buy 'em;
But sure such folks could ne'er beget
  So sweet a girl as Sally!
She is the darling of my heart,
  And she lives in our alley.

When she is by, I leave my work,
  I love her so sincerely;
My master comes like any Turk,
  And bangs me most severely:
But let him bang his bellyful,
  I'll bear it all for Sally;
She is the darling of my heart,
  And she lives in our alley.

Of all the days that's in the week
  I dearly love but one day—
And that's the day that comes
    betwixt
  A Saturday and Monday;

For then I'm dressed all in my
    best
  To walk abroad with Sally;
She is the darling of my heart,
  And she lives in our alley.

My master carries me to church,
  And often am I blamèd
Because I leave him in the lurch
  As soon as text is namèd;
I leave the church in sermon-time
  And slink away to Sally;
She is the darling of my heart,
  And she lives in our alley.

When Christmas comes about
    again,
  O, then I shall have money;
I'll hoard it up, and box it all,
  I'll give it to my honey:
I would it were ten thousand
    pound,
  I'd give it all to Sally;
She is the darling of my heart,
  And she lives in our alley.

My master and the neighbors all
  Make game of me and Sally,
And, but for her, I'd better be
  A slave and row a galley;
But when my seven long years
    are out,
  O, then I'll marry Sally;
O, then we'll wed, and then we'll bed—
  But not in our alley!

HENRY CAREY

SHALL I COMPARE THEE TO A SUMMER'S DAY?

Shall I compare thee to a summer's day?
Thou art more lovely and more temperate:
Rough winds do shake the darling buds of May,
And summer's lease hath all too short a date:
Sometime too hot the eye of heaven shines,
And often is his gold complexion dimm'd;
And every fair from fair sometime declines,
By chance, or nature's changing course untrimm'd;
But thy eternal summer shall not fade,
Nor lose possession of that fair thou ow'st,
Nor shall death brag thou wander'st in his shade,
When in eternal lines to time thou grow'st;
  So long as men can breathe, or eyes can see,
  So long lives this, and this gives life to thee.

WILLIAM SHAKESPEARE

LET ME NOT TO THE MARRIAGE OF TRUE MINDS

Let me not to the marriage of true minds
Admit impediments. Love is not love
Which alters when it alteration finds,
Or bends with the remover to remove:
O, no! it is an ever-fixed mark,
That looks on tempests and is never shaken;
It is the star to every wandering bark,
Whose worth's unknown, although his height be taken.
Love's not Time's fool, though rosy lips and cheeks
Within his bending sickle's compass come;
Love alters not with his brief hours and weeks,
But bears it out even to the edge of doom.
  If this be error, and upon me prov'd,
  I never writ, nor no man ever lov'd.

WILLIAM SHAKESPEARE

"HERE LIES JULIET"

Romeo. For here lies Juliet, and her beauty makes
This vault a feasting presence full of light.
Death, lie thou there, by a dead man interr'd.
How oft when men are at the point of death
Have they been merry! which their keepers call
A lightning before death: O, how may I
Call this a lightning? O my love! my wife!
Death, that hath suck'd the honey of thy breath,
Hath had no power yet upon thy beauty:
Thou art not conquer'd; beauty's ensign yet
Is crimson in thy lips and in thy cheeks,
And death's pale flag is not advanced there.
Tybalt, liest thou there in thy bloody sheet?
O, what more favour can I do to thee
Than with that hand that cut thy youth in twain
To sunder his that was thine enemy?
Forgive me, cousin! Ah, dear Juliet,
Why art thou yet so fair? shall I believe
That unsubstantial death is amorous,
And that the lean abhorred monster keeps
Thee here in dark to be his paramour?
For fear of that, I still will stay with thee;
And never from this dim palace of dim night
Depart again: here, here will I remain
With worms that are thy chamber-maids; O, here
Will I set up my everlasting rest,
And shake the yoke of inauspicious stars
From this world-wearied flesh. Eyes, look your last!
Arms, take your last embrace! and lips, O you
The doors of breath, seal with a righteous kiss
A dateless bargain to engrossing death!
Come, bitter conduct, come, unsavoury guide!
Thou desperate pilot, now at once run on
The dashing rocks thy sea-sick weary bark.
Here's to my love! (*Drinks*) O true apothecary!
Thy drugs are quick. Thus with a kiss I die.

WILLIAM SHAKESPEARE

CYNARA

(*Non Sum Qualis Eram Bonae sub Regno Cynarae*)

Last night, ah, yesternight, betwixt her lips and mine
There fell thy shadow, Cynara! thy breath was shed
Upon my soul between the kisses and the wine;
And I was desolate and sick of an old passion,
  Yea, I was desolate and bowed my head:
I have been faithful to thee, Cynara! in my fashion.

All night upon mine heart I felt her warm heart beat,
Night-long within mine arms in love and sleep she lay;
Surely the kisses of her bought red mouth were sweet;
But I was desolate and sick of an old passion,
  When I awoke and found the dawn was gray:
I have been faithful to thee, Cynara! in my fashion.

I have forgot much, Cynara! gone with the wind,
Flung roses, roses riotously with the throng,
Dancing, to put thy pale, lost lilies out of mind;
But I was desolate and sick of an old passion,
  Yea, all the time, because the dance was long:
I have been faithful to thee, Cynara! in my fashion.

I cried for madder music and for stronger wine,
But when the feast is finished and the lamps expire,
Then falls thy shadow, Cynara! the night is thine;
And I am desolate and sick of an old passion,
  Yea hungry for the lips of my desire:
I have been faithful to thee, Cynara! in my fashion.

ERNEST DOWSON

SONG

Go and catch a falling star,
  Get with child a mandrake root,
Tell me where all past years are,
  Or who cleft the devil's foot,
Teach me to hear a mermaid's
      singing,
Or to keep off envy's stinging,
    And find
    What wind
Serves to advance an honest mind.

If thou be'st born to strange sights,
  Things invisible go see,
Ride ten thousand days and nights,
  Till Age snow white hairs on thee;
Thou, when thou return'st, wilt
    tell me

All strange wonders that befell thee,
    And swear
    No where
Lives a woman true and fair.

If thou find'st one, let me know;
  Such a pilgrimage were sweet.
Yet do not; I would not go,
  Though at next door we might
    meet.
Though she were true when you
    met her,
And last till you write your letter,
    Yet she
    Will be
False, ere I come, to two or three.

JOHN DONNE

THE GIRL I LEFT BEHIND ME

The dames of France are fond
  and free,
And Flemish lips are willing,
And soft the maids of Italy,
And Spanish eyes are thrilling;
Still, though I bask beneath their
  smile,
Their charms fail to bind me.
And my heart falls back to Erin's
  Isle,
To the girl I left behind me.

For she's as fair as Shannon's
  side,
And purer than its water,
But she refused to be my bride
Though many years I sought her;
Yet since to France I sailed
  away,
Her letters oft remind me,
That I promised never to
  gainsay
The girl I left behind me.

She says, "My own dear love come
    home,
My friends are rich and many,
Or else, abroad with you I'll roam,
A soldier stout as any;
If you'll not come, nor let me go,
I'll think you have resigned me."
My heart nigh broke when I
    answered "No,"
To the girl I left behind me.

For never shall my true love brave
A life of war and toiling,
And never as a skulking slave
I'll tread my native soil on;
But were it free or to be freed,
The battle's close would find me
To Ireland bound, nor message
    need
From the girl I left behind me.

ANONYMOUS

BOOK IV

JUST FOLKS

WHEN THE FROST IS ON THE PUNKIN

When the frost is on the punkin and the fodder's in the shock
And you hear the kyouck and gobble of the struttin' turkey-cock,
And the clackin' of the guineys, and the cluckin' of the hens,
And the rooster's hallylooyer as he tiptoes on the fence;
O, it's then's the times a feller is a-feelin' at his best,
With the risin' sun to greet him from a night of peaceful rest,
As he leaves the house, bareheaded, and goes out to feed the stock,
When the frost is on the punkin and the fodder's in the shock.

They's something kindo' harty-like about the atmusfere
When the heat of summer's over and the coolin' fall is here—
Of course we miss the flowers, and the blossums on the trees,
And the mumble of the hummin'-birds and buzzin' of the bees;
But the air's so appetizin'; and the landscape through the haze
Of a crisp and sunny morning of the airly autumn days
Is a pictur' that no painter has the colorin' to mock—
When the frost is on the punkin and the fodder's in the shock.

The husky, rusty russel of the tossels of the corn,
And the raspin' of the tangled leaves, as golden as the morn;
The stubble in the furries—kindo' lonesome-like, but still
A-preachin' sermons to us of the barns they growed to fill;
The strawstack in the medder, and the reaper in the shed;
The hosses in theyr stalls below—the clover overhead!—
O, it sets my hart a-clickin' like the tickin' of a clock,
When the frost is on the punkin and the fodder's in the shock!

Then your apples all is gethered, and the ones a feller keeps
Is poured around the celler-floor in red and yeller heaps;
And your cider-makin' 's over, and your wimmern-folks is through
With their mince and apple-butter, and theyr souse and sausage, too!
I don't know how to tell it—but ef sich a thing could be
As the Angels wantin' boardin', and they'd call around on *me*—
I'd want to 'commodate 'em—all the whole-indurin' flock—
When the frost is on the punkin and the fodder's in the shock!

JAMES WHITCOMB RILEY

HOME, SWEET HOME

Mid pleasures and palaces though
we may roam,
Be it ever so humble, there's no
place like home;
A charm from the sky seems to
hallow us there,
Which, seek through the world, is
ne'er met with elsewhere.
Home, home, sweet, sweet home!
There's no place like home, oh,
there's no place like home!

An exile from home, splendor
dazzles in vain;
Oh, give me my lowly thatched
cottage again!
The birds singing gayly, that came
at my call—
Give me them—and the peace of
mind, dearer than all!
Home, home, sweet, sweet home!
There's no place like home, oh,
there's no place like home!

I gaze on the moon as I tread the
drear wild,
And feel that my mother now
thinks of her child,
As she looks on that moon from
our own cottage door

Thro' the woodbine, whose
fragrance shall cheer me no more.
Home, home, sweet, sweet home!
There's no place like home, oh,
there's no place like home!

How sweet 'tis to sit 'neath a fond
father's smile,
And the caress of a mother to
soothe and beguile!
Let others delight mid new
pleasures to roam,
But give me, oh, give me, the
pleasures of home,
Home, home, sweet, sweet home!
There's no place like home, oh,
there's no place like home!

To thee I'll return, overburdened
with care;
The heart's dearest solace will
smile on me there;
No more from that cottage again
will I roam;
Be it ever so humble, there's no
place like home.
Home, home, sweet, sweet home!
There's no place like home, oh,
there's no place like home!

JOHN HOWARD PAYNE

JUST FOLKS

We're queer folks here.
We'll talk about the weather,
The good times we've had
   together,
The good times near,
The roses buddin', an' the bees
Once more upon their nectar
   sprees;
The scarlet fever scare, an' who
Came mighty near not pullin'
   through,
An' who had light attacks, an' all
The things that int'rest, big or
   small;
But here you'll never hear of
   sinnin'
Or any scandal that's beginnin'.
We've got too many other labors
To scatter tales that harm our
   neighbors.

We're strange folks here.
We're tryin' to be cheerful,
An' keep this home from gettin'
   tearful.
We hold it dear;
Too dear for pettiness an' meanness,
An' nasty tales of men's
   uncleanness.
Here you shall come to joyous smilin',
Secure from hate and harsh revilin';
Here, where the wood fire
   brightly blazes,

You'll hear from us our neighbor's
   praises.
Here, that they'll never grow to
   doubt us,
We keep our friends always about
   us;
An' here, though storms outside
   may pelter
Is refuge for our friends, an'
   shelter.

We've one rule here,
An' that is to be pleasant.
The folks we know are always
   present,
Or very near.
An' though they dwell in many
   places,
We think we're talkin' to their
   faces;
An' that keeps us from only seein'
The faults in any human bein',
An' checks our tongues when
   they'd go trailin'
Into the mire of mortal failin'.
Flaws aren't so big when folks are
   near you;
You don't talk mean when they
   can hear you.
An' so no scandal here is started,
Because from friends we're never
   parted.

EDGAR A. GUEST

A PRAYER FOR A LITTLE HOME

God send us a little home
To come back to when we roam—
Low walls and fluted tiles,
Wide windows, a view for miles;
Red firelight and deep chairs;
Small white beds upstairs;
Great talk in little nooks;
Dim colors, rows of books;

One picture on each wall;
Not many things at all.
God send us a little ground—
Tall trees standing round,
Homely flowers in brown sod,
Overhead Thy stars, O God!
God bless, when winds blow,
Our home and all we know.

ANONYMOUS

THE HAND THAT ROCKS THE CRADLE IS THE HAND THAT RULES THE WORLD

Blessings on the hand of women!
  Angels guard its strength and
    grace,
In the palace, cottage, hovel,
  Oh, no matter where the place;
Would that never storms
    assailed it,
  Rainbows ever gently curled;
For the hand that rocks the cradle
  Is the hand that rules the world.

Infancy's the tender fountain,
  Power may with beauty flow,
Mother's first to guide the
    streamlets,
  From them souls unresting grow—
Grow on for the good or evil,
  Sunshine streamed or evil hurled;
For the hand that rocks the cradle
  Is the hand that rules the world.

Woman, how divine your mission
  Here upon our natal sod!
Keep, oh, keep the young heart
    open
  Always to the breath of God!
All true trophies of the ages
  Are from mother-love
    impearled;
For the hand that rocks the cradle
  Is the hand that rules the world.

Blessings on the hand of women!
  Fathers, sons, and daughters cry,
And the sacred song is mingled
  With the worship in the sky—
Mingles where no tempest
    darkens,
  Rainbows evermore are hurled;
For the hand that rocks the cradle
  Is the hand that rules the world.

WILLIAM ROSS WALLACE

WHEN FATHER CARVES THE DUCK

We all look on with anxious eyes
  When father carves the duck,
And mother almost always sighs
  When father carves the duck;
Then all of us prepare to rise,
And hold our bibs before our eyes,
And be prepared for some
    surprise,
  When father carves the duck.

He braces up and grabs a fork
  Whene'er he carves a duck,
And won't allow a soul to talk
  Until he's carved the duck.
The fork is jabbed into the sides,
Across the breast the knife he
    slides,
While every careful person hides
  From flying chips of duck.

The platter's always sure to slip
  When father carves a duck,
And how it makes the dishes skip!
    Potatoes fly amuck!
The squash and cabbage leap in
    space,
We get some gravy in our face,
And father mutters Hindoo grace
  Whene'er he carves a duck.

We then have learned to walk
    around
  The dining-room and pluck
From off the window-sills and walls
  Our share of father's duck.
While father growls and blows and jaws
And swears the knife was full of flaws,
And mother laughs at him because
  He couldn't carve a duck.

                                    E. V. WRIGHT

MOTHER O' MINE

If I were hanged on the highest hill,
  Mother o' mine, O mother o' mine!
I know whose love would follow me still,
  Mother o' mine, O mother o' mine!
If I were drowned in the deepest sea,
  Mother o' mine, O mother o' mine!
I know whose tears would come down to me,
  Mother o' mine, O mother o' mine!
If I were damned by body and soul,
I know whose prayers would make me whole,
  Mother o' mine, O mother o' mine!

                        RUDYARD KIPLING

A BAREFOOT BOY

A barefoot boy! I mark him at his play—
  For May is here once more, and so is he,—
  His dusty trousers, rolled half to the knee,
And his bare ankles grimy, too, as they:
Cross-hatchings of the nettle, in array
  Of feverish stripes, hint vividly to me
  Of woody pathways winding endlessly
Along the creek, where even yesterday
He plunged his shrinking body—gasped and shook—
  Yet called the water "warm," with never lack
Of joy. And so, half enviously I look
  Upon this graceless barefoot and his track,—
  His toe stubbed—ay, his big toe-nail knocked back
Like unto the clasp of an old pocketbook.

JAMES WHITCOMB RILEY

SONNET TO MY MOTHER

Most near, most dear, most loved and most far,
Under the window where I often found her
Sitting as huge as Asia, seismic with laughter,
Gin and chicken helpless in her Irish hand,
Irresistible as Rabelais but most tender for
The lame dogs and hurt birds that surround her,—
She is a procession no one can follow after
But be like a little dog following a brass band.
She will not glance up at the bomber nor condescend
To drop her gin and scuttle to a cellar,
But lean on the mahogany table like a mountain
Whom only faith can move, and so I send
O all my faith and all my love to tell her
That she will move from mourning into morning.

GEORGE BARKER

THE OLD OAKEN BUCKET

How dear to my heart are the scenes of my childhood,
    When fond recollection presents them to view!
The orchard, the meadow, the deep-tangled wildwood,
    And every loved spot which my infancy knew,
The wide-spreading pond and the mill which stood by it,
    The bridge and the rock where the cataract fell;
The cot of my father, the dairy house nigh it,
    And e'en the rude-bucket which hung in the well.
The old oaken bucket, the iron-bound bucket,
The moss-covered bucket which hung in the well.

That moss-covered vessel I hail as a treasure;
    For often at noon, when returned from the field,
I found it the source of an exquisite pleasure,
    The purest and sweetest that nature can yield.
How ardent I seized it with hands that were glowing!

And quick to the white-pebbled bottom it fell;
Then soon, with the emblem of truth overflowing,
    And dripping with coolness it rose from the well;
The old oaken bucket, the iron-bound bucket,
The moss-covered bucket, arose from the well.

How sweet from the green mossy brim to receive it,
    As poised on the curb, it inclined to my lips!
Not a full blushing goblet could tempt me to leave it,
    Though filled with the nectar that Jupiter sips.
And now, far removed from the loved situation,
    The tear of regret will intrusively swell,
As fancy reverts to my father's plantation,
    And sighs for the bucket which hangs in the well;
The old oaken bucket, the iron-bound bucket,
The moss-covered bucket which hangs in the well.

SAMUEL WOODWORTH

SOMEBODY'S MOTHER

The woman was old and ragged and gray
And bent with the chill of the Winter's day.
The street was wet with a recent snow
And the woman's feet were aged and slow.
She stood at the crossing and waited long,
Alone, uncared for, amid the throng
Of human beings who passed her by
Nor heeded the glance of her anxious eye.
Down the street, with laughter and shout,
Glad in the freedom of "school let out,"
Came the boys like a flock of sheep,
Hailing the snow piled white and deep.
Past the woman so old and gray
Hastened the children on their way.
Nor offered a helping hand to her—
So meek, so timid, afraid to stir
Lest the carriage wheels or the horses' feet
Should crowd her down in the slippery street.

At last came one of the merry troop,
The gayest laddie of all the group;
He paused beside her and whispered low,
"I'll help you cross, if you wish to go."
Her aged hand on his strong young arm
She placed, and so, without hurt or harm,
He guided the trembling feet along,
Proud that his own were firm and strong,
Then back again to his friends he went,
His young heart happy and well content.
"She's somebody's mother, boys, you know,
For all she's aged and poor and slow.
"And I hope some fellow will lend a hand
To help my mother, you understand,
"If ever she's poor and old and gray,
When her own dear boy is far away."
And "somebody's mother" bowed low her head
In her home that night, and the prayer she said
Was "God be kind to the noble boy,
Who is somebody's son, and pride and joy!"

MARY DOW BRINE

ON HIS DECEASED WIFE

Methought I saw my late espousèd Saint
Brought to me like Alcestis from the grave,
Whom Jove's great Son to her glad Husband gave,
Rescued from death by force though pale and faint.
Mine as whom washed from spot of child-bed taint,
Purification in the old Law did save,
And such, as yet once more I trust to have
Full sight of her in Heaven without restraint,
Came vested all in white, pure as her mind:
Her face was veiled, yet to my fancied sight,
Love, sweetness, goodness, in her person shined
So clear, as in no face with more delight.
But O as to embrace me she inclined
I waked, she fled, and day brought back my night.

JOHN MILTON

TO A LADY ON HER PASSION FOR OLD CHINA

What ecstasies her bosom fire!
How her eyes languish with
   desire!
How blest, how happy should I be,
Were that fond glance bestow'd
   on me!
New doubts and fears within me
   war:
What rival's near? a china jar.
  China's the passion of her soul;
A cup, a plate, a dish, a bowl,
Can kindle wishes in her breast,
Inflame with joy, or break her
   rest.
    Some gems collect; some medals
    prize,
And view the rust with lover's
   eyes;
Some court the stars at midnight
   hours;
Some dote on Nature's charms in
   flowers!
But ev'ry beauty I can trace
In Laura's mind, in Laura's face;
My stars are in this brighter
   sphere,
My lily and my rose is here.
    Philosophers more grave than
    wise
Hunt science down in butterflies;
Or fondly poring on a spider
Stretch human contemplation
   wider;
Fossils give joy to Galen's soul,

He digs for knowledge, like a
   mole;
In shells so learn'd, that all agree
No fish that swims knows more
   than he!
In such pursuits if wisdom lies,
Who, Laura, shall thy taste
   despise?
    When I some antique jar
    behold,
Or white, or blue, or speck'd with
   gold,
Vessels so pure, and so refin'd,
Appear the types of woman-kind:
Are they not valued for their
   beauty,
Too fair, too fine, for household
   duty?
With flowers and gold and azure
   dyed,
Of ev'ry house the grace and
   pride?
How white, how polish'd is their
   skin,
And valued most when only seen!
She who before was highest
   prized,
Is for a crack or flaw despised;
I grant they're frail, yet they're so
   rare,
The treasure cannot cost too dear!
But man is made of coarser stuff,
And serves convenience well
   enough;

He's a strong earthen vessel made
For drudging, labour, toil, and
   trade;
And when wives lose their other
   self,
With ease they bear the loss of
   delf.
   Husbands more covetous than
   sage
Condemn this china-buying rage;
They count that woman's
   prudence little,
Who sets her heart on things so
   brittle.
But are those wise men's
   inclinations
Fixt on more strong, more sure
   foundations?
If all that's frail we must despise,
No human view or scheme is wise.
Are not ambition's hopes as weak?

They swell like bubbles, shine
   and break.
A courtier's promise is so slight,
'Tis made at noon, and broke at
   night.
What pleasure's sure? The miss
   you keep
Breaks both your fortune and
   your sleep,
The man who loves a country life,
Breaks all the comforts of his wife;
And if he quit his farm and plough,
His wife in town may break her vow.
Love, Laura, love, while youth is
   warm,
For each new winter breaks a charm,
And woman's not like china sold,
But cheaper grows in growing old;
Then quickly choose the prudent
   part,
Or else you break a faithful heart.

JOHN GAY

THE TOYS

My little Son, who looked from
   thoughtful eyes
And moved and spoke in quiet
   grown-up wise,
Having my law the seventh time
   disobeyed,
I struck him, and dismissed
With hard words and unkissed,
—His Mother, who was patient,
   being dead.
Then, fearing lest his grief should
   hinder sleep,
I visited his bed,
But found him slumbering deep,

With darkened eyelids, and their
   lashes yet
From his late sobbing wet.
And I, with moan,
Kissing away his tears, left others
   of my own;
For, on a table drawn beside his
   head,
He had put, within his reach,
A box of counters and a red-
   veined stone,
A piece of glass abraded by the
   beach,
And six or seven shells,
A bottle with bluebells,

And two French copper coins,
  ranged there with careful art,
To comfort his sad heart.
So when that night I prayed
To God, I wept, and said:
Ah, when at last we lie with
  trancèd breath,
Not vexing Thee in death,
And Thou rememberest of what toys
We made our joys,

How weakly understood
Thy great commanded good,
Then, fatherly not less
Than I whom Thou hast moulded
  from the clay,
Thou'lt leave Thy wrath, and say,
"I will be sorry for their
  childishness."

COVENTRY PATMORE

OUT TO OLD AUNT MARY'S

Wasn't it pleasant, O brother mine,
In those old days of the lost sunshine
    Of youth—when the Saturday's chores were through,
    And the "Sunday's wood" in the kitchen, too,
    And we went visiting, "me and you,"
        Out to Old Aunt Mary's?—

"Me and you"—And the morning fair,
With the dewdrops twinkling everywhere;
    The scent of the cherry-blossoms blown
    After us, in the roadway lone,
    Our capering shadows onward thrown—
        Out to Old Aunt Mary's!

It all comes back so clear to-day!
Though I am as bald as you are gray,—
    Out by the barn-lot and down the lane
    We patter along in the dust again,
    As light as the tips of the drops of the rain,
        Out to Old Aunt Mary's.

The few last houses of the town;
Then on, up the high creek-bluffs and down;
   Past the squat toll-gate, with its well-sweep pole,
   The bridge, and "the old 'babtizin'-hole,' "
   Loitering, awed, o'er pool and shoal,
      Out to Old Aunt Mary's.

We cross the pasture, and through the wood,
Where the old gray snag of the poplar stood,
   Where the hammering "red-heads" hopped awry,
   And the buzzard "raised" in the "clearing"-sky
   And lolled and circled, as we went by
      Out to Old Aunt Mary's.

Or, stayed by the glint of the redbird's wings,
Or the glitter of song that the bluebird sings,
   All hushed we feign to strike strange trails,
   As the "big braves" do in the Indian tales,
   Till again our real quest lags and fails—
      Out to Old Aunt Mary's.—

And the woodland echoes with yells of mirth
That make old war-whoops of minor worth! . . .
   Where such heroes of war as we?—
   With bows and arrows of fantasy,
   Chasing each other from tree to tree
      Out to Old Aunt Mary's!

And then in the dust of the road again;
And the teams we met, and the countrymen;
   And the long highway, with sunshine spread
   As thick as butter on country bread,
   Our cares behind, and our hearts ahead
      Out to Old Aunt Mary's.—

For only, now, at the road's next bend
To the right we could make out the gable-end
   Of the fine old Huston homestead—not
   Half a mile from the sacred spot
   Where dwelt our Saint in her simple cot—
      Out to Old Aunt Mary's.

Why, I see her now in the open door
Where the little gourds grew up the sides and o'er
   The clapboard roof!—And her face—ah, me!
   Wasn't it good for a boy to see—
   And wasn't it good for a boy to be
         Out to Old Aunt Mary's?—

The jelly—the jam and the marmalade,
And the cherry and quince "preserves" she made!
   And the sweet-sour pickles of peach and pear,
   With cinnamon in 'em, and all things rare!—
   And the more we ate was the more to spare,
         Out to Old Aunt Mary's!

Ah! was there, ever, so kind a face
And gentle as hers, or such a grace
   Of welcoming, as she cut the cake
   Or the juicy pies that she joyed to make
   Just for the visiting children's sake—
         Out to Old Aunt Mary's!

The honey, too, in its amber comb
One only finds in an old farm-home;
   And the coffee, fragrant and sweet, and ho!
   So hot that we gloried to drink it so,
   With spangles of tears in our eyes, you know—
         Out to Old Aunt Mary's.

And the romps we took, in our glad unrest!—
Was it the lawn that we loved the best,
   With its swooping swing in the locust trees,
   Or was it the grove, with its leafy breeze,
   Or the dim haymow, with its fragrancies—
         Out to Old Aunt Mary's.

Far fields, bottom-lands, creek-banks—all,
We ranged at will.—Where the waterfall
   Laughed all day as it slowly poured
   Over the dam by the old mill-ford,
   While the tail-race writhed, and the mill-wheel roared—
         Out to Old Aunt Mary's.

But home, with Aunty in nearer call,
That was the best place, after all!—
　　The talks on the back porch, in the low
　　Slanting sun and the evening glow,
　　With the voice of counsel that touched us so,
　　　　Out to Old Aunt Mary's.

And then, in the garden—near the side
Where the beehives were and the path was wide,—
　　The apple-house—like a fairy cell—
　　With the little square door we knew so well,
　　And the wealth inside but our tongues could tell—
　　　　Out to Old Aunt Mary's.

And the old spring-house, in the cool green gloom
Of the willow trees,—and the cooler room
　　Where the swinging shelves and the crocks were kept,
　　Where the cream in a golden languor slept,
　　While the waters gurgled and laughed and wept—
　　　　Out to Old Aunt Mary's.

And as many a time have you and I—
Barefoot boys in the days gone by—
　　Knelt, and in tremulous ecstasies
　　Dipped our lips into sweets like these,—
　　Memory now is on her knees
　　　　Out to Old Aunt Mary's.—

For, O my brother so far away,
This is to tell you—she waits *to-day*
　　To welcome us:—Aunt Mary fell
　　Asleep this morning, whispering, "Tell
　　The boys to come.". . . And all is well
　　　　Out to Old Aunt Mary's.

　　　　　　　　　JAMES WHITCOMB RILEY

BOOK V

POEMS OF YOUTH AND AGE

YOUNG AND OLD

When all the world is young, lad,
  And all the trees are green;
And every goose a swan, lad,
  And every lass a queen;
Then hey for boot and horse, lad,
  And round the world away;
Young blood must have its course,
  lad,
  And every dog his day.

When all the world is old, lad,
  And all the trees are brown;
And all the sport is stale, lad,
  And all the wheels run down;
Creep home, and take your place
  there,
  The spent and maimed among:
God grant you find one face there,
  You loved when all was young.

CHARLES KINGSLEY

I REMEMBER, I REMEMBER

I remember, I remember,
The house where I was born,
The little window where the sun
Came peeping in at morn;
He never came a wink too soon,
Nor brought too long a day,
But now, I often wish the night
Had borne my breath away!

I remember, I remember,
The roses, red and white,
The violets, and the lily-cups,
Those flowers made of light!
The lilacs where the robin built,
And where my brother set
The laburnum on his birthday,—
The tree is living yet!

I remember, I remember,
Where I was used to swing,
And thought the air must rush as
  fresh
To swallows on the wing;
My spirit flew in feathers then,
That is so heavy now,
And summer pools could hardly cool
The fever on my brow!

I remember, I remember,
The fir trees dark and high;
I used to think their slender tops
Were close against the sky:
It was a childish ignorance,
But now 'tis little joy
To know I'm farther off from heaven
Than when I was a boy.

THOMAS HOOD

ON GROWING OLD

Be with me, Beauty, for the fire is dying,
My dog and I are old, too old for roving.
Man, whose young passion sets the spindrift flying,
Is soon too lame to march, too cold for loving.
I take the book and gather to the fire,
Turning old yellow leaves; minute by minute
The clock ticks to my heart; a withered wire
Moves a thin ghost of music in the spinet.
I cannot sail your seas, I cannot wander
Your cornland nor your hill-land nor your valleys
Ever again, nor share the battle yonder
Where the young knight the broken squadron rallies;
Only stay quiet, while my mind remembers
The beauty of fire from the beauty of embers.

Beauty, have pity, for the strong have power,
The rich their wealth, the beautiful their grace,
Summer of man its sunlight and its flower,
Springtime of man all April in a face.
Only, as in the jostling in the Strand,
Where the mob thrusts or loiters or is loud,
The beggar with the saucer in his hand
Asks only a penny from the passing crowd,
So, from this glittering world with all its fashion,
Its fire and play of men, its stir, its march,
Let me have wisdom, Beauty, wisdom and passion,
Bread to the soul, rain where the summers parch.
Give me but these, and though the darkness close
Even the night will blossom as the rose.

JOHN MASEFIELD

MY HEART LEAPS UP

My heart leaps up when I behold
  A rainbow in the sky;
So was it when my life began;
So is it now I am a man;
So be it when I shall grow old,
  Or let me die!

The Child is father of the Man;
And I could wish my days to be
Bound each to each by natural
  piety.

WILLIAM WORDSWORTH

TEARS, IDLE TEARS

Tears, idle tears, I know not what they mean,
Tears from the depth of some divine despair
Rise in the heart, and gather to the eyes,
In looking on the happy autumn-fields,
And thinking of the days that are no more.

Fresh as the first beam glittering on a sail,
That brings our friends up from the under-world,
Sad as the last which reddens over one
That sinks with all we love below the verge;
So sad, so fresh, the days that are no more.

Ah, sad and strange as in dark summer dawns
The earliest pipe of half-awakened birds
To dying ears, when unto dying eyes
The casement slowly grows a glimmering square;
So sad, so strange, the days that are no more.

Dear as remembered kisses after death,
And sweet as those by hopeless fancy feigned
On lips that are for others; deep as love,
Deep as first love, and wild with all regret;
O Death in Life, the days that are no more!

ALFRED, LORD TENNYSON

THE LIGHT OF OTHER DAYS

Oft in the stilly night,
  Ere slumber's chain has bound me,
Fond Memory brings the light
  Of other days around me:
    The smiles, the tears
    Of boyhood's years,
  The words of love then spoken;
    The eyes that shone,
    Now dimm'd and gone,
  The cheerful hearts now broken!
Thus in the stilly night,
  Ere slumber's chain has bound me,
Sad Memory brings the light
  Of other days around me.

When I remember all
  The friends so link'd together
I've seen around me fall
  Like leaves in wintry weather,
    I feel like one
    Who treads alone
  Some banquet-hall deserted,
    Whose lights are fled
    Whose garlands dead,
  And all but he departed!
Thus in the stilly night,
  Ere slumber's chain has bound me,
Sad Memory brings the light
  Of other days around me.

THOMAS MOORE

THE SEVEN AGES OF MAN

All the world's a stage,
And all the men and women merely players:
They have their exits and their entrances;
And one man in his time plays many parts,
His acts being seven ages. At first the infant,
Mewling and puking in the nurse's arms.
And then the whining school-boy, with his satchel,
And shining morning face, creeping like snail
Unwillingly to school. And then the lover
Sighing like furnace, with a woeful ballad
Made to his mistress' eyebrow. Then a soldier,
Full of strange oaths, and bearded like the pard,
Jealous in honour, sudden and quick in quarrel,
Seeking the bubble reputation
Even in the cannon's mouth. And then the justice,
In fair round belly with good capon lin'd,
With eyes severe, and beard of formal cut,
Full of wise saws and modern instances;
And so he plays his part. The sixth age shifts
Into the lean and slipper'd pantaloon,
With spectacles on nose and pouch on side,
His youthful hose well sav'd a world too wide
For his shrunk shank; and his big manly voice,
Turning again toward childish treble, pipes
And whistles in his sound. Last scene of all,
That ends this strange eventful history,
Is second childishness and mere oblivion,
Sans teeth, sans eyes, sans taste, sans everything.

WILLIAM SHAKESPEARE

SAILING TO BYZANTIUM

That is no country for old men. The young
In one another's arms, birds in the trees
—Those dying generations—at their song,
The salmon-falls, the mackerel-crowded seas,
Fish, flesh, or fowl, commend all summer long
Whatever is begotten, born, and dies.
Caught in that sensual music all neglect
Monuments of unaging intellect.

An aged man is but a paltry thing,
A tattered coat upon a stick, unless
Soul clap its hands and sing, and louder sing
For every tatter in its mortal dress,
Nor is there singing school but studying
Monuments of its own magnificence;
And therefore I have sailed the seas and come
To the holy city of Byzantium.

O sages standing in God's holy fire
As in the gold mosaic of a wall,
Come from the holy fire, perne in a gyre,
And be the singing-masters of my soul.
Consume my heart away; sick with desire
And fastened to a dying animal
It knows not what it is; and gather me
Into the artifice of eternity.

Once out of nature I shall never take
My bodily form from any natural thing,
But such a form as Grecian goldsmiths make
Of hammered gold and gold enameling
To keep a drowsy Emperor awake;
Or set upon a golden bough to sing
To lords and ladies of Byzantium
Of what is past, or passing, or to come.

WILLIAM BUTLER YEATS

LOVELIEST OF TREES, THE CHERRY NOW

Loveliest of trees, the cherry now
Is hung with bloom along the
    bough,
And stands about the woodland
    ride
Wearing white for Eastertide.

Now, of my threescore years and
    ten,

Twenty will not come again,
And take from seventy springs a
    score,
It only leaves me fifty more.

And since to look at things in bloom
Fifty springs are little room,
About the woodlands I will go
To see the cherry hung with snow.

A. E. HOUSMAN

WHEN I WAS ONE-AND-TWENTY

When I was one-and-twenty
  I heard a wise man say,
"Give crowns and pounds and
    guineas
  But not your heart away;
Give pearls away and rubies
  But keep your fancy free."
But I was one-and-twenty,
  No use to talk to me.

When I was one-and-twenty
  I heard him say again,
"The heart out of the bosom
  Was never given in vain;
'Tis paid with sighs a plenty.
  And sold for endless rue."
And I am two-and-twenty,
  And oh, 'tis true, 'tis true.

A. E. HOUSMAN

ON A FLY DRINKING OUT OF HIS CUP

Busy, curious, thirsty fly!
Drink with me and drink as I:
Freely welcome to my cup,
Couldst thou sip and sip it up:
Make the most of life you may,
Life is short and wears away.

Both alike are mine and thine
Hastening quick to their decline:
Thine's a summer, mine's no more,
Though repeated to threescore.
Threescore summers, when they're gone,
Will appear as short as one!

WILLIAM OLDYS

A MINUET ON REACHING THE AGE OF FIFTY

Old Age, on tiptoe, lays her jewelled hand
Lightly in mine.—Come, tread a stately measure,
Most gracious partner, nobly posed and bland.
    Ours be no boisterous pleasure,
But smiling conversation, with quick glance
And memories dancing lightlier than we dance,

    Friends who a thousand joys
Divide and double, save one joy supreme
    Which many a pang alloys.
    Let wanton girls and boys
Cry over lovers' woes and broken toys.
Our waking life is sweeter than their dream.

Dame Nature, with unwitting hand,
Has sparsely strewn the black abyss with lights
Minute, remote, and numberless. We stand
    Measuring far depths and heights,
    Arched over by a laughing heaven,
Intangible and never to be scaled.
If we confess our sins, they are forgiven.
    We triumph, if we know we failed.

    Tears that in youth you shed,
Congealed to pearls, now deck your silvery hair;
    Sighs breathed for loves long dead
Frosted the glittering atoms of the air
        Into the veils you wear
Round your soft bosom and most queenly head;
        The shimmer of your gown
Catches all tints of autumn, and the dew
Of gardens where the damask roses blew;

The myriad tapers from these arches hung
        Play on your diamonded crown;
And stars, whose light angelical caressed
        Your virgin days,
Give back in your calm eyes their holier rays.

The deep past living in your breast
Heaves these half-merry sighs;
And the soft accents of your tongue
Breathe unrecorded charities.

Hasten not; the feast will wait.
This is a master-night without a morrow.
No chill and haggard dawn, with after-sorrow,
    Will snuff the spluttering candle out,
Or blanch the revellers homeward straggling late.
    Before the rout
Wearies or wanes, will come a calmer trance.
Lulled by the poppied fragrance of this bower,
    We'll cheat the lapsing hour,
And close our eyes, still smiling, on the dance.

GEORGE SANTAYANA

THE RIVER OF LIFE

The more we live, more brief
    appear
  Our life's succeeding stages:
A day to childhood seems a year,
  And years like passing ages.
The gladsome current of our youth,
  Ere passion yet disorders,
Steals lingering like a river smooth
  Along its grassy borders.

But as the care-worn cheeks grow
    wan,
  And sorrow's shafts fly thicker,
Ye stars, that measure life to man,
  Why seem your courses quicker?

When joys have lost their bloom
    and breath
  And life itself is vapid,

Why, as we reach the Falls of
    Death,
  Feel we its tide more rapid?

It may be strange—yet who would
    change
  Time's course to slower
    speeding,
When one by one our friends have
    gone
  And left our bosoms bleeding?

Heaven gives our years of fading
    strength
  Indemnifying fleetness;
And those of youth, a seeming
    length,
  Proportion'd to their sweetness.

THOMAS CAMPBELL

GRIEVE NOT, LADIES

Oh, grieve not, Ladies, if at night
  Ye wake to feel your beauty
    going.
It was a web of frail delight,
  Inconstant as an April snowing.

In other eyes, in other lands,
  In deep fair pools, new beauty
    lingers,
But like spent water in your hands
  It runs from your reluctant fingers.

Ye shall not keep the singing lark
  That owes to earlier skies its
    duty.
Weep not to hear along the dark
  The sound of your departing
    beauty.

The fine and anguished ear of night
  Is tuned to hear the smallest
    sorrow.
Oh, wait until the morning light!
  It may not seem so gone
    to-morrow!

But honey-pale and rosy-red!
  Brief lights that made a little
    shining!
Beautiful looks about us shed—
  They leave us to the old
    repining.

Think not the watchful dim
    despair
  Has come to you, the first,
    sweet-hearted!
For oh, the gold in Helen's hair!
  And how she cried when that
    departed!

Perhaps that one that took the most,
  The swiftest borrower, wildest
    spender,
May count, as we do not, the cost—
  And grow to us more true and
    tender.

Happy are we if in his eyes
  We see no shadow of forgetting,
Nay—if our star sinks in those skies
  We shall not wholly see its setting.

Then let us laugh as do the brooks
  That such immortal youth is ours,
If memory keeps for them our looks
  As fresh as are the spring-time
    flowers.

Oh, grieve not, ladies, if at night
  Ye wake to feel the cold
    December!
Rather recall the early light
  And in your loved one's arms,
    remember.

ANNA HEMPSTEAD BRANCH

ODE ON INTIMATIONS OF IMMORTALITY

The Child is father of the Man;
And I could wish my days to be
Bound each to each by natural piety.

I

There was a time when meadow, grove, and stream,
The earth, and every common sight,
        To me did seem
        Apparelled in celestial light,
The glory and the freshness of a dream.
It is not now as it hath been of yore;—
        Turn wheresoe'er I may,
            By night or day,
The things which I have seen I now can see no more.

II

        The Rainbow comes and goes,
        And lovely is the Rose,
        The Moon doth with delight
Look round her when the heavens are bare,
        Waters on a starry night
        Are beautiful and fair;
    The sunshine is a glorious birth;
    But yet I know, where'er I go,
That there hath past away a glory from the earth.

III

Now, while the birds thus sing a joyous song,
  And while the young lambs bound
    As to the tabor's sound,
To me alone there came a thought of grief:
A timely utterance gave that thought relief,
    And I again am strong:
The cataracts blow their trumpets from the steep;
No more shall grief of mine the season wrong;
I hear the Echoes through the mountains throng,
The Winds come to me from the fields of sleep,
    And all the earth is gay;
      Land and sea
    Give themselves up to jollity,
    And with the heart of May
    Doth every beast keep holiday;—
    Thou Child of Joy,
Shout round me, let me hear thy shouts, thou happy
    Shepherd-boy!

IV

Ye blessèd Creatures, I have heard the call
  Ye to each other make; I see
The heavens laugh with you in your jubilee;
  My heart is at your festival,
  My head hath its coronal,
The fullness of your bliss, I feel—I feel it all.
  Oh evil day! if I were sullen
  While Earth herself is adorning,
    This sweet May-morning,
  And the children are culling
    On every side,
  In a thousand valleys far and wide,
  Fresh flowers; while the sun shines warm,
And the Babe leaps up on his mother's arm:—
  I hear, I hear, with joy I hear!
  —But there's a Tree, of many, one,
A single Field which I have looked upon,
Both of them speak of something that is gone:
  The Pansy at my feet

Doth the same tale repeat:
Whither is fled the visionary gleam?
Where is it now, the glory and the dream?

V

Our birth is but a sleep and a forgetting:
The Soul that rises with us, our life's Star,
        Hath had elsewhere its setting,
            And cometh from afar:
            Not in entire forgetfulness,
            And not in utter nakedness,
But trailing clouds of glory do we come
        From God, who is our home:
Heaven lies about us in our infancy!
Shades of the prison-house begin to close
        Upon the growing Boy,
But he beholds the light, and whence it flows,
        He sees it in his joy;
The Youth, who daily farther from the east
        Must travel, still is Nature's priest,
        And by the vision splendid
        Is on his way attended;
At length the Man perceives it die away,
And fade into the light of common day.

VI

Earth fills her lap with pleasures of her own;
Yearnings she hath in her own natural kind,
And, even with something of a mother's mind,
        And no unworthy aim,
        The homely nurse doth all she can
To make her Foster-child, her inmate Man,
        Forget the glories he hath known,
And that imperial palace whence he came.

VII

Behold the Child among his new-born blisses,
A six years' darling of a pigmy size!
See, where 'mid work of his own hand he lies,
Fretted by sallies of his mother's kisses,
With light upon him from his father's eyes!

See, at his feet, some little plan or chart,
Some fragment from his dream of human life,
Shaped by himself with newly-learnèd art;
  A wedding or a festival,
  A mourning or a funeral;
   And this hath now his heart,
   And unto this he frames his song:
    Then will he fit his tongue
To dialogues of business, love, or strife;
   But it will not be long
   Ere this be thrown aside,
   And with new joy and pride
The little Actor cons another part;
Filling from time to time his 'humorous stage'
With all the Persons, down to palsied Age,
That Life brings with her in her equipage;
   As if his whole vocation
   Were endless imitation.

VIII

Thou, whose exterior semblance doth belie
   Thy soul's immensity;
Thou best philosopher, who yet dost keep
Thy heritage, thou eye among the blind,
That, deaf and silent, read'st the Eternal Deep,
Haunted forever by the Eternal Mind,—
   Mighty prophet! seer blest!
   On whom those truths do rest,
Which we are toiling all our lives to find,
In darkness lost, the darkness of the grave;
Thou, over whom thy Immortality
Broods like the Day, a master o'er a slave,
A Presence which is not to be put by;
Thou little Child, yet glorious in the might
Of heaven-born freedom on thy being's height,
Why with such earnest pains dost thou provoke
The years to bring the inevitable yoke,
Thus blindly with thy blessedness at strife?
Full soon thy Soul shall have her earthly freight,
And custom lie upon thee with a weight,
Heavy as frost, and deep almost as life!

IX

O joy! that in our embers
Is something that doth live,
That nature yet remembers
What was so fugitive!
The thought of our past years in me doth breed
Perpetual benediction; not indeed
For that which is most worthy to be blest;
Delight and liberty, the simple creed
Of childhood, whether busy or at rest,
With new-fledged hope still fluttering in his breast:—
Not for these I raise
The song of thanks and praise;
But for those obstinate questionings
Of sense and outward things,
Fallings from us, vanishings;
Blank misgivings of a Creature
Moving about in worlds not realized,
High instincts before which our mortal nature
Did tremble like a guilty thing surprised:
But for those first affections,
Those shadowy recollections,
Which, be they what they may,
Are yet the fountain-light of all our day,
Are yet a master-light of all our seeing;
Uphold us, cherish, and have power to make
Our noisy years seem moments in the being
Of the Eternal Silence: truths that wake,
To perish never:
Which neither listlessness, nor mad endeavor,
Nor man nor boy,
Nor all that is at enmity with joy,
Can utterly abolish or destroy!
Hence in a season of calm weather
Though inland far we be,
Our souls have sight of that immortal sea
Which brought us hither,
Can in a moment travel thither,
And see the children sport upon the shore,
And hear the mighty waters rolling evermore.

X

Then sing, ye Birds, sing, sing a joyous song!
    And let the young Lambs bound
    As to the tabor's sound!
We in thought will join your throng,
    Ye that pipe and ye that play,
    Ye that through your hearts to-day
    Feel the gladness of the May!
What though the radiance which was once so bright
Be now forever taken from my sight,
    Though nothing can bring back the hour
Of splendor in the grass, of glory in the flower;
    We will grieve not, rather find
    Strength in what remains behind;
    In the primal sympathy
    Which having been must ever be;
    In the soothing thoughts that spring
    Out of human suffering;
    In the faith that looks through death,
In years that bring the philosophic mind.

XI

And O, ye Fountains, Meadows, Hills, and Groves,
Forebode not any severing of our loves!
Yet in my heart of hearts I feel your might;
I only have relinquished one delight
To live beneath your more habitual sway.
I love the Brooks which down their channels fret,
Even more than when I tripped lightly as they;
The innocent brightness of a new-born Day
    Is lovely yet;
The Clouds that gather round the setting sun
Do take a sober coloring from an eye
That hath kept watch o'er man's mortality;
Another race hath been, and other palms are won.
Thanks to the human heart by which we live,
Thanks to its tenderness, its joys, and fears,
To me the meanest flower that blows can give
Thoughts that do often lie too deep for tears.

             WILLIAM WORDSWORTH

MY LOST YOUTH

Often I think of the beautiful town
  That is seated by the sea;
Often in thought go up and down
The pleasant streets of that dear old town,
  And my youth comes back to me.
    And a verse of a Lapland song
    Is haunting my memory still:
    "A boy's will is the wind's will,
And the thoughts of youth are long, long thoughts."

I can see the shadowy lines of its trees,
  And catch, in sudden gleams,
The sheen of the far-surrounding seas,
And islands that were the Hesperides
  Of all my boyish dreams.
    And the burden of that old song,
    It murmurs and whispers still:
    "A boy's will is the wind's will,
And the thoughts of youth are long, long thoughts."

I remember the black wharves and the slips,
  And the sea-tides tossing free;
And Spanish sailors with bearded lips,
And the beauty and mystery of the ships,
  And the magic of the sea.
    And the voice of that wayward song
    Is singing and saying still:
    "A boy's will is the wind's will,
And the thoughts of youth are long, long thoughts."

I remember the bulwarks by the shore,
  And the fort upon the hill;
The sunrise gun, with its hollow roar,
The drum-beat repeated o'er and o'er,
  And the bugle wild and shrill.

And the music of that old song
Throbs in my memory still:
"A boy's will is the wind's will,
And the thoughts of youth are long, long thoughts."

I remember the sea-fight far away,
  How it thundered o'er the tide!
And the dead captains, as they lay
In their graves, o'crlooking the tranquil bay
  Where they in battle died.
    And the sound of that mournful song
    Goes through me with a thrill:
    "A boy's will is the wind's will,
And the thoughts of youth are long, long thoughts."

I can see the breezy dome of groves,
  The shadows of Deering's Woods;
And the friendships old and the early loves
Come back with a Sabbath sound, as of doves
  In quiet neighborhoods.
    And the verse of that sweet old song,
    It flutters and murmurs still:
    "A boy's will is the wind's will,
And the thoughts of youth are long, long thoughts."

I remember the gleams and glooms that dart
  Across the school-boy's brain;
The song and the silence in the heart,
    That in part are prophecies, and in part
    Are longings wild and vain.
    And the voice of that fitful song
    Sings on, and is never still:
    "A boy's will is the wind's will,
And the thoughts of youth are long, long thoughts."

There are things of which I may not speak;
  There are dreams that cannot die;
There are thoughts that make the strong heart weak,
And bring a pallor into the cheek,

And a mist before the eye.
  And the words of that fatal song
  Come over me like a chill:
  "A boy's will is the wind's will,
And the thoughts of youth are long, long thoughts."

Strange to me now are the forms I meet
  When I visit the dear old town;
But the native air is pure and sweet,
And the trees that o'ershadow each well-known street,
  As they balance up and down,
    Are singing the beautiful song,
    Are sighing and whispering still:
    "A boy's will is the wind's will,
And the thoughts of youth are long, long thoughts."

And Deering's Woods are fresh and fair,
  And with joy that is almost pain
My heart goes back to wander there,
And among the dreams of the days that were,
  I find my lost youth again.
    And the strange and beautiful song,
    The groves are repeating it still:
    "A boy's will is the wind's will,
And the thoughts of youth are long, long thoughts."

        HENRY WADSWORTH LONGFELLOW

REMEMBRANCE

When to the sessions of sweet silent thought
I summon up remembrance of things past,
I sigh the lack of many a thing I sought,
And with old woes new wail my dear time's waste;
Then can I drown an eye, unused to flow,
For precious friends hid in death's dateless night,
And weep afresh love's long-since-cancell'd woe,
And moan the expense of many a vanish'd sight.

Then can I grieve at grievances foregone,
And heavily from woe to woe tell o'er
The sad account of fore-bemoanéd moan,
Which I new pay as if not paid before:
—But if the while I think on thee, dear friend,
All losses are restored, and sorrows end.

WILLIAM SHAKESPEARE

THE ISLE OF THE LONG AGO

Oh, a wonderful stream is the River Time,
  As it flows through the realm of Tears,
With a faultless rhythm and a musical rhyme,
And a broader sweep and a surge sublime
  As it blends with the ocean of Years.

How the winters are drifting like flakes of snow!
  And the summers like buds between;
And the year in the sheaf—so they come and they go
On the River's breast with its ebb and flow,
  As they glide in the shadow and sheen.

There's a magical Isle up the River Time
  Where the softest of airs are playing;
There's a cloudless sky and a tropical clime,
And a voice as sweet as a vesper chime,
  And the Junes with the roses are staying.

And the name of this Isle is the Long Ago,
   And we bury our treasures there;
There are brows of beauty and bosoms of snow—
They are heaps of dust, but we loved them so!
   There are trinkets and tresses of hair.

There are fragments of song that nobody sings,
   And a part of an infant's prayer,
There's a harp unswept and a lute without strings,
There are broken vows and pieces of rings,
   And the garments that *she* used to wear.

There are hands that are waved when the fairy shore
   By the mirage is lifted in air;
And we sometimes hear through the turbulent roar
Sweet voices we heard in the days gone before,
   When the wind down the River is fair.

Oh, remembered for aye be the blessed Isle
   All the day of our life till night,
And when evening comes with its beautiful smile,
And our eyes are closing in slumber awhile,
   May that "Greenwood" of soul be in sight.

BENJAMIN FRANKLIN TAYLOR

GROWING OLD

What is it to grow old?
Is it to lose the glory of the form,
The lustre of the eye?
Is it for beauty to forego her
   wealth?
—Yes, but not this alone.

Is it to feel our strength—
Not our bloom only, but our
   strength—decay?
Is it to feel each limb
Grow stiffer, every function less
   exact,
Each nerve more loosely strung?

Yes, this, and more; but not—
Ah, 'tis not what in youth we
   dreamed 'twould be!
'Tis not to have our life
Mellowed and softened as with
   sunset glow,
A golden day's decline.

'Tis not to see the world
As from a height, with rapt
   prophetic eyes,
And heart profoundly stirred;
And weep, and feel the fulness of
   the past,
The years that are no more.

It is to spend long days
And not once feel that we were
  ever young;
It is to add, immured
In the hot prison of the present,
  month
To month with weary pain.

It is to suffer this,
And feel but half, and feebly,
  what we feel.

Deep in our hidden heart
Festers the dull remembrance of a
  change,
But no emotion—none.

It is!—last stage of all—
When we are frozen up within,
  and quite
The phantom of ourselves,
To hear the world applaud the
  hollow ghost
Which blessed the living man.

MATTHEW ARNOLD

THE OLD FAMILIAR FACES

I have had playmates, I have had
  companions,
In my days of childhood, in my
  joyful schooldays,—
All, all are gone, the old familiar
  faces.

I have been laughing, I have been
  carousing,
Drinking late, sitting late, with
  my bosom cronies,—
All, all are gone, the old familiar
  faces.

I loved a Love once, fairest among
  women:
Closed are her doors on me, I
  must not see her,—
All, all are gone, the old familiar
  faces.

I have a friend, a kinder friend
  has no man:
Like an ingrate, I left my friend
  abruptly;

Left him, to muse on the old
  familiar faces.

Ghost-like, I paced round the
  haunts of my childhood.
Earth seemed a desert I was bound
  to traverse,
Seeking to find the old familiar
  faces.

Friend of my bosom, thou more
  than a brother,
Why wert not thou born in my
  father's dwelling?
So might we talk of the old
  familiar faces—

How some they have died, and
  some they have left me,
And some are taken from me; all
  are departed,—
All, all are gone, the old familiar
  faces.

CHARLES LAMB

THE LEADEN ECHO AND THE GOLDEN ECHO
(Maidens' Song from St. Winefred's Well)

THE LEADEN ECHO

How to kéep—is there any any, is there none such, nowhere known some,
  bow or brooch or braid or brace, láce, latch or catch or key to keep
Back beauty, keep it, beauty, beauty, beauty, . . . from vanishing away?
O is there no frowning of these wrinkles, rankèd wrinkles deep,
Dówn? no waving off of these most mournful messengers, still messengers,
  sad and stealing messengers of grey?
No there's none, there's none, O no there's none,
Nor can you long be, what you now are, called fair,
Do what you may do, what, do what you may,
And wisdom is early to despair:
Be beginning; since, no, nothing can be done to keep at bay
Age and age's evils, hoar hair,
Ruck and wrinkle, drooping, dying, death's worst, winding sheets, tombs
  and worms and tumbling to decay;
So be beginning, be beginning to despair.
O there's none; no no no there's none:
Be beginning to despair, to despair,
Despair, despair, despair, despair.

THE GOLDEN ECHO

     Spare!
There ís one, yes I have one (Hush there!);
Only not within seeing of the sun,
Not within the singeing of the strong sun,
Tall sun's tingeing, or treacherous the tainting of the earth's air,
Somewhere elsewhere there is ah well where! one,
Óne. Yes I can tell such a kcy, I do know such a place,
Where whatever's prized and passes of us, everything that's fresh and fast
  flying of us, seems to us sweet of us and swiftly away with, done away
  with, undone,
Undone, done with, soon done with, and yet dearly and dangerously
  sweet
Of us, the wimpled-water-dimpled, not-by-morning-matchèd face,

The flower of beauty, fleece of beauty, too too apt to, ah! to fleet,
Never fleets móre, fastened with the tenderest truth
To its own best being and its loveliness of youth: it is an everlastingness
    of, O it is an all youth!
Come then, your ways and airs and looks, locks, maiden gear, gallantry
    and gaiety and grace,
Winning ways, airs innocent, maiden manners, sweet looks, loose locks,
    long locks, lovelocks, gaygear, going gallant, girlgrace—
Resign them, sign them, seal them, send them, motion them with breath,
And with sighs soaring, soaring síghs deliver
Them; beauty-in-the-ghost, deliver it, early now, long before death
Give beauty back, beauty, beauty, beauty, back to God, beauty's self and
    beauty's giver.
See; not a hair is, not an eyelash, not the least lash lost; every hair
Is, hair of the head, numbered.
Nay, what we had lighthanded left in surly the mere mould
Will have waked and have waxed and have walked with the wind what-
    while we slept,
This side, that side hurling a heavyheaded hundredfold
Whatwhile we, while we slumbered.
O then, weary then why should we tread? O why are we so haggard at the
    heart, so care-coiled, care-killed, so fagged, so fashed, so cogged, so
    cumbered,
When the thing we freely fórfeit is kept with fonder a care,
Fonder a care kept than we could have kept it, kept
Far with fonder a care (and we, we should have lost it) finer, fonder
A care kept.—Where kept? Do but tell us where kept, where.—
Yonder.—What high as that! We follow, now we follow.—Yonder, yes
    yonder, yonder,
Yonder.

GERARD MANLEY HOPKINS

ROCK ME TO SLEEP

Backward, turn backward, O
  Time, in your flight,
Make me a child again just for
  to-night!
Mother, come back from the
  echoless shore,
Take me again to your heart as of
  yore;
Kiss from my forehead the furrows
  of care,
Smooth the few silver threads out
  of my hair;
Over my slumbers your loving
  watch keep;—
Rock me to sleep, Mother—rock
  me to sleep!

Backward, flow backward, O tide
  of the years!
I am so weary of toil and of
  tears—
Toil without recompense, tears
  all in vain—
Take them, and give me my
  childhood again!
I have grown weary of dust and
  decay—
Weary of flinging my soul-wealth
  away;
Weary of sowing for others to
  reap;—
Rock me to sleep, Mother—rock
  me to sleep!

Tired of the hollow, the base, the
  untrue,
Mother, O Mother, my heart calls
  for you!

Many a summer the grass has
  grown green,
Blossomed and faded, our faces
  between:
Yet, with strong yearning and
  passionate pain,
Long I to-night for your presence
  again.
Come from the silence so long
  and so deep;—
Rock me to sleep, Mother—rock
  me to sleep!

Over my heart, in the days that
  are flown,
No love like mother-love ever has
  shone;
No other worship abides and
  endures—
Faithful, unselfish, and patient
  like yours:
None like a mother can charm
  away pain
From the sick soul and the world-
  weary brain.
Slumber's soft calms o'er my heavy
  lids creep;—
Rock me to sleep, Mother—rock
  me to sleep!

Come, let your brown hair, just
  lighted with gold,
Fall on your shoulders again as of
  old;
Let it drop over my forehead
  to-night,
Shading my faint eyes away from
  the light;

For with its sunny-edged shadows
  once more
Haply will throng the sweet
  visions of yore;
Lovingly, softly, its bright billows
  sweep;—
Rock me to sleep, Mother—rock
  me to sleep!

Mother, dear Mother, the years
  have been long
Since I last listened your lullaby
  song;

Sing, then, and unto my soul it
  shall seem
Womanhood's years have been
  only a dream.
Clasped to your heart in a loving
  embrace,
With your light lashes just
  sweeping my face,
Never hereafter to wake or to
  weep;—
Rock me to sleep, Mother—rock
  me to sleep!

ELIZABETH AKERS ALLEN

WHEN YOU ARE OLD

When you are old and gray and
    full of sleep
  And nodding by the fire, take
    down this book,
  And slowly read, and dream of
    the soft look
Your eyes had once, and of their
  shadows deep;

How many loved your moments of
    glad grace,
  And loved your beauty with
    love false or true;

But one man loved the pilgrim
    soul in you,
And loved the sorrows of your
  changing face.

And bending down beside the
    glowing bars,
  Murmur, a little sadly, how love
    fled
  And paced upon the mountains
    overhead,
And hid his face amid a crowd
  of stars.

WILLIAM BUTLER YEATS

THE OLD TIMES WERE THE BEST

Friends, my heart is half aweary
  Of its happiness to-night:
Though your songs are gay and
    cheery,
  And your spirits feather-light,
There's a ghostly music haunting
  Still the heart of every guest

And a voiceless chorus chanting
  That the Old Times were the best.
                CHORUS
All about is bright and pleasant
  With the sound of song and jest,
Yet a feeling's ever present
  That the Old Times were the best.

JAMES WHITCOMB RILEY

THE BALLAD OF DEAD LADIES OF FRANÇOIS VILLON

Tell me now in what hidden way is
    Lady Flora the lovely Roman?
Where's Hipparchia, and where is Thais,
    Neither of them the fairer woman?
    Where is Echo, beheld of no man,
Only heard on river and mere,—
    She whose beauty was more than human? . . .
But where are the snows of yester-year?

Where's Héloise, the learned nun,
    For whose sake Abeillard, I ween,
Lost manhood and put priesthood on?
    (From Love he won such dule and teen!)
    And where, I pray you, is the Queen
Who willed that Buridan should steer
    Sewed in a sack's mouth down the Seine? . . .
But where are the snows of yester-year?

White Queen Blanche, like a queen of lilies,
    With a voice like any mermaiden,—
Bertha Broadfoot, Beatrice, Alice,
    And Ermengarde the lady of Maine,—
    And that good Joan whom Englishmen
At Rouen doomed and burned her there,—
    Mother of God, where are they then? . . .
But where are the snows of yester-year?

Nay, never ask this week, fair lord,
    Where they are gone, nor yet this year,
Save with this much for an overword,—
    But where are the snows of yester-year?

                    DANTE GABRIEL ROSSETTI

O MISTRESS MINE

O Mistress mine, where are you
  roaming?
O, stay and hear; your true love's
  coming,
   That can sing both high and
   low:
Trip no further, pretty sweeting;
Journeys end in lovers meeting,
   Every wise man's son doth know.

What is love? 'Tis not hereafter;
Present mirth hath present
  laughter;
   What's to come is still unsure:
In delay there lies no plenty;
Then, come kiss me, sweet and
  twenty,
   Youth's a stuff will not endure.

WILLIAM SHAKESPEARE

GOOD-BYE, MY FANCY!

Good-bye, my Fancy!
Farewell, dear mate, dear love!
I am going away, I know not where,
Or to what fortune, or whether I may ever see you again,

So Good-bye, my Fancy.
Now for my last—let me look back a moment;
The slower fainter ticking of the clock is in me,
Exit, nightfall, and soon the heart-thud stopping.
Long have we lived, joy'd, caress'd together;
Delightful!—now separation—Good-bye, my Fancy.

Yet let me not be too hasty:
Long indeed have we lived, slept, filter'd, become really blended into
  one;
Then if we die we die together (yes, we'll remain one),
If we go anywhere we'll go together to meet what happens,
May-be we'll be better off and blither, and learn something,
May-be it is yourself now really ushering me to the true songs (who
  knows?),
May-be it is you the mortal knob really undoing, turning—so now
  finally,
Good-bye—and hail! my Fancy.

WALT WHITMAN

RABBI BEN EZRA

Grow old along with me!
The best is yet to be,
The last of life, for which the first
 was made:
Our times are in his hand
Who saith "A whole I planned,
Youth shows but half; trust God:
 see all, nor be afraid!"

Not that, amassing flowers,
Youth sighed, "Which rose make
 ours,
Which lily leave and then as best
 recall?"
Not that, admiring stars,
It yearned, "Nor Jove, nor Mars;
Mine be some figured flame which
 blends, transcends them all!"

Not for such hopes and fears
Annulling youth's brief years,
Do I remonstrate: folly wide the
 mark!
Rather I prize the doubt
Low kinds exist without,
Finished and finite clods,
 untroubled by a spark.

Poor vaunt of life indeed,
Were man but formed to feed
On joy, to solely seek and find and
 feast:
Such feasting ended, then
As sure an end to men;
Irks care the crop-full bird? Frets
 doubt the maw-crammed beast?

Rejoice we are allied
To that which doth provide
And not partake, effect and not
 receive!
A spark disturbs our clod;
Nearer we hold of God
Who gives, than of his tribes that
 take, I must believe.

Then, welcome each rebuff
That turns earth's smoothness
 rough,
Each sting that bids nor sit nor
 stand but go!
Be our joys three-parts pain!
Strive, and hold cheap the strain;
Learn, nor account the pang; dare,
 never grudge the throe!

For thence,—a paradox
Which comforts while it
    mocks,—
Shall life succeed in that it seems
    to fail:
What I aspired to be,
And was not, comforts me:
A brute I might have been, but
    would not sink i' the scale.

What is he but a brute
Whose flesh has soul to suit,
Whose spirit works lest arms and
    legs want play?
To man, propose this test—
Thy body at its best,
How far can that project thy soul
    on its lone way?

Yet gifts should prove their use:
I own the Past profuse
Of power each side, perfection
    every turn:
Eyes, ears took in their dole,
Brain treasured up the whole:
Should not the heart beat once
    "How good to live and learn"?

Not once beat "Praise be thine!
I see the whole design,
I, who saw power, see now Love
    perfect too:
Perfect I call thy plan:
Thanks that I was a man!
Maker, remake, complete,—I trust
    what thou shalt do!"

For pleasant is this flesh;
Our soul, in its rose-mesh
Pulled ever to the earth, still
    yearns for rest:

Would we some prize might
    hold
To match those manifold
Possessions of the brute,—gain
    most, as we did best!

Let us not always say,
    "Spite of this flesh to-day
I strove, made head, gained
    ground upon the whole!"
As the bird wings and sings,
Let us cry, "All good things
Are ours, nor soul helps flesh
    more, now, than flesh helps
    soul!"

Therefore I summon age
To grant youth's heritage,
Life's struggle having so far
    reached its term:
Thence shall I pass, approved
A man, for aye removed
From the developed brute; a God
    though in the germ.

And I shall thereupon
Take rest, ere I be gone
Once more on my adventure brave
    and new:
Fearless and unperplexed,
When I wage battle next,
What weapons to select, what
    armor to indue.

Youth ended, I shall try
My gain or loss thereby;
Leave the fire ashes, what survives
    is gold:
And I shall weigh the same,
Give life its praise or blame:
Young, all lay in dispute; I shall
    know, being old,

For note, when evening shuts,
A certain moment cuts
The deed off, calls the glory from
    the gray:
A whisper from the west
Shoots—"Add this to the rest,
Take it and try its worth: here
    dies another day."

So, still within this life,
Though lifted o'er its strife,
Let me discern, compare,
    pronounce at last,
"This rage was right i' the main,
That acquiescence vain:
The Future I may face now I
    have proved the Past."

For more is not reserved
To man, with soul just nerved
To act to-morrow what he learns
    to-day:
Here, work enough to watch
The Master work, and catch
Hints of the proper craft, tricks of
    the tool's true play.

As it was better, youth
Should strive, through acts
    uncouth,
Toward making, than repose on
    aught found made:
So, better, age, exempt
From strife, should know, than
    tempt
Further. Thou waitedest age: wait
    death nor be afraid!

Enough now, if the Right
And Good and Infinite
Be named here, as thou callest thy
    hand thine own,

With knowledge absolute,
Subject to no dispute
From fools that crowded youth,
    nor let thee feel alone.

Be there, for once and all,
Severed great minds from small,
Announced to each his station in
    the Past!
Was I, the world arraigned,
Were they, my soul disdained,
Right? Let age speak the truth
    and give us peace at last!

Now, who shall arbitrate?
Ten men love what I hate,
Shun what I follow, slight what I
    receive;
Ten, who in ears and eyes
Match me: we all surmise,
They this thing, and I that: whom
    shall my soul believe?

Not on the vulgar mass
Called "work," must sentence
    pass,
Things done, that took the eye
    and had the price;
O'er which, from level stand,
The low world laid its hand,
Found straightway to its mind,
    could value in a trice:

But all, the world's coarse
    thumb
And finger failed to plumb,
So passed in making up the main
    account;
All instincts immature,
All purposes unsure,
That weighed not as his work, yet
    swelled the man's amount:

Thoughts hardly to be packed
Into a narrow act,
Fancies that broke through
    language and escaped;
All I could never be,
All, men ignored in me,
This, I was worth to God, whose
    wheel the pitcher shaped.

Ay, note that Potter's wheel,
That metaphor! and feel
Why time spins fast, why passive
    lies our clay,—
Thou, to whom fools propound,
When the wine makes its
    round,
"Since life fleets, all is change; the
    Past gone, seize to-day!"

Fool! All that is, at all,
Lasts ever, past recall;
Earth changes, but thy soul and
    God stand sure:
What entered into thee,
That was, is, and shall be:
Time's wheel runs back or stops:
    Potter and clay endure.

He fixed thee 'mid this dance
Of plastic circumstance,
This Present, thou, forsooth,
    would fain arrest:
Machinery just meant
To give thy soul its bent,
Try thee and turn thee forth,
    sufficiently impressed.

What though the earlier grooves
Which ran the laughing loves
Around thy base, no longer pause
    and press?
What though, about thy rim,
Skull-things in order grim
Grow out, in graver mood, obey
    the sterner stress?

Look not thou down but up!
To uses of a cup,
The festal board, lamp's flash and
    trumpet's peal,
The new wine's foaming flow,
The Master's lips a-glow!
Thou, heaven's consummate cup,
    what needest thou with
    earth's wheel?

But I need, now as then,
Thee, God, who mouldest men;
And since, not even while the
    whirl was worst,
Did I,—to the wheel of life
With shapes and colors rife,
Bound dizzily,—mistake my end,
    to slake thy thirst:

So, take and use thy work:
Amend what flaws may lurk,
What strain o' the stuff, what
    warpings past the aim!
My times be in thy hand!
Perfect the cup as planned!
Let age approve of youth, and
    death complete the same!

ROBERT BROWNING

THE HUMAN SEASONS

Four seasons fill the measure of the year;
There are four seasons in the mind of man:
He has his lusty Spring, when fancy clear
Takes in all beauty with an easy span:
He has his Summer, when luxuriously
Spring's honey'd cud of youthful thought he loves
To ruminate, and by such dreaming nigh
His nearest unto heaven: quiet coves
His soul has in its Autumn, when his wings
He furleth close: contented so to look
On mists in idleness—to let fair things
Pass by unheeded as a threshold brook:
He has his Winter too of pale misfeature,
Or else he would forgo his mortal nature.

JOHN KEATS

THE ROAD NOT TAKEN

Two roads diverged in a yellow
  wood,
And sorry I could not travel both
And be one traveler, long I stood
And looked down one as far as I
  could
To where it bent in the
  undergrowth;

Then took the other, as just as
  fair,
And having perhaps the better
  claim,
Because it was grassy and wanted
  wear;
Though as for that the passing
  there
Had worn them really about the
  same,

And both that morning equally
  lay
In leaves no step had trodden
  black.
Oh, I kept the first for another
  day!
Yet knowing how way leads on to
  way,
I doubted if I should ever come
  back.

I shall be telling this with a sigh
Somewhere ages and ages hence:
Two roads diverged in a wood,
  and I—
I took the one less traveled by,
And that has made all the
  difference.

ROBERT FROST

BOOK VI

SOUND THE TRUMPETS!

THE MINSTREL BOY

The Minstrel Boy to the war is gone
  In the ranks of death you'll find him,
His father's sword he has girded on,
  And his wild harp slung behind him.
"Land of song!" said the warrior bard,
  "Tho' all the world betrays thee,
One sword, at least, thy rights shall guard,
  One faithful harp shall praise thee."
The minstrel fell! but the foeman's chain
  Could not bring that proud soul under;
The harp he loved ne'er spoke again,
  For he tore its chords asunder;
And said, "No chain shall sully thee,
  Thou soul of love and bravery.
Thy songs were made for the pure and free,
  They shall never sound in slavery."

THOMAS MOORE

THE MAN HE KILLED

"Had he and I but met
  By some old ancient inn,
We should have sat us down to wet
  Right many a nipperkin!

"But ranged as infantry,
  And staring face to face,
I shot at him as he at me,
  And killed him in his place.

"I shot him dead because—
  Because he was my foe,

Just so: my foe of course he was;
  That's clear enough; although

"He thought he'd 'list, perhaps,
  Off-hand like—just as I;
Was out of work, had sold his traps—
  No other reason why.

"Yes; quaint and curious war is!
  You shoot a fellow down
You'd treat if met where any bar is,
  Or help to half-a-crown."

THOMAS HARDY

THE CHARGE OF THE LIGHT BRIGADE

To commemorate the cavalry charge at Balaclava in the Crimean War

Half a league, half a league,
Half a league onward,
All in the valley of Death
  Rode the six hundred.
  "Forward, the Light Brigade!
Charge for the guns!" he said.
Into the valley of Death
  Rode the six hundred.

"Forward, the Light Brigade!"
Was there a man dismayed?
Not though the soldier knew
  Some one had blundered.
Theirs not to make reply,
Theirs not to reason why,
Theirs but to do and die.
Into the valley of Death
  Rode the six hundred.

Cannon to right of them,
Cannon to left of them,
Cannon in front of them
  Volleyed and thundered;
Stormed at with shot and shell,
Boldly they rode and well,
Into the jaws of Death,
Into the mouth of Hell
  Rode the six hundred.

Flashed all their sabres bare,
Flashed as they turned in air

Sabring the gunners there,
Charging an army, while
  All the world wondered:
Plunged in the battery-smoke
Right through the line they broke;
Cossack and Russian
Reeled from the sabre-stroke
  Shattered and sundered.
Then they rode back, but not,
  Not the six hundred.

Cannon to right of them,
Cannon to left of them,
Cannon behind them
  Volleyed and thundered;
Stormed at with shot and shell,
While horse and hero fell,
They that had fought so well
Came through the jaws of Death,
Back from the mouth of Hell,
All that was left of them,
  Left of six hundred.

When can their glory fade?
O the wild charge they made!
  All the world wondered.
Honor the charge they made!
Honor the Light Brigade,
  Noble six hundred!

ALFRED LORD TENNYSON

CASABIANCA

In the battle of the Nile, thirteen-year-old Casabianca, son of the Admiral of the Orient, remained at his post after the ship had taken fire and the guns had been abandoned. He perished with the ship.

The boy stood on the burning deck,
Whence all but he had fled;
The flame that lit the battle's
    wreck,
Shone round him o'er the dead.

Yet beautiful and bright he stood,
As born to rule the storm;
A creature of heroic blood,
A proud though childlike form.

The flames rolled on; he would
    not go
Without his father's word;
That father, faint in death below,
His voice no longer heard.

He called aloud, "Say, Father, say,
If yet my task is done!"
He knew not that the chieftain lay
Unconscious of his son.

"Speak, Father!" once again he
    cried,
"If I may yet be gone!"
—And but the booming shots
    replied,
And fast the flames rolled on.

Upon his brow he felt their breath,
And in his waving hair;

And looked from that lone post of
    death
In still yet brave despair;

And shouted but once more aloud,
"My Father! must I stay?"
While o'er him fast, through sail
    and shroud,
The wreathing fires made way.

They wrapt the ship in splendor
    wild,
They caught the flag on high,
And streamed above the gallant
    child,
Like banners in the sky.

There came a burst of thunder
    sound;
The boy—Oh! where was *he?*
—Ask of the winds, that far
    around
With fragments strewed the sea;—

With shroud, and mast, and
    pennon fair,
That well had borne their part,—
But the noblest thing that
    perished there
Was that young, faithful heart.

FELICIA DOROTHEA HEMANS

SHERIDAN'S RIDE

Up from the South at break of day,
Bringing to Winchester fresh dismay,
The affrighted air with a shudder bore,
Like a herald in haste, to the chieftain's door,
The terrible grumble, and rumble, and roar,
Telling the battle was on once more,
And Sheridan twenty miles away.

And wider still those billows of war
Thundered along the horizon's bar;
And louder yet into Winchester rolled
The roar of that red sea uncontrolled,
Making the blood of the listener cold,
As he thought of the stake in that fiery fray,
With Sheridan twenty miles away.

But there is a road from Winchester town,
A good, broad highway leading down;
And there, through the flush of the morning light,
A steed as black as the steeds of night
Was seen to pass, as with eagle flight;
As if he knew the terrible need,
He stretched away with the utmost speed;
Hills rose and fell; but his heart was gay,
With Sheridan fifteen miles away.

Still sprung from those swift hoofs, thundering South,
The dust, like smoke from the cannon's mouth;
Or the trail of a comet, sweeping faster and faster,
Foreboding to traitors the doom of disaster,
The heart of the steed and the heart of the master
Were beating like prisoners assaulting their walls,
Impatient to be where the battlefield calls;
Every nerve of the charger was strained to full play,
With Sheridan only ten miles away.

Under his spurning feet the road
Like an arrowy Alpine river flowed,
And the landscape sped away behind
Like an ocean flying before the wind,
And the steed, like a barque fed with furnace ire,
Swept on, with his wild eye full of fire.
But lo! he is nearing his heart's desire;
He is snuffing the smoke of the roaring fray,
With Sheridan only five miles away.

The first that the general saw were the groups
Of stragglers, and then the retreating troops;
What was done? What to do? A glance told him both,
Then striking his spurs, with a terrible oath,
He dashed down the line 'mid a storm of huzzas,
And the wave of retreat checked its course there, because
The sight of the master compelled it to pause.
With foam and with dust the black charger was gray;
By the flash of his eye and the red nostril's play,
He seemed to the whole great army to say,
"I have brought you Sheridan all the way
From Winchester down to save the day!"

Hurrah! Hurrah for Sheridan!
Hurrah! Hurrah for horse and man!
And when their statues are placed on high,
Under the dome of the Union sky,
The American soldier's Temple of Fame;
There with the glorious general's name,
Be it said, in letters both bold and bright,
"Here is the steed that saved the day,
By carrying Sheridan into the fight,
From Winchester, twenty miles away!"

Thomas Buchanan Read

ALL QUIET ALONG THE POTOMAC

"All quiet along the Potomac," they say,
   "Except, now and then, a stray picket
Is shot, as he walks on his beat to and fro,
   By a rifleman hid in the thicket."
'Tis nothing—a private or two now and then
   Will not count in the news of the battle;
Not an officer lost—only one of the men,
   Moaning out, all alone, the death-rattle.

All quiet along the Potomac to-night,
   Where the soldiers lie peacefully dreaming;
Their tents, in the rays of the clear autumn moon
   Or the light of the watch-fire, are gleaming.
A tremulous sigh of the gentle night-wind
   Through the forest-leaves softly is creeping,
While stars up above, with their glittering eyes,
   Keep guard, for the army is sleeping.

There's only the sound of the lone sentry's tread
   As he tramps from the rock to the fountain,
And thinks of the two in the low trundle-bed
   Far away in the cot on the mountain.
His musket falls slack; his face, dark and grim,
   Grows gentle with memories tender
As he mutters a prayer for the children asleep—
   For their mother; may Heaven defend her!

The moon seems to shine just as brightly as then,
   That night when the love yet unspoken
Leaped up to his lips—when low-murmured vows
   Were pledged to be ever unbroken.
Then, drawing his sleeve roughly over his eyes,
   He dashes off tears that are welling,
And gathers his gun closer up to its place,
   As if to keep down the heart-swelling.

He passes the fountain, the blasted pine tree,
  The footstep is lagging and weary;
Yet onward he goes through the broad belt of light,
  Toward the shade of the forest so dreary.
Hark! was it the night-wind that rustled the leaves?
  Was it moonlight so wondrously flashing?
It looked like a rifle—"Ha! Mary, good-bye!"
  The red life-blood is ebbing and plashing.

All quiet along the Potomac to-night,
  No sound save the rush of the river;
While soft falls the dew on the face of the dead—
  The picket's off duty for ever!

                              ETHEL LYNN BEERS

CONCORD HYMN

Sung at the completion of the Battle Monument, April 19, 1886

By the rude bridge that arched the flood,
  Their flag to April's breeze unfurled,
Here once the embattled farmers stood,
  And fired the shot heard round the world.

The foe long since in silence slept;
  Alike the conqueror silent sleeps;
And Time the ruined bridge has swept
  Down the dark stream which seaward creeps.

On this green bank, by this soft stream,
  We set today a votive stone;
That memory may their deed redeem,
  When, like our sires, our sons are gone.

Spirit, that made those spirits dare
  To die, and leave their children free,
Bid Time and Nature gently spare
  The shaft we raise to them and thee.

                              RALPH WALDO EMERSON

OLD IRONSIDES

Ay, tear her tattered ensign down!
Long has it waved on high,
And many an eye has danced to see
That banner in the sky;
Beneath it rung the battle shout,
And burst the cannon's roar;—
The meteor of the ocean air
Shall sweep the clouds no more!

Her deck, once red with heroes'
　blood,
Where knelt the vanquished foe,
When winds were hurrying o'er
　the flood,
And waves were white below,
No more shall feel the victor's
　tread,

Or know the conquered knee;—
The harpies of the shore shall
　pluck
The eagle of the sea!

O, better that her shattered hulk
Should sink beneath the wave;
Her thunders shook the mighty
　deep,
And there should be her grave;
Nail to the mast her holy flag,
Set every threadbare sail,
And give her to the god of storms,
The lightning and the gale!

OLIVER WENDELL HOLMES

IN FLANDERS FIELDS

In Flanders fields the poppies blow
Between the crosses, row on row,
That mark our place; and in the sky
The larks, still bravely singing, fly
Scarce heard amid the guns below.

We are the Dead. Short days ago
We lived, felt dawn, saw sunset glow,
Loved and were loved, and now we lie
　In Flanders fields.

Take up our quarrel with the foe!
To you from failing hands, we
　throw
The torch— Be yours to hold it
　high!
If ye break faith with us who die
We shall not sleep, though
　poppies grow
　　In Flanders fields.

CAPTAIN JOHN D. McCRAE

THE SPIRES OF OXFORD

(As seen from the train)

I saw the spires of Oxford
　As I was passing by,
The grey spires of Oxford
　Against a pearl-grey sky;
My heart was with the Oxford
　　men
　Who went abroad to die.

The years go fast in Oxford,
　The golden years and gay;
The hoary colleges look down
　On careless boys at play,
But when the bugles sounded—
　　War!
　They put their games away.

They left the peaceful river,
　The cricket field, the quad,
The shaven lawns of Oxford,
　To seek a bloody sod.
They gave their merry youth away
　For country and for God.

God rest you, happy gentlemen,
　Who laid your good lives down,
Who took the khaki and the gun
　Instead of cap and gown.
God bring you to a fairer place
　Then even Oxford town.

WINIFRED M. LETTS

THE SOLDIER

If I should die, think only this of me:
That there's some corner of a foreign field
That is forever England. There shall be
In that rich earth a richer dust concealed;
A dust whom England bore, shaped, made aware,
Gave, once, her flowers to love, her ways to roam;
A body of England's, breathing English air,
Washed by the rivers, blest by suns of home.
And think, this heart, all evil shed away,
A pulse in the eternal mind, no less
Gives somewhere back the thoughts by England given;
Her sights and sounds; dreams happy as her day;
And laughter, learnt of friends, and gentleness,
In hearts at peace, under an English heaven.

RUPERT BROOKE

I HAVE A RENDEZVOUS WITH DEATH

I have a rendezvous with Death
At some disputed barricade,
When Spring comes back with
   rustling shade
And apple-blossoms fill the air—
I have a rendezvous with Death
When Spring brings back blue
   days and fair.

It may be he shall take my hand
And lead me into his dark land
And close my eyes and quench my
   breath—
It may be I shall pass him still.
I have a rendezvous with Death
On some scarred slope of battered hill,
When Spring comes round again
   this year
And the first meadow-flowers appear.

God knows 'twere better to be deep
Pillowed in silk and scented down,
Where love throbs out in blissful
   sleep,
Pulse nigh to pulse, and breath to
   breath,
Where hushed awakenings are
   dear . . .
But I've a rendezvous with Death
At midnight in some flaming
   town,
When Spring trips north again
   this year,
And I to my pledged word am
   true,
I shall not fail that rendezvous.

ALAN SEEGER

ARMS AND THE BOY

Let the boy try along this bayonet-blade
How cold steel is, and keen with hunger of blood;
Blue with all malice, like a madman's flash;
And thinly drawn with famishing for flesh.

Lend him to stroke these blind, blunt bullet-heads
Which long to nuzzle in the hearts of lads,
Or give him cartridges of fine zinc teeth,
Sharp with the sharpness of grief and death.

For his teeth seem for laughing round an apple.
Their lurk no claws behind his fingers supple;
And God will grow no talons at his heels,
Nor antlers through the thickness of his curls.

WILFRED OWEN

A REFUSAL TO MOURN THE DEATH, BY FIRE, OF A CHILD IN LONDON

Never until the mankind making
Bird beast and flower
Fathering and all humbling
    darkness
Tells with silence the last light
    breaking
And the still hour
Is come of the sea tumbling in
    harness

And I must enter again the round
Zion of the water bead
And the synagogue of the ear of
    corn
Shall I let pray the shadow of a
    sound
Or sow my salt seed
In the least valley of sackcloth to
    mourn

The majesty and burning of the
    child's death.
I shall not murder
The mankind of her going with a
    grave truth
Nor blaspheme down the stations
    of the breath
With any further
Elegy of innocence and youth

Deep with the first dead lies
    London's daughter,
Robed in the long friends,
The grains beyond age, the dark
    veins of her mother
Secret by the unmourning water
Of the riding Thames.
After the first death, there is no
    other.

DYLAN THOMAS

ELEGY ON GORDON BARBER

Lamentably Drowned in his Eighteenth Year

When in the mirror of a permanent tear
Over the iris of your mother's eye
I beheld the dark tremor of your face, austere
With space of death, spun too benign for youth,
Icicle of the past to pierce her living sigh—
I saw you wish the last kiss of mother's mouth,
Who took the salted waters rather in the suck
Of seas, sighing yourself to fill and drench
With water the plum-rich glory of your breast
Where beat the heart escaping from war's luck.

Gordon, I mourn your wrist, your running foot,
Your curious brows, your thigh, your unborn daughters,
Yet mourn more deep the drought-caught war dry boy
Who goes, a killer, to join you in your sleep
And envy you what made you blench
Taking your purple back to drought-less waters.
What choke of terror filled you in the wet
What fierce surprise caught you when play turned fate
And all the rains you loved became your net,
Formlessly yielding, yet stronger than your breath?
Then did you dream of mother or hopes hatched
When the cold cramp held you from nape to foot
And time dissolved, promise dissolved, in Death?
Did you cry 'cruel' to all the hands that stretched
Not near, but played afar, when you sank down
Your sponge of lungs hurt to the quick
Till you had left the quick to join the dead,
Whom, now, your mother mourns, grief-sick.
You were too young to drown.

Never will you take bride to happy bed,
Who lay awash in water yet no laving
Needed, so pure so young for sudden leaving.
Gone, gone is Gordon, tall and brilliant lad
Whose mind was science. Now hollow his skull
A noble sculpture, is but sunken bone,
His cells from water come by water laid
Grave-deep, to water gone.
Lost, lost the hope he had
Washed to a cipher his splendour and his skill.

But Gordon's gone, it's other boys who live afraid.

Two years, and lads have grown to hold a gun.
In dust must splendid lads go down and choke,
Red dry their hands and dry their one day's sun
From which they earthward fall to fiery tomb
Bomb-weighted, from bloodying children's hair.

Never a boy but takes as cross Cain's crime
And goes to death by making death, to pass
Death's gate distorted with the dried brown grime—
Better the watery death than death by air
Or death by sand
Where fall hard fish of fear
Loud in unwetted dust.

Spun on a lucky wave, O early boy!
Now ocean's fish you are
As heretofore.
Perhaps you had sweet mercy's tenderness
To win so soon largesse of choice
That you, by grace, went gayly to the wave
And all our mourning should be to rejoice.

GENE DERWOOD

ANTHEM FOR DOOMED YOUTH

What passing-bells for these who die as cattle?
Only the monstrous anger of the guns.
Only the stuttering rifles' rapid rattle
Can patter out their hasty orisons.
No mockeries for them; no prayers nor bells,
Nor any voice of mourning save the choirs,—
The shrill, demented choirs of wailing shells;
And bugles calling for them from sad shires.

What candles may be held to speed them all?
Not in the hands of boys, but in their eyes
Shall shine the holy glimmers of good-byes.
The pallor of girls' brows shall be their pall;
Their flowers the tenderness of patient minds,
And each slow dusk a drawing-down of blinds.

WILFRED OWEN

HIGH FLIGHT

Written by a 19-year-old American volunteer with the Royal
Canadian Air Force, who was killed in action December 11, 1941

Oh, I have slipped the surly bonds of earth,
And danced the skies on laughter-silvered wings;
Sunward I've climbed and joined the tumbling mirth
Of sun-split clouds—and done a hundred things
You have not dreamed of—wheeled and soared and swung
High in the sunlit silence. Hov'ring there,
I've chased the shouting wind along and flung
My eager craft through footless halls of air.
Up, up the long, delirious, burning blue
I've topped the wind-swept heights with easy grace,
Where never lark, or even eagle, flew;
And, while with silent, lifting mind I've trod
The high untrespassed sanctity of space,
Put out my hand, and touched the face of God.

JOHN GILLESPIE MAGEE, JR.

ULTIMA RATIO REGUM

The guns spell money's ultimate reason
In letters of lead on the spring hillside.
But the boy lying dead under the olive trees
Was too young and too silly
To have been notable to their important eye.
He was a better target for a kiss.

When he lived, tall factory hooters never summoned him.
Nor did restaurant plate-glass doors revolve to wave him in.
His name never appeared in the papers.
The world maintained its traditional wall
Round the dead with their gold sunk deep as a well,
Whilst his life, intangible as a Stock Exchange rumour, drifted outside.

O too lightly he threw down his cap
One day when the breeze threw petals from the trees.
The unflowering wall sprouted with guns,
Machine-gun anger quickly scythed the grasses;
Flags and leaves fell from hands and branches;
The tweed cap rotted in the nettles.
Consider his life which was valueless
In terms of employment, hotel ledgers, news files.
Consider. One bullet in ten thousand kills a man.
Ask. Was so much expenditure justified
On the death of one so young and so silly
Lying under the olive tree, O world, O death?

STEPHEN SPENDER

THE DARK HILLS

Dark hills at evening in the west,
Where sunset hovers like a sound
Of golden horns that sang to rest
Old bones of warriors under ground,

Far now from all the bannered ways
Where flash the legions of the sun,
You fade—as if the last of days
Were fading, and all wars were done.

EDWIN ARLINGTON ROBINSON

ONE MORNING THE WORLD WOKE UP

One morning the world woke up and there was no news;
No gun was shelling the great ear drum of the air,
No Christian flesh spurted beneath the subtle screws,
No moaning came from the many agony-faced Jews,
Only the trees in a gauze of wind trembled and were fair.

No trucks climbed into the groove of an endless road,
No tanks were swaying drunken with death at the hilltop,
No bombs were planting their bushes of blood and mud,
And the aimless tides of unfortunates no longer flowed:
A break in the action at last . . . all had come to a stop.

Those trees danced, in their delicate selves half furled,
And a new time on the glittering atmosphere was seen;
The lightning stuttering on the closed eyelid of the world
Was gone, and an age of horizons had dawned, soft, pearled,
The world woke up to a scene like spring's first green.

Birds chirped in waterfalls of little sounds for hours,
Rainbows, in miniature nuggets, were stored in the dews,
The sky was one vast moonstone of the tenderest blues,
And the meadows lay carpeted in three heights of flowers:
One morning the world woke up and there was no news.

OSCAR WILLIAMS

GREATER LOVE

Red lips are not so red
  As the stained stones kissed by the English dead.
Kindness of wooed and wooer
Seems shame to their love pure.
O Love, your eyes lose lure
  When I behold eyes blinded in my stead!

Your slender attitude
  Trembles not exquisite like limbs knife-skewed,
Rolling and rolling there
Where God seems not to care;
Till the fierce Love they bear
  Cramps them in death's extreme decrepitude.

Your voice sings not so soft,—
  Though even as wind murmuring through raftered loft,—
Your dear voice is not dear,
Gentle, and evening clear,
As theirs whom none now hear,
  Now earth has stopped their piteous mouths that coughed.

Heart, you were never hot,
  Nor large, nor full like hearts made great with shot;
And though your hand be pale,
Paler are all which trail
Your cross through flame and hail:
  Weep, you may weep, for you may touch them not.

WILFRED OWEN

FIFE TUNE

One morning in spring
We marched from Devizes
All shapes and all sizes
Like beads on a string,
But yet with a swing
We trod the bluemetal
And full of high fettle
We started to sing.

She ran down the stair
A twelve-year-old darling
And laughing and calling
She tossed her bright hair;

Then silent to stare
At the men flowing past her—
There were all she could master
Adoring her there.

It's seldom I'll see
A sweeter or prettier;
I doubt we'll forget her
In two years or three.
And lucky he'll be
She takes for a lover
While we are far over
The treacherous sea.

JOHN MANIFOLD

BOOK VII

THE MASK OF COMEDY

JABBERWOCKY

'Twas brillig, and the slithy toves
　　Did gyre and gimble in the wabe:
All mimsy were the borogoves,
　　And the mome raths outgrabe.

"Beware the Jabberwock, my son!
　　The jaws that bite, the claws
　　　　that catch!
Beware the Jubjub bird, and shun
　　The frumious Bandersnatch!"

He took his vorpal sword in hand;
　　Long time the manxome foe he
　　　　sought—
So rested he by the Tumtum tree,
　　And stood awhile in thought.

And, as in uffish thought he stood,
　　The Jabberwock, with eyes of
　　　　flame,

Came whiffling through the tulgey
　　wood,
　　And burbled as it came!

One, two! One, two! And through
　　and through
　　The vorpal blade went snicker-
　　　　snack!
He left it dead, and with its head
　　He went galumphing back.

"And hast thou slain the
　　Jabberwock?
Come to my arms, my beamish
　　boy!
O frabjous day! Callooh, Callay!"
　　He chortled in his joy.

'Twas brillig, and the slithy toves
　　Did gyre and gimble in the wabe:
All mimsy were the borogoves,
　　And the mome raths outgrabe.

LEWIS CARROLL

THE PURPLE COW

I never saw a Purple Cow,
　　I never hope to see one;
But I can tell you, anyhow,
　　I'd rather see than be one.

GELETT BURGESS

Ah, yes, I wrote the "Purple Cow"—
　　I'm sorry, now, I wrote it!
But I can tell you, anyhow,
　　I'll kill you if you quote it.

GELETT BURGESS

PEANUTS

The boy stood on the burning deck
Eating peanuts by the peck;
His father called him, he wouldn't go,
Because he loved the peanuts so.

ANONYMOUS

THE SYCOPHANTIC FOX AND THE GULLIBLE RAVEN

A raven sat upon a tree,
  And not a word he spoke, for
His beak contained a piece of Brie,
  Or, maybe, it was Roquefort.
    We'll make it any kind you
      please—
    At all events it was a cheese.

Beneath the tree's umbrageous
    limb
  A hungry fox sat smiling;
He saw the raven watching him,
  And spoke in words beguiling:
    "J'admire," said he, "ton
      beau plumage,"
    (The which was simply
      persiflage.)

Two things there are, no doubt
    you know,
  To which a fox is used:
A rooster that is bound to crow,
  A crow that's bound to roost;
    And whichsoever he espies
    He tells the most unblushing
      lies.

"Sweet fowl," he said, "I understand
  You're more than merely natty,
I hear you sing to beat the band
  And Adelina Patti.
    Pray render with your liquid tongue
    A bit from 'Götterdämmerung.' "

This subtle speech was aimed to
    please
  The crow, and it succeeded;
He thought no bird in all the trees
  Could sing as well as he did.
    In flattery completely doused,
    He gave the "Jewel Song"
      from "Faust."

But gravitation's law, of course,
  As Isaac Newton showed it,
Exerted on the cheese its force,
  And elsewhere soon bestowed it.
    In fact, there is no need to tell
    What happened when to
      earth it fell.

I blush to add that when the bird
  Took in the situation
He said one brief, emphatic word,
  Unfit for publication.
    The fox was greatly startled, but
    He only sighed and answered "Tut."

The Moral is: A fox is bound
  To be a shameless sinner.
And also: When the cheese comes
    round
  You know it's after dinner.
    But (what is only known to few)
    The fox is after dinner, too.
        GUY WETMORE CARRYL

THIS IS THE KEY

This is the key of the kingdom:
In that kingdom there is a city.
In that city there is a town.
In that town there is a street.
In that street there is a lane.
In that lane there is a yard.
In that yard there is a house.
In that house there is a room.
In that room there is a bed.
On that bed there is a basket.
In that basket there are some
    flowers.

Flowers in a basket.
Basket in the bed.
Bed in the room.
Room in the house.
House in the yard.
Yard in the lane.
Lane in the street.
Street in the town.
Town in the city.
City in the kingdom.
Of the kingom this is the key.

ANONYMOUS

THE KILKENNY CATS

There wanst was two cats of
    Kilkenny,
Each thought there was one cat
    too many,
So they quarreled and they fit,

They scratch'd and they bit,
Till, barrin' their nails,
And the tips of their tails,
Instead of two cats, there warnt
    any.

ANONYMOUS

TO BE OR NOT TO BE

I sometimes think I'd rather crow
And be a rooster than to roost
And be a crow. But I dunno.

A rooster he can roost also,
Which don't seem fair when crows
    can't crow.
Which may help, some. Still I dunno.

Crows should be glad of one
    thing, though;
Nobody thinks of eating crow,

While roosters they are good enough
For anyone unless they're tough.

There are lots of tough old
    roosters though,
And anyway a crow can't crow,
So mebby roosters stand more
    show.
It looks that way. But I dunno.

ANONYMOUS

THE JUMBLIES

They went to sea in a sieve, they did;
  In a sieve they went to sea:
In spite of all their friends could say,
On a winter's morn, on a stormy day,
  In a sieve they went to sea.
And when the sieve turned round and round,
And everyone cried, "You'll all be drowned!"
They called aloud, "Our sieve ain't big,
But we don't care a button; we don't care a fig:
  In a sieve we'll go to sea!"
    Far and few, far and few,
      Are the lands where the Jumblies live:
      Their heads are green, and their hands are blue;
      And they went to sea in a sieve.

They sailed away in a sieve, they did,
  In a sieve they sailed so fast,
With only a beautiful pea-green veil
Tied with a ribbon, by way of a sail,
  To a small tobacco-pipe mast.
And every one said who saw them go,
"Oh! won't they be soon upset; you know!
For the sky is dark, and the voyage is long;
And, happen what may, it's extremely wrong
  In a sieve to sail so fast."

The water it soon came in, it did;
  The water it soon came in:
So, to keep them dry, they wrapped their feet
In a pinky paper all folded neat;
  And they fastened it down with a pin.
And they passed the night in a crockery-jar;
And each of them said, "How wise we are!
Though the sky be dark, and the voyage be long,
Yet we never can think we were rash or wrong
  While round in our sieve we spin."

And all night long they sailed away;
  And, when the sun went down,
They whistled and warbled a moony song
To the echoing sound of a coppery gong,
  In the shade of the mountains brown,
  "O Timballoo! how happy we are
When we live in a sieve and crockery-jar!
And all night long, in the moonlight pale,
We sail away with a pea-green sail
  In the shade of the mountains brown."

They sailed to the Western Sea, they did,—
  To a land all covered with trees:
And they bought an owl, and a useful cart,
And a pound of rice, and a cranberry-tart,
  And a hive of silvery bees;
And they bought a pig, and some green jackdaws,
And a lovely monkey with lollipop paws,
And forty bottles of ring-bo-ree,
  And no end of Stilton cheese.

And in twenty years they all came back,—
  In twenty years or more;
And every one said, "How tall they've grown!
For they've been to the Lakes, and the Torrible Zone,
  And the hills of the Chankly Bore."
And they drank their health, and gave them a feast
Of dumplings made of beautiful yeast;
And every one said, "If we only live,
We, too, will go to sea in a sieve,
  To the hills of the Chankly Bore."
    Far and few, far and few,
      Are the lands where the Jumblies live.
    Their heads are green, and their hands are blue;
      And they went to sea in a sieve.

EDWARD LEAR

THE SEA-GULL

Hark to the whimper of the sea-gull;
He weeps because he's not an ea-gull.
Suppose you were, you silly sea-gull,
Could you explain it to your she-gull?

OGDEN NASH

WHAT ARE FOLKS MADE OF?

What are little boys made of,
 made of?
What are little boys made of?
Piggins and pails and little puppy
 tails,
That's what little boys are
 made of.
What are little girls made of? etc.
Sugar and spice and all things nice
And that's what little girls are
 made of.
What are young men made of? etc.

Thorns and briars, they're all bad
 liars,
And that's what young men are
 made of.
What's young women made of? etc.
Rings and jings and all fine things
And that's what young women's
 made of.
What are old men made of? etc.
Whisky and brandy and sugar
 and candy,
And that's what old men are made of.

ANONYMOUS

THE PESSIMIST

Nothing to do but work,
 Nothing to eat but food;
Nothing to wear but clothes
 To keep one from going nude.

Nothing to breathe but air,
 Quick as a flash 'tis gone;
Nowhere to fall but off,
 Nowhere to stand but on.

Nothing to comb but hair,
 Nowhere to sleep but in bed;
Nothing to weep but tears,
 Nothing to bury but dead.

Nothing to sing but songs;
 Ah, well, alas! alack!
Nowhere to go but out,
 Nowhere to come but back.

Nothing to see but sights,
 Nothing to quench but thirst;
Nothing to have but what we've got;
 Thus thro' life we are cursed.

Nothing to strike but a gait;
 Everything moves that goes.
Nothing at all but common sense
 Can ever withstand these woes.

BEN KING

THE MODERN HIAWATHA

When he killed the Mudjokivis,
Of the skin he made him mittens,
Made them with the fur side inside
Made them with the skin side
    outside,
He, to get the warm side inside,
Put the inside skin side outside;

He, to get the cold side outside,
Put the warm side fur side inside.
That's why he put the fur side
    inside,
Why he put the skin side outside
Why he turned them inside
    outside.

ANONYMOUS

WORLD WAR

WORLD WAR I

The officers get all the steak
And all we get is the bellyache.
The general got the croix-de-
    guerre,
And the son of a gun was never
    there.

WORLD WAR II

The Wacs and Waves will win
    the war;
So what the hell are we fighting
    for?

WORLD WAR III

I won't print and you won't see
The verses written on World
    War III.

ANONYMOUS

TROUBLE

Better never trouble Trouble
Until Trouble troubles you;
For you only make your trouble
Double-trouble when you do;
And the trouble—like a bubble—
That you're troubling about,
May be nothing but a cipher
With its rim rubbed out.

DAVID KEPPEL

THE TURTLE

The turtle lives 'twixt plated
    decks
Which practically conceal its sex.
I think it clever of the turtle
In such a fix to be so fertile.

OGDEN NASH

INVESTOR'S SOLILOQUY

To buy, or not to buy; that is the question:
Whether 'tis nobler in the mind to suffer
The slings and arrows of an outrageous market,
Or to take cash against a sea of troubles,
And by selling, end them. To buy, to keep—
No more; and by this keeping, to say we end
The bear trend and the thousand natural shocks
That stocks are heir to—'tis a consummation
Devoutly to be wish'd—To buy, to keep—
To keep? Perchance on margin! Ay, there's the rub!
For in that margining what dreams may come,
When we have shuffled off our buying power,
Must give us pause. There's the respect
That makes calamity of so long a position.
For who would bear the whips and scorns of debit balances,
The broker's interest, the shorts' contumely,
The pangs of dispriz'd appreciation, the market's delay,
The insolence of bankers, and the spurns
That patient merit of the unworthy takes,
When he himself might the quietus make
With a bare short sale? Who would losses bear
To grunt and sweat under a falling market,
But that the dread of something after selling,
The undiscover'd rally—from whose bourn
No short seller returns, puzzles the will
And makes us rather bear those losses we have
Than fly to others that we know not of?
Thus ambivalence does make cowards of us all.
And thus the native hue of resolution
Is sicklied o'er with the pale cast of doubt
And enterprises of great pith and moment,
With this regard, their current turn awry,
And lose the name of
Profits.

KENNETH WARD

THE OLD OAKEN BUCKET

(As censored by the Board of Health)

With what anguish of mind I remember my childhood,
  Recalled in the light of knowledge since gained,
The malarious farm, the wet fungus-grown wildwood,
  The chills then contracted that since have remained;
The scum-covered duck-pond, the pig-sty close by it,
  The ditch where the sour-smelling house drainage fell,
The damp, shaded dwelling, the foul barnyard nigh it—
  But worse than all else was that terrible well,
And the old oaken bucket, the mold-crusted bucket,
  The moss-covered bucket that hung in the well.

Just think of it! Moss on the vessel that lifted
  The water I drank in the days called to mind;
Ere I knew what professors and scientists gifted
  In the waters of wells by analysis find;
The rotting wood-fiber, the oxide of iron,
  The algae, the frog of unusual size,
The water as clear as the verses of Byron,
  Are things I remember with tears in my eyes.

Oh, had I but realized in time to avoid them—
  The dangers that lurked in that pestilent draft—
I'd have tested for organic germs and destroyed them—
  With potassic permanganate ere I had quaffed.
Or perchance I'd have boiled it, and afterward strained it
  Through filters of charcoal and gravel combined;
Or, after distilling, condensed and regained it
  In potable form with its filth left behind.

How little I knew of the enteric fever
  Which lurked in the water I ventured to drink,
But since I've become a devoted believer
  In the teachings of science, I shudder to think.
And now, far removed from the scenes I'm describing,
  The story of warning to others I tell,
As memory reverts to my youthful imbibing
  And I gag at the thought of that horrible well,
And the old oaken bucket, the fungus-grown bucket—
  In fact, the slop-bucket—that hung in the well.

ANONYMOUS

HOW DOTH THE LITTLE CROCODILE

How doth the little crocodile
  Improve his shining tail,
And pour the waters of the Nile
  On every golden scale!

How cheerfully he seems to grin,
  How neatly spreads his claws,
And welcomes little fishes in
  With gently smiling jaws!

LEWIS CARROLL

MONEY

Workers earn it,
Spendthrifts burn it,
Bankers lend it,
Women spend it,
Forgers fake it,
Taxes take it,
Dying leave it,

Heirs receive it,
Thrifty save it,
Misers crave it,
Robbers seize it,
Rich increase it,
Gamblers lose it . . .
I could use it.

RICHARD ARMOUR

REFLECTIONS ON ICE-BREAKING

Candy
Is dandy
But Liquor
Is quicker.

OGDEN NASH

PORTRAIT OF THE ARTIST
AS A PREMATURELY OLD MAN

It is common knowledge to every schoolboy and even every Bachelor of Arts,
That all sin is divided into two parts.
One kind of sin is called a sin of commission, and that is very important,
And it is what you are doing when you are doing something you ortant,
And the other kind of sin is just the opposite and is called a sin of omis-
    sion and is equally bad in the eyes of all right-thinking people, from
    Billy Sunday to Buddha,
And it consists of not having done something you shudda.
I might as well give you my opinion of these two kinds of sin as long as, in
    a way, against each other we are pitting them,
And that is, don't bother your head about sins of commission because,
    however sinful, they must at least be fun or else you wouldn't be com-
    mitting them.
It is the sin of omission, the second kind of sin,
That lays eggs under your skin.
The way you get really painfully bitten
Is by the insurance you haven't taken out and the checks you haven't
    added up the stubs of and the appointments you haven't kept and the
    bills you haven't paid and the letters you haven't written.
Also, about sins of omission there is one particularly painful lack of beauty,
Namely, it isn't as though it had been a riotous red letter day or night
    every time you neglected to do your duty;
You didn't get a wicked forbidden thrill
Every time you let a policy lapse or forgot to pay a bill;
You didn't slap the lads in the tavern on the back and loudly cry Whee,
Let's all fail to write just one more letter before we go home, and this
    round of unwritten letters is on me.
No, you never get any fun
Out of the things you haven't done,
But they are the things that I do not like to be amid,
Because the suitable things you didn't do give you a lot more trouble than
    the unsuitable things you did.
The moral is that it is probably better not to sin at all, but if some kind
    of sin you must be pursuing,
Well, remember to do it by doing rather than by not doing.

OGDEN NASH

ALL'S WELL THAT ENDS WELL

A Friend of mine was married to
    a scold,
To me he came, and all his
    troubles told.
Said he, "She's like a woman
    raving mad."
"Alas! my friend," said I, "that's
    very bad!"
"No, not so bad," said he; "for,
    with her, true
I had both house and land, and
    money too."
  "That was well," said I;
  "No, not so well," said he;
  "For I and her own brother
  Went to law with one another;
  I was cast, the suit was lost,
And every penny went to pay the
    cost."
  "That was bad," said I;
  "No, not so bad," said he:
"For we agreed that he the house
    should keep,
And give to me four score of
    Yorkshire sheep

All fat, and fair, and fine, they
    were to be."
"Well, then," said I, "sure that
    was well for thee?"
  "No, not so well," said he;
  "For, when the sheep I got,
  They every one died of the rot."
  "That was bad," said I;
  "No, not so bad," said he;
  "For I had thought to scrape the fat
  And keep it in an oaken vat;
Then into tallow melt for winter store."
"Well, then," said I, "that's better
    than before?"
  " 'Twas not so well," said he;
  "For having got a clumsy fellow
  To scrape the fat and melt the
    tallow;
Into the melting fat the fire catches,
  And, like brimstone matches,
  Burnt my house to ashes."
  "That was bad," said I;
"No! not so bad," said he; "for,
    what is best,
My scolding wife has gone among the rest."
                ANONYMOUS

A FRIEND

Who borrows all your ready cash,
And with it cuts a mighty dash
Proving the lender weak and rash?—
    Your friend!

Who finds out every secret fault,
Misjudges every word and
  thought,
And makes you pass for worse
  than nought?—
    Your friend!

Who wins your money at deep play,
Then tells you that the world
  doth say,
" 'Twere wise from clubs you kept
  away?"—
    Your friend!

Who sells you, for the longest price,
Horses, a dealer, in a trice,
Would find unsound and full of
  vice?—
    Your friend!

Who eats your dinners, then looks
  shrewd;
Wishes you had a cook like Ude,
For then much oftener would
  intrude?—
    Your friend!

Who tells you that you've
  shocking wine,
And owns that, though he sports
  not fine,
Crockford's the only place to dine?—
    Your friend!

Who wheedles you with words
  most fond
To sign for him a heavy bond,
"Or else, by jove, must quick
  abscond?"—
    Your friend!

Who makes you all the interest pay,
With principal, some future day,
And laughs at what you then may
  say?—
    Your friend!

Who makes deep love unto your wife,
Knowing you prize her more than life,
And breeds between you hate and
  strife?—
    Your friend!

Who, when you've got into a brawl,
Insists that out your man you call,
Then gets you shot, which ends it
  all?—
    Your friend!!!

MARGUERITE POWER
COUNTESS OF BLESSINGTON

ELEGY ON THE DEATH OF A MAD DOG

Good people all, of every sort,
 Give ear unto my song;
And if you find it wond'rous short,
 It cannot hold you long.

In Islington there was a man,
 Of whom the world might say,
That still a godly race he ran,
 Whene'er he went to pray.

A kind and gentle heart he had,
 To comfort friends and foes;
The naked every day he clad,
 When he put on his clothes.

And in that town a dog was
  found,
 As many dogs there be,
Both mongrel, puppy, whelp, and
  hound,
 And curs of low degree.

This dog and man at first were
  friends;
 But when a pique began,
The dog, to gain some private ends,
 Went mad and bit the man.

Around from all the neighboring streets
 The wond'ring neighbors ran,
And swore the dog had lost its wits,
 To bite so good a man.

The wound it seem'd both sore and sad
 To every Christian eye;
And while they swore the dog was mad,
 They swore the man would die.

But soon a wonder came to light,
 That showed the rogues they lied:
The man recover'd of the bite,
 The dog it was that died.

     OLIVER GOLDSMITH

THE WISE OLD OWL

A wise old owl sat on an oak,
The more he saw the less he spoke;
The less he spoke the more he heard;
Why aren't we like that wise old bird?

   EDWARD H. RICHARDS

A BAKER'S DUZZEN
UV WIZE SAWZ

Them ez wants, must choose.
Them ez hez, must lose.
Them ez knows, won't blab.
Them ez guesses, will gab.
Them ez borrows, sorrows.
Them ez lends, spends.
Them ez gives, lives.
Them ez keeps dark, is deep.
Them ez kin earn, kin keep.
Them ez aims, hits.
Them ez hez, gits.
Them ez waits, win.
Them ez *will, kin.*

EDWARD ROWLAND SILL

TENDERHEARTEDNESS

Billy, in one of his nice new
    sashes,
Fell in the fire and was burnt to
    ashes;
Now, although the room grows
    chilly,
I haven't the heart to poke poor
    Billy.

HARRY GRAHAM

THE HARDSHIP
OF ACCOUNTING

Never ask of money spent
Where the spender thinks it went.
Nobody was ever meant
To remember or invent
What he did with every cent.

ROBERT FROST

MISFORTUNES
NEVER COME SINGLY

Making toast at the fireside,
Nurse fell in the grate and died;
And what makes it ten times
    worse,
All the toast was burnt with
    nurse.

HARRY GRAHAM

WHO DOES NOT LOVE
WINE, WOMEN AND SONG

Who does not love wine, women
    and song
Remains a fool his whole life
    long.

J. H. VOSS

FIGHT

He that is in the battle slain
Will never rise to fight again:
But he that fights and runs away
Will live to fight another day.

ANONYMOUS

FROM GREENLAND
TO ICELAND

From Greenland to Iceland
    From Sitka to Siam,
There are so many people
    More clever than I am.

ANONYMOUS

HEAVEN WILL PROTECT THE WORKING GIRL

A village maid was leaving home, with tears her eyes were wet,
Her mother dear was standing near the spot;
She says to her: "Neuralgia dear, I hope you won't forget
That I'm the only mother you have got.
The city is a wicked place as anyone can see,
And cruel dangers 'round your path may hurl;
So ev'ry week you'd better send your wages back to me
For Heaven will protect a working girl.

Chorus:
    "You are going far away, but remember what I say,
    When you are in the city's giddy whirl,
    From temptations, crimes and follies, villains, taxicabs and trolleys,
    Oh! Heaven will protect the working girl."

Her dear old mother's words proved true, for soon the poor girl met
A man who on her ruin was intent;
He treated her respectful as those villains always do,
And she supposed he was a perfect gent.
But she found different when one night she went with him to dine
Into a table d'hôte so blithe and gay.
And he says to her: "After this we'll have a demitasse!"
Then to him these brave words the girl did say:

Chorus:
    "Stand back, villain, go your way! here I will no longer stay,
    Although you were a marquis or an earl;
    You may tempt the upper classes with your villainous demitasses,
    But Heaven will protect the working girl."

EDGAR SMITH

A PROMISE MADE

A promise made
Is a debt unpaid.

ANONYMOUS

BRAVE OLD WORLD

When the last H-bomb blast has done its stuff
And stilled for good the geiger counter's voice,
When nothing's left but just a few of us
Will come the moment of my dreadful choice:
Invent the peaceful wheel? Oh dear me, no!
Let those who would, assuage the general woe—
I plan to freeze my neighbors to the marrow
By being the inventor of the bow and arrow.

ELISABETH LAMBERT

BURLESQUE

If the man who turnips cries,
Cry not when his father dies,
'Tis a proof that he had rather
Have a turnip than his father.

SAMUEL JOHNSON

ATOMIC COURTESY

To smash the simple atom
All mankind was intent.
    Now any day
    The atom may
Return the compliment.

ETHEL JACOBSON

DOCTOR FELL

I do not love thee, Doctor Fell,
The reason why I cannot tell,
But this one thing I know full
    well:
I do not love thee, Doctor Fell.

THOMAS BROWN

WOMAN'S WILL

Men dying make their wills—but wives
    Escape a work so sad;
Why should they make what all
    their lives
    The gentle dames have had?

JOHN G. SAXE

THE DYING AIRMAN

A handsome young airman lay dying,
And as on the aerodrome he lay,
To the mechanics who round him
  came sighing,
These last dying words he did say:

"Take the cylinders out of my
  kidneys,
The connecting-rod out of my brain,
Take the cam-shaft from out of
  my backbone,
And assemble the engine again."
ANONYMOUS

EVIDENCE READ AT THE TRIAL OF
THE KNAVE OF HEARTS

They told me you had been to her,
  And mentioned me to him:
She gave me a good character,
  But said I could not swim.

He sent them word I had not gone,
  (We know it to be true):
If she should push the matter on,
  What would become of you?

I gave her one, they gave him two,
  You gave us three or more;
They all returned from him to you,
  Though they were mine before.

If I or she should chance to be
  Involved in this affair,
He trusts to you to set them free,
  Exactly as we were.

My notion was that you had been
  (Before she had this fit)
An obstacle that came between
  Him, and ourselves, and it.

Don't let him know she liked
  them best,
  For this must ever be
A secret, kept from all the rest,
  Between yourself and me.
LEWIS CARROLL

THE LITTLE MAN WHO WASN'T THERE

As I was going up the stair
I met a man who wasn't there;
He wasn't there again today—
I wish, I *wish*, he'd stay away.
HUGHES MEARNS

GENIUS

A scientist living at Staines
Is searching with infinite pains
    For a new type of sound
    Which he hopes, when it's
        found,
Will travel much faster than
    planes.

R. J. P. HEWISON

FAITH-HEALER

There was a faith-healer in Deal
Who said, "Although pain isn't
    real,
    If I sit on a pin
    And it punctures my skin,
I dislike what I fancy I feel."

ANONYMOUS

BANG STREET

Bang Street—
Rattle tin can clang Street,
Garbage truck's birth pang Street,
Dog belt's howl Street,
Loud mouthed brat Street,
Pneumatic drill kill Street,
Self-starter with engine that won't
    work Street,
Wish to God I could go deaf
    Street—
Out dog! . . . And let me into
    Sputnick Number Two.

LIVINGSTON WELCH

MR. JONES

"There's been an accident," they
    said,
"Your servant's cut in half; he's
    dead!"
"Indeed!" said Mr. Jones, "and
    please,
Send me the half that's got my
    keys."

HARRY GRAHAM

ON MONSIEUR COUÉ

This very remarkable man
Commends a most practical plan;
    You can do what you want
    If you don't think you can't
So don't think you can't think
    you can.

CHARLES INGE

IT ISN'T THE COUGH

It isn't the cough
That carries you off;
It's the coffin
They carry you off in.

ANONYMOUS

AUNT ELIZA

In the drinking well
    Which the plumber built her,
Aunt Eliza fell—
    We must buy a filter.

HARRY GRAHAM

THE CRIMES OF LIZZIE BORDEN

Lizzie Borden with an axe,
Hit her father forty whacks,
When she saw what she had done,
She hit her mother forty-one.

ANONYMOUS

RELATIVITY

There was a young lady named
    Bright,
Who travelled much faster than
    light,
  She started one day
  In the relative way,
And returned on the previous
    night.

ANONYMOUS

A SHOT AT RANDOM

(*In Imitation of Longfellow*)

I shot an arrow into the air:
I don't know how it fell, or
    where;
But, strangely enough, at my
    journey's end,
I found it again in the neck of a
    friend.

D. B. WYNDHAM LEWIS

INFANT INNOCENCE

The Grizzly Bear is huge and
    wild;
He has devoured the infant child.
The infant child is not aware
It has been eaten by the bear.

A. E. HOUSMAN

TO AN ACQUAINTANCE

Thou speakest always ill of me,
I always speak well of thee:
But, spite of all our noise and
    pother,
The world believes nor one, nor
    t'other.

ANONYMOUS

THE RAIN

The rain it raineth every day,
  Upon the just and unjust fella,
But more upon the just, because
  The unjust hath the just's
    umbrella.

ANONYMOUS

LIVES OF GREAT MEN

Lives of great men all remind us
  As their pages o'er we turn,
That we're apt to leave behind us
  Letters that we ought to burn.

ANONYMOUS

FIRST FIG

My candle burns at both ends;
  It will not last the night;
But ah, my foes, and oh, my
    friends—
  It gives a lovely light!
EDNA ST. VINCENT MILLAY

MAN IS A FOOL

As a rule, man is a fool,
When it's hot, he wants it cool;
When it's cool, he wants it hot,
Always wanting what is not.
ANONYMOUS

What can't be cured
Must be endured.
ANONYMOUS

EPIGRAM

To John I owed great obligation;
  But John unhappily thought fit
To publish it to all the nation:
  So John and I are more than quit.
MATTHEW PRIOR

A DECREPIT OLD GASMAN

A decrepit old gasman, named
    Peter,
While hunting around his gas
    heater,
  Touched a leak with his light;
  He rose out of sight—
And, as everyone who knows
    anything about
    poetry can tell you, he also
    ruined the meter.
ANONYMOUS

JUST FOR THE RIDE

There was a young man of the Clyde,
Who went to a funeral and cried.
  When asked who was dead,
  He stammered and said,
"I don't know—I just came for
    the ride."
ANONYMOUS

NOT JUST FOR THE RIDE

There was a young lady of Niger
Who smiled as she rode on a tiger:
  They came back from the ride
  With the lady inside
And the smile on the face of the tiger
ANONYMOUS

THE HEIGHT OF THE RIDICULOUS

I wrote some lines once on a time
  In wondrous merry mood,
And thought, as usual, men would
    say
  They were exceeding good.

They were so queer, so very queer,
  I laughed as I would die;
Albeit, in the general way,
  A sober man am I.

I called my servant, and he came;
  How kind it was of him
To mind a slender man like me,
  He of the mighty limb!

"These to the printer," I
    exclaimed,
  And, in my humorous way,
I added (as a trifling jest),
  "There'll be the devil to pay."

He took the paper, and I watched,
  And saw him peep within;
At the first line he read, his face
  Was all upon the grin.

He read the next; the grin grew
    broad,
  And shot from ear to ear;
He read the third; a chuckling noise
  I now began to hear.

The fourth; he broke into a roar;
  The fifth; his waistband split;
The sixth; he burst five buttons off,
  And tumbled in a fit.

Ten days and nights, with
    sleepless eye,
  I watched that wretched man,
And since, I never dare to write
  As funny as I can.

OLIVER WENDELL HOLMES

MY FACE

As a beauty I'm not a great star,
There are others more handsome, by far,
But my face—I don't mind it
For I am behind it,
It's the people in front get the jar!
ANTHONY EUWER

IT PAYS

There was a young man of Montrose
Who had pockets in none of his clothes.
When asked by his lass
Where he carried his brass,
He said: "Darling, I pay through the nose."
ARNOLD BENNETT

AN OLD MAN FROM PERU

There was an old man from Peru
Who dreamed he was eating his shoe.
He woke in a fright
In the middle of the night
And found it was perfectly true.
ANONYMOUS

BASEBALL'S SAD LEXICON

These are the saddest of possible words:
"Tinker to Evers to Chance."
Trio of bear cubs, and fleeter than birds,
Tinker and Evers and Chance.
Ruthlessly pricking our gonfalon bubble,
Making a Giant hit into a double—
Words that are heavy with nothing but trouble:
"Tinker to Evers to Chance."
FRANKLIN P. ADAMS

BOOK VIII

THE WORLD OF NATURE

LETTER TO THE CITY CLERK

The Honorable the City Clerk: Dear Sir,
I got your notice. In it you refer
To the strange fact that I have not yet paid
My dog license. You say a law was made
That city officers have authority
To kill or sell my dog—Well, let us see.
When Socrates drew one foot on the bed
After his draught of hemlock Crito said
"What shall we do with you when you have died?"
To that the old philosopher replied
"Crito, you may do anything you please
If you can catch me." Now, like Socrates,
My loving dog, I grieve to say, has gone
Into that spacious mystery where soon
You and all city officers and I
Will follow. Athens doomed her sage to die.
"Nature," he said "has passed the same decree
Upon my judges that they passed on me."
So now you may do anything you please
To my dog if you catch him, except these
Two things that you have threatened, my good sir;
Because it is the special character
Of that state where he is (strange to be told)
That nothing there is ever killed or sold.

FREDERICK A. WRIGHT

TO THE CUCKOO

O blithe new-comer! I have heard,
  I hear thee and rejoice:
O Cuckoo! shall I call thee Bird,
  Or but a wandering Voice?

While I am lying on the grass
  Thy twofold shout I hear;
From hill to hill it seems to pass,
  At once far off and near.

Though babbling only to the vale
  Of sunshine and of flowers,
Thou bringest unto me a tale
  Of visionary hours.

Thrice welcome, darling of the
    Spring!
  Even yet thou art to me
No bird, but an invisible thing,
  A voice, a mystery;

The same whom in my school-boy days
  I listen'd to; that Cry
Which made me look a thousand ways
  In bush, and tree, and sky.

To seek thee did I often rove
  Through woods and on the green;
And thou wert still a hope, a love;
  Still longed for, never seen.

And I can listen to thee yet;
  Can lie upon the plain
And listen, till I do beget
  That golden time again.

O blessèd Bird! the earth we pace
  Again appears to be
An unsubstantial, fairy place,
  That is fit home for Thee!

              WILLIAM WORDSWORTH

ANIMALS

I think I could turn and live with animals, they are so placid and self-
    contained;
I stand and look at them long and long.
They do not sweat and whine about their condition;
They do not lie awake in the dark and weep for their sins;
They do not make me sick discussing their duty to God;
Not one is dissatisfied—not one is demented with the mania of owning things;
Not one kneels to another, nor to his kind that lived thousands of years ago;
Not one is respectable or industrious over the whole earth.

              WALT WHITMAN

TO A MOUSE

ON TURNING UP HER NEST WITH THE PLOUGH

Wee, sleekit,[1] cow'rin, tim'rous
    beastie,
Oh, what a panic's in thy breastie!
Thou need na start awa sae hasty
    Wi' bickerin brattle! [2]
I wad be laith to rin an' chase thee
    Wi' murd'rin pattle! [3]

I'm truly sorry man's dominion
Has broken nature's social union,
An' justifies that ill opinion
    Which makes thee startle
At me, thy poor earth-born
    companion,
    An' fellow-mortal!

I doubt na, whyles,[4] but thou may
    thieve:
What then? poor beastie, thou
    maun live!
A daimen icker in a thrave [5]
    'S a sma' request;
I'll get a blessin wi' the lave,[6]
    An' never miss 't!

Thy wee bit housie, too, in ruin!
Its silly wa's the win's are strewin
An' naething, now, to big a new ane,
    O' foggage [7] green!
An' bleak December's winds ensuin
    Baith snell [8] an' keen!

Thou saw the fields laid bare and
    waste,
An' weary winter comin' fast,
An' cozie here beneath the blast
    Thou thought to dwell,
Till crash! the cruel coulter past
    Out thro' thy cell.

That wee bit heap o' leaves an'
    stibble
Has cost thee mony a weary nibble!
Now thou's turn'd out for a' thy
    trouble,
    But house or hald,[9]
To thole the winter's sleety dribble [10]
    An' cranreuch cauld! [11]

But, Mousie, thou art no thy lane
In proving foresight may be vain:
The best laid schemes o' mice an' men
    Gang aft a-gley,[12]
An' lea'e us nought but grief an' pain
    For promis'd joy.

Still thou art blest, compar'd wi' me!
The present only toucheth thee:
But, och! I backward cast my ee
    On prospects drear!
An' forward, tho' I canna see,
    I guess an' fear!

ROBERT BURNS

[1] sleek
[2] noisy scamper
[3] plough-scraper
[4] sometimes
[5] occasional ear in 24 sheaves
[6] rest
[7] coarse grass
[8] bitter
[9] possession
[10] endure winter's sleety drizzle
[11] cold hoar-frost
[12] go oft amiss

TO THE SKYLARK

Ethereal minstrel! pilgrim of the sky!
   Dost thou despise the earth where cares abound?
Or, while the wings aspire, are heart and eye
   Both with thy nest upon the dewy ground?
Thy nest which thou canst drop into at will,
Those quivering wings composed, that music still!

To the last point of vision, and beyond,
   Mount, daring warbler!—that love-prompted strain
('Twixt thee and thine a never-failing bond),
   Thrills not the less the bosom of the plain:
Yet might'st thou seem, proud privilege! to sing
All independent of the leafy spring.

Leave to the nightingale her shady wood;
   A privacy of glorious light is thine,
Whence thou dost pour upon the world a flood
   Of harmony, with instinct more divine;
Type of the wise, who soar, but never roam—
True to the kindred points of Heaven and Home!

WILLIAM WORDSWORTH

A SONNET ON A MONKEY

O lovely O most charming pug
Thy graceful air and heavenly mug
The beauties of his mind do shine
And every bit is shaped so fine
Your very tail is most divine
Your teeth is whiter than the snow
You are a great buck and a bow
Your eyes are of so fine a shape
More like a christian's than an ape
His cheeks is like the rose's blume
Your hair is like the raven's plume
His nose's cast is of the roman
He is a very pretty woman
I could not get a rhyme for roman
And was obliged to call him woman.

MARJORY FLEMING, AGE 8

TO A SKYLARK

Hail to thee, blithe spirit!
   Bird thou never wert—
That from heaven or near it
   Pourest thy full heart
In profuse strains of unpremeditated art.

Higher still and higher
   From the earth thou springest,
Like a cloud of fire;
   The blue deep thou wingest,
And singing still dost soar, and soaring ever singest.

In the golden light'ning
   Of the sunken sun,
O'er which clouds are bright'ning,
   Thou dost float and run,
Like an unbodied joy whose race is just begun.

The pale purple even
   Melts around thy flight;
Like a star of heaven,
   In the broad daylight
Thou art unseen, but yet I hear thy shrill delight—

Keen as are the arrows
   Of that silver sphere
Whose intense lamp narrows
   In the white dawn clear,
Until we hardly see, we feel that it is there.

All the earth and air
With thy voice is loud,
As, when night is bare,
From one lonely cloud
The moon rains out her beams, and heaven is overflow'd.

What thou art we know not;
What is most like thee?
From rainbow clouds there flow not
Drops so bright to see,
As from thy presence showers a rain of melody:—

Like a poet hidden
In the light of thought,
Singing hymns unbidden,
Till the world is wrought
To sympathy with hopes and fears it heeded not:

Like a high-born maiden
In a palace tower,
Soothing her love-laden
Soul in secret hour
With music sweet as love, which overflows her bower:

Like a glow-worm golden
In a dell of dew,
Scattering unbeholden
Its aërial hue
Among the flowers and grass which screen it from the view:

Like a rose embower'd
In its own green leaves,
By warm winds deflower'd,
Till the scent it gives
Makes faint with too much sweet those heavy-wingèd thieves.

Sound of vernal showers
On the twinkling grass,
Rain-awaken'd flowers—
All that ever was
Joyous and clear and fresh—thy music doth surpass.

Teach us, sprite or bird,
    What sweet thoughts are thine:
I have never heard
    Praise of love or wine
That panted forth a flood of rapture so divine.

Chorus hymeneal,
    Or triumphal chant,
Match'd with thine would be all
    But an empty vaunt—
A thing wherein we feel there is some hidden want.

What objects are the fountains
    Of thy happy strain?
What fields, or waves, or mountains?
    What shapes of sky or plain?
What love of thine own kind? what ignorance of pain?

With thy clear keen joyance
    Languor cannot be:
Shadow of annoyance
    Never came near thee:
Thou lovest, but ne'er knew love's sad satiety.

Waking or asleep,
    Thou of death must deem
Things more true and deep
    Than we mortals dream,
Or how could thy notes flow in such a crystal stream?

We look before and after,
    And pine for what is not:
Our sincerest laughter
    With some pain is fraught;
Our sweetest songs are those that tell of saddest thought.

Yet, if we could scorn
    Hate and pride and fear,
If we were things born
    Not to shed a tear,
I know not how thy joy we ever should come near.

Better than all measures
 Of delightful sound,
Better than all treasures
 That in books are found,
Thy skill to poet were, thou scorner of the ground!

Teach me half the gladness
 That thy brain must know;
Such harmonious madness
 From my lips would flow,
The world should listen then, as I am listening now.
                    PERCY BYSSHE SHELLEY

NURSERY RHYME FOR THE TENDER-HEARTED

Scuttle, scuttle, little roach—
How you run when I approach:
Up above the pantry shelf,
Hastening to secrete yourself.

Most adventurous of vermin,
How I wish I could determine
How you spend your hours of
  ease,
Perhaps reclining on the cheese.

Cook has gone, and all is dark—
Then the kitchen is your park:
In the garbage heap that she
  leaves
Do you browse among the tea
  leaves?

How delightful to suspect
All the places you have trekked:

Does your long antenna whisk its
Gentle tip across the biscuits?

Do you linger, little soul,
Drowsing in our sugar bowl?
Or, abandonment most utter,
Shake a shimmy on the butter?

Do you chant your simple tunes
Swimming in the baby's prunes?
Then, when dawn comes, do you
  slink
Homeward to the kitchen sink?

Timid roach, why be so shy?
We are brothers, thou and I.
In the midnight, like yourself,
I explore the pantry shelf!
                    CHRISTOPHER MORLEY

TO A WATERFOWL

Whither, 'midst falling dew,
While glow the heavens with the
    last steps of day,
Far, through their rosy depths,
    dost thou pursue
    Thy solitary way!

Vainly the fowler's eye
Might mark thy distant flight to
    do thee wrong,
As, darkly painted on the crimson
    sky,
    Thy figure floats along.

Seek'st thou the plashy brink
Of weedy lake, or marge of river
    wide,
Or where the rocking billows rise
    and sink
    On the chafed ocean side?

There is a power whose care
Teaches thy way along that
    pathless coast,—
The desert and illimitable air,—
    Lone wandering, but not lost.

All day thy wings have fanned,
At that far height, the cold, thin
    atmosphere,
Yet stoop not, weary, to the
    welcome land,
    Though the dark night is near.

And soon that toil shall end;
Soon shalt thou find a summer
    home, and rest,
And scream among thy fellows;
    reeds shall bend,
    Soon, o'er thy sheltered nest.

Thou'rt gone, the abyss of heaven
Hath swallowed up thy form; yet,
    on my heart
Deeply hath sunk the lesson thou
    hast given,
    And shall not soon depart.

He who, from zone to zone,
Guides through the boundless sky
    thy certain flight,
In the long way that I must tread
    alone,
    Will lead my steps aright.

WILLIAM CULLEN BRYANT

A NARROW FELLOW IN THE GRASS
(The Snake)

A narrow fellow in the grass
Occasionally rides;
You may have met him,—did you
    not?
His notice sudden is.

The grass divides as with a comb,
A spotted shaft is seen;
And then it closes at your feet
And opens further on.

He likes a boggy acre,
A floor to cool for corn.
Yet when a child, and barefoot,
I more than once, at morn,

Have passed, I thought, a whip-
    lash
Unbraiding in the sun,—
When, stooping to secure it,
It wrinkled, and was gone.

Several of nature's people
I know, and they know me;
I feel for them a transport
Of cordiality;

But never met this fellow,
Attended or alone,
Without a tighter breathing,
And zero at the bone.

EMILY DICKINSON

MILK FOR THE CAT

When the tea is brought at five
    o'clock,
And all the neat curtains are
    drawn with care,
The little black cat with bright
    green eyes
Is suddenly purring there.

At first she pretends, having
    nothing to do,
She has come in merely to blink
    by the grate,
But, though tea may be late or the
    milk may be sour,
She is never late.

And presently her agate eyes
Take a soft large, milky haze
And her independent casual glance
Becomes a stiff, hard gaze.

Then she stamps her claws or lifts
    her ears,
Or twists her tail and begins to stir,
Till suddenly all her lithe body
    becomes
One breathing, trembling purr.

The children eat and wriggle and
    laugh,
The two old ladies stroke their silk:
But the cat is grown small and
    thin with desire,
Transformed to a creeping lust
    for milk.

The white saucer like some full
    moon descends
At last from the clouds of the
    table above;

She sighs and dreams and thrills
    and glows,
Transfigured with love.

She nestles over the shining rim,
Buries her chin in the creamy sea;
Her tail hangs loose; each drowsy
    paw
Is doubled under each bending knee.

A long, dim ecstasy holds her life;
Her world is an infinite shapeless
    white,
Till her tongue has curled the
    last holy drop,
Then she sinks back into the night,

Draws and dips her body to heap
Her sleepy nerves in the great
    armchair,
Lies defeated and buried deep
Three or four hours unconscious
    there.

                            HAROLD MONRO

THE TIGER

Tiger, tiger, burning bright
In the forests of the night,
What immortal hand or eye
Could frame thy fearful symmetry?

In what distant deeps or skies
Burnt the fire of thine eyes?
On what wings dare he aspire?
What the hand dare seize the fire?

And what shoulder and what art
Could twist the sinews of thy heart?
And, when thy heart began to beat,
What dread hand and what dread feet?

What the hammer? What the chain?
In what furnace was thy brain?
What the anvil? What dread grasp
Dare its deadly terrors clasp?

When the stars threw down their spe
And water'd heaven with their tears,
Did He smile His work to see?
Did He who made the lamb make th

Tiger, tiger, burning bright
In the forests of the night,
What immortal hand or eye
Dare frame thy fearful symmetry?

                            WILLIAM BLAKE

HOW TO TELL THE WILD ANIMALS

If ever you should go by chance
  To jungles in the East;
And if there should to you
    advance
  A large and tawny beast,
If he roars at you as you're dyin'
You'll know it is the Asian Lion.

Or if some time when roaming
    round,
  A noble wild beast greets you,
With black stripes on a yellow
    ground,
  Just notice if he eats you.
This simple rule may help you
    learn
The Bengal Tiger to discern.

If strolling forth, a beast you view,
  Whose hide with spots is
    peppered,
As soon as he has lept on you,
  You'll know it is the Leopard.
'Twill do no good to roar with
    pain,
He'll only lep and lep again.

If when you're walking round
    your yard,
  You meet a creature there,
Who hugs you very, very hard,
  Be sure it is the Bear.
If you have any doubt, I guess
He'll give you just one more
    caress.

Though to distinguish beasts of
    prey
  A novice might nonplus,
The Crocodiles you always may
  Tell from Hyenas thus:
Hyenas come with merry smiles;
But if they weep, they're
    Crocodiles.

The true Chameleon is small,
  A lizard sort of thing;
He hasn't any ears at all,
  And not a single wing.
If there is nothing in the tree,
'Tis the Chameleon you see.

CAROLYN WELLS

THE PRAYING MANTIS VISITS A PENTHOUSE

The praying Mantis with its length of straw
Out of the nowhere's forehead born full armed
Engages the century at my terrace door.
Focused at inches the dinosaur insect sends
Broadsides of epic stillness at my eye,
Above the deafening projects of the age.

My wife, who fears the thunder of its poise,
Has seen it and cries out. The clouds like curls
Fall in my faith as I seize a stick to stop
This Martian raid distilled to a straw with legs,
To wisps of prowess. Bristling with motionlessness
The Mantis prays to the Stick twice armed with Man.
I strike, the stick whistles, shearing off two legs
Which run off by themselves beneath some boards.
The Mantis spreads out tints of batlike wing,
The many colored pennants of its blood,
And hugs my weapon; the frantic greens come out,
The reds and yellows blurt out from the straw,
All sinews doubtless screaming insect death.
Against the railing's edge I knock the stick
Sending that gay mad body into the gulf.
Such noisy trappings in defeat wake doubts.
I search my mind for possible wounds and feel
The victim's body heavy on the victor's heart.

OSCAR WILLIAMS

THE SONG OF THE MISCHIEVOUS DOG

There are many who say that a dog has his day,
And a cat has a number of lives;
There are others who think that a lobster is pink,
And that bees never work in their hives.
There are fewer, of course, who insist that a horse
Has a horn and two humps on its head,
And a fellow who jests that a mare can build nests
Is as rare as a donkey that's red.
Yet in spite of all this, I have moments of bliss,
For I cherish a passion for bones,
And though doubtful of biscuits, I'm willing to risk it,
And love to chase rabbits and stones.
But my greatest delight is to take a good bite
At a calf that is plump and delicious;
And if I indulge in a bite at a bulge,
Let's hope you won't think me too vicious.

DYLAN THOMAS, AGE 11

BOOK IX

MOTHER NATURE, FATHER TIME

WHAT IS SO RARE AS A DAY IN JUNE

And what is so rare as a day in
    June?
  Then, if ever, come perfect days;
Then Heaven tries earth if it be
    in tune,
  And over it softly her warm ear
    lays:
Whether we look, or whether we
    listen,
We hear life murmur, or see it
    glisten;
Every clod feels a stir of might,
  An instinct within it that
    reaches and towers,
And, groping blindly above it for
    light,
  Climbs to a soul in grass and
    flowers;
The flush of life may well be seen
  Thrilling back over hills and
    valleys;
The cowslip startles in meadows
    green,
The buttercup catches the sun in
    its chalice,
And there's never a leaf nor a
    blade too mean
  To be some happy creature's
    palace;
The little bird sits at his door in
    the sun,
  Atilt like a blossom among the
    leaves,
And lets his illumined being
    o'errun
  With the deluge of summer it
    receives;

His mate feels the eggs beneath
    her wings,
And the heart in her dumb breast
    flutters and sings;
He sings to the wide world, and
    she to her nest,—
In the nice ear of Nature which
    song is the best?

Now is the high-tide of the year,
  And whatever of life hath
    ebbed away
Comes flooding back with a
    ripply cheer,
  Into every bare inlet and creek
    and bay;
Now the heart is so full that a
    drop overfills it,
We are happy now because God
    wills it;
No matter how barren the past
    may have been,
'Tis enough for us now that the
    leaves are green;
We sit in the warm shade and feel
    right well
How the sap creeps up and the
    blossoms swell;
We may shut our eyes but we
    cannot help knowing
That skies are clear and grass is
    growing;
The breeze comes whispering in
    our ear,
That dandelions are blossoming
    near,
  That maize has sprouted, that
    streams are flowing,

That the river is bluer than the
sky,
That the robin is plastering his
house hard by;
And if the breeze kept the good
news back,
For our couriers we should not
lack;
We could guess it all by yon
heifer's lowing,—
And hark! how clear bold
chanticleer,
Warmed with the new wine of
the year,
Tells all in his lusty crowing!

Joy comes, grief goes, we know
not how;
Everything is happy now,
Everything is upward striving;
'Tis as easy now for the heart to
be true

As for grass to be green or skies to
be blue,—
'Tis for the natural way of
living:
Who knows whither the clouds
have fled?
In the unscarred heaven they
leave no wake,
And the eyes forget the tears they
have shed,
The heart forgets its sorrow and
ache;
The soul partakes the season's
youth,
And the sulphurous rifts of
passion and woe
Lie deep 'neath a silence pure
and smooth,
Like burnt-out craters healed
with snow.

JAMES RUSSELL LOWELL

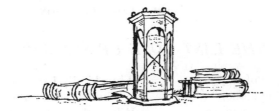

LITTLE THINGS

Little drops of water,
Little grains of sand,
Make the mighty ocean
And the pleasant land.

Thus the little minutes,
Humble though they be,
Make the mighty ages
Of eternity.

JULIA A. FLETCHER CARNEY

FOG

The fog comes
on little cat feet.

It sits looking
over harbor and city
on silent haunches
and then, moves on.

CARL SANDBURG

BLOW, BUGLE, BLOW

The splendour falls on castle walls
   And snowy summits old in story:
The long light shakes across the lakes,
   And the wild cataract leaps in glory.
Blow, bugle, blow, set the wild echoes flying,
Blow, bugle; answer, echoes, dying, dying, dying.

O hark, O hear! how thin and clear,
   And thinner, clearer, farther going!
O sweet and far from cliff and scar
   The horns of Elfland faintly blowing!
Blow, let us hear the purple glens replying:
Blow, bugle; answer, echoes, dying, dying, dying.

O love, they die in yon rich sky,
   They faint on hill or field or river:
Our echoes rolc from soul to soul,
   And grow for ever and for ever.
Blow, bugle, blow, set the wild echoes flying,
And answer, echoes, answer, dying, dying, dying.
                     ALFRED, LORD TENNYSON

THE LAST ROSE OF SUMMER

'Tis the last rose of summer
   Left blooming alone;
All her lovely companions
   Are faded and gone;
No flower of her kindred,
   No rose-bud is nigh,
To reflect back her blushes,
   Or give sigh for sigh.

I'll not leave thee, thou lone one!
   To pine on the stem;
Since the lovely are sleeping,
   Go, sleep thou with them.

Thus kindly I scatter
   Thy leaves o'er the bed
Where thy mates of the garden
   Lie scentless and dead.

So soon may I follow,
   When friendships decay,
And from Love's shining circle
   The gems drop away.
When true hearts lie withered,
   And fond ones are flown,
O! who would inhabit
   This bleak world alone?
                     THOMAS MOORE

THE OLD SWIMMIN'-HOLE

Oh! the old swimmin'-hole! whare the crick so still and deep
Looked like a baby-river that was laying half asleep,
And the gurgle of the worter round the drift jest below
Sounded like the laugh of something we onc't ust to know
Before we could remember anything but the eyes
Of the angels lookin' out as we left Paradise;
But the merry days of youth is beyond our controle,
And it's hard to part ferever with the old swimmin'-hole.

Oh! the old swimmin'-hole! In the happy days of yore,
When I ust to lean above it on the old sickamore,
Oh! it showed me a face in its warm sunny tide
That gazed back at me so gay and glorified,
It made me love myself, as I leaped to caress
My shadder smilin' up at me with sich tenderness.
But them days is past and gone, and old Time's tuck his toll
From the old man come back to the old swimmin'-hole.

Oh! the old swimmin'-hole! In the long, lazy days
When the humdrum of school made so many run-a-ways,
How plesant was the jurney down the old dusty lane,
Whare the tracks of our bare feet was all printed so plane
You could tell by the dent of the heel and the sole
They was lots o' fun on hand at the old swimmin'-hole.
But the lost joys is past! Let your tears in sorrow roll
Like the rain that ust to dapple up the old swimmin'-hole.

Thare the bulrushes growed, and the cattails so tall,
And the sunshine and shadder fell over it all;
And it mottled the worter with amber and gold
Tel the glad lilies rocked in the ripples that rolled;
And the snake-feeder's four gauzy wings fluttered by
Like the ghost of a daisy dropped out of the sky,
Or a wownded apple-blossom in the breeze's controle
As it cut acrost some orchurd to'rds the old swimmin'-hole.

Oh! the old swimmin'-hole! When I last saw the place,
The scenes was all changed, like the change in my face;
The bridge of the railroad now crosses the spot
Whare the old divin'-log lays sunk and fergot.
And I stray down the banks whare the trees ust to be—
But never again will theyr shade shelter me!
And I wish in my sorrow I could strip to the soul,
And dive off in my grave like the old swimmin'-hole.

JAMES WHITCOMB RILEY

THE WEST WIND

It's a warm wind, the west wind, full of birds' cries;
I never hear the west wind but tears are in my eyes.
For it comes from the west lands, the old brown hills,
And April's in the west wind, and daffodils.

It's a fine land, the west land, for hearts as tired as mine,
Apple orchards blossom there, and the air's like wine.
There is cool green grass there, where men may lie at rest;
And the thrushes are in song there, fluting from the nest.

"Will you not come home, brother? You have been long away.
It's April, and blossom time, and white is the spray:
And bright is the sun, brother, and warm is the rain;
Will you not come home, brother, home to us again?

"The young corn is green, brother, where the rabbits run;
It's blue sky, and white clouds, and warm rain and sun.
It's song to a man's soul, brother, fire to a man's brain,
To hear the wild bees and see the merry spring again.

"Larks are singing in the west, brother, above the green wheat,
So will you not come home, brother, and rest your tired feet?
I've a balm for bruised hearts, brother, sleep for aching eyes,"
Says the warm wind, the west wind, full of birds' cries.

It's the white road westwards is the road I must tread
To the green grass, the cool grass, and rest for heart and head,
To the violets and the brown brooks and the thrushes' song
In the fine land, the west land, the land where I belong.

JOHN MASEFIELD

WOODMAN, SPARE THAT TREE

Woodman, spare that tree!
Touch not a single bough!
In youth it sheltered me,
And I'll protect it now.
'Twas my forefather's hand
That placed it near his cot;
There, woodman, let it stand
Thy ax shall harm it not!

That old familiar tree,
Whose glory and renown
Are spread o'er land and sea,
And wouldst thou hew it down?
Woodman, forbear thy stroke!
Cut not its earth-bound ties!
Oh! spare that aged oak,
Now towering to the skies.

When but an idle boy
I sought its grateful shade;
In all their gushing joy
Here too my sisters played.
My mother kissed me here
My father pressed my hand—
Forgive this foolish tear,
But let that old oak stand!

My heart-strings round thee cling,
Close as thy bark, old friend!
Here shall the wild-bird sing,
And still thy branches bend.
Old tree, the storm still brave!
And, woodman, leave the spot!
While I've a hand to save,
Thy ax shall harm it not.

GEORGE P. MORRIS

FLOWER IN THE CRANNIED WALL

Flower in the crannied wall,
I pluck you out of the crannies,
I hold you here, root and all, in my hand,
Little flower—but *if* I could understand
What you are, root and all, and all in all,
I should know what God and man is.

ALFRED, LORD TENNYSON

ODE TO THE WEST WIND

O wild West Wind, thou breath of Autumn's being,
Thou, from whose unseen presence the leaves dead
Are driven, like ghosts from an enchanter fleeing,
Yellow, and black, and pale, and hectic red,
Pestilence-stricken multitudes: O thou
Who chariotest to their dark wintry bed
The wingéd seeds, where they lie cold and low,
Each like a corpse within its grave, until
Thine azure sister of the Spring shall blow
Her clarion o'er the dreaming earth, and fill
(Driving sweet buds like flocks to feed in air)
With living hues and odours plain and hill:
Wild spirit, which art moving everywhere;
Destroyer and preserver; Hear, oh, hear!

　　Thou on whose stream, 'mid the steep sky's commotion,
Loose clouds like earth's decaying leaves are shed,
Shook from the tangled boughs of Heaven and Ocean,
Angels of rain and lightning; there are spread
On the blue surface of thine airy surge,
Like the bright hair uplifted from the head
Of some fierce Maenad, ev'n from the dim verge
Of the horizon to the zenith's height—
The locks of the approaching storm. Thou dirge
Of the dying year, to which this closing night
Will be the dome of a vast sepulchre,
Vaulted with all thy congregated might
Of vapours, from whose solid atmosphere
Black rain, and fire, and hail, will burst; oh, hear!

　　Thou who didst waken from his summer-dreams
The blue Mediterranean, where he lay,
Lull'd by the coil of his crystalline streams,
Beside a pumice isle in Baiae's bay,
And saw in sleep old palaces and towers
Quivering within the wave's intenser day,

All overgrown with azure moss and flowers
So sweet, the sense faints picturing them! Thou
For whose path the Atlantic's level powers
Cleave themselves into chasms, while far below
The sea-blooms and the oozy woods which wear
The sapless foliage of the ocean, know
Thy voice, and suddenly grow grey with fear
And tremble and despoil themselves: oh, hear!

If I were a dead leaf thou mightest bear;
If I were a swift cloud to fly with thee;
A wave to pant beneath thy power, and share
The impulse of thy strength, only less free
Than thou, O uncontrollable! If even
I were as in my boyhood, and could be
The comrade of thy wanderings over heaven,
As then, when to outstrip thy skiey speed
Scarce seem'd a vision, I would ne'er have striven
As thus with thee in prayer in my sore need.
Oh, lift me as a wave, a leaf, a cloud!
I fall upon the thorns of life! I bleed!
A heavy weight of hours has chain'd and bow'd
One too like thee: tameless, and swift, and proud.

Make me thy lyre, ev'n as the forest is:
What if my leaves are falling like its own?
The tumult of thy mighty harmonies
Will take from both a deep autumnal tone,
Sweet though in sadness. Be thou, Spirit fierce,
My spirit! be thou me, impetuous one!
Drive my dead thoughts over the universe
Like wither'd leaves to quicken a new birth;
And, by the incantation of this verse,
Scatter, as from an unextinguish'd hearth
Ashes and sparks, my words among mankind!
Be through my lips to unawaken'd earth
The trumpet of a prophecy! O Wind,
If Winter comes, can Spring be far behind?

PERCY BYSSHE SHELLEY

HOME-THOUGHTS FROM ABROAD

Oh, to be in England
Now that April's there,
And whoever wakes in England
Sees, some morning, unaware,
That the lowest boughs and the brush-wood sheaf
Round the elm-tree bole are in tiny leaf,
While the chaffinch sings on the orchard bough
In England—now!

And after April, when May follows,
And the whitethroat builds, and all the swallows—
Hark! where my blossomed pear-tree in the hedge
Leans to the field and scatters on the clover
Blossoms and dewdrops—at the bent-spray's edge—
That's the wise thrush; he sings each song twice over,
Lest you should think he never could recapture
The first fine careless rapture!
And though the fields look rough with hoary dew,
All will be gay when noontide wakes anew
The buttercups, the little children's dower,
—Far brighter than this gaudy melon-flower!

ROBERT BROWNING

GREEN THINGS GROWING

O the green things growing, the green things growing,
The faint sweet smell of the green things growing!
I should like to live, whether I smile or grieve,
Just to watch the happy life of my green things growing.

O the fluttering and the pattering of those green things growing!
How they talk each to each, when none of us are knowing;
In the wonderful white of the weird moonlight
Or the dim dreamy dawn when the cocks are crowing.

I love, I love them so—my green things growing!
And I think that they love me, without false showing;
For by many a tender touch, they comfort me so much,
With the soft mute comfort of green things growing.

And in the rich store of their blossoms glowing
Ten for one I take they're on me bestowing:
Oh, I should like to see, if God's will it may be,
Many, many a summer of my green things growing!

But if I must be gathered for the angel's sowing,
Sleep out of sight awhile, like the green things growing,
Though dust to dust return, I think I'll scarcely mourn,
If I may change into green things growing.

DINAH MARIA MULOCK CRAIK

TREES

I think that I shall never see
A poem lovely as a tree.

A tree whose hungry mouth is
pressed
Against the earth's sweet flowing
breast;

A tree that looks at God all day
And lifts her leafy arms to pray;

A tree that may in summer wear
A nest of robins in her hair;

Upon whose bosom snow has lain;
Who intimately lives with rain.

Poems are made by fools like me,
But only God can make a tree.

JOYCE KILMER

SOLITUDE

Happy the man, whose wish and
　care
A few paternal acres bound,
Content to breathe his native air
　　In his own ground.

Whose herds with milk, whose
　fields with bread,
Whose flocks supply him with
　attire;
Whose trees in summer yield him
　shade,
　　In winter, fire.

Blest, who can unconcernedly find
Hours, days, and years slide soft away

In health of body, peace of mind;
　　Quiet by day,

Sound sleep by night; study and
　ease
Together mixed, sweet recreation,
And innocence, which most does
　please
　　With meditation.

Thus let me live, unseen,
　unknown;
Thus unlamented let me die,
Steal from the world, and not a
　stone
　　Tell where I lie.

ALEXANDER POPE

LEISURE

What is this life, if, full of care,
We have no time to stand and
　stare,

No time to stand beneath the
　boughs
And stare as long as sheep or
　cows.

No time to see, when woods we
　pass,
Where squirrels hide their nuts in
　grass.

No time to see, in broad daylight,
Streams full of stars, like skies at
　night.

No time to turn at Beauty's glance,
And watch her feet, how they can
　dance.

No time to wait till her mouth can
Enrich that smile her eyes began.

A poor life this if, full of care,
We have no time to stand and stare.

W. H. DAVIES

SONG OF THE OPEN ROAD

I

Afoot and light-hearted I take to the open road,
Healthy, free, the world before me,
The long brown path before me leading wherever I choose.
Henceforth I ask not good-fortune, I myself am good-fortune,
Henceforth I whimper no more, postpone no more, need nothing,
Done with indoor complaints, libraries, querulous criticisms,
Strong and content I travel the open road.
The earth, that is sufficient,
I do not want the constellations any nearer,
I know they are very well where they are,
I know they suffice for those who belong to them.

(Still here I carry my old delicious burdens,
I carry them, men and women, I carry them with me wherever I go,
I swear it is impossible for me to get rid of them,
I am fill'd with them; and I will fill them in return.)

II

You road I enter upon and look around, I believe you are not all that is here,
I believe that much unseen is also here.
Here the profound lesson of reception, nor preference nor denial,
The black with his woolly head, the felon, the diseas'd, the illiterate per-
    son, are not denied;
The birth, the hasting after the physician, the beggar's tramp, the drunk-
    ard's stagger, the laughing party of mechanics,
The escaped youth, the rich person's carriage, the fop, the eloping couple,

The early market-man, the hearse, the moving of furniture into the town,
the return back from the town,
They pass, I also pass, any thing passes, none can be interdicted,
None but are accepted, none but shall be dear to me.

III

You air that serves me with breath to speak!
You objects that call from diffusion my meanings and give them shape!
You light that wraps me and all things in delicate equable showers!
You paths worn in the irregular hollows by the roadsides!
I believe you are latent with unseen existences, you are so dear to me.
You flagg'd walks of the cities! you strong curbs at the edges!
You ferries! you planks and posts of wharves! you timberlined sides! you
distant ships!
You rows of houses! you window-pierc'd façades! you roofs!
You porches and entrances! you copings and iron guards!
You windows whose transparent shells might expose so much!
You doors and ascending steps! you arches!
You gray stones of interminable pavements! you trodden crossings!
From all that has touch'd you I believe you have imparted to yourselves,
and now would impart the same secretly to me,
From the living and the dead you have peopled your impassive surfaces,
and the spirits thereof would be evident and amicable with me.

IV

The earth expanding right hand and left hand,
The picture alive, every part in its best light,
The music falling in where it is wanted, and stopping where it is not
wanted,
The cheerful voice of the public road, the gay fresh sentiment of the road.
O highway I travel, do you say to me *Do not leave me?*
Do you say *Venture not—if you leave me you are lost?*
Do you say *I am already prepared, I am well-beaten and undenied, ad-
here to me?*
O public road, I say back I am not afraid to leave you, yet I love you,
You express me better than I can express myself,
You shall be more to me than my poem.
I think heroic deeds were all conceiv'd in the open air, and all free poems al
I think I could stop here myself and do miracles,
I think whatever I shall meet on the road I shall like, and whoever be-
holds me shall like me,
I think whoever I see must be happy.

V

From this hour I ordain myself loos'd of limits and imaginary lines,
Going where I list, my own master total and absolute,
Listening to others, considering well what they say,
Pausing, searching, receiving, contemplating,
Gently, but with undeniable will, divesting myself of the holds that would
    hold me.
I inhale great draughts of space,
The east and the west are mine, and the north and the south are mine.
I am larger, better than I thought,
I did not know I held so much goodness.
All seems beautiful to me,
I can repeat over to men and women You have done such good to me I
    would do the same to you,
I will recruit for myself and you as I go,
I will scatter myself among men and women as I go,
I will toss a new gladness and roughness among them,
Whoever denies me it shall not trouble me,
Whoever accepts me he or she shall be blessed and shall bless me.

VI

Now if a thousand perfect men were to appear it would not amaze me,
Now if a thousand beautiful forms of women appear'd it would not as-
    tonish me.
Now I see the secret of the making of the best persons,
It is to grow in the open air and to eat and sleep with the earth.
Here a great personal deed has room,
(Such a deed seizes upon the hearts of the whole race of men,
Its effusion of strength and will overwhelms law and mocks all authority
    and all argument against it.)

Here is the test of wisdom,
Wisdom is not finally tested in schools,
Wisdom cannot be pass'd from one having it to another not having it,
Wisdom is of the soul, is not susceptible of proof, is its own proof,
Applies to all stages and objects and qualities and is content,
Is the certainty of the reality and immortality of things, and the excel-
    lence of things;
Something there is in the float of the sight of things that provokes it out
    of the soul.

Now I re-examine philosophies and religions,
They may prove well in lecture-rooms, yet not prove at all under the
    spacious clouds and along the landscape and flowing currents.
Here is realization,
Here is a man tallied—he realizes here what he has in him,
The past, the future, majesty, love—if they are vacant of you, you are
    vacant of them.
Only the kernel of every object nourishes;
Where is he who tears off the husks for you and me?
Where is he that undoes stratagems and envelopes for you and me?
Here is adhesiveness, it is not previously fashion'd, it is apropos;
Do you know what it is as you pass to be loved by strangers?
Do you know the talk of those turning eye-balls?

VII

Here is the efflux of the soul,
The efflux of the soul comes from within through embower'd gates, ever
    provoking questions,
These yearnings why are they? these thoughts in the darkness why are
    they?
Why are there men and women that while they are nigh me the sunlight
    expands my blood?
Why when they leave me do my pennants of joy sink flat and lank?
Why are there trees I never walk under but large and melodious thoughts
    descend upon me?
(I think they hang there winter and summer on those trees and always
    drop fruit as I pass;)
What is it I interchange so suddenly with strangers?
What with some driver as I ride on the seat by his side?
What with some fisherman drawing his seine by the shore as I walk by
    and pause?
What gives me to be free to a woman's and man's good-will? what gives
    them to be free to mine?

VIII

The efflux of the soul is happiness, here is happiness,
I think it pervades the open air, waiting at all times,
Now it flows unto us, we are rightly charged.
Here rises the fluid and attaching character,

The fluid and attaching character is the freshness and sweetness of man
and woman,
(The herbs of the morning sprout no fresher and sweeter every day out
of the roots of themselves, than it sprouts fresh and sweet continually
out of itself.)
Toward the fluid and attaching character exudes the sweat of the love of
young and old,
From it falls distill'd the charm that mocks beauty and attainments,
Toward it heaves the shuddering longing ache of contact.

IX

Allons! whoever you are come travel with me!
Traveling with me you find what never tires.
The earth never tires,
The earth is rude, silent, incomprehensible at first, Nature is rude and
incomprehensible at first,
Be not discouraged, keep on, there are divine things well envelop'd,
I swear to you there are divine things more beautiful than words can tell.
Allons! we must not stop here,
However sweet these laid-up stores, however convenient this dwelling we
cannot remain here,
However shelter'd this port and however calm these waters we must not
anchor here,
However welcome the hospitality that surrounds us we are permitted to
receive it but a little while.

X

Allons! the inducements shall be greater,
We will sail pathless and wild seas,
We will go where winds blow, waves dash, and the Yankee clipper speeds
by under full sail.
Allons! with power, liberty, the earth, the elements,
Health, defiance, gayety, self-esteem, curiosity;
Allons! from all formules!
From your formules, O bat-eyed and materialistic priests.
The stale cadaver blocks up the passage—the burial waits no longer.
Allons! yet take warning!
He traveling with me needs the best blood, thews, endurance,
None may come to the trial till he or she bring courage and health,
Come not here if you have already spent the best of yourself,

Only those may come who come in sweet and determin'd bodies,
No diseas'd person, no rum-drinker or venereal taint is permitted here.
 (I and mine do not convince by arguments, similes, rhymes,
We convince by our presence.)

XI

Listen! I will be honest with you,
I do not offer the old smooth prizes, but offer rough new prizes,
These are the days that must happen to you:
You shall not heap up what is call'd riches,
You shall scatter with lavish hand all that you earn or achieve,
You but arrive at the city to which you were destin'd, you hardly settle
    yourself to satisfaction before you are call'd by an irresistible call to
    depart,
You shall be treated to the ironical smiles and mockings of those who re-
    main behind you,
What beckonings of love you receive you shall only answer with passion-
    ate kisses of parting,
You shall not allow the hold of those who spread their reach'd hands
    toward you.

XII

Allons! after the great Companions, and to belong to them!
They too are on the road—they are the swift and majestic men—they
    are the greatest women,
Enjoyers of calms of seas and storms of seas,
Sailors of many a ship, walkers of many a mile of land,
Habitués of many distant countries, habitués of far-distant dwellings,
Trusters of men and women, observers of cities, solitary toilers,
Pausers and contemplators of tufts, blossoms, shells of the shore,
Dancers at wedding-dances, kissers of brides, tender helpers of children,
    bearers of children,
Soldiers of revòlts, standers by gaping graves, lowerers-down of coffins,
Journeyers over consecutive seasons, over the years, the curious years
    each emerging from that which preceded it,
Journeyers as with companions, namely their own diverse phases,
Forth-steppers from the latent unrealized baby-days,
Journeyers gayly with their own youth, journeyers with their bearded and
    well-grain'd manhood,
Journeyers with their womanhood, ample, unsurpass'd, content,
Journeyers with their own sublime old age of manhood or womanhood,
Old age, calm, expanded, broad with the haughty breadth of the universe,
Old age, flowing free with the delicious near-by freedom of death.

XIII

Allons! to that which is endless as it was beginningless,
To undergo much, tramps of days, rests of nights,
To merge all in the travel they tend to, and the days and nights they
    tend to,
Again to merge them in the start of superior journeys,
To see nothing anywhere but what you may reach it and pass it,
To conceive no time, however distant, but what you may reach it and
    pass it,
To look up or down no road but it stretches and waits for you, however
    long but it stretches and waits for you,
To see no being, not God's or any, but you also go thither,
To see no possession but you may possess it, enjoying all without labor or
    purchase, abstracting the feast yet not abstracting one particle of it,
To take the best of the farmer's farm and the rich man's elegant villa,
    and the chaste blessings of the well-married couple, and the fruits of
    orchards and flowers of gardens,
To take to your use out of the compact cities as you pass through,
To carry buildings and streets with you afterward wherever you go,
To gather the minds of men out of their brains as you encounter them,
    to gather the love out of their hearts,
To take your lovers on the road with you, for all that you leave them be-
    hind you,
To know the universe itself as a road, as many roads, as roads for travel-
    ing souls.
All parts away for the progress of souls,
All religion, all solid things, arts, governments—all that was or is ap-
    parent upon this globe or any globe, falls into niches and corners be-
    fore the procession of souls along the grand roads of the universe.
Of the progress of the souls of men and women along the grand roads of
    the universe, all other progress is the needed emblem and sustenance.
Forever alive, forever forward,
Stately, solemn, sad, withdrawn, baffled, mad, turbulent, feeble, dissatisfied,
Desperate, proud, fond, sick, accepted by men, rejected by men,
They go! they go! I know that they go, but I know not where they go,
But I know that they go toward the best—toward something great.

Whoever you are, come forth! or man or woman come forth!
You must not stay sleeping and dallying there in the house, though you
    built it, or though it has been built for you.

Out of the dark confinement! out from behind the screen!
It is useless to protest. I know all and expose it.
Behold through you as bad as the rest,
Through the laughter, dancing, dining, supping, of people,
Inside of dresses and ornaments, inside of those wash'd and trimm'd faces,
Behold a secret silent loathing and despair.

No husband, no wife, no friend, trusted to hear the confession,
Another self, a duplicate of every one, skulking and hiding it goes,
Formless and wordless through the streets of the cities, polite and bland
  in the parlors,
In the cars of railroads, in steamboats, in the public assembly,
Home to the houses of men and women, at the table, in the bedroom,
  everywhere,
Smartly attired, countenance smiling, form upright, death under the
  breast-bones, hell under the skull-bones,
Under the broadcloth and gloves, under the ribbons and artificial flowers,
Keeping fair with the customs, speaking not a syllable of itself,
Speaking of any thing else but never of itself.

XIV

Allons! through struggles and wars!
The goal that was named cannot be countermanded.
Have the past struggles succeeded?
What has succeeded? yourself? your nation? Nature?
Now understand me well—it is provided in the essence of things that
  from any fruition of success, no matter what, shall come forth some-
  thing to make a greater struggle necessary.
My call is the call of battle, I nourish active rebellion,
He going with me must go well arm'd,
He going with me goes often with spare diet, poverty, angry enemies,
  desertions.

XV

Allons! the road is before us!
It is safe—I have tried it—my own feet have tried it well—be not de-
  tain'd!
Let the paper remain on the desk unwritten, and the book on the shelf
  unopen'd!

WALT WHITMAN

BLOW, THOU WINTER WIND

Blow, blow, thou winter wind,
Thou art not so unkind
    As man's ingratitude;
Thy tooth is not so keen,
Because thou art not seen,
    Although thy breath be rude.

Heigh-ho! sing, heigh-ho! unto
    the green holly:
Most friendship is feigning, most
    loving mere folly:

Then, heigh-ho, the holly!
    This life is most jolly.

Freeze, freeze, thou bitter sky,
That dost not bite so nigh
    As benefits forgot:
Though thou the waters warp,
Thy sting is not so sharp
    As friend remember'd not.

WILLIAM SHAKESPEARE

STOPPING BY WOODS ON A SNOWY EVENING

Whose woods these are I think I know.
His house is in the village though;
He will not see me stopping here
To watch his woods fill up with snow.

My little horse must think it queer
To stop without a farmhouse near
Between the woods and frozen lake
The darkest evening of the year.

He gives his harness bells a shake
To ask if there is some mistake.
The only other sound's the sweep
Of easy wind and downy flake.

The woods are lovely, dark and deep.
But I have promises to keep,
And miles to go before I sleep,
And miles to go before I sleep.

ROBERT FROST

THE LAKE ISLE OF INNISFREE

I will arise and go now, and go to Innisfree,
And a small cabin build there, of clay and wattles made:
Nine bean-rows will I have there, a hive for the honey-bee,
And live alone in the bee-loud glade.

And I shall have some peace there, for peace comes dropping slow,
Dropping from the veils of the morning to where the cricket sings;
There midnight's all a glimmer, and noon a purple glow,
And evening full of linnet's wings.

I will arise and go now, for always night and day
I hear lake water lapping with low sounds by the shore;
While I stand on the roadway, or on the pavements grey,
I hear it in the deep heart's core.

WILLIAM BUTLER YEATS

DAFFODILS

I wandered lonely as a cloud
　　That floats on high o'er vales
　　　and hills,
When all at once I saw a crowd,
　A host, of golden daffodils;
Beside the lake, beneath the trees,
Fluttering and dancing in the breeze.

Continuous as the stars that shine
　And twinkle on the Milky Way,
They stretched in never-ending line
　Along the margin of a bay:
Ten thousand saw I at a glance,
Tossing their heads in sprightly
　　dance.

The waves beside them danced,
　　but they
　　Out-did the sparkling waves in glee:
A poet could not but be gay,
　In such a jocund company:
I gazed—and gazed—but little thought
What wealth the show to me had
　　brought:

For oft, when on my couch I lie
　In vacant or in pensive mood,
They flash upon that inward eye
　Which is the bliss of solitude;
And then my heart with pleasure fills,
And dances with the daffodils.

WILLIAM WORDSWORTH

THE BROOK'S SONG

I come from haunts of coot and
    hern,
  I make a sudden sally,
And sparkle out among the fern,
  To bicker down a valley.

By thirty hills I hurry down,
  Or slip between the ridges,
By twenty thorps, a little town,
  And half a hundred bridges.

Till last by Philip's farm I flow
  To join the brimming river,
For men may come and men may
    go,
  But I go on for ever.

I chatter over stony ways,
  In little sharps and trebles,
I bubble into eddying bays,
  I babble on the pebbles.

With many a curve my banks I
    fret
  By many a field and fallow,
And many a fairy foreland set
  With willow-weed and mallow.

I chatter, chatter, as I flow
  To join the brimming river,
For men may come and men may
    go,
  But I go on for ever.

I wind about, and in and out,
  With here a blossom sailing,

And here and there a lusty trout,
  And here and there a grayling,

And here and there a foamy flake
  Upon me, as I travel
With many a silvery water-break
  Above the golden gravel,

And draw them all along, and
    flow
  To join the brimming river,
For men may come and men may
    go,
  But I go on for ever.

I steal by lawns and grassy plots,
  I slide by hazel covers;
I move the sweet forget-me-nots
  That grow for happy lovers.

I slip, I slide, I gloom, I glance,
  Among my skimming swallows;
I make the netted sunbeam dance
  Against my sandy shallows.

I murmur under moon and stars
  In brambly wildernesses;
I linger by my shingly bars;
  I loiter round my cresses;

And out again I curve and flow
  To join the brimming river,
For men may come and men may
    go,
  But I go on for ever

    ALFRED, LORD TENNYSON

THE TIDE RISES, THE TIDE FALLS

The tide rises, the tide falls,
The twilight darkens, the curlew
    calls;
Along the sea-sands damp and
    brown
The traveller hastens toward the
    town,
    And the tide rises, the tide falls.

Darkness settles on roofs and walls,
But the sea, the sea in the
    darkness calls;

The little waves, with their soft,
    white hands,
Efface the footprints in the sands,
    And the tide rises, the tide falls.

The morning breaks; the steeds in
    their stalls
Stamp and neigh, as the hostler
    calls;
The day returns, but nevermore
Returns the traveller to the shore,
    And the tide rises, the tide falls.

HENRY WADSWORTH LONGFELLOW

FEAR NO MORE

Fear no more the heat o' th' sun,
    Nor the furious winter's rages;
Thou thy worldly task hast done,
    Home art gone, and ta'en thy
        wages:
Golden lads and girls all must,
As chimney-sweepers, come to dust.

Fear no more the frown o' th' great;
    Thou art past the tyrant's stroke;
Care no more to clothe and eat;
    To thee the reed is as the oak;

The Sceptre, Learning, Physic,
    must
All follow this, and come to dust.

Fear no more the lightning-flash,
    Nor th' all-dreaded thunder-
      stone;
Fear not slander, censure rash;
    Thou hast finished joy and
      moan:
All lovers young, all lovers must
Consign to thee, and come to dust.

WILLIAM SHAKESPEARE

LIKE AS THE WAVES

Like as the waves make towards the pebbled shore,
So do our minutes hasten to their end;
Each changing place with that which goes before,
In sequent toil all forwards do contend.
Nativity, once in the main light,
Crawls to maturity, wherewith being crown'd,
Crooked eclipses 'gainst his glory fight,
And Time that gave doth now his gift confound.

Time doth transfix the flourish set on youth
And delves the parallels in beauty's brow,
Feeds on the rarities of nature's truth,
And nothing stands but for his scythe to mow:
And yet to times in hope my verse shall stand,
Praising thy worth, despite his cruel hand.

WILLIAM SHAKESPEARE

WHEN I HAVE SEEN BY TIME'S FELL HAND

When I have seen by Time's fell hand defaced
The rich proud cost of outworn buried age;
When sometime lofty towers I see down-razed
And brass eternal slave to mortal rage;
When I have seen the hungry ocean gain
Advantage on the kingdom of the shore,
And the firm soil win of the watery main,
Increasing store with loss and loss with store;

When I have seen such interchange of state,
Or state itself confounded to decay;
Ruin hath taught me thus to ruminate,
That Time will come and take my love away.
This thought is as a death, which cannot choose
But weep to have that which it fears to lose.

WILLIAM SHAKESPEARE

WHEN I DO COUNT THE CLOCK

When I do count the clock that tells the time,
And see the brave day sunk in hideous night;
When I behold the violet past prime,
And sable curls all silvered o'er with white;
When lofty trees I see barren of leaves,
Which erst from heat did canopy the herd,
And summer's green all girded up in sheaves
Borne on the bier with white and bristly beard,
Then of thy beauty do I question make,
That thou among the wastes of time must go,
Since sweets and beauties do themselves forsake
And die as fast as they see others grow;
    And nothing 'gainst Time's scythe can make defence
    Save breed, to brave him when he takes thee hence.

WILLIAM SHAKESPEARE

FULL MANY A GLORIOUS MORNING

Full many a glorious morning have I seen
Flatter the mountain-tops with sovereign eye,
Kissing with golden face the meadows green,
Gilding pale streams with heavenly alchemy;
Anon permit the basest clouds to ride
With ugly rack on his celestial face,
And from the forlorn world his visage hide,
Stealing unseen to west with this disgrace:

Even so my sun one early morn did shine
With all-triumphant splendour on my brow;
But out, alack! he was but one hour mine;
The region cloud hath mask'd him from me now.
Yet him for this my love no whit disdaineth;
Suns of the world may stain when heaven's sun staineth.

WILLIAM SHAKESPEARE

OUT WHERE THE WEST BEGINS

Out where the handclasp's a little stronger,
Out where the smile dwells a little longer,
   That's where the West begins;
Out where the sun is a little brighter,
Where the snows that fall are a trifle whiter,
Where the bonds of home are a wee bit tighter,—
   That's where the West begins.

Out where the skies are a trifle bluer,
Out where friendship's a little truer,
   That's where the West begins;
Out where a fresher breeze is blowing,
Where there's laughter in every streamlet flowing,
Where there's more of reaping and less of sowing,—
   That's where the West begins.

Out where the world is in the making,
Where fewer hearts in despair are aching,
   That's where the West begins;
Where there's more of singing and less of sighing,
Where there's more of giving and less of buying,
And a man makes friends without half trying—
   That's where the West begins.

                  ARTHUR CHAPMAN

UNDER THE GREENWOOD TREE

Under the greenwood tree
Who loves to lie with me,
And turn his merry note
Unto the sweet bird's throat—
Come hither, come hither, come
   hither!
   Here shall he see
   No enemy
But winter and rough weather.

Who doth ambition shun
And loves to live i' the sun,
Seeking the food he eats
And pleased with what he gets—
Come hither, come hither, come
   hither!
   Here shall he see
   No enemy
But winter and rough weather.

                  WILLIAM SHAKESPEARE

A THING OF BEAUTY

A thing of beauty is a joy for ever:
Its loveliness increases; it will never
Pass into nothingness; but still will keep
A bower quiet for us, and a sleep
Full of sweet dreams, and health, and quiet breathing.
Therefore, on every morrow, are we wreathing
A flowery band to bind us to the earth,
Spite of despondence, of the inhuman dearth
Of noble natures, of the gloomy days,
Of all the unhealthy and o'er-darkened ways
Made for our searching: yes, in spite of all,
Some shape of beauty moves away the pall
From our dark spirits. Such the sun, the moon,
Trees old and young, sprouting a shady boon
For simple sheep; and such are daffodils
With the green world they live in; and clear rills
That for themselves a cooling covert make
'Gainst the hot season; the mid-forest brake,
Rich with a sprinkling of fair musk-rose blooms:
And such too is the grandeur of the dooms
We have imagined for the mighty dead;
All lovely tales that we have heard or read:
An endless fountain of immortal drink,
Pouring unto us from the heaven's brink.
Nor do we merely feel these essences
For one short hour; no, even as the trees
That whisper round a temple become soon
Dear as the temple's self, so does the moon,
The passion poesy, glories infinite,
Haunt us till they become a cheering light
Unto our souls, and bound to us so fast,
That, whether there be shine, or gloom o'ercast,
They always must be with us, or we die.

JOHN KEATS

BOOK X

THE EVERYDAY SCENE

OVER THE HILL TO THE POOR-HOUSE

Over the hill to the poor-house I'm trudgin' my weary way—
I, a woman of seventy, and only a trifle gray—
I, who am smart an' chipper, for all the years I've told,
As many another woman that's only half as old.

Over the hill to the poor-house—I can't quite make it clear!
Over the hill to the poor-house—it seems so horrid queer!
Many a step I've taken a-toilin' to and fro,
But this is a sort of journey I never thought to go.

What is the use of heapin' on me a pauper's shame?
Am I lazy or crazy? am I blind or lame?
True, I am not so supple, nor yet so awful stout;
But charity ain't no favor, if one can live without.

I am willin' and anxious an' ready any day
To work for a decent livin', an' pay my honest way;
For I can earn my victuals, an' more too, I'll be bound,
If anybody only is willin' to have me round.

Once I was young an' han'some—I was, upon my soul—
Once my cheeks was roses, my eyes as black as coal;
And I can't remember, in them days, of hearin' people say,
For any kind of a reason, that I was in their way.

'T ain't no use of boastin', or talkin' over free,
But many a house an' home was open then to me;
Many a han'some offer I had from likely men,
And nobody ever hinted that I was a burden then.

And when to John I was married, sure he was good and smart,
But he and all the neighbors would own I done my part;
For life was all before me, an' I was young an' strong,
And I worked the best that I could in tryin' to get along.

And so we worked together: and life was hard, but gay,
With now and then a baby for to cheer us on our way;
Till we had half a dozen, an' all growed clean an' neat,
An' went to school like others, an' had enough to eat.

So we worked for the child'rn, and raised 'em every one;
Worked for 'em summer and winter, just as we ought to've done;
Only perhaps we humored 'em, which some good folks condemn,
But every couple's child'rn's a heap the best to them.

Strange how much we think of our blessed little ones!—
I'd have died for my daughters, I'd have died for my sons!
And God he made that rule of love; but when we're old and gray,
I've noticed it sometimes somehow fails to work the other way.

So they have shirked and slighted me, an' shifted me about—
So they have well-nigh soured me, an' wore my old heart out;
But still I've borne up pretty well, an' wasn't much put down,
Till Charley went to the poor-master, an' put me on the town.

Over the hill to the poor-house—my child'rn dear, good-by!
Many a night I've watched you when only God was nigh;
And God'll judge between us; but I will al'ays pray
That you shall never suffer the half I do today.

WILL CARLETON

THE WORLD IS TOO MUCH WITH US

The world is too much with us; late and soon,
Getting and spending, we lay waste our powers:
Little we see in Nature that is ours;
We have given our hearts away, a sordid boon!
This Sea that bares her bosom to the moon;
The winds that will be howling at all hours,
And are up-gathered now like sleeping flowers;
For this, for everything, we are out of tune;
It moves us not.—Great God! I'd rather be
A Pagan suckled in a creed outworn;
So might I, standing on this pleasant lea,
Have glimpses that would make me less forlorn;
Have sight of Proteus rising from the sea;
Or hear old Triton blow his wreathèd horn.

WILLIAM WORDSWORTH

FOR A' THAT AND A' THAT

Is there for honest poverty
That hings his head, and a' that?
The coward slave, we pass him
   by;
We dare be poor for a' that!
For a' that, and a' that,
Our toils obscure, and a' that;
The rank is but the guinea
   stamp—
The man's the gowd for a' that!

What tho' on hamely fare we
   dine,
Wear hodden gray, and a' that?
Gie fools their silks, and knaves
   their wine—
A man's a man for a' that!
For a' that, and a' that,
Their tinsel show, and a' that;
The honest man, though e'er sae
   poor,
Is king o' men, for a' that!

Ye see yon birkie ca'd a lord,
Wha struts, an' stares, an' a'
   that—
Tho' hundreds worship at his
   word,

He's but a coof for a' that;
For a' that, and a' that,
His riband, star, and a' that;
The man of independent mind,
He looks an' laughs at a' that.

A prince can mak a belted knight,
A marquis, duke, and a' that;
But an honest man's aboon his
   might—
Gude faith, he mauna fa' that!
For a' that, and a' that,
Their dignities, an' a' that;
The pith o' sense, and pride o'
   worth,
Are higher rank than a' that.

Then let us pray that come it
   may,—
As come it will for a' that,—
That sense and worth, o'er a' the
   earth,
May bear the gree, an' a' that.
For a' that, and a' that,
It's comin' yet, for a' that—
That man to man, the warld o'er,
Shall brithers be for a' that.

ROBERT BURNS

THE GOLF LINKS

The golf links lie so near the mill
That almost every day
The laboring children can look out
And see the men at play.

SARAH N. CLEGHORN

THE MAN WITH THE HOE

Bowed by the weight of centuries he leans
Upon his hoe and gazes on the ground,
The emptiness of ages in his face,
And on his back the burden of the world.
Who made him dead to rapture and despair,
A thing that grieves not and that never hopes,
Stolid and stunned, a brother to the ox?
Who loosened and let down this brutal jaw?
Whose was the hand that slanted back this brow?
Whose breath blew out the light within this brain?

Is this the Thing the Lord God made and gave
To have dominion over sea and land;
To trace the stars and search the heavens for power;
To feel the passion of Eternity?
Is this the dream He dreamed who shaped the suns
And marked their ways upon the ancient deep?
Down all the caverns of Hell to their last gulf
There is no shape more terrible than this—
More tongued with censure of the world's blind greed—
More filled with signs and portents for the soul—
More packt with danger to the universe.

What gulfs between him and the seraphim!
Slave of the wheel of labor, what to him
Are Plato and the swing of Pleiades?
What the long reaches of the peaks of song,
The rift of dawn, the reddening of the rose?

Through this dread shape the suffering ages look;
Time's tragedy is in that aching stoop;
Through this dread shape humanity betrayed,
Plundered, profaned, and disinherited,
Cries protest to the Judges of the World,
A protest that is also prophecy.

O masters, lords and rulers in all lands,
Is this the handiwork you give to God,
This monstrous thing distorted and soul-quenched?
How will you ever straighten up this shape;
Touch it again with immortality;
Give back the upward looking and the light;
Rebuild in it the music and the dream;
Make right the immemorial infamies,
Perfidious wrongs, immedicable woes?
O masters, lords and rulers in all lands,
How will the Future reckon with this man?
How answer his brute question in that hour
When whirlwinds of rebellion shake all shores?
How will it be with kingdoms and with kings—
With those who shaped him to the thing he is—
When this dumb terror shall rise to judge the world,
After the silence of the centuries?

EDWIN MARKHAM

COMPOSED UPON WESTMINSTER BRIDGE
SEPT. 3, 1802

Earth has not anything to show more fair:
Dull would he be of soul who could pass by
A sight so touching in its majesty:
This city now doth like a garment wear
The beauty of the morning; silent, bare,
Ships, towers, domes, theaters, and temples lie
Open unto the fields, and to the sky;
All bright and glittering in the smokeless air.
Never did sun more beautifully steep
In his first splendor, valley, rock, or hill;
Ne'er saw I, never felt, a calm so deep!
The river glideth at his own sweet will:
Dear God! the very houses seem asleep;
And all that mighty heart is lying still!

WILLIAM WORDSWORTH

THIRTY BOB A WEEK

I couldn't touch a step and turn a screw,
　And set the blooming world a-work for me,
Like such as cut their teeth—I hope, like you—
　On the handle of a skeleton gold key;
I cut mine on a leek, which I eat it every week:
　I'm a clerk at thirty bob as you can see.

But I don't allow it's luck and all a toss;
　There's no such thing as being starred and crossed;
It's just the power of some to be a boss,
　And the bally power of others to be bossed:
I face the music, sir; you bet I ain't a cur;
　Strike me lucky if I don't believe I'm lost!

For like a mole I journey in the dark,
　A-travelling along the underground
From my Pillar'd Halls and broad Suburban Park,
　To come the daily dull official round;
And home again at night with my pipe all alight,
　A-scheming how to count ten bob a pound.

And it's often very cold and very wet,
　And my missis stitches towels for a hunks;
And the Pillar'd Halls is half of it to let—
　Three rooms about the size of travelling trunks.
And we cough, my wife and I, to dislocate a sigh,
　When the noisy little kids are in their bunks.

But you never hear her do a growl or whine,
　For she's made of flint and roses, very odd;
And I've got to cut my meaning rather fine,
　Or I'd blubber, for I'm made of greens and sod:
So p'r'aps we are in Hell for all that I can tell,
　And lost and damn'd and served up hot to God

I ain't blaspheming, Mr. Silver-tongue;
   I'm saying things a bit beyond your art:
Of all the rummy starts you ever sprung,
   Thirty bob a week's the rummiest start!
With your science and your books and your the'ries about spooks,
   Did you ever hear of looking in your heart?

I didn't mean your pocket, Mr., no:
   I mean that having children and a wife,
With thirty bob on which to come and go,
   Isn't dancing to the tabor and the fife:
When it doesn't make you drink, by Heaven! it makes you think,
   And notice curious items about life.

I step into my heart and there I meet
   A god-almighty devil singing small,
Who would like to shout and whistle in the street,
   And squelch the passers flat against the wall;
If the whole world was a cake he had the power to take,
   He would take it, ask for more, and eat it all.

And I meet a sort of simpleton beside,
   The kind that life is always giving beans;
With thirty bob a week to keep a bride
   He fell in love and married in his teens:
At thirty bob he stuck; but he knows it isn't luck:
   He knows the seas are deeper than tureens.

And the god-almighty devil and the fool
   That meet me in the High Street on the strike,
When I walk about my heart a-gathering wool,
   Are my good and evil angels if you like.
And both of them together in every kind of weather
   Ride me like a double-seated bike.

That's rough a bit and needs its meaning curled.
   But I have a high old hot un in my mind—
A most engrugious notion of the world,
   That leaves your lightning 'rithmetic behind:
I give it at a glance when I say "There ain't no chance,
   Nor nothing of the lucky-lottery kind."

And it's this way I make it out to be:
   No fathers, mothers, countries, climates—none;
Not Adam was responsible for me,
   Nor society, nor systems, nary one:
A little sleeping seed, I woke—I did, indeed—
   A million years before the blooming sun.

I woke because I thought the time had come;
   Beyond my will there was no other cause;
And every where I found myself at home,
   Because I chose to be the thing I was;
And in what ever shape of mollusc or of ape
   I always went according to the laws.

I was the love that chose my mother out;
   I joined two lives and from the union burst;
My weakness and my strength without a doubt
   Are mine alone for ever from the first:
It's just the very same with a difference in the name
   As "Thy will be done." You say it if you durst!

They say it daily up and down the land
   As easy as you take a drink, it's true;
But the difficultest go to understand,
   And the difficultest job a man can do,
Is to come it brave and meek with thirty bob a week,
   And feel that that's the proper thing for you.

It's a naked child against a hungry wolf;
   It's playing bowls upon a splitting wreck;
It's walking on a string across a gulf
   With millstones fore-and-aft about your neck;
But the thing is daily done by many and many a one;
   And we fall, face forward, fighting, on the deck.

JOHN DAVIDSON

A MAN OF WORDS

A man of words and not of deeds,
Is like a garden full of weeds;
And when the weeds begin to grow,
It's like a garden full of snow;
And when the snow begins to fall,
It's like a bird upon the wall;
And when the bird away does fly,
It's like an eagle in the sky;
And when the sky begins to roar,
It's like a lion at the door;
And when the door begins to
    crack,
It's like a stick across your back;
And when your back begins to
    smart,
It's like a penknife in your heart;
And when your heart begins to
    bleed,
You're dead, and dead, and dead
    indeed.

ANONYMOUS

FACTORY WINDOWS ARE ALWAYS BROKEN

Factory windows are always broken.
Somebody's always throwing bricks,
Somebody's always heaving cinders,
Playing ugly Yahoo tricks.

Factory windows are always broken.
Other windows are let alone.
No one throws through the chapel-window
The bitter, snarling derisive stone.

Factory windows are always broken.
Something or other is going wrong.
Something is rotten—I think, in Denmark.
End of the factory-window song.

VACHEL LINDSAY

MAN'S INHUMANITY TO MAN

Many and sharp the numerous ills
    Inwoven with our frame;
More pointed still, we make ourselves
    Regret, remorse and shame;
And man, whose heaven-erected face
    The smiles of love adorn,
Man's inhumanity to man,
    Makes countless thousands mourn.

ROBERT BURNS

THE VILLAGE BLACKSMITH

Under a spreading chestnut-tree
  The village smithy stands;
The smith, a mighty man is he,
  With large and sinewy hands;
And the muscles of his brawny arms
  Are strong as iron bands.

His hair is crisp, and black, and long,
  His face is like the tan;
His brow is wet with honest sweat,
  He earns whate'er he can,
And looks the whole world in the
    face,
  For he owes not any man.

Week in, week out, from morn
    till night,
  You can hear his bellows blow;
You can hear him swing his heavy
    sledge
  With measured beat and slow,
Like a sexton ringing the village bell,
  When the evening sun is low.

And children coming home from
    school
  Look in at the open door;
They love to see the flaming forge,
  And hear the bellows roar,
And catch the burning sparks that fly
  Like chaff from a threshing-floor.

He goes on Sunday to the church,
  And sits among his boys;
He hears the parson pray and
    preach,
  He hears his daughter's voice,
Singing in the village choir,
  And it makes his heart rejoice.

It sounds to him like her mother's
    voice,
  Singing in Paradise!
He needs must think of her once more,
  How in the grave she lies;
And with his hard, rough hand he wipes
  A tear out of his eyes.

Toiling,—rejoicing,—sorrowing,
  Onward through life he goes;
Each morning sees some task
    begin,
  Each evening sees its close;
Something attempted, something
    done,
  Has earned a night's repose.

Thanks, thanks to thee, my
    worthy friend,
  For the lesson thou hast taught!
Thus at the flaming forge of life
  Our fortunes must be wrought;
Thus on its sounding anvil shaped
  Each burning deed and
    thought!

HENRY WADSWORTH LONGFELLOW

MENDING WALL

Something there is that doesn't love a wall,
That sends the frozen-ground-swell under it,
And spills the upper boulders in the sun;
And makes gaps even two can pass abreast.
The work of hunters is another thing:
I have come after them and made repair
Where they have left not one stone on a stone,
But they would have the rabbit out of hiding,
To please the yelping dogs. The gaps I mean,
No one has seen them made or heard them made,
But at spring mending-time we find them there.
I let my neighbour know beyond the hill;
And on a day we meet to walk the line
And set the wall between us once again.
We keep the wall between us as we go.
To each the boulders that have fallen to each.
And some are loaves and some so nearly balls
We have to use a spell to make them balance:
'Stay where you are until our backs are turned!'
We wear our fingers rough with handling them.
Oh, just another kind of out-door game,
One on a side. It comes to little more:
There where it is we do not need the wall:
He is all pine and I am apple orchard.
My apple trees will never get across
And eat the cones under his pines, I tell him.

He only says, 'Good fences make good neighbours.'
Spring is the mischief in me, and I wonder
If I could put a notion in his head:
'*Why* do they make good neighbours? Isn't it
Where there are cows? But here there are no cows.
Before I built a wall I'd ask to know
What I was walling in or walling out,
And to whom I was like to give offence.
Something there is that doesn't love a wall,
That wants it down.' I could say 'Elves' to him,
But it's not elves exactly, and I'd rather
He said it for himself. I see him there
Bringing a stone grasped firmly by the top
In each hand, like an old-stone savage armed.
He moves in darkness as it seems to me,
Not of woods only and the shade of trees.
He will not go behind his father's saying,
And he likes having thought of it so well
He says again, 'Good fences make good neighbours.'

ROBERT FROST

THE BELLS

I

Hear the sledges with the bells—
Silver bells!
What a world of merriment their melody foretells!
How they tinkle, tinkle, tinkle,
In the icy air of night!
While the stars that oversprinkle
All the heavens, seem to twinkle
With a crystalline delight;
Keeping time, time, time,
In a sort of Runic rhyme,
To the tintinnabulation that so musically wells
From the bells, bells, bells, bells,
Bells, bells, bells—
From the jingling and the tinkling of the bells.

II

Hear the mellow wedding bells—
Golden bells!
What a world of happiness their harmony foretells!
Through the balmy air of night
How they ring out their delight!—
From the molten-golden notes,
And all in tune,
What a liquid ditty floats
To the turtle-dove that listens, while she gloats
On the moon!
Oh, from out the sounding cells,
What a gush of euphony voluminously wells!
How it swells!
How it dwells
On the Future!—how it tells
Of the rapture that impels
To the swinging and the ringing
Of the bells, bells, bells—
Of the bells, bells, bells, bells,
Bells, bells, bells—
To the rhyming and the chiming of the bells!

III

Hear the loud alarum bells—
Brazen bells!
What a tale of terror, now their turbulency tells!
In the startled ear of night
How they scream out their affright!
Too much horrified to speak,
They can only shriek, shriek,
Out of tune,
In a clamorous appealing to the mercy of the fire,
In a mad expostulation with the deaf and frantic fire,
Leaping higher, higher, higher,
With a desperate desire,
And a resolute endeavor
Now—now to sit, or never,
By the side of the pale-faced moon.
Oh, the bells, bells, bells!

What a tale their terror tells
   Of Despair!
How they clang, and clash, and roar!
What a horror they outpour
On the bosom of the palpitating air!
  Yet the ear, it fully knows,
    By the twanging,
    And the clanging,
  How the danger ebbs and flows;
  Yet the ear distinctly tells,
    In the jangling,
    And the wrangling,
  How the danger sinks and swells,
By the sinking or the swelling in the anger of the bells—
    Of the bells—
  Of the bells, bells, bells, bells,
    Bells, bells, bells—
  In the clamor and the clanging of the bells!

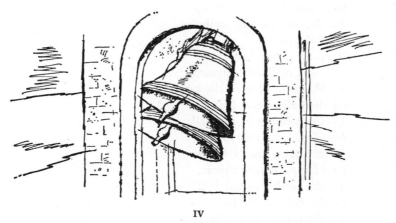

IV

Hear the tolling of the bells—
   Iron bells!
What a world of solemn thought their monody compels!
   In the silence of the night,
   How we shiver with affright
At the melancholy menace of their tone!
For every sound that floats
From the rust within their throats
  Is a groan.

And the people—ah, the people—
They that dwell up in the steeple,
     All alone,
And who, tolling, tolling, tolling,
In that muffled monotone,
Feel a glory in so rolling
On the human heart a stone—
They are neither man nor woman—
They are neither brute nor human—
          They are Ghouls:—
And their king it is who tolls:—
And he rolls, rolls, rolls,
          Rolls
A pæan from the bells!
And his merry bosom swells
With the pæan of the bells!
And he dances, and he yells;
Keeping time, time, time,
In a sort of Runic rhyme,
To the pæan of the bells:—
     Of the bells:
Keeping time, time, time,
In a sort of Runic rhyme,
To the throbbing of the bells:—
Of the bells, bells, bells—
To the sobbing of the bells:—
Keeping time, time, time,
As he knells, knells, knells,
In a happy Runic rhyme,
To the rolling of the bells—
Of the bells, bells, bells:—
To the tolling of the bells—
Of the bells, bells, bells, bells,
          Bells, bells, bells—
To the moaning and the groaning of the bells.

                    EDGAR ALLAN POE

BOOK XI

MY COUNTRY, 'TIS OF THEE

O CAPTAIN! MY CAPTAIN!

O Captain! my Captain! our fearful trip is done;
The ship has weather'd every rack, the prize we sought is won;
The port is near, the bells I hear, the people all exulting,
While follow eyes the steady keel, the vessel grim and daring:

But O heart! heart! heart!
O the bleeding drops of red,
Where on the deck my Captain lies,
Fallen cold and dead.

O Captain! my Captain! rise up and hear the bells;
Rise up—for you the flag is flung—for you the bugle trills;
For you bouquets and ribbon'd wreaths—for you the shores a-crowding;
For you they call, the swaying mass, their eager faces turning:

Here Captain! dear father!
This arm beneath your head;
It is some dream that on the deck
You've fallen cold and dead.

My Captain does not answer, his lips are pale and still;
My father does not feel my arm, he has no pulse or will;
The ship is anchor'd safe and sound, its voyage closed and done;
From fearful trip the victor ship comes in with object won:

Exult, O shores, and ring, O bells!
But I, with mournful tread,
Walk the deck my Captain lies,
Fallen cold and dead.

WALT WHITMAN

THE STAR-SPANGLED BANNER

O! say can you see by the dawn's early light,
What so proudly we hail'd at the twilight's last gleaming,
Whose broad stripes and bright stars, through the perilous fight,
O'er the ramparts we watched were so gallantly streaming?
And the rocket's red glare, the bombs bursting in air,
Gave proof through the night that our flag was still there;
O! say does that star-spangled banner yet wave,
O'er the land of the free, and the home of the brave?

On the shore dimly seen through the mists of the deep,
Where the foe's haughty host in dread silence reposes,
What is that which the breeze, o'er the towering steep,
As it fitfully blows, half conceals, half discloses?
Now it catches the gleam of the morning's first beam,
In full glory reflected now shines in the stream.
'Tis the star-spangled banner, O! long may it wave
O'er the land of the free, and the home of the brave.

And where is that band who so vauntingly swore
That the havoc of war and the battle's confusion,
A home and a country, shall leave us no more?
Their blood has wash'd out their foul footsteps pollution;
No refuge could save the hireling and slave,
From the terror of flight, or the gloom of the grave;
And the star-spangled banner in triumph doth wave,
O'er the land of the free, and the home of the brave.

O, thus be it ever when freemen shall stand,
Between their lov'd home and the war's desolation,
Blest with vict'ry and peace, may the heav'n-rescued land,
Praise the Power that hath made and preserved us a nation.
Then conquer we must, when our cause it is just,
And this be our motto,—"In God is our trust,"
And the star-spangled banner in triumph shall wave,
O'er the land of the free, and the home of the brave.

FRANCIS SCOTT KEY

ABRAHAM LINCOLN WALKS AT MIDNIGHT

In Springfield, Illinois

It is portentous, and a thing of state
That here at midnight, in our little town
A mourning figure walks, and will not rest,
Near the old court-house pacing up and down,

Or by his homestead, or in shadowed yards
He lingers where his children used to play,
Or through the market, on the well-worn stones
He stalks until the dawn-stars burn away.

A bronzed, lank man! His suit of ancient black,
A famous high top-hat and plain worn shawl
Make him the quaint great figure that men love,
The prairie-lawyer, master of us all.

He cannot sleep upon his hillside now.
He is among us:—as in times before!
And we who toss and lie awake for long
Breathe deep, and start, to see him pass the door.

His head is bowed. He thinks on men and kings.
Yea, when the sick world cries, how can he sleep?
Too many peasants fight, they know not why,
Too many homesteads in black terror weep.

The sins of all the war-lords burn his heart.
He sees the dreadnaughts scouring every main.
He carries on his shawl-wrapped shoulders now
The bitterness, the folly and the pain.

He cannot rest until a spirit-dawn
Shall come;—the shining hope of Europe free:
The league of sober folk, the Workers' Earth,
Bringing long peace to Cornland, Alp and Sea.

It breaks his heart that kings must murder still,
That all his hours of travail here for men
Seem yet in vain. And who will bring white peace
That he may sleep upon his hill again?

VACHEL LINDSAY

BURIAL OF SIR JOHN MOORE

Not a drum was heard, not a funeral note,
  As his corse to the rampart we hurried;
Not a soldier discharged his farewell shot
  O'er the grave where our hero we buried.

We buried him darkly, at dead of night,
  The sods with our bayonets turning;
By the struggling moonbeams' misty light,
  And the lantern dimly burning.

No useless coffin enclosed his breast,
  Not in sheet or in shroud we wound him;
But he lay, like a warrior taking his rest,
  With his martial cloak around him.

Few and short were the prayers we said,
  And we spoke not a word of sorrow;
But we steadfastly gazed on the face of the dead,
  And we bitterly thought of the morrow.

We thought, as we hollowed his narrow bed,
  And smoothed down his lonely pillow,
That the foe and the stranger would tread o'er his head,
And we far away on the billow!

Lightly they'll talk of the spirit that's gone,
  And o'er his cold ashes upbraid him;
But little he'll reck, if they let him sleep on
  In the grave where a Briton has laid him!

But half of our heavy task was done,
  When the clock struck the hour for retiring;
And we heard the distant and random gun
  That the foe was suddenly firing.

Slowly and sadly we laid him down,
  From the field of his fame fresh and gory!
We carved not a line, and we raised not a stone,
  But we left him alone with his glory.

                              CHARLES WOLFE

BREATHES THERE THE MAN
WITH SOUL SO DEAD

Breathes there the man with soul
  so dead
Who never to himself hath said,
This is my own, my native land!
Whose heart hath ne'er within
  him burned,
As home his footsteps he hath
  turned
From wandering on a foreign
  strand?
If such there breathe, go, mark
  him well;
For him no minstrel raptures swell;

High though his titles, proud his
  name,
Boundless his wealth as wish can
  claim,
Despite those titles, power, and pelf,
The wretch, concentred all in self,
Living, shall forfeit fair renown,
And, doubly dying, shall go down
To the vile dust from whence he
  sprung,
Unwept, unhonored, and unsung.

                  SIR WALTER SCOTT

THE AMERICAN FLAG

When Freedom, from her
    mountain height,
  Unfurled her standard to the
    air,
She tore the azure robe of night,
  And set the stars of glory there!
She mingled with its gorgeous dyes
The milky baldric of the skies,
And striped its pure, celestial
  white
With streakings of the morning
  light;
Then, from his mansion in the sun,
She called her eagle-bearer down,
And gave into his mighty hand
    The symbol of her chosen land!

Majestic monarch of the cloud!
  Who rear'st aloft thy regal form,
To hear the tempest trumping loud,
And see the lightning lances driven,
  When strive the warriors of the
    storm,
And rolls the thunder-drum of
  heaven,—
Child of the Sun! to thee 't is given
  To guard the banner of the free,
To hover in the sulphur smoke,
To ward away the battle-stroke,
And bid its blendings shine afar,
Like rainbows on the cloud of war,
  The harbingers of victory!
Flag of the brave! thy folds shall fly,

The sign of hope and triumph high!
When speaks the signal-trumpet
    tone,
And the long line comes gleaming on,
Ere yet the life-blood, warm and wet,
Has dimmed the glistening
    bayonet,
Each soldier's eye shall brightly turn
To where thy sky-born glories burn,
And, as his springing steps
    advance,
    Catch war and vengeance from
      the glance.

And when the cannon-mouthings
    loud
Heave in wild wreaths the battle
    shroud,
And gory sabres rise and fall
Like shoots of flame on midnight's pall,
Then shall thy meteor glances glow,
    And cowering foes shall shrink
      beneath
Each gallant arm that strikes below

That lovely messenger of death.
Flag of the seas! on ocean wave
Thy stars shall glitter o'er the
    brave;
When death, careering on the gale,
Sweeps darkly round the bellied
    sail,
And frighted waves rush wildly
    back
Before the broadside's reeling rack,
Each dying wanderer of the sea
Shall look at once to heaven and
    thee,
And smile to see thy splendors fly
    In triumph o'er his closing eye.

Flag of the free heart's hope and
    home,
    By angel hands to valor given!
Thy stars have lit the welkin dome,
    And all thy hues were born in
      heaven.

JOSEPH RODMAN DRAKE

ANNE RUTLEDGE

Out of me unworthy and
    unknown
The vibrations of deathless music;
'With malice toward none, with
    charity for all.'
Out of me the forgiveness of
    millions toward millions,
And the beneficent face of a
    nation
Shining with justice and truth.

I am Anne Rutledge who sleep
    beneath these weeds,
Beloved in life of Abraham
    Lincoln,
Wedded to him, not through
    union,
But through separation.
Bloom forever, O Republic,
From the dust of my bosom!

EDGAR LEE MASTERS

A SONG FOR OUR FLAG

A bit of color against the blue:
Hues of the morning, blue for
    true,
And red for the kindling light of
    flame,
And white for a nation's stainless
    fame.
Oh! fling it forth to the winds afar,
With hope in its every shining
    star:
Under its folds wherever found,
Thank God, we have freedom's
    holy ground.

Don't you love it, as out it floats
From the schoolhouse peak, and
    glad young throats
Sing of the banner that aye
    shall be
Symbol of honor and victory?
Don't you thrill when the
    marching feet
Of jubilant soldiers shake the
    street,
And the bugles shrill, and the
    trumpets call,

And the red, white and blue is
    over us all?
Don't you pray, amid starting
    tears,
It may never be furled through
    age-long years?

A song for our flag, our country's
    boast,
That gathers beneath it a mighty
    host;
Long may it wave o'er the goodly
    land
We hold in fee 'neath our Father's
    hand.
For God and liberty evermore
May that banner stand from shore
    to shore,
Never to those high meanings lost,
Never with alien standards
    crossed,
But always valiant and pure and
    true,
Our starry flag: red, white, and
    blue.

MARGARET E. SANGSTER

THE NEW COLOSSUS
INSCRIPTION ON THE STATUE OF LIBERTY

Not like the brazen giant of Greek fame,
With conquering limbs astride from land to land,
Here at our sea-washed, sunset gates shall stand
A mighty woman with a torch, whose flame
Is the imprisoned lightning, and her name
Mother of Exiles. From her beacon-hand
Glows world-wide welcome; her mild eyes command
The air-bridged harbor that twin cities frame.
"Keep, ancient lands, your storied pomp!" cries she
With silent lips. "Give me your tired, your poor,
Your huddled masses yearning to breathe free,
The wretched refuse of your teeming shore.
Send these, the homeless, tempest-tost to me,
I lift my lamp beside the golden door!"

EMMA LAZARUS

I HEAR AMERICA SINGING

I hear America singing, the varied carols I hear;
Those mechanics—each one singing his, as it should be, blithe and
    strong;
The carpenter singing his, as he measures his plank or beam,
The mason singing his, as he makes ready for work, or leaves off work;
The boatman singing what belongs to him in his boat—the deckhand
    singing on the steamboat deck;
The shoemaker singing as he sits on his bench—the hatter singing as
    he stands;
The wood-cutter's song—the ploughboy's, on his way in the morning,
    or at the noon intermission, or at sundown;
The delicious singing of the mother—or of the young wife at work—
    or of the girl sewing or washing;
Each singing what belongs to him or her, and to none else;
The day what belongs to the day—at night, the party of young fellows,
    robust, friendly,
Singing, with open mouths, their strong melodious songs.

WALT WHITMAN

DIXIE*

I wish I was in de land ob cotton,
Old time dar am not forgotten;
  Look away, look away, look away, Dixie land!
In Dixie whar I was born in,
Early on one frosty mornin',
  Look away, look away, look away, Dixie land!

Chorus:
    Den I wish I was in Dixie! Hooray! Hooray!
    In Dixie land we'll take our stand, to lib an' die in Dixie,
    Away, away, away down south in Dixie!
    Away, away, away down south in Dixie!

Old missus marry Will de weaber,
William was a gay deceaber,
When he put his arm around 'er,
He looked as fierce as a forty-pounder. (*Chorus.*)

His face was as sharp as a butcher cleaber,
But dat did not seem to greab 'er;
Will run away, missus took a decline, O,
Her face was the color of bacon rhine, O. (*Chorus.*)

While missus libbed, she libbed in clover,
When she died, she died all over;
How could she act de foolish part,
An' marry a man to break her heart? (*Chorus.*)

Buck wheat cakes an' stony batter
Makes you fat or a little fatter;
Here's a health to de next old missus,
An' all de gals dat want to kiss us. (*Chorus.*)

Now if you want to drive 'way sorrow,
Come an' hear dis song to-morrow;
Den hoe it down an' scratch your grabble,
To Dixie's land I'm bound to trabble. (*Chorus.*)

DANIEL DECATUR EMMETT

*The original version.

HAIL COLUMBIA

Hail, Columbia! happy land!
Hail, ye heroes! heaven-born band!
  Who fought and bled in
    freedom's cause,
  Who fought and bled in
    freedom's cause,
And when the storm of war was
    gone,
Enjoyed the peace your valor won.
  Let independence be our boast,
  Ever mindful what it cost;
  Ever grateful for the prize,
  Let its altar reach the skies.

Cho.: Firm, united, let us be,
    Rallying round our liberty;
    As a band of brothers joined
    Peace and safety we shall find.

Immortal patriots! rise once more:
Defend your rights, defend your
    shore:
  Let no rude foe, with impious
    hand,
  Let no rude foe, with impious
    hand,
Invade the shrine where sacred lies
Of toil and blood the well-earned
    prize.
  While offering peace sincere
    and just,
  In Heaven we place a manly trust,
  That truth and justice will
    prevail,
  And every scheme of bondage fail.

Sound, sound the trumpet of
    fame!
Let Washington's great name
  Ring through the world with
    loud applause;
  Ring through the world with
    loud applause;
Let every clime to freedom dear,
Listen with joyful ear.
  With equal skill, and godlike
    power,
  He governed in the fearful hour
  Of horrid war; or guides, with ease,
  The happier times of honest peace.

Behold the chief who now
    commands,
Once more to serve his country,
    stands—
  The rock on which the storm
    will beat;
  The rock on which the storm
    will beat;
But, armed in virtue firm and
    true,
His hopes are fixed on Heaven
    and you.
  When hope was sinking in
    dismay,
  And glooms obscured
    Columbia's day,
  His steady mind, from changes
    free,
  Resolved on death or liberty.
                JOSEPH HOPKINSON

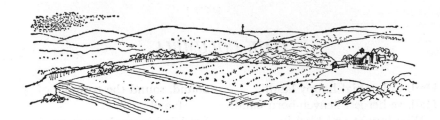

AMERICA FOR ME

'Tis fine to see the Old World, and travel up and down
Among the famous palaces and cities of renown,
To admire the crumbly castles and the statues of the kings,—
But now I think I've had enough of antiquated things.

So it's home again, and home again, America for me!
My heart is turning home again, and there I long to be,
In the land of youth and freedom beyond the ocean bars,
Where the air is full of sunlight and the flag is full of stars.

Oh, London is a man's town, there's power in the air;
And Paris is a woman's town, with flowers in her hair;
And it's sweet to dream in Venice, and it's great to study Rome;
But when it comes to living, there is no place like home.

I like the German fir-woods, in green battalions drilled;
I like the garden of Versailles, with flashing fountains filled;
But oh, to take your hand, my dear, and ramble for a day
In the friendly Western woodland where Nature has her way!

I know that Europe's wonderful, yet something seems to lack;
The Past is too much with her, and the people looking back.
But the glory of the Present is to make the Future free,—
We love our land for what she is and what she is to be.

Oh, it's home again, and home again, America for me!
I want a ship that's westward bound to plow the rolling sea,
To the blessed Land of Room Enough beyond the ocean bars,
Where the air is full of sunlight and the flag is full of stars.

HENRY VAN DYKE

AMERICA

My country, 'tis of thee,
Sweet land of liberty,
　Of thee I sing;
Land where my fathers died,
Land of the pilgrims' pride.
From every mountain-side
　Let Freedom ring.

My native country, thee,
Land of the noble free,—
　Thy name I love;
I love thy rocks and rills
Thy woods and templed hills:
My heart with rapture thrills
　Like that above.

Let music swell the breeze,
And ring from all the trees,
　Sweet Freedom's song;
Let mortal tongues awake,
Let all that breathe partake,
Let rocks their silence break,—
　The sound prolong.

Our fathers' God, to Thee,
Author of liberty,
　To thee we sing;
Long may our land be bright
With Freedom's holy light;
Protect us by Thy might,
　Great God, our King.

SAMUEL FRANCIS SMITH

AMERICA THE BEAUTIFUL

O beautiful for spacious skies,
For amber waves of grain,
For purple mountain majesties
Above the fruited plain!
America! America!
God shed His grace on thee
And crown thy good with
　brotherhood
From sea to shining sea!

O beautiful for pilgrim feet,
Whose stern, impassioned stress
A thoroughfare for freedom beat
Across the wilderness!
America! America!
God mend thine every flaw,
Confirm thy soul in self-control,
Thy liberty in law!

O beautiful for heroes proved
In liberating strife,
Who more than self their country
　loved,
And mercy more than life!
America! America!
May God thy gold refine
Till all success be nobleness
And every gain divine!

O beautiful for patriot dream
That sees beyond the years
Thine alabaster cities gleam
Undimmed by human tears!
America! America!
God shed His grace on thee
And crown thy good with
　brotherhood
From sea to shining sea!

KATHARINE LEE BATES

THE FLAG GOES BY

Hats off!
Along the street there comes
A blare of bugles, a ruffle of drums,
A flash of color beneath the sky:
Hats off!
The flag is passing by!

Blue and crimson and white it shines,
Over the steel-tipped, ordered lines.
Hats off!
The colors before us fly;
But more than the flag is passing by:

Sea-fights and land-fights, grim
and great,
Fought to make and to save the State;
Weary marches and sinking ships;
Cheers of victory on dying lips;

Days of plenty and years of peace;
March of a strong land's swift
increase;
Equal justice, right and law,
Stately honor and reverend awe;

Sign of a nation great and strong
To ward her people from foreign
wrong;
Pride and glory and honor,—all
Live in the colors to stand or fall.
Hats off!

Along the street there comes
A blare of bugles, a ruffle of drums;
And loyal hearts are beating high:
Hats off!
The flag is passing by!

HENRY HOLCOMB BENNETT

O SHIP OF STATE

Thou, too, sail on, O Ship of State!
Sail on, O Union, strong and great!
Humanity with all its fears,
With all the hopes of future years,
Is hanging breathless on thy fate!
We know what Master laid thy keel,
What Workmen wrought thy ribs of steel,
Who made each mast, and sail, and rope,
What anvils rang, what hammers beat,
In what a forge and what a heat
Were shaped the anchors of thy hope!
Fear not each sudden sound and shock,

'Tis of the wave and not the rock;
'Tis but the flapping of the sail,
And not a rent made by the gale!
In spite of rock and tempest's roar,
In spite of false lights on the shore,
Sail on, nor fear to breast the sea!
Our hearts, our hopes, are all with thee,
Our hearts, our hopes, our
prayers, our tears,
Our faith triumphant o'er our fears,
Are all with thee,—are all with thee!

HENRY WADSWORTH LONGFELLOW

GOD SAVE THE FLAG

Washed in the blood of the brave and the blooming,
   Snatched from the altars of insolent foes,
Burning with star-fires, but never consuming,
   Flash its broad ribbons of lily and rose.

Vainly the prophets of Baal would rend it,
   Vainly his worshippers pray for its fall;
Thousands have died for it, millions defend it,
   Emblem of justice and mercy to all:

Justice that reddens the sky with her terrors,
   Mercy that comes with her white-handed train,
Soothing all passions, redeeming all errors,
   Sheathing the sabre and breaking the chain.

Borne on the deluge of old usurpations,
   Drifted our Ark o'er the desolate seas,
Bearing the rainbow of hope to the nations,
   Torn from the storm-cloud and flung to the breeze!

God bless the Flag and its loyal defenders,
   While its broad folds o'er the battle-field wave,
Till the dim star-wreath rekindle its splendors,
   Washed from its stains in the blood of the brave!

OLIVER WENDELL HOLMES

THE WEARING OF THE GREEN

Oh Paddy dear, and did you hear the news that's going round?
The shamrock is forbid by law to grow on Irish ground:
Saint Patrick's day no more we'll keep, his color can't be seen,
For there's a cruel law agin the wearing of the Green.
I met with Napper Tandy and he took me by the hand,
And said he, How's poor old Ireland, and how does she stand?
She's the most distressful country that ever yet was seen;
They're hanging men and women for the wearing of the Green.

Then since the color we must wear is England's cruel Red,
'Twill serve us to remind us of the blood that has been shed;
You may take the shamrock from your hat and cast it on the sod,
But never fear, 'twill take root there, though underfoot 'tis trod.
When laws can stop the blades of grass from growing as they grow.
And when the leaves in summertime their verdure dare not show,
Then I will change the color that I wear in my caubeen;
But till that day, please God, I'll stick to wearing of the Green.

ANONYMOUS

LANDING OF THE PILGRIM FATHERS

The breaking waves dashed high
On a stern and rock-bound coast;
And the woods against a stormy sky,
Their giant branches tossed;
And the heavy night hung dark
The hills and waters o'er—
When a band of exiles moored
    their bark
On a wild New England shore.

Not as the conqueror comes,
They, the true-hearted, came;—
Not with the roll of stirring
    drums,
And the trumpets that sing of
    fame;—
Not as the flying come,
In silence and in fear;
They shook the depths of the
    desert's gloom
With their hymns of lofty cheer.

Amidst the storm they sang,
And the stars heard, and the sea!
And the sounding aisles of the
    dim woods rang
To the anthem of the free;

The ocean eagle soared
From his nest by the white wave's
    foam,
And the rocking pines of the
    forest roared:—
This was their welcome home!

There were men with hoary hair
Amidst that pilgrim band;
Why had they come to wither there,
Away from their childhood's land?
There was woman's fearless eye,
Lit by her deep love's truth;
There was manhood's brow
    serenely high,
And the fiery heart of youth.

What sought they thus afar?
Bright jewels of the mine?
The wealth of seas? the spoils of war?
They sought a faith's pure shrine!
Ay, call it holy ground,
The soil where first they trod!
They left unstained what there
    they found
Freedom to worship God!

FELICIA DOROTHEA HEMANS

YOUR FLAG AND MY FLAG

Your flag and my flag,
  And how it flies today,
In your land and my land,
  And half a world away!

Rose-red and blood-red,
  The stripes forever gleam;
Snow-white and soul-white—
  The good forefather's dream;
Sky-blue and true-blue,
  With stars to gleam aright—
The gloried guidon of the day;
  A shelter through the night.

Your flag and my flag!
  To every star and stripe
The drums beat as hearts beat
  And fifers shrilly pipe!
Your flag and my flag—
  A blessing in the sky;

Your hope and my hope—
  It never hid a lie!

Home land and far land
  And half the world around,
Old Glory hears our glad salute
  And ripples to the sound.

Your flag and my flag!
  And, Oh! how much it holds—
Your land and my land—
  Secure within its folds!
Your heart and my heart
  Beat quicker at the sight.
Sun-kissed and wind-tossed—
  Red and blue and white.
The one flag—the great flag—
  The flag for me and you
Glorified all else beside,
  The red and white and blue.

WILBUR D. NESBIT

COLUMBUS

Behind him lay the gray Azores,
Behind the Gates of Hercules;
Before him not the ghost of shores
Before him only shoreless seas.
The good mate said: "Now we
   must pray,
For lo! the very stars are gone.
Brave Admiral, speak, what shall
   I say?"
"Why, say, 'Sail on! sail on! and
   on!' "

"My men grow mutinous day by
   day;
My men grow ghastly wan and
   weak."
The stout mate thought of home;
   a spray
Of salt wave washed his swarthy
   cheek.
"What shall I say, brave Admiral,
   say,
If we sight naught but seas at
   dawn?"
"Why, you shall say at break of
   day,
'Sail on! sail on! and on!' "

They sailed and sailed, as winds
   might blow,
Until at last the blanched mate
   said:
"Why, now not even God would
   know
Should I and all my men fall
   dead.

These very winds forget their way,
For God from these dread seas is
   gone.
Now speak, brave Admiral, speak
   and say"—
He said, "Sail on! sail on! and
   on!"

They sailed. They sailed. Then
   spake the mate:
"This mad sea shows his teeth
   tonight.
He curls his lip, he lies in wait,
With lifted teeth, as if to bite!
Brave Admiral, say but one good
   word:
What shall we do when hope is
   gone?"
The words leapt like a leaping
   sword:
"Sail on! sail on! sail on! and on!"

Then pale and worn, he kept his
   deck,
And peered through darkness. Ah,
   that night
Of all dark nights! And then a
   speck—
A light! a light! at last a light!
It grew, a starlit flag unfurled!
It grew to be Time's burst of
   dawn.
He gained a world; he gave that
   world
Its grandest lesson: "On! sail on!"

JOAQUIN MILLER

BOOK XII

STORY POEMS AND BALLADS

THE CONGO

(*A Study of the Negro Race*)

I—THEIR BASIC SAVAGERY

A deep roll-ing bass

Fat black bucks in a wine-barrel room,
Barrel-house kings, with feet unstable,
Sagged and reeled and pounded on the table,
Pounded on the table,
Beat an empty barrel with the handle of a broom,
Hard as they were able,
Boom, boom, BOOM,
With a silk umbrella and the handle of a broom,

*More delib-erate.
Solemnly chanted*

Boomlay, boomlay, boomlay, BOOM.
THEN I had religion, THEN I had a vision.
I could not turn from their revel in derision.
THEN I SAW THE CONGO, CREEPING THROUGH THE BLACK,
CUTTING THROUGH THE JUNGLE WITH A GOLDEN TRACK.
Then along that riverbank
A thousand miles
Tattooed cannibals danced in files;
Then I heard the boom of the blood-lust song
And a thigh-bone beating on a tin-pan gong.
And "BLOOD!" screamed the whistles and the fifes of the
     warriors,

A rapidly piling climax of speed and racket

"BLOOD!" screamed the skull-faced, lean witch-doctors;
"Whirl ye the deadly voo-doo rattle,
Harry the uplands,
Steal all the cattle,
Rattle-rattle, rattle-rattle, Bing!

With a philosophic pause

Boomlay, boomlay, boomlay, BOOM!"
A roaring, epic, rag-time tune
From the mouth of the Congo
To the Mountains of the Moon.
Death is an Elephant,

Shrilly and with a heavily accented metre

Torch-eyed and horrible,
Foam-flanked and terrible.
Boom, steal the pygmies,
Boom, kill the Arabs,
Boom, kill the white men,
Hoo, Hoo, Hoo,

Like the wind in the chimney

Listen to the yell of Leopold's ghost
Burning in Hell for his hand-maimed host.
Hear how the demons chuckle and yell
Cutting his hands off down in Hell.
Listen to the creepy proclamation,
Blown through the lairs of the forest-nation,
Blown past the white-ants' hill of clay,
Blown past the marsh where the butterflies play:—

All the O sounds very golden. Heavy accents very heavy. Light accents very light. Last line whispered

"Be careful what you do,
Or Mumbo-Jumbo, god of the Congo,
And all of the other
Gods of the Congo,
Mumbo-Jumbo will hoo-doo you,
Mumbo-Jumbo will hoo-doo you,
Mumbo-Jumbo will hoo-doo you."

II—THEIR IRREPRESSIBLE HIGH SPIRITS

Rather shrill and high

Wild crap-shooters with a whoop and a call
Danced the juba in their gambling-hall,
And laughed fit to kill, and shook the town,
And guyed the policemen and laughed them down
With a boomlay, boomlay, boomlay, Boom.
THEN I SAW THE CONGO, CREEPING THROUGH THE BLACK,
CUTTING THROUGH THE JUNGLE WITH A GOLDEN TRACK.

Read exactly as in first section. Lay emphasis on the delicate ideas. Keep as light-footed as possible

A Negro fairyland swung into view,
A minstrel river
Where dreams come true.
The ebony palace soared on high
Through the blossoming trees to the evening sky.
The inlaid porches and casements shone
With gold and ivory and elephant-bone.
And the black crowd laughed till their sides were sore
At the baboon butler in the agate door,
And the well-known tunes of the parrot band
That trilled on the bushes of that magic land.

With pom-
posity
A troupe of skull-faced witch-men came
Through the agate doorway in suits of flame—
Yea, long-tailed coats with a gold-leaf crust
And hats that were covered with diamond dust.
And the crowd in the court gave a whoop and a call
And danced the juba from wall to wall.

With a great
deliberation
and ghostli-
ness
But the witch-men suddenly stilled the throng
With a stern cold glare, and a stern old song:
"Mumbo-Jumbo will hoo-doo you.". . .

With over-
whelming
assurance,
good cheer,
and pomp
Just then from the doorway, as fat as shotes
Came the cake-walk princes in their long red coats,
Canes with a brilliant lacquer shine,
And tall silk hats that were red as wine.

With grow-
ing speed
and sharply
marked
dance-
rhythm
And they pranced with their butterfly partners there,
Coal-black maidens with pearls in their hair,
Knee-skirts trimmed with the jassamine sweet,
And bells on their ankles and little black feet.
And the couples railed at the chant and the frown
Of the witch-men lean, and laughed them down.
(Oh, rare was the revel, and well worth while
That made those glowering witch-men smile.)
The cake-walk royalty then began

With a touch
of negro dia-
lect, and as
rapidly as
possible to-
ward the end
To walk for a cake that was tall as a man
To the tune of "Boomlay, boomlay, Boom,"
While the witch-men laughed, with a sinister air,
And sang with the scalawags prancing there:
"Walk with care, walk with care,
Or Mumbo-Jumbo, god of the Congo,
And all of the other
Gods of the Congo,
Mumbo-Jumbo will hoo-doo you.
Beware, beware, walk with care,
Boomlay, boomlay, boomlay, boom,
Boomlay, boomlay, boomlay, boom,
Boomlay, boomlay, boomlay, boom,
Boomlay, boomlay, boomlay,
Boom."

Slow philo-
sophic calm
Oh, rare was the revel, and well worth while
That made those glowering witch-men smile.

III—THE HOPE OF THEIR RELIGION

Heavy bass.
With a literal
imitation of
camp-meet-
ing racket
and trance

A good old Negro in the slums of the town
Preached at a sister for her velvet gown.
Howled at a brother for his low-down ways,
His prowling, guzzling, sneak-thief days.
Beat on the Bible till he wore it out
Starting the jubilee revival shout.
And some had visions, as they stood on chairs,
And sang of Jacob, and the golden stairs.
And they all repented, a thousand strong,
From their stupor and savagery and sin and wrong,
And slammed with their hymn-books till they shook the
    room
With "Glory, glory, glory,"
And "Boom, boom, Boom."

THEN I SAW THE CONGO, CREEPING THROUGH THE BLACK,
CUTTING THROUGH THE JUNGLE WITH A GOLDEN TRACK.

Exactly as in
the first sec-
tion. Begin
with terror
and power,
end with joy

And the gray sky opened like a new-rent veil
And showed the apostles with their coats of mail.
In bright white steel they were seated round,
And their fire-eyes watched where the Congo wound.

Sung to the
tune of
"Hark, ten
thousand
harps and
voices"

And the twelve Apostles, from their thrones on high,
Thrilled all the forest with their heavenly cry:
"Mumbo-Jumbo will die in the jungle;
Never again will he hoo-doo you,
Never again will he hoo-doo you."

With grow-
ing delibera-
tion and joy

Then along that river, a thousand miles,
The vine-snared trees fell down in files.
Pioneer angels cleared the way
For a Congo paradise, for babes at play,
For sacred capitals, for temples clean.
Gone were the skull-faced witch-men lean;

In a rather
high key—as
delicately as
possible

There, where the wild ghost-gods had wailed,
A million boats of the angels sailed
With oars of silver, and prows of blue,
And silken pennants that the sun shone through;
'Twas a land transfigured, 'twas a new creation.
Oh, a singing wind swept the Negro nation,

And on through the backwoods clearing flew:—

To the tune of "Hark, ten thousand harps and voices"

"Mumbo-Jumbo is dead in the jungle.
Never again will he hoo-doo you,
Never again will he hoo-doo you."

Redeemed were the forests, the beasts and the men,
And only the vulture dared again

Dying down into a penetrating, terrified whisper

By the far lone mountains of the moon
To cry, in the silence, the Congo tune:
"Mumbo-Jumbo will hoo-doo you,
Mumbo-Jumbo will hoo-doo you.
Mumbo . . . Jumbo . . . will . . . hoo-doo . . . you."

VACHEL LINDSAY

MR. FLOOD'S PARTY

Old Eben Flood, climbing alone
   one night
Over the hill between the town
   below
And the forsaken upland hermitage
That held as much as he should
   ever know
On earth again of home, paused
   warily.
The road was his with not a
   native near;
And Eben, having leisure, said aloud,
For no man else in Tilbury Town
   to hear:

"Well, Mr. Flood, we have the
   harvest moon
Again, and we may not have many
   more;
The bird is on the wing, the poet
   says,
And you and I have said it here
   before.
Drink to the bird." He raised up
   to the light
The jug that he had gone so far to fill
And answered huskily: "Well, Mr.
   Flood,
Since you propose it, I believe I will."

Alone, as if enduring to the end
A valiant armor of scarred hopes
  outworn,
He stood there in the middle of
  the road
Like Roland's ghost winding a
  silent horn.
Below him, in the town among
  the trees,
Where friends of other days had
  honored him,
A phantom salutation of the dead
Rang thinly till old Eben's eyes
  were dim.

Then, as a mother lays her
  sleeping child
Down tenderly, fearing it may
  awake,
He set the jug down slowly at his
  feet
With trembling care, knowing
  that most things break;
And only when assured that on
  firm earth
It stood, as the uncertain lives of
  men
Assuredly did not, he paced away,
And with his hand extended
  paused again:

"Well, Mr. Flood, we have not
  met like this
In a long time; and many a
  change has come
To both of us, I fear, since last it was
We had a drop together. Welcome
  home!"

Convivially returning with
  himself,
Again he raised the jug up to the
  light;
And with an acquiescent quaver
  said:
"Well, Mr. Flood, if you insist, I
  might.

"Only a very little, Mr. Flood—
For auld lang syne. No more, sir;
  that will do."
So, for the time, apparently it did,
And Eben evidently thought so too;
For soon amid the silver loneliness
Of night he lifted up his voice
  and sang,
Secure, with only two moons
  listening,
Until the whole harmonious
  landscape rang—

"For auld lang syne." The weary
  throat gave out,
The last word wavered; and the
  song being done,
He raised again the jug regretfully
And shook his head, and was
  again alone.
There was not much that was
  ahead of him,
And there was nothing in the
  town below—
Where strangers would have shut
  the many doors
That many friends had opened
  long ago.
EDWIN ARLINGTON ROBINSON

THE BALLAD OF THE OYSTERMAN

It was a tall young oysterman lived by the river-side,
His shop was just upon the bank, his boat was on the tide;
The daughter of a fisherman, that was so straight and slim,
Lived over on the other bank, right opposite to him.

It was the pensive oysterman that saw a lovely maid,
Upon a moonlight evening, a-sitting in the shade;
He saw her wave her handkerchief, as much as if to say,
'I 'm wide awake, young oysterman, and all the folks away.'

Then up arose the oysterman, and to himself said he,
'I guess I 'll leave the skiff at home, for fear that folks should see;
I read it in the story-book, that, for to kiss his dear,
Leander swam the Hellespont,—and I will swim this here.'

And he has leaped into the waves, and crossed the shining stream,
And he has clambered up the bank, all in the moonlight gleam;
Oh there were kisses sweet as dew, and words as soft as rain,—
But they have heard her father's step, and in he leaps again!

Out spoke the ancient fisherman,—'Oh, what was that, my daughter?'
' 'T was nothing but a pebble, sir, I threw into the water.'
'And what is that, pray tell me, love, that paddles off so fast?'
'It 's nothing but a porpoise, sir, that 's been a-swimming past.'

Out spoke the ancient fisherman,—'Now bring me my harpoon!
I 'll get into my fishing-boat, and fix the fellow soon.'
Down fell that pretty innocent, as falls a snow-white lamb,
Her hair drooped round her pallid cheeks, like seaweed on a clam.

Alas for those two loving ones! she waked not from her swound,
And he was taken with the cramp, and in the waves was drowned;
But Fate has metamorphosed them, in pity of their woe,
And now they keep an oyster-shop for mermaids down below.

OLIVER WENDELL HOLMES

JIM BLUDSO

Wall, no! I can't tell whar he lives,
  Becase he don't live, you see;
Leastways, he's got out of the
    habit
  Of livin' like you and me.
Whar have you been for the last
    three year
  That you haven't heard folks tell
How Jimmy Bludso passed in his
    checks
  The night of the Prairie Belle?

He weren't no saint—them
    engineers
  Is all pretty much alike—
One wife in Natchez-under-the-
    Hill
  And another one here, in Pike;
A keerless man in his talk was Jim,
  And an awkward hand in a row,
But he never flunked, and he
    never lied—
  I reckon he never knowed how.

And this was all the religion he
    had—
  To treat his engine well;
Never be passed on the river;
  To mind the pilot's bell;

And if ever the Prairie Belle took fire,
  A thousand times he swore
He'd hold her nozzle agin the bank
  Till the last soul got ashore.

All boats has their day on the
    Mississip,
  And her day come at last,—
The Movastar was a better boat,
  But the Belle she *wouldn't* be
    passed.
And so she come tearin' along
    that night—
  The oldest craft on the line—
With a nigger squat on her safety-
    valve,
  And her furnace crammed,
    rosin and pine.

The fire bust out as she cl'ared the bar
  And burnt a hole in the night,
And quick as a flash she turned,
    and made
  For that willer-bank on the right.
There was runnin' an' cursin', but
    Jim yelled out
  Over all the infernal roar,
"I'll hold her nozzle agin the bank
  Till the last galoot's ashore!"

Through the hot, black breath of
    the burnin' boat
  Jim Bludso's voice was heard,
And they all had trust in his
    cussedness,
  And knowed he would keep his
    word.
And, sure's you're born, they all
    got off
  Afore the smokestacks fell,—
And Bludso's ghost went up alone
  In the smoke of the Prairie
    Belle.

He weren't no saint—but at
    jedgment
  I'd run my chance with Jim,
'Longside of some pious
    gentlemen
  That wouldn't shook hands
    with him.
He seen his duty, a dead-sure
    thing,—
  And went for it, thar and then;
And Christ ain't a-goin' to be too
    hard
  On a man that died for men.

                JOHN HAY

THE YARN OF THE "NANCY BELL"

'Twas on the shores that round
    our coast
  From Deal to Ramsgate span,
That I found alone, on a piece of
    stone,
  An elderly naval man.

His hair was weedy, his beard was
    long,
  And weedy and long was he;
And I heard this wight on the
    shore recite,
  In a singular minor key:—

"Oh, I am a cook and a captain
    bold,
  And the mate of the Nancy brig,
And a bo'sun tight, and a
    midshipmite,
  And the crew of the captain's gig."

And he shook his fists and he tore
    his hair,
  Till I really felt afraid,
For I couldn't help thinking the
    man had been drinking,
  And so I simply said:—

"Oh, elderly man, it's little I know
  Of the duties of men of the sea,
And I'll eat my hand if I
    understand
  How ever you can be

"At once a cook and a captain
    bold,
  And the mate of the Nancy brig,
And a bo'sun tight, and a
    midshipmite,
  And the crew of the captain's
    gig!"

Then he gave a hitch to his
    trousers, which
Is a trick all seamen larn,
And having got rid of a thumping
    quid,
    He spun this painful yarn:—

" 'Twas in the good ship Nancy
    Bell
That we sailed to the Indian sea,
And there on a reef we come to
    grief,
    Which has often occurred to me.

"And pretty nigh all o' the crew
    was drowned
    (There was seventy-seven o' soul) ;
And only ten of the Nancy's men
    Said 'Here!' to the muster-roll.

"There was me, and the cook, and
    the captain bold,
And the mate of the Nancy brig,
And the bo'sun tight and a
    midshipmite,
And the crew of the captain's gig.

"For a month we'd neither wittles
    nor drink,
    Till a-hungry we did feel,
So we drawed a lot, and,
    accordin', shot
    The captain for our meal.

"The next lot fell to the Nancy's
    mate,
    And a delicate dish he made;
Then our appetite with the
    midshipmite
We seven survivors stayed.

"And then we murdered the
    bo'sun tight,
    And he much resembled pig;
Then we wittled free, did the
    cook and me,
    On the crew of the captain's gig.

"Then only the cook and me was
    left,
    And the delicate question, 'Which
Of us two goes to the kettle?' arose,
    And we argued it out as sich.

"For I loved that cook as a
    brother, I did,
    And the cook he worshipped me;
But we'd both be blowed if we'd
    either be stowed
    In the other chap's hold, you see.

" 'I'll be eat if you dines off me,'
    says Tom.
    'Yes, that,' says I, 'you'll be.
I'm boiled if I die, my friend,'
    quoth I;
    And 'Exactly so,' quoth he.

"Says he: 'Dear James, to murder me
    Were a foolish thing to do,
For don't you see that you can't
    cook *me*,
    While I can—and will—cook *you?'*

"So he boils the water, and takes
    the salt
    And the pepper in portions true
(Which he never forgot) , and
    some chopped shalot,
    And some sage and parsley too.

" 'Come here,' says he, with a
    proper pride,
  Which his smiling features tell;
' 'Twill soothing be if I let you see
    How extremely nice you'll smell.'

"And he stirred it round and
    round and round,
  And he sniffed at the foaming
    froth;
When I ups with his heels, and
    smothers his squeals
  In the scum of the boiling broth.

"And I eat that cook in a week or
    less,
  And as I eating be

The last of his chops, why I
    almost drops,
For a wessel in sight I see.—

"And I never larf, and I never
    smile,
  And I never lark nor play;
But sit and croak, and a single joke
  I have—which is to say:

"Oh, I am a cook and a captain
    bold,
  And the mate of the Nancy brig,
And a bo'sun tight, and a
    midshipmite,
  And the crew of the captain's gig!"
                          W. S. GILBERT

CHARLEMAGNE

Olger the Dane and Desiderio,
King of the Lombards, on a lofty tower
Stood gazing northward o'er the rolling plains,
League after league of harvest, to the foot
Of the snow-crested Alps, and saw approach
A mighty army, thronging all the roads
That led into the city. And the King
Said unto Olger, who had passed his youth
As hostage at the court of France, and knew
The Emperor's form and face: "Is Charlemagne
Among the host?" And Olger answered: "No."

And still the innumerable multitude
Flowed onward and increased, until the King
Cried in amazement: "Surely Charlemagne
Is coming in the midst of all these knights!"
And Olger answered slowly: "No; not yet;
He will not come so soon." Then much disturbed
King Desiderio asked: "What shall we do,
If he approach with a still greater army?"
And Olger answered: "When he shall appear,

You will behold what manner of man he is;
But what will then befall us I know not."

Then came the guard that never knew repose,
The Paladins of France! and at the sight
The Lombard King o'ercome with terror cried:
"This must be Charlemagne!" and as before
Did Olger answer: "No; not yet, not yet."

And then appeared in panoply complete
The Bishops and the Abbots and the Priests
Of the imperial chapel, and the Counts;
And Desiderio could no more endure
The light of day, nor yet encounter death,
But sobbed aloud and said: "Let us go down
And hide us in the bosom of the earth,
Far from the sight and anger of a foe
So terrible as this!" And Olger said:
"When you behold the harvests in the fields
Shaking with fear, the Po and the Ticino
Lashing the city walls with iron waves,
Then may you know that Charlemagne is come."
And even as he spake, in the northwest,
Lo! there uprose a black and threatening cloud,
Out of whose bosom flashed the light of arms
Upon the people pent up in the city;
A light more terrible than any darkness,
And Charlemagne appeared;—a Man of Iron!

His helmet was of iron, and his gloves
Of iron, and his breastplate and his greaves
And tassets were of iron, and his shield.
In his left hand he held an iron spear,
In his right hand his sword invincible.
The horse he rode on had the strength of iron,
And color of iron. All who went before him,
Beside him and behind him, his whole host,
Were armed with iron, and their hearts within them
Were stronger than the armor that they wore.
The fields and all the roads were filled with iron,
And points of iron glistened in the sun
And shed a terror through the city streets.

This at a single glance Olger the Dane
Saw from the tower, and turning to the King
Exclaimed in haste: "Behold; this is the man
You looked for with such eagerness!" and then
Fell as one dead at Desiderio's feet.

HENRY WADSWORTH LONGFELLOW

THE RAVEN

Once upon a midnight dreary, while I pondered, weak and weary,
Over many a quaint and curious volume of forgotten lore—
While I nodded, nearly napping, suddenly there came a tapping,
As of some one gently rapping, rapping at my chamber door.
' 'T is some visitor,' I muttered, 'tapping at my chamber door—
    Only this and nothing more.'

Ah, distinctly I remember it was in the bleak December;
And each separate dying ember wrought its ghost upon the floor.
Eagerly I wished the morrow;—vainly I had sought to borrow
From my books surcease of sorrow—sorrow for the lost Lenore—
For the rare and radiant maiden whom the angels name Lenore—
    Nameless *here* for evermore.

And the silken, sad, uncertain rustling of each purple curtain
Thrilled me—filled me with fantastic terrors never felt before;
So that now, to still the beating of my heart, I stood repeating,
' 'T is some visitor entreating entrance at my chamber door—
Some late visitor entreating entrance at my chamber door;—
    This it is and nothing more.'

Presently my soul grew stronger; hesitating then no longer,
'Sir,' said I, 'or Madam, truly your forgiveness I implore;
But the fact is I was napping, and so gently you came rapping,
And so faintly you came tapping, tapping at my chamber door,
That I scarce was sure I heard you'—here I opened wide the door;—
    Darkness there and nothing more.

Deep into that darkness peering, long I stood there wondering, fearing,
Doubting, dreaming dreams no mortal ever dared to dream before;
But the silence was unbroken, and the stillness gave no token,
And the only word there spoken was the whispered word, 'Lenore?'
This I whispered, and an echo murmured back the word, 'Lenore!'
    Merely this and nothing more.

Back into the chamber turning, all my soul within me burning,
Soon again I heard a tapping somewhat louder than before.
'Surely,' said I, 'surely that is something at my window lattice;
Let me see, then, what thereat is, and this mystery explore—
Let my heart be still a moment and this mystery explore;—
    'T is the wind and nothing more!'

Open here I flung the shutter, when, with many a flirt and flutter,
In there stepped a stately Raven of the saintly days of yore;
Not the least obeisance made he; not a minute stopped or stayed he;
But, with mien of lord or lady, perched above my chamber door—
Perched upon a bust of Pallas just above my chamber door—
    Perched, and sat, and nothing more.

Then this ebony bird beguiling my sad fancy into smiling,
By the grave and stern decorum of the countenance it wore,
'Though thy crest be shorn and shaven, thou,' I said, 'art sure no
    craven,
Ghastly grim and ancient Raven wandering from the Nightly shore—
Tell me what thy lordly name is on the Night's Plutonian shore!'
    Quoth the Raven, 'Nevermore.'

Much I marvelled this ungainly fowl to hear discourse so plainly,
Though its answer little meaning—little relevancy bore;
For we cannot help agreeing that no living human being
Ever yet was blessed with seeing bird above his chamber door—
Bird or beast upon the sculptured bust above his chamber door,
    With such name as 'Nevermore.'

But the Raven, sitting lonely on the placid bust, spoke only
That one word, as if his soul in that one word he did outpour.
Nothing farther then he uttered—not a feather then he fluttered—
Till I scarcely more than muttered, 'Other friends have flown before—
On the morrow *he* will leave me, as my Hopes have flown before.'
    Then the bird said, 'Nevermore.'

Startled at the stillness broken by reply so aptly spoken,
'Doubtless,' said I, 'what it utters is its only stock and store
Caught from some unhappy master whom unmerciful Disaster
Followed fast and followed faster till his songs one burden bore—
Till the dirges of his Hope that melancholy burden bore
    Of "Never—nevermore." '

But the Raven still beguiling my sad fancy into smiling,
Straight I wheeled a cushioned seat in front of bird and bust and door;
Then, upon the velvet sinking, I betook myself to linking
Fancy unto fancy, thinking what this ominous bird of yore—
What this grim, ungainly, ghastly, gaunt, and ominous bird of yore
    Meant in croaking 'Nevermore.'

This I sat engaged in guessing, but no syllable expressing
To the fowl whose fiery eyes now burned into my bosom's core;
This and more I sat divining, with my head at ease reclining
On the cushion's velvet lining that the lamp-light gloated o'er,
But whose velvet-violet lining with the lamp-light gloating o'er,
    She shall press, ah, nevermore!

Then, methought, the air grew denser, perfumed from an unseen
    censer
Swung by seraphim whose foot-falls tinkled on the tufted floor.
'Wretch,' I cried, 'thy God hath lent thee—by these angels he hath
    sent thee
Respite—respite and nepenthe from thy memories of Lenore;
Quaff, oh, quaff this kind nepenthe and forget this lost Lenore!'
    Quoth the Raven, 'Nevermore.'
'Prophet!' said I, 'thing of evil!—prophet still, if bird or devil!—
Whether Tempter sent, or whether tempest tossed thee here ashore,
Desolate yet all undaunted, on this desert land enchanted—
On this home by Horror haunted—tell me truly, I implore—
Is there—*is* there balm in Gilead?—tell me—tell me, I implore!'
    Quoth the Raven, 'Nevermore.'

'Prophet!' said I, 'thing of evil!—prophet still, if bird or devil!
By that Heaven that bends above us—by that God we both adore—
Tell this soul with sorrow laden if, within the distant Aidenn,
It shall clasp a sainted maiden whom the angels name Lenore—
Clasp a rare and radiant maiden whom the angels name Lenore.'
      Quoth the Raven, 'Nevermore.'

'Be that word our sign of parting, bird or fiend!' I shrieked,
      upstarting—
'Get thee back into the tempest and the Night's Plutonian shore!
Leave no black plume as a token of that lie thy soul hath spoken!
Leave my loneliness unbroken!—quit the bust above my door!
Take thy beak from out my heart, and take thy form from off my
      door!'
      Quoth the Raven, 'Nevermore.'

And the Raven, never flitting, still is sitting, *still* is sitting
On the pallid bust of Pallas just above my chamber door;
And his eyes have all the seeming of a demon's that is dreaming,
And the lamp-light o'er him streaming throws his shadow on the floor;
And my soul from out that shadow that lies floating on the floor
      Shall be lifted—nevermore!

                                        EDGAR ALLAN POE

BARBARA ALLEN

In scarlet town, where I was born,
    There was a fair maid dwellin',
Made every youth cry *Well-a-way!*
    Her name was Barbara Allen.

All in the merry month of May
    When green buds they were
        swellin',
Young Jemmy Grove on his
        death-bed lay,
    For love of Barbara Allen.

He sent his man in to her then,
    To the town where she was
        dwellin',

"O haste and come to my master
        dear,
    If your name be Barbara Allen."

So slowly, slowly rase she up,
    And slowly she came nigh him,
And when she drew the curtain by—
    "Young man, I think you're
        dyin'."

"O it's I'm sick and very very sick,
    And it's all for Barbara Allen."
"O the better for me ye'se never be,
    Tho' your heart's blood were
        a-spillin'!

"O dinna ye mind young man,"
   says she,
  "When the red wine ye were
    fillin',
That ye made the healths go
   round and round,
  And slighted Barbara Allen?"

He turn'd his face unto the wall,
  And death was with him
   dealin':
"Adieu, adieu, my dear friends all,
  And be kind to Barbara Allen!"

As she was walking o'er the fields,
  She heard the dead-bell knellin';

And every jow the dead-bell gave
  Cried "Woe to Barbara Allen."

"O mother, mother, make my
   bed,
  O make it saft and narrow:
My love has died for me today,
  I'll die for him to-morrow.

"Farewell," she said, "ye virgins
   all,
  And shun the fault I fell in:
Henceforth take warning by the
   fall
  Of cruel Barbara Allen."

              ANONYMOUS

LOCHINVAR

Oh, young Lochinvar is come out of the West,—
Through all the wide Border his steed was the best,
And, save his good broadsword, he weapon had none,—
He rode all unarmed, and he rode all alone.
So faithful in love, and so dauntless in war,
There never was knight like the young Lochinvar.

He stayed not for brake, and he stopped not for stone,
He swam the Eske river where ford there was none,
But, ere he alighted at Netherby gate,
The bride had consented, the gallant came late;
For a laggard in love, and a dastard in war,
Was to wed the fair Ellen of brave Lochinvar.

So boldly he entered the Netherby hall,
Among bridesmen, and kinsmen, and brothers, and all.
Then spoke the bride's father, his hand on his sword,
(For the poor craven bridegroom said never a word),
"Oh, come ye in peace here, or come ye in war,
Or to dance at our bridal, young Lord Lochinvar?"

"I long wooed your daughter, my suit you denied;—
Love swells like the Solway, but ebbs like its tide;—
And now am I come, with this lost love of mine,
To lead but one measure, drink one cup of wine.
There are maidens in Scotland more lovely by far,
That would gladly be bride to the young Lochinvar."

The bride kissed the goblet, the knight took it up,
He quaffed off the wine, and he threw down the cup.
She looked down to blush, and she looked up to sigh,
With a smile on her lips, and a tear in her eye.
He took her soft hand ere her mother could bar:
"Now tread we a measure," said young Lochinvar.

So stately his form, and so lovely her face,
That never a hall such a galliard did grace;
While her mother did fret, and her father did fume,
And the bridegroom stood dangling his bonnet and plume,
And the bridemaidens whispered, " 'Twere better by far
To have matched our fair cousin with young Lochinvar."

One touch to her hand, and one word in her ear,
When they reached the hall-door, and the charger stood near;
So light to the croupe the fair lady he swung,
So light to the saddle before her he sprung!
"She is won! we are gone! over bank, bush, and scaur;
They'll have fleet steeds that follow," quoth young Lochinvar.

There was mounting 'mong Græmes of the Netherby clan;
Forsters, Fenwicks, and Musgraves, they rode and they ran;
There was racing and chasing on Cannobie Lee,
But the lost bride of Netherby ne'er did they see.
So daring in love, and so dauntless in war,
Have ye e'er heard of gallant like young Lochinvar?

SIR WALTER SCOTT

THE RIME OF THE ANCIENT MARINER

An ancient Mariner meeteth three gallants bidden to a wedding feast, and detaineth one.

It is an ancient Mariner,
And he stoppeth one of three.
"By thy long grey beard and glittering eye,
Now wherefore stopp'st thou me?

The Bridegroom's doors are open'd wide,
And I am next of kin;
The guests are met, the feast is set:
May'st hear the merry din."

The Wedding-Guest is spell-bound by the eye of the old seafaring man, and constrained to hear his tale.

He holds him with his skinny hand,
"There was a ship," quoth he.
"Hold off! Unhand me, grey-beard loon!"
Eftsoons his hand dropt he.

He holds him with his glittering eye—
The Wedding-Guest stood still,
And listens like a three years' child:
The Mariner hath his will.

The Wedding-Guest sat on a stone:
He cannot choose but hear;
And thus spake on that ancient man,
The bright-eyed Mariner.

The Mariner tells how the ship sailed southward with a good wind and fair weather, till it reached the Line.

"The ship was cheer'd, the harbour clear'd,
Merrily did we drop
Below the kirk, below the hill,
Below the lighthouse top.

The Sun came up upon the left,
Out of the sea came he!
And he shone bright, and on the right
Went down into the sea.

Higher and higher every day,
Till over the mast at noon——"
The Wedding-Guest here beat his breast,
For he heard the loud bassoon.

*The Wedding-
Guest heareth
the bridal
music; but the
Mariner con-
tinueth his tale.*

The bride hath pac'd into the hall,
Red as a rose is she;
Nodding their heads before her goes
The merry minstrelsy.

The Wedding-Guest he beat his breast,
Yet he cannot choose but hear;
And thus spake on that ancient man,
The bright-ey'd Mariner.

*The ship driven
by a storm to-
ward the South
Pole.*

"And now the Storm-blast came, and he
Was tyrannous and strong:
He struck with his o'ertaking wings,
And chas'd us south along.

With sloping masts and dipping prow,
As who pursu'd with yell and blow
Still treads the shadow of his foe,
And forward bends his head,
The ship drove fast, loud roar'd the blast,
And southward aye we fled.

And now there came both mist and snow,
And it grew wondrous cold:
And ice, mast-high, came floating by,
As green as emerald.

*The land of ice,
and of fearful
sounds, where
no living thing
was to be seen.*

And through the drifts the snowy clifts
Did send a dismal sheen:
Nor shapes of men nor beasts we ken—
The ice was all between.

The ice was here, the ice was there,
The ice was all around:
It crack'd and growl'd, and roar'd and howl'd,
Like noises in a swound!

*Till a great
sea-bird, called
the Albatross,
came through
the snow-fog,
and was re-
ceived with
great joy and
hospitality.*

At length did cross an Albatross,
Thorough the fog it came;
As if it had been a Christian soul,
We hail'd it in God's name.

It ate the food it ne'er had eat,
And round and round it flew.
The ice did split with a thunder-fit;
The helmsman steer'd us through!

*And lo! the
Albatross
proveth a bird
of good omen,
and followeth
the ship as it
returned north-
ward through
fog and float-
ing ice.*

And a good south wind sprung up behind;
The Albatross did follow,
And every day, for food or play,
Came to the mariners' hollo!

In mist or cloud, on mast or shroud,
It perch'd for vespers nine;
Whiles all the night, through fog-smoke white,
Glimmer'd the white moonshine."

*The ancient
Mariner in-
hospitably
killeth the
pious bird of
good omen.*

"God save thee, ancient Mariner,
From the fiends, that plague thee thus!—
Why look'st thou so?"—"With my crossbow
I shot the Albatross."

Part II

"The Sun now rose upon the right:
Out of the sea came he,
Still hid in mist, and on the left
Went down into the sea.

And the good south wind still blew behind,
But no sweet bird did follow,
Nor any day for food or play
Came to the mariners' hollo!

*His shipmates
cry out against
the ancient
Mariner for
killing the bird
of good luck.*

And I had done an hellish thing,
And it would work 'em woe:
For all averr'd I had kill'd the bird
That made the breeze to blow.

Ah wretch! said they, the bird to slay,
That made the breeze to blow!

But when the fog cleared off, they justify the same, and thus make themselves accomplices in the crime.

Nor dim nor red, like God's own head,
The glorious Sun uprist:
Then all averr'd I had kill'd the bird
That brought the fog and mist.
'Twas right, said they, such birds to slay,
That bring the fog and mist.

The fair breeze continues; the ship enters the Pacific Ocean, and sails northward, even till it reaches the Line.

The fair breeze blew, the white foam flew,
The furrow follow'd free;
We were the first that ever burst
Into that silent sea.

The ship hath been suddenly becalmed.

Down dropt the breeze, the sails dropt down,
'Twas sad as sad could be;
And we did speak only to break
The silence of the sea!

All in a hot and copper sky,
The bloody Sun, at noon,
Right up above the mast did stand,
No bigger than the Moon.

Day after day, day after day,
We stuck, nor breath nor motion;
As idle as a painted ship
Upon a painted ocean.

And the Albatross begins to be avenged.

Water, water, everywhere,
And all the boards did shrink;
Water, water, everywhere,
Nor any drop to drink.

A Spirit had followed them, one of the invisible inhabitants of this planet, neither departed souls nor angels; concerning whom the learned Jews, Josephus, and the Platonic Constantinopolitan, Michael

The very deep did rot: O Christ!
That ever this should be!
Yea, slimy things did crawl with legs
Upon the slimy sea.

About, about, in reel and rout
The death-fires danc'd at night;
The water, like a witch's oils,
Burnt green, and blue, and white.

Psellus, may be consulted. They are very numerous, and there is no climate or element without one or more.

And some in dreams assurèd were
Of the Spirit that plagued us so;
Nine fathom deep he had follow'd us
From the land of mist and snow.

The shipmates, in their sore distress, would fain throw the whole guilt on the ancient Mariner: in sign whereof they hang the dead sea-bird round his neck.

And every tongue, through utter drought,
Was wither'd at the root;
We could not speak, no more than if
We had been chok'd with soot.

Ah! well a-day! what evil looks
Had I from old and young!
Instead of the cross, the Albatross
About my neck was hung."

PART III

"There passed a weary time. Each throat
Was parch'd, and glaz'd each eye.
A weary time! a weary time!
How glaz'd each weary eye!

The ancient Mariner beholdeth a sign in the element afar off.

When, looking westward, I beheld
A something in the sky.

At first it seem'd a little speck,
And then it seem'd a mist;
It moved and moved, and took at last
A certain shape, I wist.

A speck, a mist, a shape, I wist!
And still it near'd and near'd:
As if it dodged a water-sprite,
It plung'd, and tack'd and veer'd.

At its nearer approach, it seemeth him to be a ship; and at a dear ransom he freeth his speech from the bonds of thirst.

With throats unslak'd, with black lips bak'd,
We could nor laugh nor wail;
Through utter drought all dumb we stood!
I bit my arm, I suck'd the blood,
And cried, A sail! a sail!

A flash of joy;

With throats unslak'd, with black lips bak'd,
Agape they heard me call:
Gramercy! they for joy did grin,
And all at once their breath drew in,
As they were drinking all.

*And horror
follows. For
can it be a
ship that comes
onward without
wind or tide?*
See! see! (I cried) she tacks no more!
Hither to work us weal—
Without a breeze, without a tide,
She steadies with upright keel!

The western wave was all aflame,
The day was wellnigh done!
Almost upon the western wave
Rested the broad, bright Sun;
When that strange shape drove suddenly
Betwixt us and the Sun.

*It seemeth him
but the skele-
ton of a ship.*
And straight the Sun was fleck'd with bars
  (Heaven's Mother send us grace!),
As if through a dungeon-grate he peer'd
With broad and burning face.

Alas! (thought I, and my heart beat loud)
How fast she nears and nears!
Are those her sails that glance in the Sun,
Like restless gossameres?

*And its ribs
are seen as
bars on the
face of the
setting Sun.
The Spectre-
Woman and
her Death-
mate, and no
other, on
board the
skeleton ship.
Like vessel,
like crew!*
Are those her ribs through which the Sun
Did peer, as through a grate?
And is that Woman all her crew
Is that a Death? and are there two?
Is Death that Woman's mate?

Her lips were red, her looks were free,
Her locks were yellow as gold:
Her skin was as white as leprosy,
The Nightmare Life-in-Death was she,
Who thicks man's blood with cold.

*Death and
Life-in-Death
have diced for
the ship's crew
and she (the
latter) winneth
the ancient
Mariner.*
The naked hulk alongside came,
And the twain were casting dice;
'The game is done! I've won! I've won!'
Quoth she, and whistles thrice.

*No twilight
within the
courts of the
Sun.*
The Sun's rim dips; the stars rush out:
At one stride comes the dark;
With far-heard whisper, o'er the sea,
Off shot the spectre-bark.

We listen'd and look'd sideways up!
Fear at my heart, as at a cup,
My life-blood seem'd to sip!
The stars were dim, and thick the night,
The steersman's face by his lamp gleam'd white;

At the rising of the Moon,

From the sails the dew did drip—
Till clomb above the eastern bar
The hornèd Moon, with one bright star
Within the nether tip.

One after another,

One after one, by the star-dogg'd Moon,
Too quick for groan or sigh,
Each turn'd his face with a ghastly pang,
And curs'd me with his eye.

His shipmates drop down dead.

Four times fifty living men
  (And I heard nor sigh nor groan),
With heavy thump, a lifeless lump,
They dropp'd down one by one.

But Life-in-Death begins her work on the ancient Mariner.

The souls did from their bodies fly—
They fled to bliss or woe!
And every soul, it pass'd me by
Like the whizz of my crossbow!"

PART IV

The Wedding-Guest feareth that a spirit is talking to him.

"I fear thee, ancient Mariner!
I fear thy skinny hand!
And thou art long, and lank, and brown,
As is the ribb'd sea-sand.

I fear thee and thy glittering eye,
And thy skinny hand so brown."—

But the ancient Mariner assureth him of his bodily life, and proceedeth to relate his horrible penance.

"Fear not, fear not, thou Wedding-Guest!
This body dropt not down.

Alone, alone, all, all alone,
Alone on a wide, wide sea!
And never a saint took pity on
My soul in agony.

He despiseth the creatures of the calm.

The many men, so beautiful!
And they all dead did lie:
And a thousand thousand slimy things
Liv'd on; and so did I.

And envieth that they should live, and so many lie dead.

I look'd upon the rotting sea,
And drew my eyes away;
I look'd upon the rotting deck,
And there the dead men lay.

I look'd to heaven, and tried to pray;
But or ever a prayer had gusht,
A wicked whisper came, and made
My heart as dry as dust.

I clos'd my lids, and kept them close,
And the balls like pulses beat;
But the sky and the sea, and the sea and the sky,
Lay like a load on my weary eye,
And the dead were at my feet.

But the curse liveth for him in the eye of the dead men.

The cold sweat melted from their limbs,
Nor rot nor reek did they:
The look with which they look'd on me
Had never pass'd away.

*In his loneli-
ness and
fixedness he
yearneth
towards the
journeying
Moon, and the
stars that still
sojourn, yet still
move onward;
and everywhere
the blue sky
belongs to them,
and is their
appointed rest
and their native
country and their
own natural
homes, which
they enter un-
announced, as
lords that are
certainly ex-
pected, and yet
there is a silent
joy at their
arrival.*

An orphan's curse would drag to hell
A spirit from on high;
But oh! more horrible than that
Is the curse in a dead man's eye!
Seven days, seven nights, I saw that curse,
And yet I could not die.

The moving Moon went up the sky,
And nowhere did abide;
Softly she was going up,
And a star or two beside—

Her beams bemock'd the sultry main,
Like April hoar-frost spread;
But where the ship's huge shadow lay,
The charmèd water burnt alway
A still and awful red.

*By the light
of the Moon
he beholdeth
God's crea-
tures of the
great calm.*

Beyond the shadow of the ship,
I watch'd the water-snakes:
They moved in tracks of shining white
And when they rear'd, the elfish light
Fell off in hoary flakes.

Within the shadow of the ship
I watch'd their rich attire:
Blue, glossy green, and velvet black,
They coil'd and swam; and every track
Was a flash of golden fire.

*Their beauty
and their
happiness.*

O happy living things! no tongue
Their beauty might declare:
A spring of love gush'd from my heart,
And I bless'd them unaware:
Sure my kind saint took pity on me,
And I bless'd them unaware.

*He blesseth
them in his
heart.*

*The spell
begins to
break.*

The selfsame moment I could pray;
And from my neck so free
The Albatross fell off, and sank
Like lead into the sea."

PART V

"O sleep! it is a gentle thing,
Beloved from pole to pole!
To Mary Queen the praise be given!
She sent the gentle sleep from Heaven,
That slid into my soul.

By grace of the holy Mother, the ancient Mariner is refreshed with rain.

The silly buckets on the deck,
That had so long remain'd,
I dreamt that they were fill'd with dew;
And when I awoke, it rain'd.

My lips were wet, my throat was cold,
My garments all were dank;
Sure I had drunken in my dreams,
And still my body drank.

I moved, and could not feel my limbs:
I was so light—almost
I thought that I had died in sleep,
And was a blessèd ghost.

He heareth sounds and seeth strange sights and commotions in the sky and the element.

And soon I heard a roaring wind:
It did not come anear;
But with its sound it shook the sails,
That were so thin and sere.

The upper air burst into life;
And a hundred fire-flags sheen;
To and fro they were hurried about!
And to and fro, and in and out,
The wan stars danced between.

And the coming wind did roar more loud,
And the sails did sigh like sedge;
And the rain pour'd down from one black cloud;
The Moon was at its edge.

The thick black cloud was cleft, and still
The Moon was at its side;
Like waters shot from some high crag,
The lightning fell with never a jag,
A river steep and wide.

*The bodies of
the ship's crew
are inspired,
and the ship
moves on;*

The loud wind never reach'd the ship,
Yet now the ship moved on!
Beneath the lightning and the Moon
The dead men gave a groan.

They groan'd, they stirr'd, they all uprose,
Nor spake, nor moved their eyes;
It had been strange, even in a dream,
To have seen those dead men rise.

The helmsman steer'd, the ship moved on;
Yet never a breeze up-blew;
The mariners all 'gan work the ropes,
Where they were wont to do;
They raised their limbs like lifeless tools—
We were a ghastly crew.

The body of my brother's son
Stood by me, knee to knee:
The body and I pull'd at one rope,
But he said naught to me."

*But not by
the souls of
the men, nor
by demons of
earth or mid-
dle air, but by
a blessed troop
of angelic
spirits, sent
down by the
invocation of
the guardian
saint.*

"I fear thee, ancient Mariner!"
"Be calm, thou Wedding-Guest:
'Twas not those souls that fled in pain,
Which to their corses came again,
But a troop of spirits blest:

For when it dawn'd—they dropp'd their arms,
And cluster'd round the mast;
Sweet sounds rose slowly through their mouths,
And from their bodies pass'd.

Around, around, flew each sweet sound,
Then darted to the Sun;
Slowly the sounds came back again,
Now mix'd, now one by one.

Sometimes a-dropping from the sky
I heard the skylark sing;
Sometimes all little birds that are,
How they seem'd to fill the sea and air
With their sweet jargoning!

And now 'twas like all instruments,
Now like a lonely flute;
And now it is an angel's song,
That makes the Heavens be mute.

It ceased; yet still the sails made on
A pleasant noise till noon,
A noise like of a hidden brook
In the leafy month of June,
That to the sleeping woods all night
Singeth a quiet tune.

Till noon we quietly sail'd on,
Yet never a breeze did breathe:
Slowly and smoothly went the ship,
Moved onward from beneath.

The lonesome Spirit from the South Pole carries on the ship as far as the Line, in obedience to the angelic troop, but still requireth vengeance.

Under the keel nine fathom deep,
From the land of mist and snow,
The Spirit slid: and it was he
That made the ship to go.
The sails at noon left off their tune,
And the ship stood still also.

The Sun, right up above the mast,
Had fix'd her to the ocean:
But in a minute she 'gan stir,
With a short uneasy motion—
Backwards and forwards half her length
With a short uneasy motion.

Then like a pawing horse let go,
She made a sudden bound:
It flung the blood into my head,
And I fell down in a swound.

The Polar Spirit's fellow demons, the invisible inhabitants of the element, take part in his wrong; and two of them relate, one to the other, that penance long and heavy for the ancient Mariner hath been accorded to the Polar Spirit, who returneth southward.

How long in that same fit I lay,
I have not to declare;
But ere my living life return'd,
I heard, and in my soul discern'd
Two voices in the air.

'Is it he?' quoth one, 'is this the man?
By Him who died on cross,
With his cruel bow he laid full low
The harmless Albatross.

The Spirit who bideth by himself
In the land of mist and snow,
He loved the bird that loved the man
Who shot him with his bow.'

The other was a softer voice,
As soft as honey-dew:
Quoth he, 'The man hath penance done,
And penance more will do.' "

PART VI

"First Voice:
'But tell me, tell me! speak again,
Thy soft response renewing—
What makes that ship drive on so fast?
What is the Ocean doing?'

Second Voice:
'Still as a slave before his lord,
The Ocean hath no blast;
His great bright eye most silently
Up to the Moon is cast—

If he may know which way to go;
For she guides him smooth or grim.
See, brother, see! how graciously
She looketh down on him.'

*The Mariner
hath been cast
into a trance;
for the angelic
power causeth
the vessel to
drive northward
faster than
human life
could endure.*

First Voice:
'But why drives on that ship so fast,
Without or wave or wind?'

Second Voice:
'The air is cut away before,
And closes from behind.

Fly, brother, fly! more high, more high!
Or we shall be belated:
For slow and slow that ship will go,
When the Mariner's trance is abated.'

*The supernat-
ural motion
is retarded;
the Mariner
awakes, and
his penance
begins anew.*

I woke, and we were sailing on
As in a gentle weather:
'Twas night, calm night, the Moon was high;
The dead men stood together.

All stood together on the deck,
For a charnel-dungeon fitter:
All fix'd on me their stony eyes,
That in the Moon did glitter.

The pang, the curse, with which they died,
Had never pass'd away:
I could not draw my eyes from theirs,
Nor turn them up to pray.

And now this spell was snapt: once more
I viewed the ocean green,
And look'd far forth, yet little saw
Of what had else been seen—

The curse is finally expiated.

Like one that on a lonesome road
Doth walk in fear and dread,
And having once turn'd round, walks on,
And turns no more his head;
Because he knows a frightful fiend
Doth close behind him tread.

But soon there breathed a wind on me,
Nor sound nor motion made:
Its path was not upon the sea,
In ripple or in shade.

It raised my hair, it fann'd my cheek
Like a meadow-gale of spring—
It mingled strangely with my fears,
Yet if felt like a welcoming.

Swiftly, swiftly flew the ship,
Yet she sail'd softly too:
Sweetly, sweetly blew the breeze—
On me alone it blew.

And the ancient Mariner beholdeth his native country.

O dream of joy! is this indeed
The lighthouse top I see?
Is this the hill? is this the kirk?
Is this mine own countree?

We drifted o'er the harbour-bar,
And I with sobs did pray—
O let me be awake, my God!
Or let me sleep alway.

The harbour-bay was clear as glass,
So smoothly it was strewn!
And on the bay the moonlight lay,
And the shadow of the Moon.

The rock shone bright, the kirk no less
That stands above the rock:
The moonlight steep'd in silentness
The steady weathercock.

The angelic spirits leave the dead bodies,

And the bay was white with silent light
Till rising from the same,
Full many shapes, that shadows were,
In crimson colours came.

And appear in their own forms of light.

A little distance from the prow
Those crimson shadows were:
I turn'd my eyes upon the deck—
O Christ! what saw I there!

Each corse lay flat, lifeless and flat,
And, by the holy rood!
A man all light, a seraph-man,
On every corse there stood.

This seraph-band, each waved his hand:
It was a heavenly sight!
They stood as signals to the land,
Each one a lovely light;

This seraph-band, each waved his hand,
No voice did they impart—
No voice; but O, the silence sank
Like music on my heart.

But soon I heard the dash of oars,
I heard the Pilot's cheer;
My head was turn'd perforce away,
And I saw a boat appear.

The Pilot and the Pilot's boy,
I heard them coming fast:
Dear Lord in Heaven! it was a joy
The dead men could not blast.

I saw a third—I heard his voice:
It is the Hermit good!
He singeth loud his godly hymns
That he makes in the wood.
He'll shrieve my soul, he'll wash away
The Albatross's blood."

PART VII

The Hermit of the Wood

"This Hermit good lives in that wood
Which slopes down to the sea.
How loudly his sweet voice he rears!
He loves to talk with marineres
That come from a far countree.

He kneels at morn, and noon, and eve—
He hath a cushion plump;
It is the moss that wholly hides
The rotted old oak-stump.

The skiff-boat near'd: I heard them talk,
'Why, this is strange, I trow!
Where are those lights so many and fair,
That signal made but now?'

Approacheth the ship with wonder.

'Strange, by my faith!' the Hermit said—
'And they answer'd not our cheer!
The planks look warp'd! and see those sails,
How thin they are and sere!
I never saw aught like to them,
Unless perchance it were

Brown skeletons of leaves that lag
My forest-brook along;
When the ivy-tod is heavy with snow,
And the owlet whoops to the wolf below,
That eats the she-wolf's young.'

'Dear Lord! it hath a fiendish look—
(The Pilot made reply)
I am a-fear'd.'—'Push on, push on!'
Said the Hermit cheerily.

The boat came closer to the ship,
But I nor spake nor stirr'd;
The boat came close beneath the ship,
And straight a sound was heard.

The ship sud-
denly sinketh.

Under the water it rumbled on
Still louder and more dread:
It reach'd the ship, it split the bay;
The ship went down like lead.

The ancient
Mariner is
saved in the
Pilot's boat.

Stunn'd by that loud and dreadful sound,
Which sky and ocean smote,
Like one that hath been seven days drown'd
My body lay afloat;
But swift as dreams, myself I found
Within the Pilot's boat.

Upon the whirl, where sank the ship,
The boat spun round and round;
And all was still, save that the hill
Was telling of the sound.

I moved my lips—the Pilot shriek'd
And fell down in a fit;
The holy Hermit raised his eyes,
And pray'd where he did sit.

I took the oars: the Pilot's boy,
Who now doth crazy go,
Laugh'd loud and long, and all the while
His eyes went to and fro.
'Ha! ha!' quoth he, 'full plain I see
The Devil knows how to row.'

And now, all in my own countree,
I stood on the firm land!
The Hermit stepp'd forth from the boat,
And scarcely he could stand.

The ancient
Mariner
earnestly en-
treateth the
Hermit to
shrieve him;
and the pen-
ance of life
falls on him.

'O shrieve me, shrieve me, holy man!'
The Hermit cross'd his brow.
'Say quick,' quoth he, 'I bid thee say—
What manner of man art thou?'

Forthwith this frame of mine was wrench'd
With a woeful agony,
Which forced me to begin my tale;
And then it left me free.

*And ever
and anon
throughout
his future life
an agony
constraineth
him to travel
from land to
land;*

Since then, at an uncertain hour,
That agony returns:
And till my ghastly tale is told,
This heart within me burns.

I pass, like night, from land to land;
I have strange power of speech;
That moment that his face I see,
I know the man that must hear me:
To him my tale I teach.

What loud uproar bursts from that door!
The wedding-guests are there:
But in the garden-bower the bride
And bride-maids singing are:
And hark, the little vesper bell,
Which biddeth me to prayer!

O Wedding-Guest! this soul hath been
Alone on a wide, wide sea:
So lonely 'twas, that God Himself
Scarce seemèd there to be.

O sweeter than the marriage-feast,
'Tis sweeter far to me,
To walk together to the kirk
With a goodly company!—

To walk together to the kirk,
And all together pray,
While each to his great Father bends,
Old men, and babes, and loving friends,
And youths and maidens gay!

*And to teach,
by his own
example, love
and reverence
to all things
that God
made and
loveth.*

Farewell, farewell! but this I tell
To thee, thou Wedding-Guest!
He prayeth well, who loveth well
Both man and bird and beast.

He prayeth best, who loveth best
All things both great and small;
For the dear God who loveth us,
He made and loveth all."

The Mariner, whose eye is bright,
Whose beard with age is hoar,
Is gone: and now the Wedding-Guest
Turn'd from the bridegroom's door.

He went like one that hath been stunn'd,
And is of sense forlorn:
A sadder and a wiser man
He rose the morrow morn.

SAMUEL TAYLOR COLERIDGE

RICHARD CORY

Whenever Richard Cory went
    down town,
  We people on the pavement
    looked at him:
He was a gentleman from sole to
    crown,
  Clean favored, and imperially slim.

And he was always quietly arrayed,
  And he was always human
    when he talked;
But still he fluttered pulses when
    he said,
  "Good-morning," and he
    glittered when he walked.

And he was rich—yes, richer than a king,
  And admirably schooled in
    every grace:
In fine, we thought that he was
    everything.
  To make us wish that we were
    in his place.

So on we worked, and waited for
    the light,
  And went without the meat,
    and cursed the bread;
And Richard Cory, one calm
    summer night,
  Went home and put a bullet
    through his head.

EDWIN ARLINGTON ROBINSON

THE COWBOY'S LAMENT

As I walked out in the streets of Laredo,
As I walked out in Laredo one day,
I spied a poor cowboy wrapped up in white linen,
Wrapped up in white linen as cold as the clay.

"Oh, beat the drum slowly and play the fife lowly,
Play the dead march as you carry me along;
Take me to the green valley, there lay the sod o'er me,
For I'm a young cowboy and I know I've done wrong.

"I see by your outfit that you are a cowboy"—
These words he did say as I boldly stepped by.
"Come sit down beside me and hear my sad story;
I am shot in the breast and I know I must die.

"Let sixteen gamblers come handle my coffin,
Let sixteen cowboys come sing me a song.
Take me to the graveyard and lay the sod o'er me,
For I'm a poor cowboy and I know I've done wrong.

"My friends and relations they live in the Nation,
They know not where their boy has gone.
He first came to Texas and hired to a ranchman,
Oh, I'm a young cowboy and I know I've done wrong.

"It was once in the saddle I used to go dashing;
It was once in the saddle I used to go gay;
First to the dram-house and then to the card-house;
Got shot in the breast and I am dying today.

"Get six jolly cowboys to carry my coffin;
Get six pretty maidens to bear up my pall.
Put bunches of roses all over my coffin,
Put roses to deaden the sods as they fall.

"Then swing your rope slowly and rattle your spurs lowly,
And give a wild whoop as you carry me along;
And in the grave throw me and roll the sod o'er me
For I'm a young cowboy and I know I've done wrong.

"Oh, bury beside me my knife and six-shooter,
My spurs on my heel, my rifle by my side,
And over my coffin put a bottle of brandy
That the cowboys may drink as they carry me along.

"Go bring me a cup, a cup of cold water,
To cool my parched lips," the cowboy then said;
Before I returned his soul had departed,
And gone to the round-up—the cowboy was dead.

We beat the drum slowly and played the fife lowly,
And bitterly wept as we bore him along;
For we all loved our comrade, so brave, young, and handsome,
We all loved our comrade although he'd done wrong.

Where men lived raw, in the desert's maw,
And hell was nothing to shun;
Where they buried 'em neat, without preacher or sheet,
And writ on their foreheads, crude but sweet,
"This Jasper was slow with a gun."

ANONYMOUS

FAIR HELEN

I wish I were where Helen lies;
Night and day on me she cries;
O that I were where Helen lies
  On fair Kirconnell lea!

Curst be the heart that thought
    the thought,
And curst the hand that fired the shot,
When in my arms burd Helen dropt,
    And died to succour me!

O think na but my heart was sair
When my Love dropt down and
    spak nae mair!
I laid her down wi' meikle care
  On fair Kirconnell lea.

As I went down the water-side,
None but my foe to be my guide,
None but my foe to be my guide,
  On fair Kirconnell lea;

I lighted down my sword to draw,
I hackéd him in pieces sma',
I hackéd him in pieces sma',
  For her sake that died for me.

O Helen fair, beyond compare!
I'll make a garland of thy hair
Shall bind my heart for evermair
  Until the day I die.

O that I were where Helen lies!
Night and day on me she cries;
Out of my bed she bids me rise,
  Says, 'Haste and come to me!'

O Helen fair! O Helen chaste!
If I were with thee, I were blest
Where thou lies low and takes thy rest
  On fair Kirconnell lea.

I wish my grave were growing green,
A winding-sheet drawn ower my een,
And I in Helen's arms lying,
  On fair Kirconnell lea.

I wish I were where Helen lies;
Night and day on me she cries;
And I am weary of the skies,
  Since my Love died for me.

           ANONYMOUS

THE LADY OF SHALOTT

PART I

On either side the river lie
Long fields of barley and of rye,
That clothe the wold and meet
  the sky;
And thro' the field the road runs by
  To many-tower'd Camelot;
And up and down the people go,
Gazing where the lilies blow
Round an island there below,
  The island of Shalott.

Willows whiten, aspens quiver,
Little breezes dusk and shiver
Thro' the wave that runs for ever
By the island in the river
  Flowing down to Camelot.
Four gray walls, and four gray
  towers,
Overlook a space of flowers,
And the silent isle imbowers
  The Lady of Shalott.

By the margin, willow-veil'd,
Slide the heavy barges trail'd
By slow horses; and unhail'd
The shallop flitteth silken-sail'd
    Skimming down to Camelot:
But who hath seen her wave her
    hand?
Or at the casement seen her
    stand?
Or is she known in all the land,
    The Lady of Shalott?

Only reapers, reaping early
In among the bearded barley,
Hear a song that echoes cheerly
From the river winding clearly,
    Down to tower'd Camelot;
And by the moon the reaper
    weary,
Piling sheaves in uplands airy,
Listening, whispers " 'Tis the
    fairy
    Lady of Shalott."

PART II

There she weaves by night and
    day
A magic web with colors gay.
She has heard a whisper say,
A curse is on her if she stay
    To look down to Camelot.
She knows not what the curse
    may be,
And so she weaveth steadily,
And little other care hath she,
    The Lady of Shalott.

And moving thro' a mirror clear
That hangs before her all the
    year,
Shadows of the world appear.

There she sees the highway near
    Winding down to Camelot;
There the river eddy whirls,
And there the surly village-churls,
And the red cloaks of market
    girls,
    Pass onward from Shalott.

Sometimes a troop of damsels
    glad,
Or an abbot or an ambling pad,
Sometimes a curly shepherd-lad,
Or long-hair'd page in crimson
    clad,
    Goes by to tower'd Camelot;
And sometimes thro' the mirror
    blue
The knights come riding two and
    two:
She hath no loyal knight and
    true,
    The Lady of Shalott.

But in her web she still delights
To weave the mirror's magic
    sights,
For often thro' the silent nights
A funeral, with plumes and lights
    And music, went to Camelot;
Or when the moon was overhead,
Came two young lovers lately
    wed:
"I am half sick of shadows," said
    The Lady of Shalott.

PART III

A bow-shot from her bower-eaves,
He rode between the barley-
    sheaves,
The sun came dazzling thro' the
    leaves,

And flamed upon the brazen
   greaves
Of bold Sir Lancelot.
A red-cross knight for ever
   kneel'd
To a lady in his shield,
That sparkled on the yellow field,
   Beside remote Shalott.

The gemmy bridle glitter'd free,
Like to some branch of stars we see
Hung in the golden Galaxy.
The bridle bells rang merrily
   As he rode down to Camelot;
And from his blazon'd baldric
   slung
A mighty silver bugle hung,
And as he rode his armor rung,
   Beside remote Shalott.

All in the blue unclouded weather
Thick-jewell'd shone the saddle-
   leather,
The helmet and the helmet-
   feather
Burn'd like one burning flame
   together,
   As he rode down to Camelot;
As often thro' the purple night,
Below the starry clusters bright,
Some bearded meteor, trailing
   light,
   Moves over still Shalott.

His broad clear brow in sunlight
   glow'd;
On burnish'd hooves his war-
   horse trode;
From underneath his helmet flow'd
His cowl-black curls as on he rode,
   As he rode down to Camelot.

From the bank and from the river
He flash'd into the crystal mirror,
"Tirra lirra," by the river
   Sang Sir Lancelot.

She left the web, she left the
   loom,
She made three paces thro' the
   room,
She saw the water-lily bloom,
She saw the helmet and the
   plume,
   She look'd down to Camelot.
Out flew the web and floated
   wide;
The mirror crack'd from side to
   side:
"The curse is come upon me,"
   cried
   The Lady of Shalott.

PART IV

In the stormy east-wind straining,
The pale yellow woods were
   waning,
The broad stream in his banks
   complaining,
Heavily the low sky raining
   Over tower'd Camelot;
Down she came and found a boat
Beneath a willow left afloat,
And round about the prow she
   wrote
   The Lady of Shalott.

And down the river's dim
   expanse
Like some bold seër in a trance,
Seeing all his own mischance—
With a glassy countenance
   Did she look to Camelot.

And at the closing of the day
She loosed the chain, and down
   she lay;
The broad stream bore her far away,
  The Lady of Shalott.

Lying, robed in snowy white
That loosely flew to left and right—
The leaves upon her falling light—
Thro' the noises of the night
  She floated down to Camelot:
And as the boat-head wound
   along
The willowy hills and fields
   among,
They heard her singing her last
   song,
  The Lady of Shalott.

Heard a carol, mournful, holy,
Chanted loudly, chanted lowly,
Till her blood was frozen slowly,
And her eyes were darkened
   wholly,
  Turn'd to tower'd Camelot.

For ere she reach'd upon the tide
The first house by the water-side,
Singing in her song she died,
  The Lady of Shalott.

Under tower and balcony,
By garden-wall and gallery,
A gleaming shape she floated by,
Dead-pale between the houses high,
  Silent into Camelot.
Out upon the wharfs they came,
Knight and burgher, lord and dame,
And round the prow they read
   her name,
  The Lady of Shalott.

Who is this? and what is here?
And in the lighted palace near
Died the sound of royal cheer:
And they cross'd themselves for fear,
  All the knights at Camelot:
But Lancelot mused a little space;
He said, "She has a lovely face;
God in his mercy lend her grace,
  The Lady of Shalott."

ALFRED, LORD TENNYSON

BEN BOLT

Don't you remember sweet Alice,
  Ben Bolt,—
Sweet Alice whose hair was so brown,
Who wept with delight when you
  gave her a smile,
And trembled with fear at your frown?
In the old church-yard in the
  valley, Ben Bolt,
In a corner obscure and alone,
They have fitted a slab of the
  granite so gray,
And Alice lies under the stone.

Under the hickory tree, Ben Bolt,
Which stood at the foot of the
  hill,
Together we've lain in the
  noonday shade,
And listened to Appleton's mill.
The mill-wheel has fallen to
  pieces, Ben Bolt,
The rafters have tumbled in,
And a quiet which crawls round
  the walls as you gaze
Has followed the olden din.

Do you mind of the cabin of logs,
    Ben Bolt,
At the edge of the pathless wood,
And the button-ball tree with its
    motley limbs,
Which nigh by the doorstep
    stood?
The cabin to ruin has gone, Ben
    Bolt,
The tree you would seek for in
    vain;
And where once the lords of the
    forest waved
Are grass and golden grain.

And don't you remember the
    school, Ben Bolt,
With the master so cruel and
    grim,
And the shaded nook in the
    running brook
Where the children went to
    swim?

Grass grows on the master's grave,
    Ben Bolt,
The spring of the brook is dry,
And of all the boys who were
    schoolmates then
There are only you and I.

There is a change in the things I
    loved, Ben Bolt,
They have changed from the old
    to the new;
But I feel in the deeps of my
    spirit the truth,
There never was change in you.
Twelvemonths twenty have past,
    Ben Bolt,
Since first we were friends—yet I
    hail
Your presence a blessing, your
    friendship a truth,
Ben Bolt of the salt-sea gale.
                THOMAS DUNN ENGLISH

THE HIGHWAYMAN

Part One

The wind was a torrent of darkness among the gusty trees,
The moon was a ghostly galleon tossed upon cloudy seas,
The road was a ribbon of moonlight over the purple moor,
And the highwayman came riding—
    Riding—riding—
The highwayman came riding, up to the old inn-door.

He'd a French cock-hat on his forehead, a bunch of lace at his chin,
A coat of the claret velvet, and breeches of brown doe-skin;
They fitted with never a wrinkle: his boots were up to the thigh!
And he rode with a jeweled twinkle,
    His pistol butts a-twinkle,
His rapier hilt a-twinkle, under the jeweled sky.

Over the cobbles he clattered and clashed in the dark inn-yard,
And he tapped with his whip on the shutters, but all was locked and
    barred;
He whistled a tune to the window, and who should be waiting there
But the landlord's black-eyed daughter,
    Bess, the landlord's daughter,
Plaiting a dark red love-knot into her long black hair.

And dark in the dark old inn-yard, a stable-wicket creaked
Where Tim the ostler listened; his face was white and peaked;
His eyes were hollows of madness, his hair like mouldy clay,
But he loved the landlord's daughter,
    The landlord's red-lipped daughter,
Dumb as a dog he listened, and he heard the robber say—

"One kiss, my bonny sweetheart, I'm after a prize to-night,
But I shall be back with the yellow gold before the morning light;
Yet, if they press me sharply, and harry me through the day,
Then look for me by moonlight,
    Watch for me by moonlight,
I'll come to thee by moonlight, though hell should bar the way."

He rose upright in his stirrups; he scarce could reach her hand,
But she loosened her hair i' the casement! His face burnt like a brand
As the black cascade of perfume came tumbling over his breast;
And he kissed its waves in the moonlight,
    (Oh, sweet black waves in the moonlight!)
Then he tugged at his reins in the moonlight, and galloped away to the
    West.

Part Two

He did not come in the dawning; he did not come at noon;
And out o' the tawny sunset, before the rise o' the moon,
When the road was a gipsy's ribbon, looping the purple moor,
A red-coat troop came marching—
    Marching—marching—
King George's men came marching, up to the old inn-door.

They said no word to the landlord, they drank his ale instead,
But they gagged his daughter and bound her to the foot of her narrow
    bed;

Two of them knelt at her casement, with muskets at their side!
There was death at every window;
   And hell at one dark window;
For Bess could see, through her casement, the road that *he* would ride.

They had tied her up to attention, with many a sniggering jest;
They had bound a musket beside her, with the barrel beneath her breast!
"Now keep good watch!" and they kissed her.
   She heard the dead man say—
Look for me by moonlight;
  Watch for me by moonlight;
I'll come to thee by moonlight, though hell should bar the way!

She twisted her hands behind her; but all the knots held good!
She writhed her hands till her fingers were wet with sweat or blood!
They stretched and strained in the darkness, and the hours crawled by
    like years,
Till, now, on the stroke of midnight,
  Cold, on the stroke of midnight,
The tip of one finger touched it! The trigger at least was hers!

The tip of one finger touched it; she strove no more for the rest!
Up, she stood up to attention, with the barrel beneath her breast,
She would not risk their hearing; she would not strive again;
For the road lay bare in the moonlight;
And the blood of her veins in the moonlight throbbed to her love's refrain.

Tlot-tlot; tlot-tlot! Had they heard it? The horse-hoofs ringing clear;
Tlot-tlot, tlot-tlot, in the distance? Were they deaf that they did not hear?
Down the ribbon of moonlight, over the brow of the hill,
The highwayman came riding,
  Riding, riding!
The red coats looked to their priming! She stood up, straight and still!

Tlot-tlot, in the frosty silence! *Tlot-tlot,* in the echoing night!
Nearer he came and nearer! Her face was like a light!
Her eyes grew wide for a moment; she drew one last deep breath,
Then her finger moved in the moonlight,
  Her musket shattered the moonlight,
Shattered her breast in the moonlight and warned him—with her death.

He turned; he spurred to the West; he did not know who stood
Bowed, with her head o'er the musket, drenched with her own red blood!
Not till the dawn he heard it, his face grew gray to hear
How Bess, the landlord's daughter,
  The landlord's black-eyed daughter,
Had watched for her love in the moonlight, and died in the darkness
    there.

Back he spurred like a madman, shrieking a curse to the sky,
With the white road smoking behind him and his rapier brandished
    high!
Blood-red were his spurs i' the golden noon; wine-red was his velvet coat,
When they shot him down in the highway,
  Down like a dog in the highway,
And he lay in his blood on the highway, with the bunch of lace at his
    throat.

.   .   .   .

And still of a winter's night, they say, when the wind is in the trees,
When the moon is a ghostly galleon tossed upon cloudy seas,
When the road is a ribbon of moonlight over the purple moor,
A highwayman comes riding—
  Riding—riding—
A highwayman comes riding, up to the old inn-door.

Over the cobbles he clatters and clangs in the dark inn-yard;
He taps with his whip on the shutters, but all is locked and barred;
He whistles a tune at the window, and who should be waiting there
But the landlord's black-eyed daughter,
  Bess, the landlord's daughter,
Plaiting a dark red love-knot into her long black hair.

ALFRED NOYES

THE DESTRUCTION OF SENNACHERIB

The Assyrian came down like the wolf on the fold,
And his cohorts were gleaming in purple and gold;
And the sheen of their spears was like stars on the sea,
When the blue wave rolls nightly on deep Galilee.

Like the leaves of the forest when summer is green,
That host with their banners at sunset were seen:
Like the leaves of the forest when autumn hath blown,
That host on the morrow lay withered and strown.

For the Angel of Death spread his wings on the blast,
And breathed in the face of the foe as he passed;
And the eyes of the sleepers waxed deadly and chill,
And their hearts but once heaved, and forever grew still!

And there lay the steed with his nostril all wide,
But through it there rolled not the breath of his pride:
And the foam of his gasping lay white on the turf,
And cold as the spray of the rock-beating surf.

And there lay the rider distorted and pale,
With the dew on his brow, and the rust on his mail;
And the tents were all silent, the banners alone,
The lances unlifted, the trumpet unblown.

And the widows of Ashur are loud in their wail,
And the idols are broke in the temple of Baal;
And the might of the Gentile, unsmote by the sword,
Hath melted like snow in the glance of the Lord!

GEORGE GORDON, LORD BYRON

THE LEAK IN THE DIKE

The good dame looked from her
    cottage
  At the close of the pleasant
    day,
And cheerily called to her little son
  Outside the door at play:
"Come, Peter! come! I want you
    to go,
  While there is light to see,
To the hut of the blind old man
    who lives
  Across the dike, for me;
And take these cakes I made for
    him—
  They are hot and smoking yet;
You have time enough to go and
    come
  Before the sun is set."

Then the good wife turned to her
    labor,
  Humming a simple song,
And thought of her husband
    working hard
  At the sluices all day long;
And set the turf a-blazing,
  And brought the coarse black
    bread:
That he might find a fire at night,
  And find the table spread.

And Peter left the brother,
  With whom all day he had
    played,

And the sister who had watched
    their sports
  In the willow's tender shade;
And told them they'd see him
    back before
  They saw a star in sight,
Though he wouldn't be afraid to go
  In the very darkest night!
For he was a brave, bright fellow,
  With eye and conscience clear;
He could do whatever a boy
    might do,
  And he had not learned to fear.
Why, he wouldn't have robbed a
    bird's nest,
  Nor brought a stork to harm,
Though never a law in Holland
  Had stood to stay his arm!

And now with his face all glowing,
  And eyes as bright as the day
With the thoughts of his pleasant
    errand,
  He trudged along the way;
And soon his joyous prattle
  Made glad a lonesome place—
Alas! if only the blind old man
  Could have seen that happy face!
Yet he somehow caught the
    brightness
  Which his voice and presence
    lent
And he felt the sunshine come and go
  As Peter came and went.

And now, as the day was sinking,
  And the winds began to rise,
The mother looked from her
    door again,
  Shading her anxious eyes,
And saw the shadows deepen
  And birds to their home come
    back,
But never a sign of Peter
  Along the level track.
But she said: "He will come at
    morning,
  So I need not fret or grieve—
Though it isn't like my boy at all
  To stay without my leave."

But where was the child delaying?
  On the homeward way was he,
And across the dike while the sun
    was up
  An hour above the sea.
He was stopping now to gather
    flowers,
  Now listening to the sound,
As the angry waters dashed
    themselves
  Against their narrow bound.
"Ah! well for us," said Peter,
  "That the gates are good and
    strong,
And my father tends them
    carefully,
  Or they would not hold you
    long!
You're a wicked sea," said Peter;
  "I know why you fret and
    chafe;
You would like to spoil our lands
    and homes;
  But our sluices keep you safe."

But hark! through the noise of
    waters
  Comes a low, clear, trickling
    sound;
And the child's face pales with
    terror,
  And his blossoms drop to the
    ground.
He is up the bank in a moment,
  And, stealing through the sand,
He sees a stream not yet so large
  As his slender, childish hand.

'Tis a leak in the dike!—He is
    but a boy,
  Unused to fearful scenes;
But, young as he is, he has
    learned to know
  The dreadful thing that means.
A leak in the dike! The stoutest
    heart
  Grows faint that cry to hear,
And the bravest man in all the
    land
  Turns white with mortal fear.
For he knows the smallest leak
    may grow
  To a flood in a single night;
And he knows the strength of the
    cruel sea
  When loosed in its angry
    might.

And the Boy! he has seen the
    danger
  And, shouting a wild alarm,
He forces back the weight of the
    sea
  With the strength of his single
    arm!

He listens for the joyful sound
  Of a footstep passing nigh;
And lays his ear to the ground, to
    catch
  The answer to his cry.
And he hears the rough winds
    blowing,
  And the waters rise and fall,
But never an answer comes to him
  Save the echo of his call.
He sees no hope, no succor,
  His feeble voice is lost;
Yet what shall he do but watch
    and wait
  Though he perish at his post!

So, faintly calling and crying
  Till the sun is under the sea;
Crying and moaning till the stars
  Come out for company;
He thinks of his brother and
    sister,
  Asleep in their safe warm bed;
He thinks of his father and mother,
  Of himself as dying—and dead;
And of how, when the night is over,
  They must come and find him
    at last;
But he never thinks he can leave
    the place
  Where duty holds him fast.

The good dame in the cottage
  Is up and astir with the light,
For the thought of her little Peter
  Has been with her all night.
And now she watches the pathway,
  As yester-eve she had done;
But what does she see so strange
    and black
  Against the rising sun?

Her neighbors are bearing
    between them
  Something straight to her door;
Her child is coming home, but not
  As he ever came before!

"He is dead!" she cries, "my
    darling!"
  And the startled father hears,
And comes and looks the way she
    looks,
  And fears the thing she fears;
Till a glad shout from the bearers
  Thrills the stricken man and wife—
"Give thanks, for your son has
    saved our land,
  And God has saved his life!"
So, there in the morning sunshine
  They knelt about the boy;
And every head was bared and bent
  In tearful, reverent joy.

'Tis many a year since then; but still,
  When the sea roars like a flood,
The boys are taught what a boy can do
  Who is brave and true and good;
For every man in that country
  Takes his son by the hand
And tells him of little Peter,
  Whose courage saved the land.

They have many a valiant hero,
  Remembered through the years;
But never one whose name so oft
  Is named with loving tears.
And his deed shall be sung by
    the cradle,
  And told to the child on the knee,
So long as the dikes of Holland
  Divide the land from the sea!
                    PHOEBE CARY

GRANDFATHER'S CLOCK

My grandfather's clock was too large for the shelf,
  So it stood ninety years on the floor;
It was taller by half than the old man himself,
  Though it weighed not a pennyweight more.
It was bought on the morn of the day that he was born
  And was always his treasure and pride.
But it stopped short—never to go again—
  When the old man died.

    Ninety years without slumbering
     Tick, tick, tick, tick.
    His life-seconds numbering
     Tick, tick, tick, tick.
    It stopped short—never to go again—
     When the old man died.

In watching its pendulum swing to and fro
  Many hours had he spent while a boy;
And in childhood and manhood the clock seemed to know
  And to share both his grief and his joy,
For it struck twenty-four when he entered the door
  With a blooming and beautiful bride,
But it stopped short—never to go again—
  When the old man died.

My grandfather said of those he could hire,
  Not a servant so faithful he found,
For it wasted no time and had but one desire—
  At the close of each week to be wound.
And it kept in its place—not a frown upon its face,
  And its hands never hung by its side;
But it stopped short—never to go again—
  When the old man died.

It rang an alarm in the dead of night—
  An alarm that for years had been dumb.
And we knew that his spirit was pluming for flight
  That his hour for departure had come.
Still the clock kept the time with a soft and muffled chime
  As we silently stood by his side;
But it stopped short—never to go again—
  When the old man died.

HENRY CLAY WORK

CASEY AT THE BAT

It looked extremely rocky for the Mudville nine that day;
The score stood two to four, with but one inning left to play.
So, when Cooney died at second, and Burrows did the same,
A pallor wreathed the features of the patrons of the game.

A straggling few got up to go, leaving there the rest,
With that hope which springs eternal within the human breast.
For they thought: "If only Casey could get a whack at that,"
They'd put even money now, with Casey at the bat.

But Flynn preceded Casey, and likewise so did Blake,
And the former was a pudd'n, and the latter was a fake.
So on that stricken multitude a deathlike silence sat;
For there seemed but little chance of Casey's getting to the bat.

But Flynn let drive a "single," to the wonderment of all.
And the much-despisèd Blakey "tore the cover off the ball."
And when the dust had lifted, and they saw what had occurred,
There was Blakey safe at second, and Flynn a-huggin' third.

Then from the gladdened multitude went up a joyous yell—
It rumbled in the mountaintops, it rattled in the dell;
It struck upon the hillside and rebounded on the flat;
For Casey, mighty Casey, was advancing to the bat.

There was ease in Casey's manner as he stepped into his place,
There was pride in Casey's bearing and a smile on Casey's face;
And when responding to the cheers he lightly doffed his hat,
No stranger in the crowd could doubt 'twas Casey at the bat.

Ten thousand eyes were on him as he rubbed his hands with dirt,
Five thousand tongues applauded when he wiped them on his shirt;
Then when the writhing pitcher ground the ball into his hip,
Defiance glanced in Casey's eye, a sneer curled Casey's lip.

And now the leather-covered sphere came hurtling through the air,
And Casey stood a-watching it in haughty grandeur there.
Close by the sturdy batsman the ball unheeded sped;
"That ain't my style," said Casey. "Strike one," the umpire said.

From the benches, black with people, there went up a muffled roar,
Like the beating of the storm waves on the stern and distant shore.
"Kill him! kill the umpire!" shouted someone on the stand;
And it's likely they'd have killed him had not Casey raised his hand.

With a smile of Christian charity great Casey's visage shone;
He stilled the rising tumult, he made the game go on;
He signaled to the pitcher, and once more the spheroid flew;
But Casey still ignored it, and the umpire said, "Strike two."

"Fraud!" cried the maddened thousands, and the echo answered "Fraud!"
But one scornful look from Casey and the audience was awed;
They saw his face grow stern and cold, they saw his muscles strain,
And they knew that Casey wouldn't let the ball go by again.

The sneer is gone from Casey's lips, his teeth are clenched in hate,
He pounds with cruel vengeance his bat upon the plate;
And now the pitcher holds the ball, and now he lets it go,
And now the air is shattered by the force of Casey's blow.

Oh, somewhere in this favored land the sun is shining bright,
The band is playing somewhere, and somewhere hearts are light;
And somewhere men are laughing, and somewhere children shout,
But there is no joy in Mudville—Mighty Casey has struck out.

ERNEST LAWRENCE THAYER

THE PIED PIPER OF HAMELIN

I

Hamelin Town's in Brunswick,
By famous Hanover city;
  The river Weser, deep and
    wide,
  Washes its wall on the southern
    side;
  A pleasanter spot you never
    spied;
But, when begins my ditty,
  Almost five hundred years ago,
  To see the townsfolk suffer so
From vermin was a pity.

II

  Rats!
They fought the dogs and killed
    the cats,
  And bit the babies in the
    cradles,
And ate the cheeses out of the
    vats,
  And licked the soup from the
    cooks' own ladles,
Split open the kegs of salted
    sprats,

Made nests inside men's Sunday
    hats,
And even spoiled the women's
    chats
  By drowning their speaking
  With shrieking and squeaking
In fifty different sharps and flats.

III

At last the people in a body
  To the Town Hall came
    flocking:
" 'Tis clear," cried they, "our
    Mayor's a noddy;
  And as for our Corporation,
    —shocking
To think we buy gowns lined
    with ermine
For dolts that can't or won't
    determine
What's best to rid us of our
    vermin!
You hope, because you're old and
    obese,
To find in the furry civic robe
    ease?

Rouse up, sirs! Give your brains
    a racking,
To find the remedy we're lacking,
Or, sure as fate, we'll send you
    packing!"
At this the Mayor and Corporation
Quaked with a mighty
    consternation.

IV

An hour they sat in council,—
    At length the Mayor broke
    silence:
"For a guilder I'd my ermine
    gown sell;
    I wish I were a mile hence!
It's easy to bid one rack one's
    brain,—
I'm sure my poor head aches
    again,
I've scratched it so, and all in
    vain.
Oh for a trap, a trap, a trap!"
Just as he said this, what should
    hap
At the chamber-door but a gentle
    tap?
"Bless us," cried the Mayor,
    "what's that?"
(With the Corporation as he sat,
Looking little though wondrous fat;
Nor brighter was his eye, nor
    moister
Than a too-long-opened oyster,
Save when at noon his paunch
    grew mutinous
For a plate of turtle green and
    glutinous)
"Only a scraping of shoes on the mat?
Anything like the sound of a rat
Makes my heart go pit-a-pat!"

V

"Come in!" the Mayor cried,
    looking bigger:
And in did come the strangest
    figure!
His queer long coat from heel to
    head
Was half of yellow and half of red,
And he himself was tall and thin,
With sharp blue eyes, each like a
    pin,
And light loose hair, yet swarthy skin,
No tuft on cheek nor beard on
    chin,
But lips where smiles went out
    and in;
There was no guessing his kith
    and kin:
And nobody could enough
    admire
The tall man and his quaint
    attire.
Quoth one: "It's as my great-
    grandsire,
Starting up at the Trump of
    Doom's tone,
Had walked this way from his
    painted tombstone!"

VI

He advanced to the council-table:
And, "Please your honors," said
    he, "I'm able,
By means of a secret charm, to draw
All creatures living beneath the sun,
That creep or swim or fly or run,
After me so as you never saw!
And I chiefly use my charm
On creatures that do people harm,
The mole and toad and newt and
    viper;

And people call me the Pied Piper."
(And here they noticed round his
        neck
A scarf of red and yellow stripe,
To match with his coat of the
        self-same check,
And at the scarf's end hung a pipe;
And his fingers, they noticed,
        were ever straying
As if impatient to be playing
Upon this pipe, as low it dangled
Over his vesture so old-fangled.)
"Yet," said he, "poor piper as I am,
In Tartary I freed the Cham,
Last June, from his huge swarms
        of gnats;
I eased in Asia the Nizam
Of a mostrous brood of vampire-
        bats;
And as for what your brain
        bewilders,—
If I can rid your town of rats,
Will you give me a thousand
        guilders?"
"One? fifty thousand!" was the
        exclamation
Of the astonished Mayor and
        Corporation.

VII

Into the street the Piper stepped,
    Smiling first a little smile,
As if he knew what magic slept
    In his quiet pipe the while;
Then, like a musical adept,
To blow the pipe his lips he
        wrinkled,
And green and blue his sharp
        eyes twinkled,
Like a candle-flame where salt is
        sprinkled;

And ere three shrill notes the
        pipe uttered,
You heard as if an army
        muttered;
And the muttering grew to a
        grumbling;
And the grumbling grew to a
        mighty rumbling;
And out of the houses the rats
        came tumbling.
Great rats, small rats, lean rats,
        brawny rats,
Brown rats, black rats, gray rats,
        tawny rats,
Grave old plodders, gay young
        friskers,
    Fathers, mothers, uncles, cousins,
Cocking tails and pricking
        whiskers;
    Families by tens and dozens,
Brothers, sisters, husbands, wives,—
Followed the Piper for their lives.
From street to street he piped
        advancing,
And step for step they followed
        dancing,
Until they came to the river Weser,
Wherein all plunged and perished!
—Save one who, stout as Julius
        Cæsar,
Swam across and lived to carry
(As he, the manuscript he
        cherished)
To Rat-land home his
        commentary,
Which was: "At the first shrill
        notes of the pipe,
I heard a sound as of scraping
        tripe,
And putting apples, wondrous ripe,
Into a cider-press's gripe,—

And a moving away of pickle-tub-
    boards,
And a leaving ajar of conserve-
    cupboards,
And a drawing the corks of train-
    oil-flasks,
And a breaking the hoops of
    butter-casks;
And it seemed as if a voice
(Sweeter far than by harp or by
    psaltery
Is breathed) called out, 'Oh rats,
    rejoice!
The world is grown to one vast
    drysaltery!
So munch on, crunch on, take
    your nuncheon,
Breakfast, supper, dinner, luncheon!'
And just as a bulky sugar-puncheon,
Already staved, like a great sun shone
Glorious scarce an inch before me,
Just as methought it said, 'Come,
    bore me!'—
I found the Weser rolling o'er me."

VIII

You should have heard the
    Hamelin people
Ringing the bells till they rocked
    the steeple;
"Go," cried the Mayor, "and get
    long poles!
Poke out the nests and block up
    the holes!
Consult with carpenters and builders,
And leave in our town not even
    a trace
Of the rats!"—when suddenly,
    up the face
Of the Piper perked in the
    market-place,

With a "First, if you please, my
    thousand guilders!"

IX

A thousand guilders! the Mayor
    looked blue;
So did the Corporation too.
For council-dinners made rare havoc
With Claret, Moselle,
    Vin-de-Grave, Hock;
And half the money would replenish
Their cellar's biggest butt with
    Rhenish.
To pay this sum to a wandering
    fellow
With a gypsy coat of red and yellow!
"Beside," quoth the Mayor, with
    a knowing wink,
"Our business was done at the
    river's brink;
We saw with our eyes the vermin sink,
And what's dead can't come to
    life, I think.
So, friend, we're not the folks to
    shrink
From the duty of giving you
    something to drink,
And a matter of money to put in
    your poke;
But as for the guilders, what we spoke
Of them, as you very well know,
    was in joke.
Beside, our losses have made us thrifty;
A thousand guilders! Come, take fifty!"

X

The Piper's face fell, and he cried,
"No trifling! I can't wait! beside,
I've promised to visit by dinner time
Bagdat, and accept the prime
Of the Head Cook's pottage, all
    he's rich in,

For having left, in the Caliph's
    kitchen,
Of a nest of scorpions no
    survivor:
With him I proved no
    bargain-driver;
With you, don't think I'll bate a
    stiver!
And folks who put me in a
    passion
May find me pipe after another
    fashion."

XI

"How?" cried the Mayor, "d'ye
    think I brook
Being worse treated than a
    Cook?
Insulted by a lazy ribald
With idle pipe and vesture
    piebald?
You threaten us, fellow? Do your
    worst,
Blow your pipe there till you
    burst!"

XII

Once more he stepped into the
    street;
  And to his lips again
Laid his long pipe of smooth
    straight cane;

And ere he blew three notes
    (such sweet
Soft notes as yet musician's
    cunning
Never gave the enraptured air)
There was a rustling that seemed
    like a bustling
Of merry crowds justling at
    pitching and hustling;
Small feet were pattering,
    wooden shoes clattering
Little hands clapping, and little
    tongues chattering;
And, like fowls in a farm-yard
    when barley is scattering,
Out came the children running:
All the little boys and girls,
With rosy cheeks and flaxen curls,
And sparkling eyes and teeth like
    pearls,
Tripping and skipping, ran
    merrily after
The wonderful music with
    shouting and laughter.

XIII

The Mayor was dumb, and the
    Council stood
As if they were changed into
    blocks of wood,
Unable to move a step, or cry
To the children merrily skipping
    by,—

And could only follow with the eye
That joyous crowd at the Piper's
    back.
But how the Mayor was on the rack,
And the wretched Council's
    bosoms beat,
As the Piper turned from the
    High Street
To where the Weser rolled its
    waters
Right in the way of their sons
    and daughters!
However, he turned from south
    to west,
And to Koppelberg Hill his steps
    addressed,
And after him the children
    pressed;
Great was the joy in every breast.
"He never can cross that mighty top!
He's forced to let the piping
    drop,
And we shall see our children stop!"
When, lo, as they reached the
    mountain-side,
A wondrous portal opened wide,
As if a cavern was suddenly
    hollowed;
And the Piper advanced and the
    children followed;
And when all were in, to the very last,
The door in the mountain-side
    shut fast.
Did I say, all? No! One was lame,
And could not dance the whole
    of the way;
And in after years, if you would
    blame
His sadness, he was used to say,—
"It's dull in our town since my
    playmates left!

I can't forget that I'm bereft
Of all the pleasant sights they see,
Which the Piper also promised me;
For he led us, he said, to a
    joyous land,
Joining the town and just at hand,
Where waters gushed, and
    fruit-trees grew,
And flowers put forth a fairer hue,
And everything was strange and
    new;
The sparrows were brighter than
    peacocks here,
And their dogs outran our fallow
    deer,
And honey-bees had lost their stings,
And horses were born with
    eagles' wings;
And just as I became assured
My lame foot would be speedily
    cured,
The music stopped and I stood still,
And found myself outside the hill,
Left alone against my will,
To go now limping as before,
And never hear of that country more!"

XIV

Alas, alas for Hamelin!
    There came into many a
        burgher's pate
    A text which says that heaven's
        gate
    Opes to the rich at as easy rate
As the needle's eye takes a camel
    in!
The Mayor sent East, West,
    North and South,
To offer the Piper, by word of
    mouth,

Wherever it was men's lot to
  find him,
Silver and gold to his heart's
  content,
If he'd only return the way he
  went,
  And bring the children behind
    him.
But when they saw 'twas a lost
  endeavor,
And piper and dancers were gone
  forever,
They made a decree that lawyers
  never
  Should think their records
    dated duly
If, after the day of the month
  and year,
These words did not as well
  appear,
"And so long after what
  happened here
  On the Twenty-second of July,
Thirteen hundred and seventy-six:"
And the better in memory to fix
The place of the children's last
  retreat,
They called it, the Pied Piper's
  Street—
Where any one playing on pipe
  or tabor
Was sure for the future to lose
  his labor.
Nor suffered they hostlery or tavern
  To shock with mirth a street
    so solemn;
But opposite the place of the
  cavern

They wrote the story on a
  column,
And on the great church-window
  painted
The same, to make the world
  acquainted
How their children were stolen
  away,
And there it stands to this very
  day.
And I must not omit to say
That in Transylvania there's a
  tribe
Of alien people who ascribe
The outlandish ways and dress
On which their neighbors lay
  such stress,
To their fathers and mothers
  having risen
Out of some subterraneous
  prison
Into which they were trepanned
Long time ago in a mighty band
Out of Hamelin town in
  Brunswick land,
But how or why, they don't
  understand.

xv

So, Willy, let me and you be
  wipers
Of scores out with all men—
  especially pipers!
And, whether they pipe us free
  fróm rats or fróm mice,
If we've promised them aught,
  let us keep our promise!
          ROBERT BROWNING

KUBLA KHAN

In Xanadu did Kubla Khan
A stately pleasure-dome decree:
Where Alph, the sacred river, ran
Through caverns measureless to
    man
  Down to a sunless sea.
So twice five miles of fertile
    ground
With walls and towers were
    girdled round:
And there were gardens bright
    with sinuous rills,
Where blossomed many an
    incense-bearing tree;
And here were forests ancient as
    the hills,
Enfolding sunny spots of
    greenery.

But oh! that deep romantic
    chasm which slanted
Down the green hill athwart a
    cedarn cover!
A savage place! as holy and
    enchanted
As e'er beneath a waning moon
    was haunted
By woman wailing for her
    demon-lover!
And from this chasm, with
    ceaseless turmoil seething,
As if this earth in fast thick pants
    were breathing,
A mighty fountain momently was
    forced:

Amid whose swift half-intermitted
    burst
Huge fragments vaulted like
    rebounding hail,
Or chaffy grain beneath the
    thresher's flail:
And 'mid these dancing rocks at
    once and ever
It flung up momently the sacred
    river.
Five miles meandering with a
    mazy motion
Through wood and dale the
    sacred river ran,
Then reached the caverns
    measureless to man,
And sank in tumult to a lifeless
    ocean:
And 'mid this tumult Kubla
    heard from far
Ancestral voices prophesying war!

  The shadow of the dome of
    pleasure
  Floated midway on the waves;
  Where was heard the mingled
    measure
  From the fountain and the
    caves.
It was a miracle of rare device,
A sunny pleasure-dome with
    caves of ice!

  A damsel with a dulcimer
  In a vision once I saw:

It was an Abyssinian maid,
And on her dulcimer she
    played,
Singing of Mount Abora.
Could I revive within me
Her symphony and song,
  To such a deep delight 'twould
    win me,
That with music loud and long,
I would build that dome in air,
That sunny dome! those caves of ice!

And all who heard should see
    them there,
And all should cry, Beware!
    Beware!
His flashing eyes, his floating
    hair!
Weave a circle round him thrice,
And close your eyes with holy
    dread,
For he on honey-dew hath fed,
And drunk the milk of Paradise.

SAMUEL TAYLOR COLERIDGE

THE BATTLE OF WATERLOO

There was a sound of revelry by night,
And Belgium's capital had gathered then
Her beauty and her chivalry, and bright
The lamps shone o'er fair women and brave men;
A thousand hearts beat happily; and when
Music arose with its voluptuous swell,
Soft eyes looked love to eyes which spake again,
And all went merry as a marriage-bell;
But hush! hark! a deep sound strikes like a rising knell!

Did ye not hear it?—No; 'twas but the wind,
Or the car rattling o'er the stony street;
On with the dance! let joy be unconfined;
No sleep till morn, when Youth and Pleasure meet
To chase the glowing Hours with flying feet.
But hark! that heavy sound breaks in once more,
As if the clouds its echo would repeat;
And nearer, clearer, deadlier than before!
Arm! arm! it is—it is—the cannon's opening roar!

Within a windowed niche of that high hall
Sate Brunswick's fated chieftain; he did hear
That sound, the first amidst the festival,
And caught its tone with Death's prophetic ear;

And when they smiled because he deemed it near,
His heart more truly knew that peal too well
Which stretched his father on a bloody bier,
And roused the vengeance blood alone could quell:
He rushed into the field, and, foremost fighting, fell.

Ah! then and there was hurrying to and fro,
And gathering tears, and tremblings of distress,
And cheeks all pale, which but an hour ago
Blushed at the praise of their own loveliness;
And there were sudden partings, such as press
The life from out young hearts, and choking sighs
Which ne'er might be repeated: who would guess
If evermore should meet those mutual eyes,
Since upon night so sweet such awful morn could rise!

And there was mounting in hot haste: the steed,
The mustering squadron, and the clattering car,
Went pouring forward with impetuous speed,
And swiftly forming in the ranks of war;
And the deep thunder peal on peal afar;
And near, the beat of the alarming drum
Roused up the soldier ere the morning star;
While thronged the citizens with terror dumb,
Or whispering with white lips,—"The foe! they come! they come!"

And wild and high the "Cameron's gathering" rose,
The war-note of Lochiel, which Albyn's hills
Have heard,—and heard, too, have her Saxon foes;
How in the noon of night that pibroch thrills
Savage and shrill! But with the breath which fills
Their mountain pipe, so fill the mountaineers
With the fierce native daring which instils
The stirring memory of a thousand years,
And Evan's, Donald's fame rings in each clansman's ears!

And Ardennes waves above them her green leaves,
Dewy with nature's tear-drops, as they pass,
Grieving, if aught inanimate e'er grieves,
Over the unreturning brave,—alas!

Ere evening to be trodden like the grass
Which now beneath them, but above shall grow
In its next verdure, when this fiery mass
Of living valor, rolling on the foe,
And burning with high hope, shall moulder cold and low.

Last noon beheld them full of lusty life,
Last eve in Beauty's circle proudly gay,
The midnight brought the signal-sound of strife,
The morn the marshalling in arms—the day
Battle's magnificently stern array!
The thunder-clouds close o'er it, which when rent
The earth is covered thick with other clay,
Which her own clay shall cover, heaped and pent,
Rider and horse,—friend, foe,—in one red burial blent!

Their praise is hymned by loftier harps than mine;
Yet one I would select from that proud throng,
Partly because they blend me with his line,
And partly that I did his sire some wrong,
And partly that bright names will hallow song!
And his was of the bravest, and when showered
The death-bolts deadliest the thinned files along,
Even where the thickest of war's tempest lowered,
They reached no nobler breast than thine, young, gallant Howard!

There have been tears and breaking hearts for thee,
And mine were nothing, had I such to give;
But when I stood beneath the fresh green tree,
Which living waves where thou didst cease to live,
And saw around me the wide field revive
With fruits and fertile promise, and the Spring
Come forth her work of gladness to contrive,
With all her reckless birds upon the wing,
I turned from all she brought to those she could not bring.

I turned to thee, to thousands, of whom each
And one as all a ghastly gap did make
In his own kind and kindred, whom to teach
Forgetfulness were mercy for their sake;

The Archangel's trump, not glory's, must awake
Those whom they thirst for; though the sound of Fame
May for a moment soothe, it cannot slake
The fever of vain longing, and the name
So honored, but assumes a stronger, bitterer claim.

They mourn, but smile at length; and, smiling, mourn;
The tree will wither long before it fall;
The hull drives on, though mast and sail be torn;
The roof-tree sinks, but moulders on the hall
In massy hoariness; the ruined wall
Stands when its wind-worn battlements are gone;
The bars survive the captive they inthrall;
The day drags through though storms keep out the sun;
And thus the heart will break, yet brokenly live on:

Even as a broken mirror, which the glass
In every fragment multiplies; and makes
A thousand images of one that was,
The same, and still the more, the more it breaks;
And thus the heart will do which not forsakes,
Living in shattered guise, and still, and cold,
And bloodless, with its sleepless sorrow aches,
Yet withers on till all without is old,
Showing no visible sign, for such things are untold.

GEORGE GORDON, LORD BYRON

THE SPELL OF THE YUKON

I wanted the gold, and I sought it;
I scrabbled and mucked like a slave.
Was it famine or scurvy—I fought it;
I hurled my youth into a grave.
I wanted the gold, and I got it—
Came out with a fortune last fall—
Yet somehow life's not what I
thought it,
And somehow the gold isn't all.

No! There's the land. (Have
you seen it?)
It's the cussedest land that I
know,
From the big, dizzy mountains
that screen it
To the deep, deathlike valleys
below.

Some say God was tired when He
    made it;
    Some say it's a fine land to shun;
Maybe; but there's some as would
    trade it
    For no land on earth—and I'm
    one.

You come to get rich (damned
    good reason) ;
    You feel like an exile at first;
You hate it like hell for a season,
    And then you are worse than
    the worst.
It grips you like some kinds of
    sinning;
    It twists you from foe to a friend;
It seems it's been since the
    beginning;
    It seems it will be to the end.

I've stood in some
    mighty-mouthed hollow
    That's plumb-full of hush to
    the brim;
I've watched the big, husky sun
    wallow
    In crimson and gold, and
    grow dim,
Till the moon set the pearly
    peaks gleaming,
    And the stars tumbled out,
    neck and crop;
And I've thought that I surely
    was dreaming,
    With the peace o' the world
    piled on top.
The summer—no sweeter was ever;
    The sunshiny woods all athrill;
The grayling aleap in the river,
    The bighorn asleep on the hill.

The strong life that never knows
    harness;
    The wilds where the caribou
    call;
The freshness, the freedom, the
    farness—
    O God! how I'm stuck on it all.

The winter! the brightness that
    blinds you,
    The white land locked tight as
    a drum,
The cold fear that follows and
    finds you,
    The silence that bludgeons you
    dumb,
The snows that are older than
    history,
    The woods where the weird
    shadows slant;
The stillness, the moonlight, the
    mystery,
    I've bade 'em good-bye—but I
    can't.

There's a land where the
    mountains are nameless,
    And the rivers all run God
    knows where;
There are lives that are erring
    and aimless,
    And deaths that just hang by
    a hair;
There are hardships that nobody
    reckons;
    There are valleys unpeopled
    and still;
There's a land—oh, it beckons
    and beckons,
    And I want to go back—and
    I will.

They're making my money
  diminish;
 I'm sick of the taste of
 champagne.
Thank God! when I'm skinned to
 a finish
 I'll pike to the Yukon again.
I'll fight—and you bet it's no
  sham-fight;
 It's hell!—but I've been there
 before;
And it's better than this by a
  damsite—
 So me for the Yukon once more.

There's gold, and it's haunting
  and haunting;
 It's luring me on as of old;
Yet it isn't the gold that I'm
  wanting
 So much as just finding the
 gold.
It's the great, big, broad land
  'way up yonder,
 It's the forests where silence
 has lease;
It's the beauty that thrills me
  with wonder,
 It's the stillness that fills me
 with peace.

ROBERT W. SERVICE

PAUL REVERE'S RIDE

Listen, my children, and you shall hear
Of the midnight ride of Paul Revere,
On the eighteenth of April, in Seventy-five;
Hardly a man is now alive
Who remembers that famous day and year.

He said to his friend, "If the British march
By land or sea from the town tonight,
Hang a lantern aloft in the belfry arch
Of the North Church tower as a signal light,—
One, if by land, and two, if by sea;
And I on the opposite shore will be,
Ready to ride and spread the alarm
Through every Middlesex village and farm,
For the country folk to be up and to arm."

Then he said, "Good night!" and with muffled oar
Silently rowed to the Charlestown shore,
Just as the moon rose over the bay,
Where swinging wide at her moorings lay
The *Somerset,* British man-of-war;
A phantom ship, with each mast and spar
Across the moon like a prison bar,
And a huge black hulk, that was magnified
By its own reflection in the tide.

Meanwhile, his friend through alley and street
Wanders and watches, with eager ears,
Till in the silence around him he hears
The muster of men at the barrack door,
The sound of arms, and the tramp of feet,

And the measured tread of the grenadiers,
Marching down to their boats on the shore.

Then he climbed the tower of the Old North Church,
By the wooden stairs, with stealthy tread,
To the belfry-chamber overhead,
And startled the pigeons from their perch
On the sombre rafters, that round him made
Masses and moving shapes of shade,—
By the trembling ladder, steep and tall,
To the highest window in the wall,
Where he paused to listen and look down
A moment on the roofs of the town
And the moonlight flowing over all.

Beneath, in the churchyard, lay the dead,
In their night-encampment on the hill,
Wrapped in silence so deep and still
That he could hear, like a sentinel's tread,
The watchful night-wind, as it went
Creeping along from tent to tent,
And seeming to whisper, "All is well!"
A moment only he feels the spell
Of the place and the hour, and the secret dread
Of the lonely belfry and the dead;
For suddenly all his thoughts are bent
On a shadowy something far away,
Where the river widens to meet the bay,—
A line of black that bends and floats
On the rising tide, like a bridge of boats.

Meanwhile, impatient to mount and ride,
Booted and spurred, with a heavy stride
On the opposite shore walked Paul Revere.
Now he patted his horse's side,
Now gazed at the landscape far and near,
Then, impetuous, stamped the earth,
And turned and tightened his saddle girth;
But mostly he watched with eager search
The belfry's tower of the Old North Church,
As it rose above the graves on the hill,
Lonely and spectral and sombre and still.

And lo! as he looks, on the belfry height
A glimmer, and then a gleam of light!
He springs to the saddle, the bridle he turns,
But lingers and gazes, till full on his sight
A second lamp in the belfry burns!

A hurry of hoofs in a village street,
A shape in the moonlight, a bulk in the dark,
And beneath, from the pebbles, in passing, a spark
Struck out by a steed flying fearless and fleet;
That was all! And yet, through the gloom and the light,
The fate of a nation was riding that night;
And the spark struck out by that steed, in his flight,
Kindled the land into flame with its heat.
He has left the village and mounted the steep,
And beneath him, tranquil and broad and deep,
Is the Mystic, meeting the ocean tides;
And under the alders that skirt its edge,
Now soft on the sand, now loud on the ledge,
Is heard the tramp of his steed as he rides.

It was twelve by the village clock,
When he crossed the bridge into Medford town.
He heard the crowing of the cock,
And the barking of the farmer's dog,
And he felt the damp of the river fog,
That rises after the sun goes down.

It was one by the village clock,
When he galloped into Lexington.
He saw the gilded weathercock
Swim in the moonlight as he passed,
And the meeting-house windows, blank and bare,
Gaze at him with a spectral glare,
As if they already stood aghast
At the bloody work they would look upon.

It was two by the village clock,
When he came to the bridge in Concord town.
He heard the bleating of the flock,
And the twitter of birds among the trees,
And felt the breath of the morning breeze
Blowing over the meadows brown.

And one was safe and asleep in his bed
Who at the bridge would be first to fall,
Who that day would be lying dead,
Pierced by a British musket-ball.

You know the rest. In books you have read,
How the British Regulars fired and fled,—
How the farmers gave them ball for ball,
From behind each fence and farmyard wall,
Chasing the redcoats down the lane,
Then crossing the fields to emerge again
Under the trees at the turn of the road,
And only pausing to fire and load.
So through the night rode Paul Revere;
And so through the night went his cry of alarm
To every Middlesex village and farm,—
A cry of defiance, and not of fear,
A voice in the darkness, a knock at the door,
And a word that shall echo for evermore!
For, borne on the night-wind of the Past,
Through all our history, to the last,
In the hour of darkness and peril and need,
The people will waken and listen to hear
The hurrying hoof-beats of that steed,
And the midnight message of Paul Revere.

HENRY WADSWORTH LONGFELLOW

GUNGA DIN

You may talk o' gin and beer
When you're quartered safe out 'ere,
An' you're sent to penny-fights an' Aldershot it;
But when it comes to slaughter
You will do your work on water,
An' you'll lick the bloomin' boots of 'im that's got it.
Now in Injia's sunny clime,
Where I used to spend my time
A-servin' 'Er Majesty the Queen,
Of all them blackfaced crew
The finest man I knew
Was our regimental bhisti, Gunga Din.
    He was "Din! Din! Din!

"You limpin' lump o' brick-dust, Gunga Din!
    "Hi! slippery *hitherao!*
    "Water, get it! *Panee lao!*
"You squidgy-nosed old idol, Gunga Din."

The uniform 'e wore
Was nothin' much before,
An' rather less than 'arf o' that be'ind,
For a piece o' twisty rag
An' a goatskin water-bag
Was all the field-equipment 'e could find.
When the sweatin' troop-train lay
In a sidin' through the day,
Where the 'eat would make your bloomin' eyebrows crawl.
We shouted "Harry By!"
Till our throats were bricky-dry,
Then we wopped 'im 'cause 'e couldn't serve us all.
        It was "Din! Din! Din!
    "You 'eathen, where the mischief 'ave you been?
        "You put some *juldee* in it
        "Or I'll *marrow* you this minute
    "If you don't fill up my helmet, Gunga Din!"

'E would dot an' carry one
Till the longest day was done;
An' 'e didn't seem to know the use o' fear.
If we charged or broke or cut,
You could bet your bloomin' nut,
'E'd be waitin' fifty paces right flank rear.
With 'is mussick on 'is back,
'E would skip with our attack,
An' watch us till the bugles made "Retire"
An' for all 'is dirty 'ide
'E was white, clear white, inside
When 'e went to tend the wounded under fire!
        It was "Din! Din! Din!"
    With the bullets kickin' dust-spots on the green
        When the cartridges ran out,
        You could hear the front-ranks shout,
    "Hi! ammunition-mules an' Gunga Din!"

I shan't forgit the night
When I dropped be'ind the fight
With a bullet where my belt-plate should 'a' been.
I was chokin' mad with thirst,
An' the man that spied me first
Was our good old grinnin', gruntin' Gunga Din.
'E lifted up my 'ead,
An' he plugged me where I bled,
An' 'e guv me 'arf-a-pint of water green:
It was crawlin' and it stunk,
But of all the drinks I've drunk,
I'm gratefullest to one from Gunga Din.
  It was "Din! Din! Din!
 " 'Ere's a beggar with a bullet through 'is spleen;
  " 'E's chawin' up the ground,
  "An' 'e's kickin' all around:
 "For Gawd's sake git the water, Gunga Din!"

'E carried me away
To where a dooli lay,
An' a bullet come an' drilled the beggar clean.
'E put me safe inside,
An' just before he died,
"I 'ope you liked your drink," sez Gunga Din.
So I'll meet 'im later on
At the place where 'e is gone—
Where it's always double drill and no canteen;
'E'll be squattin' on the coals
Givin' drinks to poor damned souls,
An' I'll get a swig in hell from Gunga Din!
  Yes, Din! Din! Din!
 You Lazarushian-leather Gunga Din!
  Though I've belted you and flayed you,
  By the livin' Gawd that made you,
 You're a better man than I am, Gunga Din!
      RUDYARD KIPLING

MY LAST DUCHESS

FERRARA

That's my last Duchess painted on the wall,
Looking as if she were alive. I call
That piece a wonder, now: Frà Pandolf's hands
Worked busily a day, and there she stands.
Will 't please you sit and look at her? I said
"Frà Pandolf" by design, for never read
Strangers like you that pictured countenance,
The depth and passion of its earnest glance,
But to myself they turned (since none puts by
The curtain I have drawn for you, but I)
And seemed as they would ask me, if they durst,
How such a glance came there; so, not the first
Are you to turn and ask thus. Sir, 't was not
Her husband's presence only, called that spot
Of joy into the Duchess' cheek: perhaps
Frà Pandolf chanced to say, "Her mantle laps
Over my lady's wrist too much," or "Paint
Must never hope to reproduce the faint
Half-flush that dies along her throat:" such stuff
Was courtesy, she thought, and cause enough
For calling up that spot of joy. She had
A heart—how shall I say?—too soon made glad,
Too easily impressed; she liked whate'er
She looked on, and her looks went everywhere.
Sir, 't was all one! My favor at her breast,
The dropping of the daylight in the West,
The bough of cherries some officious fool
Broke in the orchard for her, the white mule
She rode with round the terrace—all and each
Would draw from her alike the approving speech,
Or blush, at least. She thanked men,—good! but thanked
Somehow—I know not how—as if she ranked
My gift of a nine-hundred-years-old name
With anybody's gift. Who'd stoop to blame

This sort of trifling? Even had you skill
In speech— (which I have not) —to make your will
Quite clear to such an one, and say, "Just this
Or that in you disgusts me; here you miss,
Or there exceed the mark"—and if she let
Herself be lessoned so, nor plainly set
Her wits to yours, forsooth, and made excuse,
—E'en then would be some stooping; and I choose
Never to stoop. Oh, sir, she smiled, no doubt,
Whene'er I passed her; but who passed without
Much the same smile? This grew; I gave commands;
Then all smiles stopped together. There she stands
As if alive. Will 't please you rise? We'll meet
The company below, then. I repeat,
The Count your master's known munificence
Is ample warrant that no just pretense
Of mine for dowry will be disallowed;
Though his fair daughter's self, as I avowed
At starting, is my object. Nay, we'll go
Together down, sir. Notice Neptune, though,
Taming a sea-horse, thought a rarity,
Which Claus of Innsbruck cast in bronze for me!

ROBERT BROWNING

THE DEACON'S MASTERPIECE OR, THE WONDERFUL "ONE-HOSS SHAY"

A Logical Story

Have you heard of the wonderful
  one-hoss shay,
That was built in such a logical
  way
It ran a hundred years to a day,
And then, of a sudden, it—ah,
  but stay,
I'll tell you what happened
  without delay,
Scaring the parson into fits,
Frightening people out of their
  wits,—
Have you ever heard of that, I say?

Seventeen hundred and fifty-five.
Georgius Secundus was then alive,—
Snuffy old drone from the
  German hive.
That was the year when Lisbon-town
Saw the earth open and gulp her down,
And Braddock's army was done so
  brown,
Left without a scalp to its crown.
It was on the terrible
  Earthquake-day
That the Deacon finished the
  one-hoss shay.

Now in building of chaises, I tell
you what,
There is always *somewhere* a
weakest spot,—
In hub, tire, felloe, in spring or thill,
In panel, or crossbar, or floor, or sill,
In screw, bolt, thoroughbrace,—
lurking still,
Find it somewhere you must and
will,—
Above or below, or within or
without,—
And that's the reason, beyond a
doubt,
That a chaise *breaks down,* but
doesn't *wear out.*

But the Deacon swore (as
Deacons do,
With an "I dew vum," or an "I
tell *yeou*")
He would build one shay to beat
the taown
'n' the keounty 'n' all the kentry
raoun';
It should be so built that it
couldn' break daown:
"Fur," said the Deacon, " 't 's
mighty plain
Thut the weakes' place mus' stan'
the strain;
'n' the way t' fix it, uz I maintain,
is only jest
T' make that place uz strong uz
the rest."

So the Deacon inquired of the
village folk
Where he could find the strongest
oak,
That couldn't be split nor bent
nor broke,—

That was for spokes and floor
and sills;
He sent for lancewood to make
the thills;
The crossbars were ash, from the
straightest trees,
The panels of whitewood, that
cuts like cheese,
But lasts like iron for things like
these;
The hubs of logs from the
"Settler's ellum,"—
Last of its timber,—they couldn't
sell 'em,
Never an axe had seen their chips,
And the wedges flew from
between their lips,
Their blunt ends frizzled like
celery-tips;
Step and prop-iron, bolt and
screw,
Spring, tire, axle, and linchpin
too,
Steel of the finest, bright and blue;
Thoroughbrace bison-skin, thick
and wide;
Boot, top, dasher, from tough old
hide
Found in the pit when the tanner
died.
That was the way he "put her
through."
"There!" said the Deacon, "naow
she'll dew!"

Do! I tell you, I rather guess
She was a wonder, and nothing
less!
Colts grew horses, beards turned
gray,
Deacon and deaconess dropped
away,

Children and grandchildren—
 where were they?
But there stood the stout old
 one-hoss shay
As fresh as on Lisbon-earthquake-
 day!

EIGHTEEN HUNDRED;—it came and
 found
The Deacon's masterpiece strong
 and sound.
Eighteen hundred increased by
 ten;—
"Hahnsum kerridge" they called
 it then.
Eighteen hundred and twenty
 came;—
Running as usual; much the
 same.
Thirty and forty at last arrive,
And then come fifty, and FIFTY-
 FIVE.

Little of all we value here
Wakes on the morn of its
 hundredth year
Without both feeling and looking
 queer.
In fact, there's nothing that keeps
 its youth,
So far as I know, but a tree and
 truth.
(This is a moral that runs at large;
Take it.—You're welcome.—No
 extra charge.)

FIRST OF NOVEMBER,—the
 Earthquake-day,—
There are traces of age in the
 one-hoss shay,
A general flavor of mild decay,
But nothing local, as one may say.

There couldn't be,—for the
 Deacon's art
Had made it so like in every part
That there wasn't a chance for
 one to start.
For the wheels were just as strong
 as the thills
And the floor was just as strong
 as the sills,
And the panels just as strong as
 the floor,
And the whippletree neither less
 nor more,
And the back-crossbar as strong as
 the fore,
And spring and axle and hub
 encore.
And yet, *as a whole,* it is past a
 doubt
In another hour it will be *worn
 out!*

First of November, fifty-five!
This morning the parson takes a
 drive.
Now, small boys, get out of the way!
Here comes the wonderful one-
 hoss shay,
Drawn by a rat-tailed, ewe-necked
 bay.
"Huddup!" said the parson.—Off
 went they.
The parson was working his
 Sunday's text,—
Had got to *fifthly,* and stopped
 perplexed
At what the—Moses—was coming
 next.
All at once the horse stood still,
Close by the meet'n'-house on the
 hill.
First a shiver, and then a thrill,

Then something decidedly like a
   spill,—
And the parson was sitting upon
   a rock,
At half past nine by the meet'n'-
   house clock,—
Just the hour of the Earthquake
   shock!

What do you think the parson
   found,
When he got up and stared
   around?
The poor old chaise in a heap or
   mound,

As if it had been to the mill and
   ground!
You see, of course, if you're not a
   dunce,
How it went to pieces all at
   once,—
All at once, and nothing first,—
Just as bubbles do when they
   burst.

End of the wonderful one-hoss
   shay.
Logic is logic. That's all I say.
     OLIVER WENDELL HOLMES

HOW THEY BROUGHT THE GOOD NEWS
FROM GHENT TO AIX

I sprang to the stirrup, and Joris and he;
I galloped, Dirck galloped, we galloped all three;
"Good speed!" cried the watch as the gate-bolts undrew,
"Speed!" echoed the wall to us galloping through.
Behind shut the postern, the lights sank to rest,
And into the midnight we galloped abreast.

Not a word to each other; we kept the great pace
Neck by neck, stride by stride, never changing our place;
I turned in my saddle and made its girths tight,
Then shortened each stirrup and set the pique right,
Rebuckled the cheek-strap, chained slacker the bit,
Nor galloped less steadily Roland a whit.

'Twas a moonset at starting; but while we drew near
Lokeren, the cocks crew and twilight dawned clear;
At Boom a great yellow star came out to see;
At Düffeld 'twas morning as plain as could be;
And from Mecheln church-steeple we heard the half-chime,—
So Joris broke silence with "Yet there is time!"

At Aerschot up leaped of a sudden the sun,
And against him the cattle stood black every one,
To stare through the mist at us galloping past;
And I saw my stout galloper Roland at last,
With resolute shoulders, each butting away
The haze, as some bluff river headland its spray;

And his low head and crest, just one sharp ear bent back
For my voice, and the other pricked out on his track;
And one eye's black intelligence,—ever that glance
O'er its white edge at me, his own master, askance;
And the thick heavy spume-flakes, which aye and anon
His fierce lips shook upward in galloping on.

By Hasselt Dirck groaned; and cried Joris, "Stay spur!
Your Roos galloped bravely, the fault's not in her;
We'll remember at Aix,"—for one heard the quick wheeze
Of her chest, saw the stretched neck, and staggering knees,
And sunk tail, and horrible heave of the flank,
As down on her haunches she shuddered and sank.

So we were left galloping, Joris and I,
Past Looz and past Tongres, no cloud in the sky;
The broad sun above laughed a pitiless laugh;
'Neath our feet broke the brittle, bright stubble like chaff;
Till over by Dalhem a dome-spire sprang white,
And "Gallop," gasped Joris, "for Aix is in sight!"

"How they'll greet us!"—and all in a moment his roan
Rolled neck and croup over, lay dead as a stone;
And there was my Roland to bear the whole weight
Of the news which alone could save Aix from her fate,
With his nostrils like pits full of blood to the brim,
And with circles of red for his eye-sockets' rim.

Then I cast loose my buff-coat, each holster let fall,
Shook off both my jack-boots, let go belt and all,
Stood up in the stirrup, leaned, patted his ear,
Called my Roland his pet name, my horse without peer,—
Clapped my hands, laughed and sung, any noise, bad or good,
Till at length into Aix Roland galloped and stood.

And all I remember is friends flocking round,
As I sat with his head 'twixt my knees on the ground;
And no voice but was praising this Roland of mine,
As I poured down his throat our last measure of wine,
Which (the burgesses voted by common consent)
Was no more than his due who brought good news from Ghent.

ROBERT BROWNING

BARBARA FRIETCHIE

Up from the meadows rich with
    corn,
Clear in the cool September morn,
The clustered spires of Frederick
    stand
Green-walled by the hills of
    Maryland.
Round about them orchards
    sweep,
Apple and peach tree fruited
    deep,
Fair as the garden of the Lord
To the eyes of the famished rebel
    horde,
On that pleasant morn of the
    early fall
When Lee marched over the
    mountain-wall;
Over the mountains winding
    down,
Horse and foot, into Frederick
    town.

Forty flags with their silver stars,
Forty flags with their crimson bars,
Flapped in the morning wind:
    the sun
Of noon looked down, and saw
    not one.
Up rose old Barbara Frietchie
    then,
Bowed with her fourscore years
    and ten;
Bravest of all in Frederick town
She took up the flag the men
    hauled down;
In her attic window the staff she set,
To show that one heart was loyal
    yet.
Up the street came the rebel tread,
Stonewall Jackson riding ahead.
Under his slouched hat left and
    right
He glanced; the old flag met his
    sight.

"Halt!"—the dust-brown ranks
stood fast.
"Fire!"—out blazed the rifle-blast.
It shivered the window, pane and
sash;
It rent the banner with seam and
gash.
Quick, as it fell, from the broken
staff
Dame Barbara snatched the silken
scarf.
She leaned far out on the window-
sill,
And shook it forth with a royal will.
"Shoot, if you must, this old gray
head,
But spare your country's flag," she
said.

A shade of sadness, a blush of
shame,
Over the face of the leader came;
The nobler nature within him
stirred
To life at that woman's deed and
word;
"Who touches a hair of yon gray head
Dies like a dog! March on!" he said.

All day long through Frederick
street
Sounded the tread of marching
feet:
All day long that free flag tost
Over the heads of the rebel host.
Ever its torn folds rose and fell
On the loyal winds that loved it
well;
And through the hill-gaps sunset
light
Shone over it with a warm good-
night.

Barbara Frietchie's work is o'er,
And the Rebel rides on his raids
no more.
Honor to her! and let a tear
Fall, for her sake, on Stonewall's
bier.
Over Barbara Frietchie's grave,
Flag of Freedom and Union, wave!
Peace and order and beauty draw
Round thy symbol of light and law;
And ever the stars above look down
On thy stars below in Frederick
town!

JOHN GREENLEAF WHITTIER

THE SHOOTING OF DAN MC GREW

A bunch of the boys were whooping
it up in the Malamute saloon;
The kid that handles the music-box
was hitting a jag-time tune;
Back of the bar, in a solo game, sat
Dangerous Dan McGrew;
And watching his luck was his light-
o'-love, the lady that's known as
Lou.

When out of the night, which was
fifty below, and into the din and
the glare,
There stumbled a miner fresh from
the creeks, dog-dirty, and loaded
for bear.
He looked like a man with a foot
in the grave and scarcely the
strength of a louse,
Yet he tilted a poke of dust on the
bar, and he called for drinks for
the house.
There was none could place the
stranger's face, though we
searched ourselves for a clue;
But we drank his health, and the
last to drink was Dangerous Dan
McGrew.

There's men that somehow just
grip your eyes, and hold them
hard like a spell;
And such was he, and he looked to
me like a man who had lived in
hell;

With a face most hair, and the
dreary stare of a dog whose day
is done,
As he watered the green stuff in his
glass, and the drops fell one by
one.
Then I got to figgering who he was,
and wondering what he'd do,
And I turned my head—and there
watching him was the lady that's
known as Lou.

His eyes went rubbering round the
room, and he seemed in a kind of
daze,
Till at last that old piano fell in the
way of his wandering gaze.
The rag-time kid was having a
drink: there was no one else on
the stool,
So the stranger stumbles across the
room, and flops down there like
a fool.
In a buckskin shirt that was glazed
with dirt he sat, and I saw him
sway;
Then he clutched the keys with his
talon hands—my God! but that
man could play.

Were you ever out in the Great
Alone, when the moon was awful
clear,
And the icy mountains hemmed
you in with a silence you most
could *hear*;

With only the howl of a timber wolf, and you camped there in the cold,

A half-dead thing in a stark, dead world, clean mad for the muck called gold;

While high overhead, green, yellow and red, the North Lights swept in bars?—

Then you've a hunch what the music meant . . . hunger and night and the stars.

And hunger not of the belly kind, that's banished with bacon and beans,

But the gnawing hunger of lonely men for a home and all that it means:

For a fireside far from the cares that are, four walls and a roof above;

But oh! so cramful of cosy joy, and crowned with a woman's love—

A woman dearer than all the world, and true as Heaven is true—

(God! how ghastly she looks through her rouge,—the lady that's known as Lou.)

Then on a sudden the music changed, so soft that you scarce could hear;

But you felt that your life had been looted clean of all that it once held dear;

That someone had stolen the woman you loved; that her love was a devil's lie;

That your guts were gone, and the best for you was to crawl away and die.

'Twas the crowning cry of a heart's despair, and it thrilled you through and through—

"I guess I'll make it a spread misere," said Dangerous Dan McGrew.

The music almost died away . . . then it burst like a pent-up flood;

And it seemed to say, "Repay, repay," and my eyes were blind with blood.

The thought came back of an ancient wrong, and it stung like a frozen lash,

And the lust awoke to kill, to kill . . . then the music stopped with a crash,

And the stranger turned, and his eyes they burned in a most peculiar way;

In a buckskin shirt that was glazed with dirt he sat, and I saw him sway;

Then his lips went in in a kind of grin, and he spoke, and his voice was calm,

And "Boys," says he, "you don't know me, and none of you care a damn;

But I want to state, and my words are straight, and I'll bet my poke they're true,

That one of you is a hound of hell . . . and that one is Dan McGrew."

Then I ducked my head, and the lights went out, and two guns blazed in the dark,

And a woman screamed, and the
lights went up, and two men lay
stiff and stark.
Pitched on his head, and pumped
full of lead, was Dangerous Dan
McGrew,
While the man from the creeks lay
clutched to the breast of the lady
that's known as Lou.
These are the simple facts of the
case, and I guess you ought to
know.

They say that the stranger was
crazed with "hooch," and I'm not
denying it's so.
I'm not so wise as the lawyer guys,
but strictly between us two—
The woman that kissed him and—
pinched his poke—was the lady
that's known as Lou.
ROBERT W. SERVICE

MINIVER CHEEVY

Miniver Cheevy, child of scorn,
Grew lean while he assailed the
seasons;
He wept that he was ever born,
And he had reasons.

Miniver loved the days of old
When swords were bright and
steeds were prancing.
The vision of a warrior bold
Would set him dancing.

Miniver sighed for what was not,
And dreamed, and rested from
his labors;
He dreamed of Thebes and
Camelot,
And Priam's neighbors.

Miniver mourned the ripe renown
That made so many a name so
fragrant;
He mourned Romance, now on
the town,
And Art, a vagrant.

Miniver loved the Medici,
Albeit he had never seen one;
He would have sinned incessantly
Could he have been one.

Miniver cursed the commonplace
And eyed a khaki suit with
loathing;
He missed the mediæval grace
Of iron clothing.

Miniver scorned the gold he
sought,
But sore annoyed was he
without it;
Miniver thought, and thought,
and thought,
And thought about it.

Miniver Cheevy, born too late,
Scratched his head and kept on
thinking:
Miniver coughed, and called it
fate,
And kept on drinking.
EDWIN ARLINGTON ROBINSON

THE WRECK OF THE HESPERUS

It was the schooner Hesperus,
That sailed the wintry sea;
And the skipper had taken his
  little daughter,
To bear him company.

Blue were her eyes as the fairy
  flax,
Her cheeks like the dawn of day,
And her bosom white as the
  hawthorn buds
That ope in the month of May.

The skipper he stood beside the
  helm,
His pipe was in his mouth,
And he watched how the veering
  flaw did blow
The smoke now West, now South.

Then up and spake an old Sailor,
Had sailed to the Spanish Main,
"I pray thee, put into yonder port,
For I fear a hurricane.

"Last night, the moon had a
  golden ring,
And to-night no moon we see!"
The skipper, he blew a whiff from
  his pipe,
And a scornful laugh laughed he.

Colder and louder blew the wind,
A gale from the Northeast;
The snow fell hissing in the brine,
And the billows frothed like yeast.

Down came the storm, and smote
  amain
The vessel in its strength;
She shuddered and paused, like a
  frightened steed
Then leaped her cable's length.

"Come hither! come hither! my
  little daughter,
And do not tremble so;
For I can weather the roughest gale
That ever wind did blow."

He wrapped her warm in his
    seaman's coat
Against the stinging blast;
He cut a rope from a broken spar,
And bound her to the mast.

"O father! I hear the church-bells ring,
Oh say, what may it be?"
" 'Tis a fog-bell on a rock-bound
    coast!"
And he steered for the open sea.

"O father! I hear the sound of guns,
Oh say, what may it be?"
"Some ship in distress, that cannot live
In such an angry sea!"

"O father! I see a gleaming light,
Oh say, what may it be?"
But the father answered never a word,—
A frozen corpse was he.

Lashed to the helm, all stiff and stark,
With his face turned to the skies,
The lantern gleamed through the
    gleaming snow
On his fixed and glassy eyes.

Then the maiden clasped her
    hands and prayed
That saved she might be;
And she thought of Christ, who
    stilled the waves
On the Lake of Galilee.

And fast through the midnight
    dark and drear,
Through the whistling sleet and snow,
Like a sheeted ghost, the vessel swept
Towards the reef of Norman's Woe.

And ever the fitful gusts between
A sound came from the land;

It was the sound of the trampling
    surf,
On the rocks and the hard sea-sand.

The breakers were right beneath
    her bows,
She drifted a dreary wreck,
And a whooping billow swept the
    crew
Like icicles from her deck.

She struck where the white and
    fleecy waves
Looked soft as carded wool,
But the cruel rocks, they gored
    her side
Like the horns of an angry bull.

Her rattling shrouds, all sheathed
    in ice,
With the masts went by the board;
Like a vessel of glass, she stove
    and sank,
Ho! Ho! the breakers roared!

At daybreak, on the bleak sea-beach,
A fisherman stood aghast,
To see the form of a maiden fair,
Lashed close to a drifting mast!

The salt sea was frozen on her breast,
The salt tears in her eyes;
And he saw her hair, like the
    brown sea-weed,
On the billows fall and rise.

Such was the wreck of the Hesperus,
In the midnight and the snow!
Christ save us all from a death
    like this,
On the reef of Norman's Woe!

HENRY WADSWORTH LONGFELLOW

HORATIUS AT THE BRIDGE

Lars Porsena of Clusium,
  By the Nine Gods he swore
That the great house of Tarquin
  Should suffer wrong no more.
By the Nine Gods he swore it,
  And named a trysting-day,
And bade his messengers ride forth,
East and west and south and north,
  To summon his array.

East and west and south and
    north
  The messengers ride fast,
And tower and town and cottage
  Have heard the trumpet's blast.
Shame on the false Etruscan
  Who lingers in his home,
When Porsena of Clusium
  Is on the march for Rome!

The horsemen and the footmen
  Are pouring in amain
From many a stately market-place,
  From many a fruitful plain,
From many a lonely hamlet,
  Which, hid by beech and pine,
Like an eagle's nest hangs on the
    crest
  Of purple Apennine:

From lordly Volaterræ,
  Where scowls the far-famed hold
Piled by the hands of giants
  For godlike kings of old;

From sea-girt Populonia,
  Whose sentinels descry
Sardinia's snowy mountain-tops
  Fringing the southern sky;

From the proud mart of Pisæ,
  Queen of the western waves,
Where ride Massilia's triremes,
  Heavy with fair-haired slaves;
From where sweet Clanis wanders
  Through corn and vines and
    flowers,
From where Cortona lifts to
    heaven
  Her diadem of towers.

Tall are the oaks whose acorns
  Drop in dark Auser's rill;
Fat are the stags that champ the
    boughs
  Of the Ciminian hill;
Beyond all streams, Clitumnus
  Is to the herdsman dear;
Best of all pools the fowler loves
  The great Volsinian mere.

But now no stroke of woodman
  Is heard by Auser's rill;
No hunter tracks the stag's green
    path
  Up to Ciminian hill;
Unwatched along Clitumnus
  Grazes the milk-white steer;
Unharmed the water-fowl may dip
  In the Volsinian mere.

The harvests of Arretium,
  This year, old men shall reap;
This year, young boys in Umbro
  Shall plunge the struggling
    sheep;
And in the vats of Luna,
  This year, the must shall foam
Round the white feet of laughing
    girls
  Whose sires have marched to
    Rome.

There be thirty chosen prophets,
  The wisest of the land,
Who always by Lars Porsena
  Both morn and evening stand.
Evening and morn the Thirty
  Have turned the verses o'er,
Traced from the right on linen
    white
  By mighty seers of yore;

And with one voice the Thirty
  Have their glad answer given:
"Go forth, go forth, Lars
    Porsena,—
  Go forth, beloved of Heaven!
Go, and return in glory
  To Clusium's royal dome,
And hang round Nurscia's altars
  The golden shields of Rome!"

And now hath every city
  Sent up her tale of men;
The foot are fourscore thousand,
  The horse are thousands ten.
Before the gates of Sutrium
  Is met the great array;
A proud man was Lars Porsena
  Upon the trysting-day.

For all the Etruscan armies
  Were ranged beneath his eye,
And many a banished Roman,
  And many a stout ally;
And with a mighty following,
  To join the muster, came
The Tusculan Mamilius,
  Prince of the Latian name.

But by the yellow Tiber
  Was tumult and affright;
From all the spacious champaign
  To Rome men took their flight.
A mile around the city
  The throng stopped up the
    ways;
A fearful sight it was to see
  Through two long nights and
    days.

For aged folk on crutches,
  And women great with child,
And mothers, sobbing over babes
  That clung to them and smiled,
And sick men borne in litters
  High on the necks of slaves,
And troops of sunburned
    husbandmen
  With reaping-hooks and staves,

And droves of mules and asses
  Laden with skins of wine,
And endless flocks of goats and
    sheep,
  And endless herds of kine,
And endless trains of wagons,
  That creaked beneath the
    weight
Of corn-sacks and of household
    goods,
  Choked every roaring gate.

Now, from the rock Tarpeian,
    Could the wan burghers spy
The line of blazing villages
    Red in the midnight sky.
The Fathers of the City,
    They sat all night and day,
For every hour some horseman
        came
    With tidings of dismay.

To eastward and to westward
    Have spread the Tuscan bands,
Nor house, nor fence, nor
        dovecote
    In Crustumerium stands.
Verbenna down to Ostia
    Hath wasted all the plain;
Astur hath stormed Janiculum,
    And the stout guards are slain.

I wis, in all the Senate
    There was no heart so bold
But sore it ached, and fast it beat,
    When that ill news was told.
Forthwith up rose the Consul,
    Up rose the Fathers all;
In haste they girded up their
        gowns,
    And hied them to the wall.

They held a council, standing
    Before the River-gate;
Short time was there, ye well may
        guess,
    For musing or debate.
Out spake the Consul roundly:
    "The bridge must straight go
        down;
For, since Janiculum is lost,
    Naught else can save the town."

Just then a scout came flying,
    All wild with haste and fear:
"To arms! to arms! Sir Consul,—
    Lars Porsena is here."
On the low hills to westward
    The Consul fixed his eye,
And saw the swarthy storm of dust
    Rise fast along the sky.

And nearer fast and nearer
    Doth the red whirlwind come;
And louder still, and still more
        loud,
From underneath that rolling
        cloud,
Is heard the trumpets' war-note
        proud,
    The trampling and the hum.
And plainly and more plainly
    Now through the gloom
        appears,
Far to left and far to right,
In broken gleams of dark-blue
        light,
The long array of helmets bright,
    The long array of spears.

And plainly and more plainly,
    Above that glimmering line,
Now might ye see the banners
    Of twelve fair cities shine;
But the banner of proud Clusium
    Was highest of them all,—
The terror of the Umbrian,
    The terror of the Gaul.

And plainly and more plainly
    Now might the burghers know,
By port and vest, by horse and
        crest,

Each warlike Lucumo:
There Cilnius of Arretium
On his fleet roan was seen;
And Astur of the fourfold shield,
Girt with the brand none else
    may wield;
Tolumnius with the belt of gold,
And dark Verbenna from the hold
    By reedy Thrasymene.

Fast by the royal standard,
    O'erlooking all the war,
Lars Porsena of Clusium
    Sat in his ivory car.
By the right wheel rode Mamilius,
    Prince of the Latian name;
And by the left false Sextus,
    That wrought the deed of
        shame.

But when the face of Sextus
    Was seen among the foes,
A yell that rent the firmament
    From all the town arose.
On the house-tops was no woman
    But spat towards him and
        hissed,
No child but screamed out curses,
    And shook its little fist.

But the Consul's brow was sad,
    And the Consul's speech was
        low,
And darkly looked he at the wall,
    And darkly at the foe:
"Their van will be upon us
    Before the bridge goes down;
And if they once may win the
        bridge,
    What hope to save the town?"

Then out spake brave Horatius,
    The Captain of the gate:
"To every man upon this earth
    Death cometh soon or late.
And how can man die better
    Than facing fearful odds
For the ashes of his fathers
    And the temples of his gods,

"And for the tender mother
    Who dandled him to rest,
And for the wife who nurses
    His baby at her breast,
And for the holy maidens
    Who feed the eternal flame,—
To save them from false Sextus
    That wrought the deed of
        shame?

"Hew down the bridge, Sir
        Consul,
    With all the speed ye may;
I, with two more to help me,
    Will hold the foe in play.
In yon strait path a thousand
    May well be stopped by three:
Now who will stand on either
        hand,
    And keep the bridge with me?"

Then out spake Spurius Lartius,—
    A Ramnian proud was he:
"Lo, I will stand at thy right
        hand,
    And keep the bridge with thee."
And out spake strong
        Herminius,—
    Of Titian blood was he:
"I will abide on thy left side,
    And keep the bridge with thee."

"Horatius," quoth the Consul,
  "As thou sayest so let it be."
And straight against that great
    array
  Went forth the dauntless three.
For Romans in Rome's quarrel
  Spared neither land nor gold,
Nor son nor wife, nor limb nor
    life,
  In the brave days of old.

Then none was for a party—
  Then all were for the state;
Then the great man helped the
    poor,
  And the poor man loved the
    great;
Then lands were fairly portioned!
  Then spoils were fairly sold:
The Romans were like brothers
  In the brave days of old.

Now Roman is to Roman
  More hateful than a foe,
And the tribunes beard the high,
  And the fathers grind the low.
As we wax hot in faction,
  In battle we wax cold;
Wherefore men fight not as they
    fought
  In the brave days of old.

Now while the three were
    tightening
  Their harness on their backs,
The Consul was the foremost man
  To take in hand an axe;
And fathers, mixed with commons,
  Seized hatchet, bar, and crow,
And smote upon the planks above,
  And loosed the props below.

Meanwhile the Tuscan army,
  Right glorious to behold,
Came flashing back the noonday
    light,
Rank behind rank, like surges bright
  Of a broad sea of gold.
Four hundred trumpets sounded
  A peal of warlike glee,
As that great host with measured
    tread,
And spears advanced, and ensigns
    spread
Rolled slowly towards the bridge's
    head,
  Where stood the dauntless three.

The three stood calm and silent,
  And looked upon the foes,
And a great shout of laughter
  From all the vanguard rose;
And forth three chiefs came spurring
  Before that deep array;
To earth they sprang, their swords
    they drew,
And lifted high their shields, and
    flew
  To win the narrow way.

Aunus, from green Tifernum,
  Lord of the Hill of Vines;
And Seius, whose eight hundred
    slaves
  Sicken in Ilva's mines;
And Picus, long to Clusium
  Vassal in peace and war,
Who led to fight his Umbrian
    powers
From that gray crag where, girt
    with towers,
The fortress of Nequinum lowers
  O'er the pale waves of Nar.

Stout Lartius hurled down Aunus
    Into the stream beneath;
Herminius struck at Seius,
    And clove him to the teeth;
At Picus brave Horatius
    Darted one fiery thrust,
And the proud Umbrian's gilded
      arms
    Clashed in the bloody dust.

No more, aghast and pale,
From Ostia's walls the crowd shall
    mark
The track of thy destroying bark;
No more Campania's hinds shall
    fly
To woods and caverns, when they
    spy
    Thy thrice-accursèd sail!"

Then Ocnus of Falerii
    Rushed on the Roman three;
And Lausulus of Urgo,
    The rover of the sea;
And Aruns of Volsinium,
    Who slew the great wild boar,—
The great wild boar that had his den
Amidst the reeds of Cosa's fen,
And wasted fields, and slaughtered
    men,
    Along Albinia's shore.

Herminius smote down Aruns;
    Lartius laid Ocnus low;
Right to the heart of Lausulus
    Horatius sent a blow:
"Lie there," he cried, "fell pirate!

But now no sound of laughter
    Was heard among the foes;
A wild and wrathful clamor
    From all the vanguard rose.
Six spears' length from the
    entrance,
    Halted that deep array,
And for a space no man came
    forth
    To win the narrow way.

But, hark! the cry is Astur:
    And lo! the ranks divide;
And the great lord of Luna
    Comes with his stately stride.
Upon his ample shoulders
    Clangs loud the fourfold shield,

And in his hand he shakes the
   brand
  Which none but he can wield.

He smiled on those bold Romans,
  A smile serene and high;
He eyed the flinching Tuscans,
  And scorn was in his eye.
Quoth he, "The she-wolf's litter
  Stand savagely at bay;
But will ye dare to follow,
  If Astur clears the way?"

Then, whirling up his broadsword
  With both hands to the height,
He rushed against Horatius,
  And smote with all his might.
With shield and blade Horatius
  Right deftly turned the blow.
The blow, though turned, came
   yet too nigh;
It missed his helm, but gashed his
   thigh.
The Tuscans raised a joyful cry
  To see the red blood flow.

He reeled, and on Herminius
  He leaned one breathing-space,
Then, like a wild-cat mad with
   wounds,
  Sprang right at Astur's face.
Through teeth and skull and
   helmet
  So fierce a thrust he sped,
The good sword stood a
   handbreadth out
  Behind the Tuscan's head.

And the great lord of Luna
  Fell at that deadly stroke,
As falls on Mount Avernus
  A thunder-smitten oak.

Far o'er the crashing forest
  The giant arms lie spread;
And the pale augurs, muttering low
  Gaze on the blasted head.
On Astur's throat Horatius
  Right firmly pressed his heel,
And thrice and four times tugged
   amain,
  Ere he wrenched out the steel.
And "See," he cried, "the welcome,
  Fair guests, that waits you here!
What noble Lucumo comes next
  To taste our Roman cheer?"

But at his haughty challenge
  A sullen murmur ran,
Mingled with wrath and shame
   and dread,
  Along that glittering van.
There lacked not men of prowess,
  Nor men of lordly race,
For all Etruria's noblest
  Were round the fatal place.

But all Etruria's noblest
  Felt their hearts sink to see
On the earth the bloody corpses,
  In the path of the dauntless
   three;
And from the ghastly entrance,
  Where those bold Romans
   stood,
All shrank,—like boys who,
   unaware,
Ranging the woods to start a hare,
Come to the mouth of the dark
   lair
Where, growling low, a fierce old
   bear
  Lies amidst bones and blood.

Was none who would be foremost
　To lead such dire attack;
But those behind cried "Forward!"
　And those before cried "Back!"
And backward now and forward
　Wavers the deep array;
And on the tossing sea of steel
To and fro the standards reel,
And the victorious trumpet-peal
　Dies fitfully away.

Yet one man for one moment
　Strode out before the crowd;
Well known was he to all the three,
　And they gave him greeting loud:
"Now welcome, welcome, Sextus!
　Now welcome to thy home!
Why dost thou stay, and turn
　　away?
　Here lies the road to Rome."

Thrice looked he at the city;
　Thrice looked he at the dead;
And thrice came on in fury,
　And thrice turned back in dread;
And, white with fear and hatred,
　Scowled at the narrow way
Where, wallowing in a pool of
　　blood,
　The bravest Tuscans lay.

But meanwhile axe and lever
　Have manfully been plied;
And now the bridge hangs
　　tottering
　Above the boiling tide.
"Come back, come back,
　　Horatius!"
Loud cried the Fathers all,—
"Back, Lartius! back, Herminius!
　Back, ere the ruin fall!"

Back darted Spurius Lartius,—
　Herminius darted back;
And, as they passed, beneath their
　　feet
　They felt the timbers crack.
But when they turned their faces,
　And on the farther shore
Saw brave Horatius stand alone,
　They would have crossed once
　　more;

But with a crash like thunder
　Fell every loosened beam,
And, like a dam, the mighty wreck
　Lay right athwart the stream;
And a long shout of triumph
　Rose from the walls of Rome,
As to the highest turret-tops
　Was splashed the yellow foam.

And like a horse unbroken,
　When first he feels the rein,
The furious river struggled hard,
　And tossed his tawny mane,
And burst the curb, and bounded,
　Rejoicing to be free;
And whirling down, in fierce
　　career,
Battlement and plank and pier,
　Rushed headlong to the sea.

Alone stood brave Horatius,
　But constant still in mind,—
Thrice thirty thousand foes before,
　And the broad flood behind.
"Down with him!" cried false
　　Sextus,
　With a smile on his pale face;
"Now yield thee," cried Lars
　　Porsena,
　"Now yield thee to our grace!"

Round turned he, as not deigning
  Those craven ranks to see;
Naught spake he to Lars Porsena,
  To Sextus naught spake he;
But he saw on Palatinus
  The white porch of his home;
And he spake to the noble river
  That rolls by the towers of Rome:

"O Tiber! Father Tiber!
  To whom the Romans pray,
A Roman's life, a Roman's arms,
  Take thou in charge this day!"
So he spake, and, speaking,
    sheathed
  The good sword by his side,
And, with his harness on his back,
  Plunged headlong in the tide.

No sound of joy or sorrow
  Was heard from either bank,
But friends and foes in dumb
    surprise,
With parted lips and straining
    eyes,
  Stood gazing where he sank;
And when above the surges
  They saw his crest appear,
All Rome sent forth a rapturous
    cry,
And even the ranks of Tuscany
  Could scarce forbear to cheer.

But fiercely ran the current,
  Swollen high by months of rain;
And fast his blood was flowing,
  And he was sore in pain,
And heavy with his armor,
  And spent with clanging blows;
And oft they thought him sinking,
  But still again he rose.

Never, I ween, did swimmer,
  In such an evil case,
Struggle through such a raging flood
  Safe to the landing-place;
But his limbs were borne up bravely
  By the brave heart within,
And our good Father Tiber
  Bare bravely up his chin.

"Curse on him!" quoth false
    Sextus,—
  "Will not the villain drown?
But for this stay, ere close of day
  We should have sacked the
    town!"
"Heaven help him!" quoth Lars
    Porsena,
  "And bring him safe to shore;
For such a gallant feat of arms
  Was never seen before."

And now he feels the bottom;
  Now on dry earth he stands;
Now round him throng the
    Fathers
  To press his gory hands;
And now, with shouts and
    clapping,
  And noise of weeping loud,
He enters through the River-gate,
  Borne by the joyous crowd.

They gave him of the corn-land,
  That was of public right,
As much as two strong oxen
  Could plough from morn till
    night;
And they made a molten image,
  And set it up on high,—
And there it stands unto this day
  To witness if I lie.

It stands in the Comitium,
  Plain for all folk to see,—
Horatius in his harness,
  Halting upon one knee;
And underneath is written,
  In letters all of gold,
How valiantly he kept the bridge
  In the brave days of old.

And still his name sounds stirring
  Unto the men of Rome,
As the trumpet-blast that cries to
    them
  To charge the Volscian home;
And wives still pray to Juno
  For boys with hearts as bold
As his who kept the bridge so well
  In the brave days of old.

And in the nights of winter,
  When the cold north-winds
    blow,
And the long howling of the
    wolves
  Is heard amidst the snow;

When round the lonely cottage
  Roars loud the tempest's din,
And the good logs of Algidus
  Roar louder yet within;

When the oldest cask is opened,
  And the largest lamp is lit;
When the chestnuts glow in the
    embers,
  And the kid turns on the spit;
When young and old in circle
  Around the firebrands close;
When the girls are weaving baskets,
  And the lads are shaping bows;

When the goodman mends his
    armor,
  And trims his helmet's plume;
When the goodwife's shuttle merrily
  Goes flashing through the loom;
With weeping and with laughter
  Still is the story told,
How well Horatius kept the bridge
  In the brave days of old.

THOMAS BABINGTON MACAULAY

THE FACE ON THE FLOOR

'Twas a balmy summer evening, and a goodly crowd was there,
Which well-nigh filled Joe's bar-room, on the corner of the square;
And as songs and witty stories came through the open door,
A vagabond crept slowly in and posed upon the floor.

"Where did it come from?" someone said. "The wind has blown it in."
"What does it want?" another cried. "Some whiskey, rum or gin?"
"Here, Toby, seek 'em, if your stomach's equal to the work—
I wouldn't touch him with a fork, he's filthy as a Turk."

This badinage the poor wretch took with stoical good grace;
In fact, he smiled as tho' he thought he'd struck the proper place.
"Come, boys, I know there's kindly hearts among so good a crowd—
To be in such good company would make a deacon proud.

"Give me a drink—that's what I want—I'm out of funds, you know,
When I had the cash to treat the gang this hand was never slow.
What? You laugh as if you thought this pocket never held a sou;
I once was fixed as well, my boys, as any one of you.

"There, thanks, that's braced me nicely; God bless you one and all;
Next time I pass this good saloon I'll make another call.
Give you a song? No, I can't do that; my singing days are past;
My voice is cracked, my throat's worn out, and my lungs are going fast.

"Say! Give me another whiskey, and I'll tell you what I'll do—
I'll tell you a funny story, and a fact, I promise, too,
That ever I was a decent man not one of you would think;
But I was, some four or five years back. Say, give me another drink.

"Fill her up, Joe, I want to put some life into my frame—
Such little drinks to a bum like me are miserably tame;
Five fingers—there, that's the scheme—and corking whiskey, too.
Well, here's luck, boys, and landlord, my best regards to you.

"You've treated me pretty kindly and I'd like to tell you how
I came to be the dirty sot you see before you now.
As I told you, once I was a man, with muscle, frame and health,
And, but for a blunder ought to have made considerable wealth.

"I was a painter—not one that daubed on bricks and wood,
But an artist, and for my age, was rated pretty good.
I worked hard at my canvas, and was bidding fair to rise,
For gradually I saw the star of fame before my eyes.

"I made a picture perhaps you've seen, 'tis called the 'Chase of Fame.'
It brought me fifteen hundred pounds and added to my name.
And then I met a woman—now comes the funny part—
With eyes that petrified my brain, and sunk into my heart.

"Why don't you laugh? 'Tis funny that the vagabond you see
Could ever love a woman, and expect her love for me;
But 'twas so, and for a month or two, her smiles were freely given,
And when her loving lips touched mine, it carried me to heaven.

"Boys, did you ever see a girl for whom your soul you'd give,
With a form like the Milo Venus, too beautiful to live;
With eyes that would beat the Koh-i-noor, and a wealth of chestnut hair?
If so, 'twas she, for there never was another half so fair.

"I was working on a portrait, one afternoon in May,
Of a fair-haired boy, a friend of mine, who lived across the way;
And Madeline admired it, and, much to my surprise,
She said she'd like to know the man that had such dreamy eyes.

"It didn't take long to know him, and before the month had flown
My friend had stole my darling, and I was left alone;
And ere a year of misery had passed above my head,
The jewel I had treasured so had tarnished and was dead.

"That's why I took to drink, boys. Why, I never saw you smile,
I thought you'd be amused, and laughing all the while.
Why, what's the matter, friend? There's a tear-drop in your eye,
Come, laugh like me; 'tis only babes and women that should cry.

"Say, boys, if you give me just another whiskey I'll be glad,
And I'll draw right here a picture of the face that drove me mad.
Give me that piece of chalk with which you mark the baseball score—
You shall see the lovely Madeline upon the bar-room floor."

Another drink, and with chalk in hand, the vagabond began
To sketch a face that might well buy the soul of any man.
Then, as he placed another lock upon the shapely head,
With a fearful shriek, he leaped and fell across the picture—dead.

                                                    HUGH D'ARCY

THE CREMATION OF SAM MC GEE

There are strange things done in the midnight sun
  By the men who toil for gold;
The Arctic trails have their secret tales
  That would make your blood run cold;

The Northern Lights have seen queer sights,
  But the queerest they ever did see
Was the night on the marge of Lake Lebarge
  I cremated Sam McGee.

Now Sam McGee was from Tennessee, where the cotton blooms and
  blows,
Why he left his home in the South to roam 'round the Pole, God only
  knows.
He was always cold, but the land of gold seemed to hold him like a spell;
Though he'd often say in his homely way that "he'd sooner live in hell."

On Christmas Day we were mushing our way over the Dawson Trail;
Talk of your cold! through the parka's fold it stabbed like a driven nail.
If our eyes we'd close, then the lashes froze till sometimes we couldn't see;
It wasn't much fun, but the only one to whimper was Sam McGee.

And that very night, as we lay packed tight in our robes beneath the
    snow,
And the dogs were fed, and the stars o'erhead were dancing heel and toe,
He turned to me, and "Cap," says he, "I'll cash in this trip, I guess;
And if I do, I'm asking that you won't refuse my last request."

Well, he seemed so low that I couldn't say no; then he says with a sort of
    moan;
"It's the cursed cold, and it's got right hold till I'm chilled clean through
    to the bone.
Yet 'tain't being dead—it's my awful dread of the icy grave that pains;
So I want you to swear that, foul or fair, you'll cremate my last remains."

A pal's last need is a thing to heed, so I swore I would not fail;
And we started on at the streak of dawn; but God! he looked ghastly pale.
He crouched on the sleigh, and he raved all day of his home in Tennes-
    see;
And before nightfall a corpse was all that was left of Sam McGee.

There wasn't a breath in that land of death, and I hurried, horror-driven,
With a corpse half hid that I couldn't get rid, because of a promise I'd
    given;
It was lashed to the sleigh, and it seemed to say: "You may tax your
    brawn and brains,
But you promised true, and it's up to you to cremate those last remains."

Now a promise made is a debt unpaid, and the trail has its own stern
    code.
In the days to come, though my lips were dumb, in my heart how I cursed
    that load.
In the long, long night, by the lone firelight, while the huskies round in a
    ring,
Howled out their woes to the homeless snows—O God! how I loathed the
    thing.

And every day that quiet clay seemed heavier and heavier to grow;
And on I went, though the dogs were spent and the grub was getting low;
The trail was bad, and I felt half mad, but I swore I would not give in;
And I'd often sing to the hateful thing, and it hearkened with a grin.

Till I came to the marge of Lake Lebarge, and a derelict there lay;
It was jammed in the ice, but I saw in a trice it was called the "Alice
    May."
And I looked at it, and I thought a bit, and I looked at my frozen chum;
Then "Here," said I, with a sudden cry, "is my cremator-e-um."

Some planks I tore from the cabin floor, and I lit the boiler fire;
Some coal I found that was lying around, and I heaped the fuel higher;
The flames just soared, and the furnace roared—such a blaze you seldom see;
And I burrowed a hole in the glowing coal, and I stuffed in Sam McGee.

Then I made a hike, for I didn't like to hear him sizzle so;
And the heavens scowled, and the huskies howled, and the winds began
    to blow.
It was icy cold, but the hot sweat rolled down my cheeks, and I don't
    know why;
And the greasy smoke in an inky cloak went streaking down the sky.

I do not know how long in the snow I wrestled with grisly fear;
But the stars came out and they danced about ere again I ventured near;
I was sick with dread, but I bravely said: "I'll just take a peep inside.
I guess he's cooked, and it's time I looked," . . . then the door I opened wide.

And there sat Sam, looking cold and calm, in the heart of the furnace
    roar;
And he wore a smile you could see a mile, and he said: "Please close that
    door!
It's fine in here, but I greatly fear you'll let in the cold and storm—
Since I left Plumtree down in Tennessee, it's the first time I've been
    warm."

There are strange things done in the midnight sun
    By the men who toil for gold;
The Arctic trails have their secret tales
    That would make your blood run cold;

The Northern Lights have seen queer sights,
    But the queerest they ever did see
Was that night on the marge of Lake Lebarge
    I cremated Sam McGee.

ROBERT W. SERVICE

FRANKIE AND JOHNNY

Frankie and Johnny were lovers.
O my Gawd how they did love!
They swore to be true to each
    other,
As true as the stars above.
He was her man but he done her
    wrong.

Frankie and Johnny went walking,
Johnny in a brand new suit.
Frankie went walking with Johnny,
Said: "O Gawd don't my Johnny
    look cute."
He was her man but he done her
    wrong.

Frankie went down to Memphis,
Went on the morning train,
Paid a hundred dollars,
Bought Johnny a watch and chain.
He was her man but he done her
    wrong.

Frankie lived in a crib-house,
Crib-house with only two doors,
Gave her money to Johnny,
He spent it on those parlor whores.
He was her man but he done her
    wrong.

Frankie went down to the hock-
    shop,
Went for a bucket of beer,
Said: "O, Mr. Bartender,
Has my loving Johnny been here?
He is my man but he's doing me
    wrong."

"I don't want to make you no
    trouble.
I don't want to tell you no lie,
But I saw Johnny an hour ago
With a girl name Nelly Bly.
He is your man but he's doing
    you wrong."

Frankie went down to the hotel.
She didn't go there for fun,
'Cause underneath her kimono
She toted a 44 gun.
He was her man but he done her
    wrong.

Frankie went down to the hotel.
She rang the front-door bell,
Said: "Stand back all you chippies
Or I'll blow you all to hell.
I want my man for he's doing me
    wrong."

Frankie looked in through the
  keyhole
And there before her eye
She saw her Johnny on the sofa
A-loving up Nelly Bly.
He was her man; he was doing
  her wrong.

Frankie threw back her kimono,
Took out a big 44,
Root-a-toot-toot, three times she
  shoot
Right through that hardware door.
He was her man but was doing
  her wrong.

Johnny grabbed up his Stetson,
Said, "O my Gawd Frankie don't
  shoot."
But Frankie pulled hard on the
  trigger
And the gun went root-a-toot-toot.
She shot her man who was doing
  her wrong.

"Roll me over easy,
Roll me over slow,
Roll me over on my right side
'Cause my left side hurts me so.
I was her man but I done her
  wrong."

Johnny he was a gambler,
He gambled for the gain;
The very last words he ever said
Were—"High-low Jack and the
  game."
He was her man but he done her
  wrong.

"Bring out your rubber-tired buggy,
Bring out your rubber-tired hack;

I'll take my Johnny to the
  graveyard
But I won't bring him back.
He was my man but he done me
  wrong.

"Lock me in that dungeon,
Lock me in that cell,
Lock me where the north-east wind
Blows from the corner of Hell.
I shot my man 'cause he done me
  wrong."

Frankie went down to the
  Madame,
She went down on her knees.
"Forgive me, Mrs. Halcombe,
Forgive me if you please
For shooting my man 'cause he
  done me wrong."

"Forgive you Frankie darling,
Forgive you I never can,
Forgive you, Frankie darling,
For shooting your only man,
For he was your man though he
  done you wrong."

It was not murder in the first
  degree,
It was not murder in the third.
A woman simply shot her man
As a hunter drops a bird.
She shot her man 'cause he done
  her wrong.

Frankie said to the Sheriff,
"What do you think they'll do?"
The Sheriff said to Frankie,
"It's the electric chair for you.
You shot your man 'cause he done
  you wrong."

Frankie sat in the jailhouse,
Had no electric fan,
Told her little sister:
"Don't you marry no sporting
    man.
I had a man but he done me
    wrong."

Frankie heard a rumbling,
Away down in the ground;
Maybe it was little Johnny
Where she had shot him down.
He was her man, but he done her
    wrong.

Once more I saw Frankie,
She was sitting in the chair
Waiting for to go and meet her God
With the sweat dripping out of
    her hair.
He was her man, but he done her
    wrong.

This story has no moral,
This story has no end,
This story only goes to show
That there ain't no good in men.
He was her man but he done her
    wrong.

ANONYMOUS

CAPTAIN JINKS

I'm Captain Jinks of the Horse
    Marines,
I feed my horse on corn and
    beans,
And sport young ladies in their
    teens,
    Though a captain in the army.
I teach young ladies how to
    dance,
How to dance, how to dance,
I teach young ladies how to
    dance,
    For I'm the pet of the army.

Chorus:
Captain Jinks of the Horse
    Marines,
I feed my horse on corn and
    beans,
And often live beyond my means,
    Though a captain in the army.

I joined my corps when twenty-
    one,
Of course I thought it capital fun;
When the enemy came, of course
    I run,
    For I'm not cut out for the army.
When I left home, mama she cried,
Mama she cried, mama she cried,
When I left home, mama she cried:
    "He's not cut out for the army."

The first time I went out to drill,
The bugle sounding made me ill;
Of the battle field I'd had my fill,
    For I'm not cut out for the army.
The officers they all did shout,
They all did shout, they all did
    shout,
The officers they all did shout:
    "Why, kick him out of the army."

ANONYMOUS

FARE THEE WELL

Fare thee well! and if for ever,
  Still for ever, fare thee well:
Even though unforgiving, never
  'Gainst thee shall my heart
    rebel.
Would that breast were bared
    before thee
  Where thy head so oft hath lain,
While that placid sleep came o'er
    thee
  Which thou ne'er canst know
    again:
Would that breast, by thee
    glanced over,
  Every inmost thought could show!
Then thou wouldst at last discover
  'Twas not well to spurn it so.
Though the world for this
    commend thee—
  Though it smile upon the blow,
Even its praises must offend thee,
  Founded on another's woe:
Though my many faults defaced me,
  Could no other arm be found,
Than the one which once
    embraced me,
  To inflict a cureless wound?
Yet, oh yet, thyself deceive not—
  Love may sink by slow decay,

But by sudden wrench, believe
    not
  Hearts can thus be torn away:
Still thine own its life retaineth—
  Still must mine, though
    bleeding, beat;
And the undying thought which
    paineth
  Is—that we no more may meet.
These are words of deeper sorrow
  Than the wail above the dead;
Both shall live—but every
    morrow
  Wake us from a widowed bed.
And when thou wouldst solace
    gather,
  When our child's first accents
    flow
Wilt thou teach her to say "Father!"
  Though his care she must forego?
When her little hands shall press
    thee,
  When her lip to thine is pressed,
Think of him whose prayer shall
    bless thee,
  Think of him thy love had
    blessed!
Should her lineaments resemble
  Those thou never more mayst see,

Then thy heart will softly tremble
　With a pulse yet true to me.
All my faults perchance thou
　　knowest,
　All my madness none can know;
All my hopes—where'er thou goest—
　Wither, yet with *thee* they go.
Every feeling hath been shaken;
　Pride—which not a world
　　could bow—
Bows to thee—by thee forsaken,
　Even my soul forsakes me now.

But 'tis done—all words are
　　idle—
　Words from me are vainer still;
But the thoughts we cannot bridle
　Force their way without the
　　will.
Fare thee well! thus disunited,
　Torn from every nearer tie,—
Sear'd in heart, and lone, and
　　blighted,
　More than this I scarce can die.

　　　　GEORGE GORDON, LORD BYRON

THE LISTENERS

"Is there anybody there?" said the
　　Traveller,
　Knocking on the moonlit door;
And his horse in the silence
　　champed the grasses
　Of the forest's ferny floor;
And a bird flew up out of the
　　turret,
　Above the Traveller's head;
And he smote upon the door
　　again a second time;
　"Is there anybody there?" he
　　said.
But no one descended to the
　　Traveller;
　No head from the leaf-fringed sill
Leaned over and looked into his
　　grey eyes,
　Where he stood perplexed and
　　still.

But only a host of phantom
　　listeners
　That dwelt in the lone house
　　then
Stood listening in the quiet of the
　　moonlight
　To that voice from the world of
　　men:
Stood thronging the faint
　　moonbeams on the dark stair,
　That goes down to the empty
　　hall,
Hearkening in an air stirred and
　　shaken
　By the lonely Traveller's call.

And he felt in his heart their
　　strangeness,
　Their stillness answering his
　　cry,

While his horse moved, cropping
    the dark turf,
  'Neath the starred and leafy sky;
For he suddenly smote on the
    door, even
  Louder, and lifted his head:
"Tell them I came, and no one
    answered
  That I kept my word," he said.
Never the least stir made the
    listeners,

Though every word he spake
Fell echoing through the
    shadowiness of the still house
  From the one man left awake:
Ay, they heard his foot upon the
    stirrup,
  And the sound of iron on stone,
And how the silence surged softly
    backward,
  When the plunging hoofs were
    gone.

          WALTER DE LA MARE

JOHN HENRY

John Henry was a lil baby,
Sittin' on his mama's knee,
Said: "De Big Bend Tunnel on
  de C. & O. road
Gonna cause de death of me,
Lawd, lawd, gonna cause de
  death of me."

Cap'n says to John Henry,
"Gonna bring me a steam drill
  'round,
Gonna take dat steam drill out on
  de job,
Gonna whop dat steel on down,
Lawd, Lawd, gonna whop dat
  steel on down."

John Henry tol' his cap'n,
Lightnin' was in his eye:
"Cap'n, bet yo' las' red cent on me,
Fo' I'll beat it to de bottom or
  I'll die,
Lawd, Lawd, I'll beat it to de
  bottom or I'll die."

Sun shine hot an' burnin',
Wer'n't no breeze a-tall,
Sweat ran down like water down
  a hill,
Dat day John Henry let his
  hammer fall,
Lawd, Lawd, dat day John Henry
  let his hammer fall.

John Henry went to de tunnel,
An' dey put him in de lead to drive,
De rock so tall an' John Henry so small,
Dat he lied down his hammer an'
  he cried,
Lawd, Lawd, dat he lied down
  his hammer an' he cried.

John Henry started on de right hand,
De steam drill started on de lef'—
"Before I'd let dis steam drill beat
  me down,
I'd hammer my fool self to death,
Lawd, Lawd, I'd hammer my fool
  self to death."

White man tol' John Henry,
"Driver, cuss yo' soul,
You might beat dis steam an' drill
    of mine,
When de rocks in dis mountain
    turn to gol',
Lawd, Lawd, when de rocks in dis
    mountain turn to gol'."

John Henry said to his shaker,
"Shaker, why don' you sing?
I'm throwin' twelve poun's from
    my hips on down,
Jes' listen to de col' steel ring,
Lawd, Lawd, jes' listen to de col'
    steel ring."

Oh, de captain said to John Henry,
"I b'lieve this mountain's sinkin'
    in."
John Henry said to his captain,
    oh my!
"Ain' nothin' but my hammer
    suckin' win',
Lawd, Lawd, ain' nothin' but my
    hammer suckin' win'."

John Henry tol' his shaker,
"Shaker, you better pray,
For, if I miss dis six-foot steel,
Tomorrow'll be yo' buryin' day,
Lawd, Lawd, tomorrow'll be yo'
    buryin' day."

John Henry tol' his captain,
"Look yonder what I see—
Yo' drill's done broke an' yo'
    hole's done choke,
An' you cain' drive steel like me,
Lawd, Lawd, an' you cain' drive
    steel like me."

De man dat invented de steam drill,
Thought he was mighty fine.
John Henry drove his fifteen feet,
An' de steam drill only made nine,
Lawd, Lawd, an' de steam drill
    only made nine.

De hammer dat John Henry swung,
It weighed over nine pound;
He broke a rib in his lef'-han' side,
An' his intrels fell on de groun',
Lawd, Lawd, an' his intrels fell
    on de groun'.

All de womens in de Wes',
When dey heared of John Henry's
    death,
Stood in de rain, flagged de
    eas'-boun' train,
Goin' where John Henry fell dead,
Lawd, Lawd, goin' where John
    Henry fell dead.

John Henry's lil mother,
She was all dressed in red,
She jumped in bed, covered up
    her head,
Said she didn' know her son was
    dead,
Lawd, Lawd, didn' know her son
    was dead.

Dey took John Henry to de
    graveyard,
An' dey buried him in de san',
An' every locomotive come
    roarin' by,
Says, "Dere lays a steel-drivin' man,
Lawd, Lawd, dere lays a steel-
    drivin' man."

                              ANONYMOUS

LA BELLE DAME SANS MERCI

O what can ail thee, knight-at-arms,
  Alone and palely loitering?
The sedge has withered from the
    lake,
  And no birds sing.

O what can ail thee, knight-at-arms,
  So haggard and so woe-begone?
The squirrel's granary is full,
  And the harvest's done.

I see a lily on thy brow
  With anguish moist and fever
    dew,
And on thy cheek a fading rose
  Fast withereth too.

I met a lady in the meads,
  Full beautiful—a faery's child;
Her hair was long, her foot was
    light,
  And her eyes were wild.

I made a garland for her head,
  And bracelets too, and fragrant
    zone;
She looked at me as she did love,
  And made sweet moan.

I set her on my pacing steed,
  And nothing else saw all day
    long,
For sidelong would she bend, and
    sing
  A faery's song.

She found me roots of relish sweet,
  And honey wild, and manna dew,
And sure in language strange she
    said—
  "I love thee true!"

She took me to her elfin grot,
  And there she wept and sighed
    full sore,
And there I shut her wild wild eyes
  With kisses four.

And there she lullèd me asleep,
  And there I dreamed—ah! woe
    betide!
The latest dream I ever dreamed
  On the cold hill's side.

I saw pale kings and princes too,
  Pale warriors, death-pale were
    they all;
They cried—"La Belle Dame sans
    Merci
  Hath thee in thrall!"

I saw their starved lips in the gloam,
  With horrid warning gapèd wide,
And I awoke and found me here,
  On the cold hill's side.

And this is why I sojourn here,
  Alone and palely loitering,
Though the sedge is withered
    from the lake
  And no birds sing.

JOHN KEATS

THE DESERTED VILLAGE

Sweet Auburn! loveliest village of the plain;
Where health and plenty cheered the laboring swain,
Where smiling spring its earliest visit paid,
And parting summer's lingering blooms delayed:
Dear lovely bowers of innocence and ease,
Seats of my youth, when every sport could please,
How often have I loitered o'er thy green,
Where humble happiness endeared each scene!
How often have I paused on every charm,
The sheltered cot, the cultivated farm,
The never-failing brook, the busy mill,
The decent church that topped the neighboring hill,
The hawthorn bush, with seats beneath the shade,
For talking age and whispering lovers made!
How often have I blest the coming day,
When toil remitting lent its turn to play,
And all the village train, from labor free,
Led up their sports beneath the spreading tree,
While many a pastime circled in the shade,
The young contending as the old surveyed;
And many a gambol frolicked o'er the ground,
And sleights of art and feats of strength went round.
And still, as each repeated pleasure tired,
Succeeding sports the mirthful band inspired;
The dancing pair that simply sought renown,
By holding out to tire each other down;
The swain mistrustless of his smutted face,
While secret laughter tittered round the place;
The bashful virgin's side-long looks of love,
The matron's glance that would those looks reprove:

These were thy charms, sweet village! sports like these
With sweet succession, taught even toil to please:
These round thy bowers their cheerful influence shed:
These were thy charms—but all these charms are fled.

    Sweet smiling village, loveliest of the lawn,
Thy sports are fled, and all thy charms withdrawn;
Amidst thy bowers the tyrant's hand is seen,
And desolation saddens all thy green:
One only master grasps the whole domain,
And half a tillage stints thy smiling plain.
No more thy glassy brook reflects the day,
But, choked with sedges, works its weedy way;
Along thy glades, a solitary guest,
The hollow sounding bittern guards its nest:
Amidst thy desert walks the lapwing flies,
And tires their echoes with unvaried cries;
Sunk are thy bowers in shapeless ruin all,
And the long grass o'ertops the moldering wall;
And trembling, shrinking from the spoiler's hand,
Far, far away thy children leave the land.
    Ill fares the land, to hastening ills a prey,
Where wealth accumulates, and men decay:
Princes and lords may flourish, or may fade;
A breath can make them, as a breath has made:
But a bold peasantry, their country's pride,
When once destroyed, can never be supplied.
    A time there was, ere England's griefs began,
When every rood of ground maintained its man;
For him light labor spread her wholesome store,
Just gave what life required, but gave no more:
His best companions, innocence and health;
And his best riches, ignorance of wealth.
    But times are altered; trade's unfeeling train
Usurp the land and dispossess the swain;
Along the lawn, where scattered hamlets rose,
Unwieldy wealth and cumbrous pomp repose,
And every want to opulence allied,
And every pang that folly pays to pride.
Those gentle hours that plenty bade to bloom,
Those calm desires that asked but little room,
Those healthful sports that graced the peaceful scene,
Lived in each look, and brightened all the green;

These, far departing, seek a kinder shore,
And rural mirth and manners are no more.
　　Sweet Auburn! parent of the blissful hour,
Thy glades forlorn confess the tyrant's power.
Here, as I take my solitary rounds
Amidst thy tangling walks and ruined grounds,
And, many a year elapsed, return to view
Where once the cottage stood, the hawthorn grew,
Remembrance wakes with all her busy train,
Swells at my breast, and turns the past to pain.
　　In all my wanderings round this world of care,
In all my griefs—and God has given my share—
I still had hopes, my latest hours to crown,
Amidst these humble bowers to lay me down;
To husband out life's taper at the close,
And keep the flame from wasting by repose;
I still had hopes, for pride attends us still,
Amidst the swains to show my book-learned skill,
Around my fire an evening group to draw,
And tell of all I felt, and all I saw;
And, as a hare whom hounds and horns pursue
Pants to the place from whence at first she flew,
I still had hopes, my long vexations past,
Here to return—and die at home at last.
　　O blest retirement, friend to life's decline,
Retreats from care, that never must be mine,
How happy he who crowns in shades like these
A youth of labor with an age of ease;
Who quits a world where strong temptations try,
And, since 'tis hard to combat, learns to fly!
For him no wretches, born to work and weep,
Explore the mine, or tempt the dangerous deep;
No surly porter stands in guilty state,
To spurn imploring famine from the gate;
But on he moves to meet his latter end,
Angels around befriending virtue's friend;
Bends to the grave with unperceived decay,
While resignation gently slopes the way;
And, all his prospects brightening to the last,
His heaven commences ere the world be past!

Sweet was the sound, when oft at evening's close
Up yonder hill the village murmur rose;
There, as I passed with careless steps and slow,
The mingling notes came softened from below:
The swain responsive as the milk-maid sung,
The sober herd that lowed to meet their young,
The noisy geese that gabbled o'er the pool,
The playful children just let loose from school,
The watch-dog's voice that bayed the whispering wind,
And the loud laugh that spoke the vacant mind;—
These all in sweet confusion sought the shade,
And filled each pause the nightingale had made.
But now the sounds of population fail,
No cheerful murmurs fluctuate in the gale,
No busy steps the grass-grown footway tread,
For all the bloomy flush of life is fled.
All but yon widowed, solitary thing,
That feebly bends beside the plashy spring:
She, wretched matron, forced in age, for bread,
To strip the brook with mantling cresses spread,
To pick her wintry faggot from the thorn,
To seek her nightly shed, and weep till morn;
She only left of all the harmless train,
The sad historian of the pensive plain.

Near yonder copse, where once the garden smiled,
And still where many a garden flower grows wild;
There, where a few torn shrubs the place disclose,
The village preacher's modest mansion rose.
A man he was to all the country dear,
And passing rich with forty pounds a year;
Remote from towns he ran his godly race,
Nor e'er had changed, nor wished to change his place;
Unpractised he to fawn, or seek for power,
By doctrines fashioned to the varying hour;
Far other aims his heart had learned to prize,
More skilled to raise the wretched than to rise.
His house was known to all the vagrant train;
He chid their wanderings but relieved their pain:
The long-remembered beggar was his guest,
Whose beard descending swept his aged breast;

The ruined spendthrift, now no longer proud,
Claimed kindred there, and had his claims allowed;
The broken soldier, kindly bade to stay,
Sat by his fire, and talked the night away,
Wept o'er his wounds or, tales of sorrow done,
Shouldered his crutch and showed how fields were won.
Pleased with his guests, the good man learned to glow,
And quite forgot their vices in their woe;
Careless their merits or their faults to scan,
His pity gave ere charity began.
    Thus to relieve the wretched was his pride,
And e'en his failings leaned to Virtue's side;
But in his duty prompt at every call,
He watched and wept, he prayed and felt for all;
And, as a bird each fond endearment tries
To tempt its new-fledged offspring to the skies,
He tried each art, reproved each dull delay,
Allured to brighter worlds, and led the way.

    Beside the bed where parting life was laid,
And sorrow, guilt, and pain by turn dismayed,
The reverend champion stood. At his control
Despair and anguish fled the struggling soul;
Comfort came down the trembling wretch to raise,
And his last faltering accents whispered praise.
    At church, with meek and unaffected grace,
His looks adorned the venerable place;
Truth from his lips prevailed with double sway,
And fools, who came to scoff, remained to pray.
The service past, around the pious man,
With steady zeal, each honest rustic ran;
Even children followed with endearing wile,
And plucked his gown to share the good man's smile.
His ready smile a parent's warmth exprest;
Their welfare pleased him, and their cares distrest:
To them his heart, his love, his griefs were given,
But all his serious thoughts had rest in heaven.
As some tall cliff that lifts its awful form,
Swells from the vale, and midway leaves the storm,
Though round its breast the rolling clouds are spread,
Eternal sunshine settles on its head.

Beside yon straggling fence that skirts the way,
With blossomed furze unprofitably gay,
There, in his noisy mansion, skilled to rule,
The village master taught his little school.
A man severe he was, and stern to view;
I knew him well, and every truant knew;
Well had the boding tremblers learned to trace
The day's disasters in his morning face;
Full well they laughed with counterfeited glee
At all his jokes, for many a joke had he;
Full well the busy whisper circling round
Conveyed the dismal tidings when he frowned.
Yet he was kind, or, if severe in aught,
The love he bore to learning was in fault;
The village all declared how much he knew:
'T was certain he could write, and cipher too;
Lands he could measure, terms and tides presage,
And even the story ran that he could gauge;
In arguing, too, the parson owned his skill,
For, even though vanquished, he could argue still;
While words of learned length and thundering sound
Amazed the gazing rustics ranged around;
And still they gazed, and still the wonder grew,
That one small head could carry all he knew.

But past is all his fame. The very spot
Where many a time he triumphed is forgot.
Near yonder thorn, that lifts its head on high,
Where once the sign-post caught the passing eye,
Low lies that house where nut-brown draughts inspired,
Where graybeard mirth and smiling toil retired,
Where village statesmen talked with looks profound,
And news much older than their ale went round.
Imagination fondly stoops to trace
The parlor splendors of that festive place:
The white-washed wall, the nicely sanded floor,
The varnished clock that clicked behind the door;
The chest contrived a double debt to pay,
A bed by night, a chest of drawers by day;
The pictures placed for ornament and use,
The twelve good rules, the royal game of goose;

The hearth, except when winter chill'd the day,
With aspen boughs and flowers and fennel gay;
While broken tea-cups, wisely kept for show,
Ranged o'er the chimney, glistened in a row.

Vain transitory splendors! could not all
Reprieve the tottering mansion from its fall?
Obscure it sinks, nor shall it more impart
An hour's importance to the poor man's heart.
Thither no more the peasant shall repair
To sweet oblivion of his daily care;
No more the farmer's news, the barber's tale,
No more the woodman's ballad shall prevail;
No more the smith his dusky brow shall clear,
Relax his ponderous strength, and lean to hear;
The host himself no longer shall be found
Careful to see the mantling bliss go round;
Nor the coy maid, half willing to be prest,
Shall kiss the cup to pass it to the rest.

Yes! let the rich deride, the proud disdain,
These simple blessings of the lowly train;
To me more dear, congenial to my heart,
One native charm, than all the gloss of art.
Spontaneous joys, where nature has its play,
The soul adopts, and owns their first-born sway;
Lightly they frolic o'er the vacant mind,
Unenvied, unmolested, unconfined.
But the long pomp, the midnight masquerade,
With all the freaks of wanton wealth arrayed—
In these, ere triflers half their wish obtain,
The toiling pleasure sickens into pain;
And, even while fashion's brightest arts decoy,
The heart distrusting asks if this be joy.
Ye friends to truth, ye statesmen who survey
The rich man's joys increase, the poor's decay,
'Tis yours to judge, how wide the limits stand
Between a splendid and an happy land.
Proud swells the tide with loads of freighted ore,
And shouting Folly hails them from her shore;
Hoards even beyond the miser's wish abound,
And rich men flock from all the world around.

Yet count our gains! This wealth is but a name
That leaves our useful products still the same.
Not so the loss. The man of wealth and pride
Takes up a space that many poor supplied;
Space for his lake, his park's extended bounds,
Space for his horses, equipage, and hounds:
The robe that wraps his limbs in silken sloth
Has robbed the neighboring fields of half their growth;
His seat, where solitary sports are seen,
Indignant spurns the cottage from the green:
Around the world each needful product flies,
For all the luxuries the world supplies;
While thus the land adorned for pleasure all
In barren splendor feebly waits the fall.
  As some fair female unadorned and plain,
Secure to please while youth confirms her reign,
Slights every borrowed charm that dress supplies,
Nor shares with art the triumph of her eyes;
But when those charms are past, for charms are frail,
When time advances, and when lovers fail,
She then shines forth, solicitous to bless,
In all the glaring impotence of dress.
Thus fares the land by luxury betrayed:
In nature's simplest charms at first arrayed,
But verging to decline, its splendors rise,
Its vistas strike, its palaces surprise;
While, scourged by famine from the smiling land
The mournful peasant leads his humble band,
And while he sinks, without one arm to save,
The country blooms—a garden and a grave.
  Where then, ah! where, shall poverty reside,
To 'scape the pressure of contiguous pride?
If to some common's fenceless limits strayed
He drives his flock to pick the scanty blade,
Those fenceless fields the sons of wealth divide,
And even the bare-worn common is denied.

  If to the city sped—what waits him there?
To see profusion that he must not share;
To see ten thousand baneful arts combined
To pamper luxury, and thin mankind;

To see those joys the sons of pleasure know
Extorted from his fellow-creature's woe.
Here while the courtier glitters in brocade,
There the pale artist plies the sickly trade;
Here while the proud their long-drawn pomps display,
There the black gibbet glooms beside the way.
The dome where Pleasure holds her midnight reign
Here, richly decked, admits the gorgeous train:
Tumultuous grandeur crowds the blazing square,
The rattling chariots clash, the torches glare.
Sure scenes like these no troubles e'er annoy!
Sure these denote one universal joy!
Are these thy serious thoughts?—Ah, turn thine eyes
Where the poor houseless shivering female lies.
She once, perhaps, in village plenty blest,
Has wept at tales of innocence distressed;
Her modest looks the cottage might adorn,
Sweet as the primrose peeps beneath the thorn:
Now lost to all; her friends, her virtue, fled,
Near her betrayer's door she lays her head,
And, pinched with cold, and shrinking from the shower,
With heavy heart deplores that luckless hour,
When idly first, ambitious of the town,
She left her wheel and robes of country brown.
    Do thine, sweet Auburn,—thine, the loveliest train,—
Do thy fair tribes participate her pain?
Even now, perhaps, by cold and hunger led,
At proud men's doors they ask a little bread!
    Ah, no! To distant climes, a dreary scene,
Where half the convex world intrudes between,
Through torrid tracts with fainting steps they go,
Where wild Altama murmurs to their woe.
Far different there from all that charmed before
The various terrors of that horrid shore;
Those blazing suns that dart a downward ray,
And fiercely shed intolerable day;
Those matted woods, where birds forget to sing,
But silent bats in drowsy clusters cling;
Those poisonous fields with rank luxuriance crowned,
Where the dark scorpion gathers death around;
Where at each step the stranger fears to wake
The rattling terrors of the vengeful snake;

Where crouching tigers wait their hapless prey,
And savage men more murderous still than they;
While oft in whirls the mad tornado flies,
Mingling the ravaged landscape with the skies.
Far different these from every former scene,
The cooling brook, the grassy vested green,
The breezy covert of the warbling grove,
That only sheltered thefts of harmless love.

   Good Heaven! what sorrows gloomed that parting day,
That called them from their native walks away;
When the poor exiles, every pleasure past,
Hung round the bowers, and fondly looked their last,
And took a long farewell, and wished in vain
For seats like these beyond the western main,
And shuddering still to face the distant deep,
Returned and wept, and still returned to weep.
The good old sire, the first prepared to go
To new found worlds, and wept for others' woe;
But for himself, in conscious virtue brave,
He only wished for worlds beyond the grave.
His lovely daughter, lovelier in her tears,
The fond companion of his helpless years,
Silent went next, neglectful of her charms,
And left a lover's for a father's arms.
With louder plaints the mother spoke her woes,
And blest the cot where every pleasure rose,
And kist her thoughtless babes with many a tear
And claspt them close, in sorrow doubly dear,
Whilst her fond husband strove to lend relief,
In all the silent manliness of grief.

   O luxury! thou curst by Heaven's decree,
How ill exchanged are things like these for thee!
How do thy potions, with insidious joy,
Diffuse their pleasures only to destroy!
Kingdoms by thee, to sickly greatness grown,
Boast of a florid vigor not their own.
At every draught more large and large they grow,
A bloated mass of rank, unwieldy woe;
Till sapped their strength, and every part unsound,
Down, down, they sink, and spread a ruin round.

Even now the devastation is begun,
And half the business of destruction done;
Even now, methinks, as pondering here I stand,
I see the rural virtues leave the land.
Down where yon anchoring vessel spreads the sail,
That idly waiting flaps with every gale,
Downward they move, a melancholy band,
Pass from the shore, and darken all the strand.
Contented toil, and hospitable care,
And kind connubial tenderness, are there;
And piety with wishes placed above,
And steady loyalty, and faithful love.
And thou, sweet Poetry, thou loveliest maid,
Still first to fly where sensual joys invade;
Unfit in these degenerate times of shame
To catch the heart, or strike for honest fame;
Dear charming nymph, neglected and decried,
My shame in crowds, my solitary pride;
Thou source of all my bliss, and all my woe,
That found'st me poor at first, and keep'st me so;
Thou guide by which the nobler arts excel,
Thou nurse of every virtue, fare thee well!
Farewell, and oh! where'er thy voice be tried,
On Torno's cliffs, or Pambamarca's side,
Whether where equinoctial fervors glow,
Or winter wraps the polar world in snow,
Still let thy voice, prevailing over time,
Redress the rigors of the inclement clime;
Aid slighted truth with thy persuasive strain;
Teach erring man to spurn the rage of gain:
Teach him, that states of native strength possest,
Though very poor, may still be very blest;
That trade's proud empire hastes to swift decay,
As ocean sweeps the labored mole away;
While self-dependent power can time defy,
As rocks resist the billows and the sky.

                                OLIVER GOLDSMITH

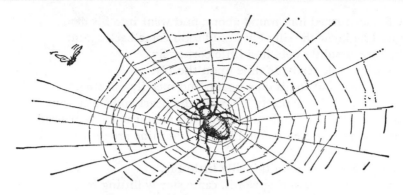

THE SPIDER AND THE FLY

"Will you walk into my parlor?" said the Spider to the Fly,
" 'Tis the prettiest little parlor that ever you did spy;
The way into my parlor is up a winding stair,
And I've many curious things to show when you are there."
"Oh no, no," said the little Fly, "to ask me is in vain,
For who goes up your winding stair can ne'er come down again."

"I'm sure you must be weary, dear, with soaring up so high;
Will you rest upon my little bed?" said the Spider to the Fly.
"There are pretty curtains drawn around; the sheets are fine and thin,
And if you like to rest a while, I'll snugly tuck you in!"
"Oh, no, no," said the little Fly, "for I've often heard it said,
They never, never wake again, who sleep upon your bed!"

Said the cunning Spider to the Fly, "Dear Friend, what can I do
To prove the warm affection I've always felt for you?
I have within my pantry good store of all that's nice;
I'm sure you're very welcome—will you please to take a slice?"
"Oh no, no," said the little Fly, "kind sir, that cannot be;
I've heard what's in your pantry, and I do not wish to see!"

"Sweet creature," said the Spider, "you're witty and you're wise,
How handsome are your gauzy wings, how brilliant are your eyes!
I have a little looking-glass upon my parlor shelf,
If you'll step in one moment, dear, you shall behold yourself."
"I thank you, gentle sir," she said, "for what you're pleased to say,
And bidding you good morning now, I'll call another day."

The Spider turned him round about, and went into his den,
For well he knew the silly Fly would soon come back again:
So he wove a subtle web, in a little corner sly,
And set his table ready, to dine upon the Fly.
Then he came out to his door again, and merrily did sing,
"Come hither, hither, pretty Fly, with the pearl and silver wing;
Your robes are green and purple—there's a crest upon your head;
Your eyes are like the diamond bright, but mine are dull as lead!"

Alas, alas! how very soon this silly little Fly,
Hearing his wily, flattering words, came slowly flitting by;
With buzzing wings she hung aloft, then near and nearer drew,
Thinking only of her brilliant eyes, and green and purple hue—
Thinking only of her crested head—poor foolish thing! At last,
Up jumped the cunning Spider, and fiercely held her fast.
He dragged her up his winding stair, into his dismal den,
Within his little parlor—but she ne'er came out again!

And now, dear little children, who may this story read,
To idle, silly, flattering words, I pray you ne'er give heed;
Unto an evil counsellor, close heart and ear and eye,
And take a lesson from this tale of the Spider and the Fly.

MARY HOWITT

BOOK XIII

OLD SONGS AND NEW

MY HEART'S IN THE HIGHLANDS

Farewell to the Highlands, farewell to the North,
The birth-place of valor, the country of worth!
Wherever I wander, wherever I rove,
The hills of the Highlands for ever I love.

My heart's in the Highlands, my heart is not here,
My heart's in the Highlands, a-chasing the deer,
A-chasing the wild deer and following the roe—
My heart's in the Highlands, wherever I go!

Farewell to the mountains high-covered with snow,
Farewell to the straths and green valleys below,
Farewell to the forests and wild-hanging woods,
Farewell to the torrents and loud-pouring floods!

My heart's in the Highlands, my heart is not here,
My heart's in the Highlands, a-chasing the deer,
A-chasing the wild deer and following the roe—
My heart's in the Highlands, wherever I go!

ROBERT BURNS

TO CELIA

Drink to me only with thine eyes,
　And I will pledge with mine;
Or leave a kiss but in the cup
　And I'll not look for wine.
The thirst that from the soul doth
　rise
　Doth ask a drink divine;
But might I of Jove's nectar sup,
　I would not change for thine.

I sent thee late a rosy wreath,
　Not so much honouring thee
As giving it a hope that there
　It could not withered be;
But thou thereon didst only breathe
　And sent'st it back to me;
Since when it grows, and smells,
　I swear,
　Not of itself but thee!

BEN JONSON

AULD LANG SYNE

Should auld acquaintance be
    forgot,
  And never brought to mind?
Should auld acquaintance be
    forgot,
  And auld lang syne?

Cho.—For auld lang syne, my
    dear,
  For auld lang syne,
We'll tak a cup o' kindness yet
  For auld lang syne!

And surely ye'll be your pint-
    stowp,
  And surely I'll be mine,

And we'll tak a cup o' kindness
    yet
  For auld lang syne!

We twa hae run about the braes
  And pou'd the gowans fine,
But we've wandered monie a
    weary fit
  Sin' auld lang syne.

We two hae paidl'd in the burn
  Frae morning sun till dine,
But seas between us braid hae
    roared
  Sin' auld lang syne.

ROBERT BURNS

Auld, old; *syne,* since; *pint-stowp,* pint-cup; *gowans,* daisies; *fit,* foot;
paidl'd, paddled; *burn,* stream; *dine,* dinner.

ANNIE LAURIE

Maxwelton's braes are bonnie
Where early fa's the dew,
And it's there that Annie Laurie
Gie'd me her promise true;
Gie'd me her promise true,
Which ne'er forgot will be;
And for bonnie Annie Laurie
I'd lay me doun and dee.

Her brow is like the snaw drift;
Her throat is like the swan;
Her face it is the fairest
That e'er the sun shone on—

That e'er the sun shone on—
And dark blue is her ee;
And for bonnie Annie Laurie
I'd lay me doun and dee.

Like dew on the gowan lying
Is the fa' o' her fairy feet;
And like the winds in summer sighing,
Her voice is low and sweet—
Her voice is low and sweet—
And she's a' the world to me;
And for bonnie Annie Laurie
I'd lay me doun and dee.

WILLIAM DOUGLAS

JEANIE WITH THE LIGHT BROWN HAIR

I dream of Jeanie with the light brown hair,
Borne, like a vapor, on the summer air;
I see her tripping where the bright streams play,
Happy as the daisies that dance on her way.

Many were the wild notes her merry voice would pour,
Many were the blithe birds that warbled them o'er:
Oh! I dream of Jeanie with the light brown hair,
Floating, like a vapor, on the summer air.

I long for Jeanie with the day-dawn smile,
Radiant in gladness, warm with winning guile;
I hear her melodies, like joys gone by,
Sighing round my heart o'er the fond hopes that die:—

Sighing like the wind and sobbing like the rain,—
Wailing for the lost one that comes not again:
Oh! I long for Jeanie, and my heart bows low,
Never more to find her where the bright waters flow.

STEPHEN FOSTER

GREEN GROW THE RASHES

Green grow the rashes, O;
Green grow the rashes, O;
The sweetest hours that e'er I spend,
  Are spent amang the lasses, O.

There's nought but care on every han
  In every hour that passes, O:
What signifies the life o' man,
  An 'twere na for the lasses, O.

The war'ly race may riches chase,
  An' riches still may fly them, O;
An' though at last they catch
      them fast,
  Their hearts can ne'er enjoy
      them, O.

But gie me a cannie hour at e'en,
  My arms about my dearie, O,
An' war'ly cares, an' war'ly men
  May a' gae tapsalteerie, O!

For you sae douce, ye sneer at this;
  Ye're nought but senseless
      asses, O;
The wisest man the warl' e'er saw,
  He dearly loved the lasses, O.

Auld Nature swears, the lovely dears
  Her noblest work she classes, O:
Her 'prentice han' she tried on man,
  An' then she made the lasses, O.
                    ROBERT BURNS

SILVER THREADS AMONG THE GOLD

Darling, I am growing old,
Silver threads among the gold,
Shine upon my brow today,
Life is fading fast away;
But, my darling, you will be
Always young and fair to me.
Yes! my darling, you will be
Always young and fair to me.

Chorus:
  Darling, I am growing old,
  Silver threads among the gold,
  Shine upon my brow today;
  Life is fading fast away.

When your hair is silver white,
And your cheeks no longer bright,
With the roses of the May,
I will kiss your lips and say;
Oh! my darling mine alone,
You have never older grown.
  (*Chorus.*)

Love can never more grow old,
Locks may lose their brown and
    gold,
Cheeks may fade and hollow
    grow,
But the hearts that love will
    know;
Never, never, winter's frost and
    chill,
Summer warmth is in them still.
  (*Chorus.*)

Love is always young and fair,
What to us is silver hair,
Faded cheeks or steps grown slow,
To the heart that beats below?
Since I kissed you mine alone,
You have never older grown.
  (*Chorus.*)
                    EBEN E. REXFORD

OLD FOLKS AT HOME

Way down upon de Swanee
    ribber,
  Far, far away,
Dere's wha my heart is turning
    ebber,
  Dere's wha de old folks stay.
All up and down de whole
    creation,
  Sadly I roam,
Still longing for de old plantation,
  And for de old folks at home.

All round de little farm I
    wander'd
  When I was young,
Dem many happy days I
    squander'd,
  Many de songs I sung.
When I was playing wid my
    brudder,
  Happy was I.

Oh! take me to my kind old
    mudder,
  Dere let me live and die.

One little hut among de bushes,
  One dat I love,
Still sadly to my mem'ry rushes,
  No matter where I rove.
When will I see the bees
    a-humming,
  All round de comb?
When will I hear de banjo
    tumming,
  Down in my good old home?

CHORUS

All de world am sad and dreary,
  Ebrywhere I roam,
Oh! darkies how my heart grows
    weary,
  Far from de old folks at home.

    STEPHEN FOSTER

FLOW GENTLY, SWEET AFTON

Flow gently, sweet Afton, among thy green braes!
Flow gently, I'll sing thee a song in thy praise!
My Mary's asleep by thy murmuring stream—
Flow gently, sweet Afton, disturb not her dream!

Thou stock dove whose echo resounds through the glen,
Ye wild whistling blackbirds in yon thorny den,
Thou green-crested lapwing, thy screaming forbear—
I charge you, disturb not my slumbering fair!

How lofty, sweet Afton, thy neighboring hills,
Far marked with the courses of clear winding rills!
There daily I wander, as noon rises high,
My flocks and my Mary's sweet cot in my eye.

How pleasant thy banks and green valleys below,
Where wild in the woodlands the primroses blow;
There oft, as mild Evening weeps over the lea,
The sweet-scented birk shades my Mary and me.

Thy crystal stream, Afton, how lovely it glides,
And winds by the cot where my Mary resides!
How wanton thy waters her snowy feet lave,
As, gathering sweet flowerets, she stems thy clear wave!

Flow gently, sweet Afton, among thy green braes!
Flow gently, sweet river, the theme of my lays!
My Mary's asleep by thy murmuring stream—
Flow gently, sweet Afton, disturb not her dream!

ROBERT BURNS

OH, MY DARLING CLEMENTINE

In a cavern, in a canyon,
Excavating for a mine,
Dwelt a miner, 'Forty-Niner,
And his daughter Clementine.

Chorus:
Oh, my darling, Oh, my darling,
Oh, my darling Clementine,
You are lost and gone forever,
Dreadful sorry, Clementine.

Light she was and like a fairy,
And her shoes were number nine;
Herring boxes, without topses
Sandals were for Clementine.
(Chorus.)

Drove she ducklings to the water,
Every morning just at nine;
Hit her foot against a splinter,
Fell into the foaming brine.
(Chorus.)

Ruby lips above the water,
Blowing bubbles soft and fine;
Alas for me! I was no swimmer,
So I lost my Clementine.
(Chorus.)

In a churchyard, near the canyon,
Where the myrtle doth entwine,
There grow roses and other posies,
Fertilized by Clementine.
(Chorus.)

Then the miner, 'Forty-Niner,
Soon began to peak and pine,
Thought he oughter jine his
    daughter,
Now he's with his Clementine.
    (*Chorus.*)

In my dreams she still doth haunt
    me,
Robed in garments soaked in brine,
Though in life I used to hug her,
Now she's dead, I'll draw the line.
    (*Chorus.*)

ANONYMOUS

LITTLE BROWN JUG

My wife and I live all alone
In a little brown hut we call our
    own.
She loves gin and I love rum,
Tell you what, don't we have fun?

Chorus:
Ha, ha, ha, 'tis you and me,
Little brown jug don't I love
    thee?
Ha, ha, ha, 'tis you and me,
Little brown jug don't I love
    thee?

If I had a cow that gave such
    milk
I'd dress her in the finest silk,
Feed her on the choicest hay,
And milk her forty times a day.
    (*Chorus.*)

'Tis you that makes my friends
    my foes,
'Tis you that makes me wear old
    clothes,

But seeing you are so near my
    nose,
Tip her up and down she goes.
    (*Chorus.*)

When I go toiling on my farm,
Take little brown jug under my
    arm,
Set it under some shady tree,
Little brown jug, don't I love
    thee? (*Chorus.*)

Then came the landlord tripping
    in,
Round top hat and peaked chin,
In his hand he carried a cup,
Says I, "Old Fellow, give us a
    sup." (*Chorus.*)

If all the folks of Adam's race,
Were put together in one place,
Then I'd prepare to drop a tear
Before I'd part with you, my dear.
    (*Chorus.*)

ANONYMOUS

O! SUSANNA

I came from Alabama
Wid my banjo on my knee;
I'm gwine to Louisiana,
My true love for to see.
It rained all night the day I left,
The weather it was dry,
The sun so hot I froze to death;
Susanna, don't you cry for me.

Chorus:
O! Susanna, O don't you cry for me;
I've come from Alabama
Wid my banjo on my knee.

I jumped aboard de telegraph
And trabbled down the ribber,
De 'lectric fluid magnified
And killed five hundred nigger;
De bullgine bust, de horse run off,
I really thought I'd die;
I shut my eyes to hold my breath;
Susanna, don't you cry. (*Chorus.*)

I had a dream de odder night
When ebery t'ing was still;
I thought I saw Susanna
A-coming down the hill;
The buckwheat cake was in her
    mouth,
The tear was in her eye;
Says I, "I'm coming from the South,
Susanna, don't you cry."
    (*Chorus.*)

I soon will be in New Orleans,
And den I'll look all round,
And when I find Susanna
I will fall upon the ground;
And if I do not find her
Dis darkie'll surely die,
And when I'm dead and buried,
Susanna, don't you cry. (*Chorus.*)
                    STEPHEN FOSTER

WHO IS SILVIA

Who is Silvia? what is she,
    That all our swains commend her?
Holy, fair, and wise is she;
    The heaven such grace did lend
        her,
That she might admiréd be.

Is she kind as she is fair?
    For beauty lives with kindness.

Love doth to her eyes repair,
    To help him of his blindness,
And, being help'd, inhabits there.

Then to Silvia let us sing,
    That Silvia is excelling;
She excels each mortal thing
    Upon the dull earth dwelling:
To her let us garlands bring.
                    WILLIAM SHAKESPEARE

MY OLD KENTUCKY HOME

The sun shines bright in the old Kentucky home;
'Tis summer, the darkeys are gay;
The corn-top's ripe, and the meadow's in the bloom,
    While the birds make music all the day.
The young folks roll on the little cabin floor,
    All merry, all happy and bright;
By-'n'-by hard times comes a-knocking at the door:—
    Then my old Kentucky home, good-night!

      Weep no more, my lady,
        O, weep no more to-day!
    We will sing one song for the old Kentucky home,
      For the old Kentucky home, far away.

They hunt no more for the possum and the coon,
    On the meadow, the hill, and the shore;
They sing no more by the glimmer of the moon,
    On the bench by the old cabin door.
The day goes by like a shadow o'er the heart,
    With sorrow, where all was delight;
The time has come when the darkeys have to part:—
    Then my old Kentucky home, good-night!

The head must bow, and the back will have to bend,
    Wherever the darkey may go;
A few more days, and the trouble all will end,
    In the field where the sugar-canes grow.
A few more days for to tote the weary load,—
    No matter, 't will never be light;
A few more days till we totter on the road:—
    Then my old Kentucky home, good-night!

      Weep no more, my lady,
        O, weep no more to-day!
    We will sing one song for the old Kentucky home,
      For the old Kentucky home, far away.

STEPHEN FOSTER

WITH A LITTLE BIT OF LUCK

The Lord above gave man an arm of iron
So he could do his job and never shirk.
The Lord above gave man an arm of iron; but
With a little bit of luck,
With a little bit of luck,
Some one else'll do the blinkin' work.

    With a little bit—with a little bit—
    With a little bit of luck
    You'll never work.

The Lord above made liquor for temptation;
To see if man could turn away from sin.
The Lord above made liquor for temptation; but
With a little bit of luck,
With a little bit of luck,
When temptation comes you'll give right in.

    With a little bit—with a little bit—
    With a little bit of luck
    You'll give right in.

Oh, you can walk the straight and narrow;
But with a little bit of luck
You'll run amuck.

The gentle sex was made for man to marry;
To share his nest and see his food is cooked.
The gentle sex was made for man to marry; but
With a little bit of luck,
With a little bit of luck,
You can have it all and not get hooked.

With a little bit—with a little bit—
With a little bit of luck
You won't get hooked.
With a little bit—with a little bit—
With a little bit of bloomin' luck!

The Lord above made man to help his neighbor,
No matter where, on land or sea or foam.
The Lord above made man to help his neighbor; but
With a little bit of luck,
With a little bit of luck,
When he comes around you won't be home.

With a little bit—with a little bit—
With a little bit of luck
You won't be home.

They're always throwing goodness at you;
But with a little bit of luck
A man can duck.

Oh, it's a crime for man to go philanderin'
And fill his wife's poor heart with grief and doubt.
Oh, it's a crime for man to go philanderin'; but
With a little bit of luck,
With a little bit of luck,
You can see the bloodhound don't find out.

With a little bit—with a little bit—
With a little bit of luck
She won't find out.
With a little bit—with a little bit—
With a little bit of bloomin' luck!

ALAN JAY LERNER

YANKEE DOODLE

Father and I went down to camp,
  Along with Cap'n Gooding;
And there we saw the men and boys,
  As thick as hasty pudding.

Chorus:
  Yankee Doodle, keep it up,
    Yankee Doodle Dandy;
  Mind the music and the step,
    And with the girls be handy.

And there we see a thousand men,
  As rich as Squire David;
And what they wasted every day,
  I wish it could be savèd.

And there was Cap'n Wellington,
  And gentle folks about him;
They say he's grown so 'tarnal proud,
  He will not ride without 'em.

I saw another snarl of men
  A-digging graves, they told me;
So 'tarnal long, so 'tarnal deep,
  They 'tended they should hold me.

It scared me so, I hooked it off,
  Nor stopped, as I remember;
Nor turned about till I got home,
  Locked up in mother's chamber.

ANONYMOUS

DOWN IN THE VALLEY

Down in the valley,
  Valley so low,
  Hang your head over,
  Hear the wind blow.
  Hear the wind blow, love,
  Hear the wind blow,
  Hang your head over,
  Hear the wind blow.

If you don't love me,
  Love whom you please,
  But throw your arms around me,
  Give my heart ease.
  Give my heart ease, dear,
  Give my heart ease,
  Throw your arms round me,
  Give my heart ease.

Down in the valley
  Walking between,
  Telling our story,
  Here's what it sings—
  Roses of sunshine,
  Violets of dew,
  Angels in heaven,
  Know I love you.

Build me a castle,
  Forty feet high,
  So I can see her
  As she goes by,
  As she goes by, dear,
  As she goes by.
  So I can see her
  As she goes by.

Bird in a cage, love,
  Bird in a cage,
  Dying for freedom,
  Ever a slave.
  Ever a slave, dear,
  Ever a slave,
  Dying for freedom,
  Ever a slave.

Write me a letter;
  Send it by mail;
  And back it in care of
  The Barbourville jail.
  Barbourville jail, love,
  Barbourville jail,
  And back it in care of
  The Barbourville jail.

ANONYMOUS

DERELICT

A Reminiscence of R. L. S's. "Treasure Island" and Cap'n Billy Bones, His Song.

"Fifteen men on the dead man's
    chest—
    "Yo-ho-ho and a bottle of rum!
"Drink and the devil had done for the
    rest—
    "Yo-ho-ho and a bottle of rum!"
The mate was fixed by the bos'n's pike,
The bos'n brained with a marlinspike
And Cookey's throat was marked be-
    like
        It had been gripped
           By fingers ten;
        And there they lay,
           All good dead men,
Like break-o'-day in a boozing-ken—
    Yo-ho-ho and a bottle of rum!

Fifteen men of a whole ship's list—
    Yo-ho-ho and a bottle of rum!
Dead and be-damned and the rest
    gone whist!—
    Yo-ho-ho and a bottle of rum!
The skipper lay with his nob in gore
Where the scullion's axe his cheek had
    shore—
And the scullion he was stabbed times
    four.
        And there they lay
           And the soggy skies
        Dripped all day long
           In up-staring eyes—
At murk sunset and at foul sunrise—
    Yo-ho-ho and a bottle of rum!

Fifteen men of 'em stiff and stark—
    Yo-ho-ho and a bottle of rum!
Ten of the crew had the Murder
    mark—
    Yo-ho-ho and a bottle of rum!
'Twas a cutlass swipe, or an ounce of
    lead,
Or a yawing hole in a battered head—
And the scuppers glut with a rotting
    red.
        And there they lay—
           Aye, damn my eyes!—
        All lookouts clapped
           On paradise—
All souls bound just contrariwise—
    Yo-ho-ho and a bottle of rum!

Fifteen men of 'em good and true—
    Yo-ho-ho and a bottle of rum!
Every man jack could ha' sailed with
    Old Pew—
    Yo-ho-ho and a bottle of rum!
There was chest on chest full of
    Spanish gold,
With a ton of plate in the middle
    hold,
And the cabins riot of stuff untold.
        And they lay there
           That had took the plum,
        With sightless glare
           And their lips struck
           dumb,
While we shared all by the rule of
    thumb—
    Yo-ho-ho and a bottle of rum!

More was seen through the sternlight
*   screen—*
*   Yo-ho-ho and a bottle of rum!*
Chartings ondoubt where a woman
*   had been!*
*   Yo-ho-ho and a bottle of rum!*
A flimsy shift on a bunker cot,
With a thin dirk slot through the
*   bosom spot*
And the lace stiff-dry in a purplish
*   blot.*
*   Or was she wench . . .*
*   Or some shuddering*
*   maid . . ?*
*   That dared the knife—*
*   And that took the blade!*
By God! she was stuff for a plucky
*   jade—*
*   Yo-ho-ho and a bottle of rum!*

Fifteen men on the dead man's chest—
    Yo-ho-ho and a bottle of rum!
Drink and the devil had done for the
    rest—
    Yo-ho-ho and a bottle of rum!
We wrapped 'em all in a mains'l tight,
With twice ten turns of a hawser's
    bight,
And we heaved 'em over and out of
    sight—
        With a yo-heave-ho!
            And a fare-you-well!
        And a sullen plunge
            In the sullen swell
Ten fathoms deep on the road to hell!
    Yo-ho-ho and a bottle of rum!
            YOUNG E. ALLISON

A LOST CHORD

Seated one day at the Organ,
I was weary and ill at ease,
And my fingers wandered idly
Over the noisy keys.

I do not know what I was playing,
Or what I was dreaming then;
But I struck one chord of music,
Like the sound of a great Amen.

It flooded the crimson twilight
Like the close of an angel's Psalm,
And it lay on my fevered spirit
With a touch of infinite calm.

It quieted pain and sorrow,
Like love overcoming strife;
It seemed the harmonious echo
From our discordant life.

It linked all perplexèd meanings
Into one perfect peace,
And trembled away into silence,
As if it were loath to cease.

I have sought, but I seek it vainly,
That one lost chord divine,

That came from the soul of the Organ
And entered into mine.

It may be that Death's bright angel
Will speak in that chord again,—
It may be that only in Heaven
I shall hear that grand Amen.

ADELAIDE PROCTER

KO-KO'S SONG

On a tree by a river a little tom-tit
    Sang "Willow, titwillow, titwillow!"
And I said to him, "Dicky-bird, why do you sit
    Singing 'Willow, titwillow, titwillow'?
Is it a weakness of intellect, birdie?" I cried,
"Or a rather tough worm in your little inside?"
With a shake of his poor little head he replied,
    "Oh, willow, titwillow, titwillow!"

He slapped at his chest, as he sat on that bough,
    Singing "Willow, titwillow, titwillow!"
And a cold perspiration bespangled his brow,
    Oh, willow, titwillow, titwillow!
He sobbed and he sighed, and a gurgle he gave,
Then he threw himself into the billowy wave,
And an echo arose from the suicide's grave—
    "Oh, willow, titwillow, titwillow!"

Now, I feel just as sure as I'm sure that my name
    Isn't Willow, titwillow, titwillow,
That 'twas blighted affection that made him exclaim,
    "Oh, willow, titwillow, titwillow!"
And if you remain callous and obdurate, I
Shall perish as he did, and you will know why,
Though I probably shall not exclaim as I die,
    "Oh, willow, titwillow, titwillow!"

W. S. GILBERT

TURKEY IN THE STRAW

As I was a-gwine down the road,
Tired team and a heavy load,
Crack my whip and the leader sprung;
I says day—day to the wagon tongue.
    Turkey in the straw, turkey in the hay,
    Roll 'em up and twist 'em up a high tuckahaw,
    And hit 'em up a tune called Turkey in the Straw.

Went out to milk and I didn't know how,
I milked the goat instead of the cow.
A monkey sittin' on a pile of straw
A-winkin' at his mother-in-law.
    Turkey in the straw, *etc.*

Met Mr. Catfish comin' down the stream,
Says Mr. Catfish, "What does you mean?"
Caught Mr. Catfish by the snout
And turned Mr. Catfish wrong side out.
    Turkey in the straw, *etc.*

Came to the river and I couldn't get across
Paid five dollars for an old blind hoss
Wouldn't go ahead, nor he wouldn't stand still
So he went up and down like an old saw mill.
    Turkey in the straw, *etc.*

As I came down the new cut road
Met Mr. Bullfrog, met Miss Toad,
And every time Miss Toad would sing
Ole Bullfrog cut a pigeon wing.
    Turkey in the straw, *etc.*

O I jumped in the seat, and I gave a little yell,
The horses run away, broke the wagon all to hell;
Sugar in the gourd and honey in the horn,
I never was so happy since the hour I was born.
    Turkey in the straw, *etc.*

                                        ANONYMOUS

I'VE BEEN WORKIN' ON THE RAILROAD

I've been workin' on the railroad
All the livelong day.
I've been workin' on the railroad
Just to pass the time away.

Don't you hear the whistle blowing?
Rise up so early in the morn.
Don't you hear the Captain shouting:
"Dinah, blow your horn."

ANONYMOUS

WHERE IS MY WANDERING BOY TONIGHT?

Where is my wandering boy tonight? the boy of my tend'rest care:
The boy that was once my joy and light, the child of my love and
    prayer.

Chorus:
    Oh, where is my boy tonight? where is my boy tonight?
    My heart o'erflows, for I love him, he knows,
    Oh, where is my boy tonight?

Once he was pure as the morning dew, as he knelt at his mother's
    knee;
No face was so bright, no heart more true, and none was as sweet as he.
    (*Chorus.*)

Oh, could I see him now, my boy, as fair as in olden times,
When prattle and smile made home a joy, and life was a merry chime.
    (*Chorus.*)

Go, for my wandering boy tonight, go search for him where you will:
But bring him to me with all his blight, and tell him I love him still.
    (*Chorus.*)

ANONYMOUS

OLD BLACK JOE

Gone are the days when my heart was young and gay,
Gone are my friends from the cotton fields away;
Gone from the earth to a better land I know,
I hear their gentle voices calling "Old Black Joe."

Chorus:
> I'm coming, I'm coming, for my head is bending low;
> I hear their gentle voices calling "Old Black Joe."

Why do I weep when my heart should feel no pain?
Why do I sigh that my friends come not again?
Grieving for forms now departed long ago,
I hear their gentle voices calling "Old Black Joe."

Where are the hearts once so happy and so free?
The children so dear that I held upon my knee?
Gone to the shore where my soul has longed to go,
I hear their gentle voices calling "Old Black Joe."

STEPHEN FOSTER

MY MARYLAND

The despot's heel is on thy shore,
    Maryland!
His torch is at thy temple door,
    Maryland!
Avenge the patriotic gore
That flecked the streets of
        Baltimore,
And be the battle-queen of yore,
    Maryland, my Maryland!

Hark to an exiled son's appeal,
    Maryland!
My Mother State, to thee I kneel,
    Maryland!
For life or death, for woe or weal,
Thy peerless chivalry reveal,
And gird thy beauteous limbs
        with steel,
    Maryland, my Maryland!

Thou wilt not cower in the dust,
  Maryland!
Thy beaming sword shall never
    rust,
  Maryland!
Remember Carroll's sacred trust,
Remember Howard's warlike thrust,
And all thy slumberers with the just,
  Maryland, my Maryland!

Come! 'tis the red dawn of the day,
  Maryland!
Come with thy panoplied array,
  Maryland!
With Ringgold's spirit for the fray,
With Watson's blood at Monterrey
With fearless Lowe and dashing May,
  Maryland, my Maryland!

Dear Mother, burst the tyrant's
    chain,
  Maryland!
Virginia should not call in vain,
  Maryland!
She meets her sisters on the
    plain,—
"Sic semper!" 'tis the proud
    refrain
That baffles minions back amain,
  Maryland!
Arise in majesty again,
  Maryland, my Maryland!

Come! for thy shield is bright and
    strong,
  Maryland!
Come! for thy dalliance does thee
    wrong,
  Maryland!

Come to thine own heroic throng
Stalking with Liberty along,
And chant thy dauntless slogan-
    song,
  Maryland, my Maryland!

I see the blush upon thy cheek,
  Maryland!
For thou wast ever bravely meek,
  Maryland!
But lo! there surges forth a shriek,
From hill to hill, from creek to
    creek,
Potomac calls to Chesapeake,
  Maryland, my Maryland!

Thou wilt not yield the Vandal
    toll,
  Maryland!
Thou wilt not crook to his control,
  Maryland!
Better the fire upon thee roll,
Better the shot, the blade, the
    bowl,
Than crucifixion of the soul,
  Maryland, my Maryland!

I hear the distant thunder hum,
  Maryland!
The Old Line's bugle, fife, and
    drum,
  Maryland!
She is not dead, nor deaf, nor
    dumb;
Huzza! she spurns the Northern
    scum!
She breathes! She burns! She'll
    come! She'll come!
  Maryland, my Maryland!
            JAMES RYDER RANDALL

ABIDE WITH ME

Abide with me: fast falls the eventide;
The darkness deepens; Lord, with me abide:
When other helpers fail, and comforts flee,
Help of the helpless, oh, abide with me!

Swift to its close ebbs our life's little day;
Earth's joys grow dim, its glories pass away;
Change and decay in all around I see:
O Thou Who changeth not, abide with me!

Not a brief glance, I beg, a passing word,
But, as Thou dwell'st with Thy disciples, Lord,
Familiar, condescending, patient, free,—
Come, not to sojourn, but abide with me!

Come not in terrors, as the King of kings;
But kind and good, with healing in Thy wings:
Tears for all woes, a heart for every plea;
Come, Friend of sinners, and abide with me!

Thou on my head in early youth didst smile,
And, though rebellious and perverse meanwhile
Thou hast not left me, oft as I left Thee;
On to the close, O Lord, abide with me!

I need Thy presence every passing hour:
What but Thy grace can foil the tempter's power?
Who like Thyself my guide and stay can be?
Through cloud and sunshine, oh, abide with me!

I fear no foe with Thee at hand to bless;
Ills have no weights, and tears no bitterness;
Where is death's sting? where, grave thy victory?
I triumph still, if Thou abide with me.

Hold then Thy cross before my closing eyes;
Shine through the gloom, and point me to the skies:
Heaven's morning breaks, and earth's vain shadows flee—
In life and death, O Lord, abide with me!

HENRY F. LYTE

MAN, MAN, MAN

Man, man, man is for the woman made,
And the woman made for man;
As the spur is for the jade,
As the scabbard for the blade,
As for digging is the spade,
  As for liquor is the can,
So man, man, man, is for the
    woman made,
  And the woman made for man.

As the scepter's to be swayed,
As for Night's the serenade,
  As for pudding is the pan,
  As to cool us is the fan,
So man, man, man, is for the
    woman made,
  And the woman made for man.

ANONYMOUS

CARRY ME BACK TO OLD VIRGINNY

Carry me back to old Virginny,
There's where the cotton and the corn and taters grow,
There's where the birds warble sweet in the spring-time,
There's where the old darkey's heart am long'd to go,
There's where I labored so hard for old Massa,
Day after day in the field of yellow corn,
No place on earth do I love more sincerely
Than old Virginny, the state where I was born.

Carry me back to old Virginny,
There let me live till I wither and decay,
Long by the old Dismal Swamp have I wandered,
There's where this old darkey's life will pass away.
Massa and Missis have long gone before me,
Soon we will meet on that bright and golden shore,
There we'll be happy and free from all sorrow,
There's where we'll meet and we'll never part no more.

JAMES BLAND

BURY ME NOT ON THE LONE PRAIRIE

"O bury me not on the lone prairie!"
These words came low and mournfully
From the pallid lips of a youth why lay
On his dying bed at the close of day.

"O bury me not on the lone prairie,
Where the wild coyotes will howl o'er me,
Where the buzzards beat and the wind goes free;
O bury me not on the lone prairie!

"O bury me not on the lone prairie,
In a narrow grave six foot by three,
Where the buffalo paws o'er a prairie sea;
O bury me not on the lone prairie!

"O bury me not on the lone prairie,
Where the wild coyotes will howl o'er me,
Where the rattlesnakes hiss and the crow flies free;
O bury me not on the lone prairie!

"O bury me not," and his voice faltered there,
But we took no heed of his dying prayer;
In a narrow grave just six by three
We buried him there on the lone prairie.

ANONYMOUS

RED RIVER VALLEY

From this valley they say you are
     going,
I shall miss your sweet face and
     your smile;
Because you are weary and tired,
You are changing your range for
     a while.

I've been thinking a long time,
     my darling,
Of the sweet words you never
     would say;
Now, alas, must my fond hopes all
     vanish?
For they say you are going away.

Chorus:
Then come sit here awhile ere
   you leave us,
Do not hasten to bid us adieu,
Just remember the Red River Valley
And the cowboy who loves you so true.

I have promised you, darling, that
   never
Will words from my lips cause you pain;
And my life it will be yours forever,
If you only will love me again.
Must the past with its joys all be
   blighted
By the future of sorrow and pain?
Must the vows that were spoken
   be slighted?

Don't you think you could love
   me again?

There never could be such a
   longing
In the heart of a poor cowboy's
   breast,
As dwells in the heart you are
   breaking,
As I wait in my home in the West.
Do you think of the valley you're
   leaving?
Oh, how lonely and dreary it'll be!
Do you think of the kind hearts
   you're hurting,
And the pain you are causing to me?

ANONYMOUS

SLIDE, KELLY, SLIDE

I played a game of baseball, I belong to Casey's Nine,
The crowd was feeling jolly, and the weather it was fine;
A nobler lot of players I think were never found.
When the omnibuses landed that day upon the ground,
The game was quickly started, they sent me to the bat;
I made two strikes. Says Casey, "What are you striking at?"
I made the third, the catcher muffed, and to the ground it fell;
I run like a devil to first base, when the gang began to yell:

Chorus:
   Slide, Kelly, slide! Your running's a disgrace!
   Slide, Kelly, slide! Stay there, hold your base!
   If someone doesn't steal you, and your batting doesn't fail you,
   They'll take you to Australia! Slide, Kelly, slide!

'Twas in the second inning they called me in, I think,
To take the catcher's place, while he went to take a drink;
But something was the matter, sure I couldn't see the ball;
And the second one that came in, broke my muzzle, nose and all.
The crowd up in the grandstand they yelled with all their might,
I ran towards the club house. I thought there was a fight.
'Twas the most unpleasant feeling I ever felt before,
I knew they had me rattled, when the gang began to roar: (*Chorus*)

They sent me out to center field, I didn't want to go,
The way my nose was swelling up, I must have been a show;
They said on me depended victory or defeat.
If a blind man were to look at us he'd know that we were beat.
"Sixty-four to nothing!" was the score when we got done,
And ev'rybody there but me said they had lots of fun.
The news got home ahead of me, they heard I was knocked out,
The neighbors carried me in the house, and then began to shout:
    (*Chorus*)

J. W. KELLY

OH, GIVE ME A HOME WHERE
THE BUFFALO ROAM

Oh, give me a home where the buffalo roam,
Where the deer and the antelope play,
Where seldom is heard a discouraging word,
And the skies are not cloudy all day.

Chorus:
Home, home on the range,
Where the deer and the antelope play,
Where seldom is heard a discouraging word,
And the skies are not cloudy all day.

How often at night when the heavens are bright
With the light of the glittering stars,
Have I stood there amazed and ask'd as I gazed,
If their glory exceeds that of ours.

ANONYMOUS

JOHN BROWN'S BODY

John Brown's body lies a-mould'ring in the grave,
John Brown's body lies a-mould'ring in the grave,
John Brown's body lies a-mould'ring in the grave,
   His soul goes marching on!

Chorus:
   Glory, glory! Hallelujah!
   Glory, glory! Hallelujah!
   Glory, glory! Hallelujah!
   His soul is marching on!

He captured Harper's Ferry with his nineteen men so true,
And he frightened old Virginia till she trembled through and through.
They hung him for a traitor, themselves the traitor crew,
   But his soul is marching on!

       John Brown died that the slave might be free,
       John Brown died that the slave might be free,
       John Brown died that the slave might be free,
         And his soul is marching on!

       The stars of Heaven are looking kindly down,
       The stars of Heaven are looking kindly down,
       The stars of Heaven are looking kindly down,
         On the grave of old John Brown.

       Now has come the glorious jubilee,
       Now has come the glorious jubilee,
       Now has come the glorious jubilee,
         When all mankind are free.

                   ANONYMOUS

THE MAN ON THE FLYING TRAPEZE

Oh, the girl that I loved she was
   handsome,
I tried all I knew her to please.
But I couldn't please her a quarter
   as well
As the man on the flying trapeze.

Chorus:
Oh, he flies through the air with
   the greatest of ease,
This daring young man on the
   flying trapeze.
His figure is handsome, all girls he
   can please,
And my love he purloined her away.

Last night as usual I went to her
   home.
There sat her old father and
   mother alone.
I asked for my love and they soon
   made it known
That she-e had flown away.

She packed up her box and eloped
   in the night,
To go-o with him at his ease.

He lowered her down from a four-
   story flight,
By means of his flying trapeze.

He took her to town and he
   dressed her in tights,
That he-e might live at his ease.
He ordered her up to the tent's
   awful height,
To appear on the flying trapeze.

Now she flies through the air with
   the greatest of ease,
This daring young girl on the
   flying trapeze.
Her figure is handsome, all men
   she can please,
And my love is purloinèd away.

Once I was happy, but now I'm
   forlorn,
Like an old coat that is tattered
   and torn,
Left to this wide world to fret and
   to mourn,
Betrayed by a maid in her teens.

                       ANONYMOUS

THERE IS A TAVERN IN THE TOWN

There is a tavern in the town,
And there my dear love sits him down, sits him down,
And drinks his wine mid laughter free,
And never, never thinks of me.

Fare thee well for I must leave thee,
Do not let this parting grieve thee,
And remember that the best of friends must part, must part.
Adieu, adieu, kind friends, adieu,
I can no longer stay with you, stay with you,
I'll hang my harp on the weeping willow tree
And may the world go well with thee.

He left me for a damsel dark, damsel dark,
Each Friday night they used to spark, used to spark,
And now my love once true to me
Takes that dark damsel on his knee.

O dig my grave both wide and deep, wide and deep,
Put tombstones at my head and feet, head and feet.
And on my breast carve a turtle dove
To signify I died of love.

ANONYMOUS

THE BLUE-TAIL FLY

When I was young I used to wait
On master and hand him his plate,
And pass the bottle when he got dry,
And brush away the blue-tail fly.

Chorus: Jimmie crack corn and I don't care,
        Jimmie crack corn and I don't care,
        Jimmie crack corn and I don't care,
        My master's gone away!

And when he'd ride in the afternoon,
I'd follow after with a hickory broom;
The pony being like to shy
When bitten by a blue-tail fly. (*Cho.*)

One day he ride around the farm,
The flies so numerous, they did swarm.
One chanced to bite him on the thigh;
The devil take the blue-tail fly! (*Cho.*)

The pony run, he jump, he pitch;
He threw my master in the ditch.
He died—and the jury wondered why—
The verdict was the blue-tail fly. (*Cho.*)

They laid him under a 'simmon tree;
His epitaph is there to see:
"Beneath this stone I'm forced to lie,
A victim of the blue-tail fly." (*Cho.*)

ANONYMOUS

ON TOP OF OLD SMOKY

On top of old Smoky, all covered with snow,
I lost my true lover by a-courting too slow.
Now courting is pleasure, parting is grief;
But a false-hearted lover is worse than a thief.

A thief he will rob you and take what you have,
But a false-hearted lover will take you to your grave.
The grave will decay you and turn you to dust,
But where is the young man a poor girl can trust?

They'll hug you and kiss you and tell you more lies
Than the cross-ties on railroads or the stars in the skies;
They'll tell you they love you to give your heart ease,
But the minute your back's turned, they'll court who they please.

On top of old Smoky, all covered with snow,
I lost my true lover by courting too slow;
Bury me on old Smoky, old Smoky so high,
Where the wild birds in heaven can hear my sad cry.

ANONYMOUS

BOOK XIV

THE FAITH WITHIN US

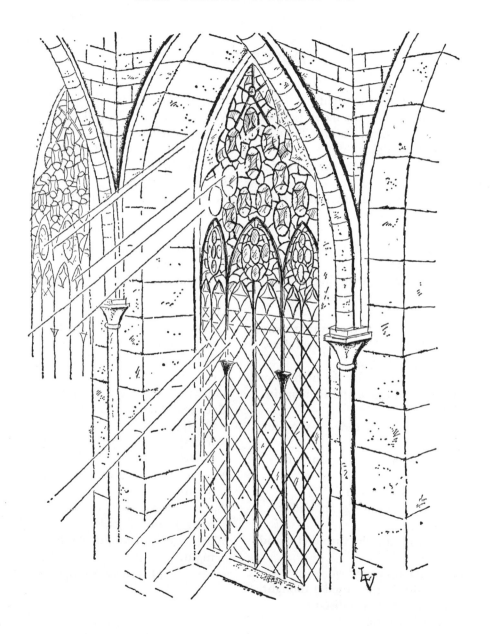

DOVER BEACH

The sea is calm to-night.
The tide is full, the moon lies fair
Upon the straits;—on the French
   coast the light
Gleams and is gone; the cliffs of
   England stand
Glimmering and vast, out in the
   tranquil bay.

Come to the window, sweet is the
   night-air!
Only, from the long line of spray
Where the sea meets the moon-
   blanch'd land,
Listen! you hear the grating roar
Of pebbles which the waves draw
   back, and fling,
At their return, up the high strand,
Begin, and cease, and then again
   begin,
With tremulous cadence slow, and
   bring
The eternal note of sadness in.

Sophocles long ago
Heard it on the Ægean, and it
   brought
Into his mind the turbid ebb and
   flow
Of human misery; we
Find also in the sound a thought,
Hearing it by this distant
   northern sea.

The Sea of Faith
Was once, too, at the full, and
   round earth's shore
Lay like the folds of a bright
   girdle furl'd.
But now I only hear
Its melancholy, long, withdrawing
   roar,
Retreating, to the breath
Of the night-wind, down the vast
   edges drear
And naked shingles of the world.

Ah, love, let us be true
To one another! for the world,
   which seems
To lie before us like a land of
   dreams,
So various, so beautiful, so new,
Hath really neither joy, nor love,
   nor light,
Nor certitude, nor peace, nor help
   for pain;
And we are here as on a darkling
   plain
Swept with confused alarms of
   struggle and flight,
Where ignorant armies clash by
   night.

MATTHEW ARNOLD

MORNING HYMN

Awake, my soul, and with the sun
Thy daily stage of duty run;
Shake off dull sloth, and joyful
    rise
To pay thy morning sacrifice.

Wake, and lift up thyself, my
    heart,
And with the angels bear thy part,
Who all night long unwearied
    sing
High praise to the Eternal King.

All praise to Thee, Who safe hast
    kept
And hast refreshed me while I
    slept!
Grant, Lord, when I from death
    shall wake,
I may of endless life partake!

Lord, I my vows to Thee renew;
Disperse my sins as morning dew:
Guard my first springs of thought
    and will,
And with Thyself my spirit fill.

Direct, control, suggest this day
All I design, or do, or say;
That all my powers, with all their
    might,
In Thy sole glory may unite.

Praise God, from Whom all
    blessings flow!
Praise Him, all creatures here
    below!
Praise Him above, ye heavenly
    host!
Praise Father, Son, and Holy
    Ghost!

THOMAS KEN

THE DARKLING THRUSH

I leant upon a coppice gate
    When Frost was spectre-gray,
And Winter's dregs made desolate
    The weakening eye of day.
The tangled vine-stems scored the sky
    Like strings of broken lyres,
And all mankind that haunted nigh
    Had sought their household fires.

The land's sharp features seemed
    to be
    The Century's corpse outleant,
His crypt the cloudy canopy,
    The wind his death-lament.
The ancient pulse of germ and birth
    Was shrunken hard and dry,
And every spirit upon earth
    Seemed fervorless as I.

At once a voice arose among
  The bleak twigs overhead
In a full-hearted evensong
  Of joy illimited;
An aged thrush, frail, gaunt, and
    small,
  In blast-beruffled plume,
Had chosen thus to fling his soul
  Upon the growing gloom.

So little cause for carolings
  Of such ecstatic sound
Was written on terrestrial things
  Afar or nigh around,
That I could think there trembled
    through
  His happy good-night air
Some blessed Hope, whereof he knew
  And I was unaware.

THOMAS HARDY

NEARER HOME

One sweetly solemn thought
  Comes to me o'er and o'er;
I am nearer home to-day
  Than I ever have been before;

Nearer my Father's house,
  Where the many mansions be;
Nearer the great white throne,
  Nearer the crystal sea;

Nearer the bound of life,
  Where we lay our burdens
    down;
Nearer leaving the cross,
  Nearer gaining the crown!

But lying darkly between,
  Winding down through the
    night,

Is the silent, unknown stream,
  That leads at last to the light.

Closer and closer my steps
  Come to the dread abysm:
Closer Death to my lips
  Presses the awful chrism.

Oh, if my mortal feet
  Have almost gained the brink;
If it be I am nearer home
  Even to-day than I think;

Father, perfect my trust;
  Let my spirit feel in death,
That her feet are firmly set
  On the rock of a living faith!

PHOEBE CARY

PERFECTION

Who seeks perfection in the art
Of driving well an ass and cart,
Or painting mountains in a mist,
Seeks God, although an Atheist.

FRANCIS CARLIN

REMEMBRANCE

Cold in the earth—and the deep snow piled above thee,
Far, far removed, cold in the dreary grave!
Have I forgot, my only Love, to love thee,
Severed at last by Time's all-severing wave?

Now, when alone, do my thoughts no longer hover
Over the mountains, on that northern shore,
Resting their wings where heath and fern-leaves cover
The noble heart for ever, ever more?

Cold in the earth—and fifteen wild Decembers,
From those brown hills, have melted into spring:
Faithful, indeed, is the spirit that remembers
After such years of change and suffering!

Sweet Love of youth, forgive, if I forget thee,
While the world's tide is bearing me along;
Other desires and other hopes beset me,
Hopes which obscure, but cannot do thee wrong!

No later light has lightened up my heaven,
No second morn has ever shone for me;
All my life's bliss from thy dear life was given,
All my life's bliss is in the grave with thee.

But, when the days of golden dreams had perished,
And even Despair was powerless to destroy;
Then did I learn how existence could be cherished,
Strengthened and fed without the aid of joy.

Then did I check the tears of useless passion—
Weaned my young soul from yearning after thine;
Sternly denied its burning wish to hasten
Down to that tomb already more than mine.

And, even yet, I dare not let it languish,
Dare not indulge in memory's rapturous pain;
Once drinking deep of that divinest anguish,
How could I seek the empty world again?

EMILY BRONTË

ON THE PROSPECT OF PLANTING ARTS
AND LEARNING IN AMERICA

The Muse, disgusted at an age
    and clime
  Barren of every glorious theme,
In distant lands now waits a
    better time,
  Producing subjects worthy fame:

In happy climes where from the
    genial sun
  And virgin earth such scenes
    ensue,
The force of art by nature seems
    outdone,
  And fancied beauties by the true:

In happy climes, the seat of
    innocence,
  Where nature guides and virtue
    rules,
Where men shall not impose for
    truth and sense
  The pedantry of courts and
    schools:

There shall be sung another
    golden age,
  The rise of empire and of arts,
The good and great inspiring epic
    rage,
  The wisest heads and noblest
    hearts.

Not such as Europe breeds in her
    decay;
  Such as she bred when fresh
    and young,
When heavenly flame did animate
    her clay,
  By future poets shall be sung.

Westward the course of empire
    takes its way;
  The four first acts already past,
A fifth shall close the drama with
    the day;
  Time's noblest offspring is the
    last.

GEORGE BERKELEY

NO COWARD SOUL IS MINE

No coward soul is mine
No trembler in the world's storm-
   troubled sphere:
I see Heaven's glories shine,
And Faith shines equal arming
   me from Fear.

O God within my breast,
Almighty ever-present Deity!
Life, that in me hast rest,
As I Undying Life, have power in
   Thee!

Vain are the thousand creeds
That move men's hearts,
   unutterably vain,
Worthless as withered weeds,
Or idlest froth amid the boundless
   main,

To waken doubt in one
Holding so fast by thy infinity,
So surely anchored on
The steadfast rock of Immortality.

With wide-embracing love
Thy spirit animates eternal years,
Pervades and broods above,
Changes, sustains, dissolves,
   creates and rears.

Though Earth and moon were
   gone,
And suns and universes ceased to
   be,
And thou wert left alone,
Every Existence would exist in
   thee.

There is not room for Death
Nor atom that his might could
   render void:
Since thou art Being and Breath,
And what thou art may never be
   destroyed.

EMILY BRONTË

THE CAPTAIN'S DAUGHTER

We were crowded in the cabin,
   Not a soul would dare to
   sleep,—
It was midnight on the waters,
   And a storm was on the deep.

'Tis a fearful thing in winter
   To be shattered by the blast,
And to hear the rattling trumpet
   Thunder, "Cut away the mast!"

So we shuddered there in silence,—
   For the stoutest held his breath,
While the hungry sea was roaring
   And the breakers talked with
   death.

As thus we sat in darkness,
   Each one busy with his prayers,
"We are lost!" the captain shouted,
   As he staggered down the stairs.

But his little daughter whispered,
　As she took his icy hand,
"Isn't God upon the ocean,
　Just the same as on the land?"

Then we kissed the little maiden,
　And we spake in better cheer,
And we anchored safe in harbor
　When the morn was shining clear.

JAMES T. FIELDS

SAY NOT THE STRUGGLE NOUGHT AVAILETH

Say not the struggle nought
　availeth,
　The labour and the wounds are
　vain,
The enemy faints not, nor faileth,
　And as things have been they
　remain.

If hopes were dupes, fears may be
　liars;
　It may be, in yon smoke
　concealed,
Your comrades chase e'en now the
　fliers,
　And, but for you, possess the
　field.

For while the tired waves, vainly
　breaking,
　Seem here no painful inch to
　gain,
Far back, through creeks and
　inlets making,
　Comes silent, flooding in, the
　main.

And not by eastern windows only,
　When daylight comes, comes in
　the light;
In front, the sun climbs slow, how
　slowly,
　But westward, look, the land is
　bright.

ARTHUR HUGH CLOUGH

INVICTUS

Out of the night that covers me,
　Black as the Pit from pole to
　pole,
I thank whatever gods may be
　For my unconquerable soul.

In the fell clutch of circumstance
　I have not winced nor cried aloud.
Under the bludgeonings of chance
　My head is bloody, but unbowed.

Beyond this place of wrath and tears
　Looms but the horror of the shade,
And yet the menace of the years
　Finds, and shall find me, unafraid.

It matters not how strait the gate,
　How charged with punishments
　the scroll,
I am the master of my fate:
　I am the captain of my soul.

WILLIAM ERNEST HENLEY

LIGHT SHINING OUT OF DARKNESS

God moves in a mysterious way,
  His wonders to perform;
He plants his footsteps in the sea,
  And rides upon the storm.

Deep in unfathomable mines
  Of never failing skill,
He treasures up his bright designs,
  And works his sovereign will.

Ye fearful saints fresh courage take;
  The clouds ye so much dread
Are big with mercy, and shall break
  In blessings on your head.

Judge not the Lord by feeble sense,
  But trust him for his grace;
Behind a frowning providence,
  He hides a smiling face.

His purposes will ripen fast,
  Unfolding every hour:
The bud may have a bitter taste,
  But sweet will be the flower.

Blind unbelief is sure to err,
  And scan his work in vain;
God is his own interpreter,
  And he will make it plain.

WILLIAM COWPER

PIED BEAUTY

Glory be to God for dappled things—
  For skies of couple-colour as a brinded cow;
    For rose-moles all in stipple upon trout that swim;
Fresh-firecoal chestnut-falls; finches' wings;
  Landscape plotted and pieced—fold, fallow, and plough;
    And áll trádes, their gear and tackle and trim.
All things counter, original, spare, strange;
  Whatever is fickle, freckled (who knows how?)
    With swift, slow; sweet, sour; adazzle, dim;
He fathers-forth whose beauty is past change:
      Praise him.

GERARD MANLEY HOPKINS

ELEGY WRITTEN IN A COUNTRY CHURCHYARD

The curfew tolls the knell of parting day,
   The lowing herd wind slowly o'er the lea,
The plowman homeward plods his weary way,
   And leaves the world to darkness and to me.

Now fades the glimmering landscape on the sight,
   And all the air a solemn stillness holds,
Save where the beetle wheels his droning flight,
   And drowsy tinklings lull the distant folds;

Save that from yonder ivy-mantled tow'r
   The moping owl does to the moon complain
Of such as, wand'ring near her secret bow'r,
   Molest her ancient solitary reign.

Beneath those rugged elms, that yew-tree's shade,
   Where heaves the turf in many a mould'ring heap,
Each in his narrow cell for ever laid,
   The rude Forefathers of the hamlet sleep.

The breezy call of incense-breathing morn,
   The swallow twitt'ring from the straw-built shed,
The cock's shrill clarion, or the echoing horn,
   No more shall rouse them from their lowly bed.

For them no more the blazing hearth shall burn,
   Or busy housewife ply her evening care:
No children run to lisp their sire's return,
   Or climb his knees the envied kiss to share.

Oft did the harvest to their sickle yield,
　Their furrow oft the stubborn glebe has broke:
How jocund did they drive their team afield!
　How bow'd the woods beneath their sturdy stroke!

Let not Ambition mock their useful toil,
　Their homely joys, and destiny obscure;
Nor Grandeur hear with a disdainful smile
　The short and simple annals of the poor.

The boast of heraldry, the pomp of pow'r,
　And all that beauty, all that wealth e'er gave,
Awaits alike th' inevitable hour:
　The paths of glory lead but to the grave.

Nor you, ye Proud, impute to these the fault,
　If Memory o'er their tomb no trophies raise,
Where through the long-drawn aisle and fretted vault
　The pealing anthem swells the note of praise.

Can storied urn or animated bust
　Back to its mansion call the fleeting breath?
Can Honour's voice provoke the silent dust,
　Or Flatt'ry soothe the dull cold ear of death?

Perhaps in this neglected spot is laid
　Some heart once pregnant with celestial fire;
Hands, that the rod of empire might have sway'd,
　Or waked to ecstasy the living lyre.

But Knowledge to their eyes her ample page
　Rich with the spoils of time did ne'er unroll;
Chill Penury repress'd their noble rage,
　And froze the genial current of the soul.

Full many a gem of purest ray serene
　The dark unfathom'd caves of ocean bear:
Full many a flower is born to blush unseen,
　And waste its sweetness on the desert air.

Some village Hampden that with dauntless breast
　The little tyrant of his fields withstood,
Some mute inglorious Milton, here may rest,
　Some Cromwell guiltless of his country's blood.

Th' applause of list'ning senates to command,
  The threats of pain and ruin to despise,
To scatter plenty o'er a smiling land,
  And read their history in a nation's eyes,

Their lot forbade: nor circumscribed alone
  Their growing virtues, but their crimes confined;
Forbade to wade through slaughter to a throne,
  And shut the gates of mercy on mankind,

The struggling pangs of conscious truth to hide,
  To quench the blushes of ingenuous shame,
Or heap the shrine of Luxury and Pride
  With incense kindled at the Muse's flame.

Far from the madding crowd's ignoble strife
  Their sober wishes never learn'd to stray;
Along the cool sequester'd vale of life
  They kept the noiseless tenor of their way.

Yet ev'n these bones from insult to protect
  Some frail memorial still erected nigh,
With uncouth rhymes and shapeless sculpture deck'd,
  Implores the passing tribute of a sigh.

Their name, their years, spelt by th' unletter'd muse,
  The place of fame and elegy supply:
And many a holy text around she strews,
  That teach the rustic moralist to die.

For who, to dumb Forgetfulness a prey,
  This pleasing anxious being e'er resign'd,
Left the warm precincts of the cheerful day,
  Nor cast one longing ling'ring look behind?

On some fond breast the parting soul relies,
  Some pious drops the closing eye requires;
E'en from the tomb the voice of Nature cries,
  E'en in our ashes live their wonted fires.

For thee, who, mindful of th' unhonour'd dead,
  Dost in these lines their artless tale relate;
If chance, by lonely contemplation led,
  Some kindred spirit shall inquire thy fate,

Haply some hoary-headed Swain may say,
   "Oft have we seen him at the peep of dawn
Brushing with hasty steps the dews away
   To meet the sun upon the upland lawn.

"There at the foot of yonder nodding beech
   That wreathes its old fantastic roots so high,
His listless length at noontide would he stretch,
   And pore upon the brook that babbles by.

"Hard by yon wood, now smiling as in scorn,
   Mutt'ring his wayward fancies he would rove,
Now drooping, woeful wan, like one forlorn,
   Or crazed with care, or cross'd in hopeless love.

"One morn I miss'd him on the custom'd hill,
   Along the heath and near his fav'rite tree;
Another came, nor yet beside the rill,
   Nor up the lawn, nor at the wood was he;

"The next with dirges due in sad array
   Slow through the church-way path we saw him borne.
Approach and read (for thou canst read) the lay
   Graved on the stone beneath yon aged thorn."

THE EPITAPH

Here rests his head upon the lap of Earth
   A Youth to Fortune and to Fame unknown.
Fair Science frown'd not on his humble birth,
   And Melancholy mark'd him for her own.

Large was his bounty, and his soul sincere,
   Heav'n did a recompense as largely send:
He gave to Mis'ry all he had, a tear,
   He gain'd from Heav'n ('twas all he wish'd) a friend.

No farther seek his merits to disclose,
   Or draw his frailties from their dread abode,
(There they alike in trembling hope repose,)
   The bosom of his Father and his God.

THOMAS GRAY

THE LAST SUPPER

I

Apostles of the hidden sun
Are come unto the room of breath
Hung with the banging blinds of death,
The body twelve, the spirit one,
Far as the eye, in earth arrayed,
The night shining, the supper laid.

II

The wine shone on the table that evening of history
Like an enormous ruby in the bauble and mystery.

In the glowing walls of the flickering decanter
There moved His face as at the world's center.

The hands of Judas showed up red and hurried
And the light hit them so, like a cross carried.

The faces of the others were there and moving
In the crystal of the dome, swiftly hovering.

The saints, under a lens, shrunken to pigmies,
Gesticulated in birds or in colored enigmas.

Outside there was a storm, the sound of temblors,
The blood bubbled and sprang into the tumblers.

When the morning came like a white wall of stone,
The day lay in the glass and the blood was gone.

OSCAR WILLIAMS

NOW I LAY ME DOWN TO SLEEP

Now I lay me down to sleep,
I pray The Lord my soul to keep;
If I should die before I wake
I pray The Lord my soul to take.

ANONYMOUS

GOD'S GRANDEUR

The world is charged with the grandeur of God.
It will flame out, like shining from shook foil;
It gathers to a greatness, like the ooze of oil
Crushed. Why do men then now not reck his rod?

Generations have trod, have trod, have trod;
And all is seared with trade; bleared, smeared with toil;
And wears man's smudge and shares man's smell: the soil
Is bare now, nor can foot feel, being shod.

And for all this, nature is never spent;
There lives the dearest freshness deep down things;
And though the last lights off the black West went
Oh, morning, at the brown brink eastward, springs—
Because the Holy Ghost over the bent
World broods with warm breast and with ah! bright wings.

GERARD MANLEY HOPKINS

"ROCKED IN THE CRADLE OF THE DEEP"

Rocked in the cradle of the deep
I lay me down in peace to sleep;
Secure I rest upon the wave,
For Thou, O Lord! hast power to
    save.
I know Thou wilt not slight my call,
For Thou dost mark the sparrow's
    fall;
And calm and peaceful shall I sleep,
Rocked in the cradle of the deep.

When in the dead of night I lie
And gaze upon the trackless sky,
The star-bespangled heavenly scroll,
The boundless waters as they roll,—

I feel Thy wondrous power to save
From perils of the stormy wave:
Rocked in the cradle of the deep,
I calmly rest and soundly sleep.

And such the trust that still were
    mine,
Though stormy winds swept o'er
    the brine,
Or though the tempest's fiery breath
Roused me from sleep to wreck
    and death.
In ocean cave, still safe with Thee
The germ of immortality!
And calm and peaceful shall I sleep,
Rocked in the cradle of the deep.

EMMA HART WILLARD

BATTER MY HEART

Batter my heart, three personed God; for you
As yet but knock, breathe, shine, and seek to mend;
That I may rise and stand, o'erthrow me and bend
Your force to break, blow, burn and make me new.
I, like an usurped town, to another due,
Labour to admit you, but Oh, to no end;
Reason, your viceroy in me, me should defend,
But is captived and proves weak or untrue.

Yet dearly I love you and would be loved fain,
But am betrothed unto your enemy:
Divorce me, untie or break that knot again,
Take me to you, imprison me, for I,
Except you enthrall me, never shall be free,
Nor ever chaste, except you ravish me.

JOHN DONNE

THE RHODORA

(On being asked whence is the flower)

In May, when sea-winds pierced our solitudes,
I found the fresh Rhodora in the woods,
Spreading its leafless blooms in a damp nook,
To please the desert and the sluggish brook.
The purple petals, fallen in the pool,
Made the black water with their beauty gay;
Here might the red-bird come his plumes to cool,
And court the flower that cheapens his array.
Rhodora! if the sages ask thee why
This charm is wasted on the earth and sky,
Tell them, dear, that if eyes were made for seeing,
Then Beauty is its own excuse for being:
Why thou wert there, O rival of the rose!
I never thought to ask, I never knew:
But, in my simple ignorance, suppose
The self-same Power that brought me there brought you.

RALPH WALDO EMERSON

THE BATTLE-HYMN OF THE REPUBLIC

Mine eyes have seen the glory of the coming of the Lord;
He is trampling out the vintage where the grapes of wrath are stored;
He hath loosed the fateful lightning of His terrible swift sword;
          His truth is marching on.

I have seen Him in the watch-fires of a hundred circling camps;
They have builded Him an altar in the evening dews and damps;
I can read His righteous sentence by the dim and flaring lamps;
          His day is marching on.

I have read a fiery gospel, writ in burnished rows of steel:
"As ye deal with my contemners, so with you my grace shall deal;
Let the Hero, born of woman, crush the serpent with his heel,
          Since God is marching on."

He has sounded forth the trumpet that shall never call retreat;
He is sifting out the hearts of men before His judgment-seat:
Oh, be swift, my soul, to answer Him! be jubilant, my feet!
          Our God is marching on.

In the beauty of the lilies Christ was born across the sea,
With a glory in His bosom that transfigures you and me:
As He died to make men holy, let us die to make men free,
          While God is marching on.

                        JULIA WARD HOWE

THE HOUND OF HEAVEN

I fled Him, down the nights and down the days;
  I fled Him, down the arches of the years;
I fled Him, down the labyrinthine ways
  Of my own mind; and in the midst of tears
I hid from Him, and under running laughter.
        Up vistaed hopes I sped;
        And shot, precipitated,
Adown Titanic glooms of chasmèd fears,
  From those strong Feet that followed, followed after.
      But with unhurrying chase,
      And unperturbèd pace,
   Deliberate speed, majestic instancy,
      They beat—and a Voice beat
      More instant than the Feet—
  "All things betray thee, who betrayest Me."

      I pleaded, outlaw-wise,
By many a hearted casement, curtained red,
  Trellised with intertwining charities;
(For, though I knew His love Who followèd,
     Yet was I sore adread
Lest, having Him, I must have naught beside) ;
But, if one little casement parted wide,
  The gust of His approach would clash it to.
  Fear wist not to evade, as Love wist to pursue.
Across the margent of the world I fled,
  And troubled the gold gateways of the stars,
  Smiting for shelter on their clangèd bars;
    Fretted to dulcet jars
And silvern chatter the pale ports o' the moon.
I said to Dawn: Be sudden—to Eve: Be soon;
  With thy young skiey blossoms heap me over
    From this tremendous Lover—
Float thy vague veil about me, lest He see!
  I tempted all His servitors, but to find
My own betrayal in their constancy,
In faith to Him their fickleness to me,
  Their traitorous trueness, and their loyal deceit.

To all swift things for swiftness did I sue;
    Clung to the whistling mane of every wind.
        But whether they swept, smoothly fleet,
      The long savannahs of the blue;
          Or whether, Thunder-driven,
        They clanged his chariot 'thwart a heaven
Plashy with flying lightnings round the spurn o' their feet:—
    Fear wist not to evade as Love wist to pursue.
        Still with unhurrying chase,
      And unperturbèd pace,
    Deliberate speed, majestic instancy,
        Came on the following Feet,
        And a Voice above their beat—
"Naught shelters thee, who wilt not shelter Me."

I sought no more that after which I strayed
        In face of man or maid;
But still within the little children's eyes
      Seems something, something that replies,
They at least are for me, surely for me!
I turned me to them very wistfully;
But just as their young eyes grew sudden fair
      With dawning answers there,
Their angel plucked them from me by the hair.
"Come then, ye other children, Nature's—share
With me" (said I) "your delicate fellowship;
      Let me greet you lip to lip,
      Let me twine with you caresses,
        Wantoning
      With our Lady-Mother's vagrant tresses,
        Banqueting
      With her in her wind-walled palace,
      Underneath her azured daïs,
      Quaffing, as your taintless way is,
        From a chalice
Lucent-weeping out of the dayspring.
        So it was done:
I in their delicate fellowship was one—
Drew the bolt of Nature's secrecies.
        I knew all the swift importings
      On the willful face of skies;

I knew how the clouds arise
Spumèd of the wild sea-snortings;
   All that's born or dies
Rose and drooped with; made them shapers
Of mine own moods, or wailful or divine;
   With them joyed and was bereaven.
   I was heavy with the even,
   When she lit her glimmering tapers
   Round the day's dead sanctities.
   I laughed in the morning's eyes.
I triumphed and I saddened with all weather,
   Heaven and I wept together,
And its sweet tears were salt with mortal mine.
Against the red throb of its sunset-heart
   I laid my own to beat,
   And share commingling heat;
But not by that, by that, was eased my human smart.
In vain my tears were wet on Heaven's grey cheek.
For ah! we know not what each other says,
   These things and I; in sound I speak—
Their sound is but their stir, they speak by silences.
Nature, poor stepdame, cannot slake my drouth;
   Let her, if she would owe me,
Drop yon blue bosom-veil of sky, and show me
   The breasts o' her tenderness:
Never did any milk of hers once bless
   My thirsting mouth.
   Nigh and nigh draws the chase,
   With unperturbèd pace,
   Deliberate speed, majestic instancy;
   And past those noisèd Feet
   A Voice comes yet more fleet—
"Lo! naught contents thee, who content'st not Me."

Naked I wait Thy love's uplifted stroke!
My harness piece by piece Thou hast hewn from me,
   And smitten me to my knee;
   I am defenceless utterly.
   I slept, methinks, and woke,
And, slowly gazing, find me stripped in sleep.

In the rash lustihead of my young powers,
    I shook the pillaring hours
And pulled my life upon me; grimed with smears,
I stand amid the dust o' the mounded years—
My mangled youth lies dead beneath the heap,
My days have crackled and gone up in smoke,
Have puffed and burst as sun-starts on a stream.
    Yea, faileth now even dream
The dreamer, and the lute the lutanist;
Even the linked fantasies, in whose blossomy twist
I swung the earth a trinket at my wrist,
Are yielding; cords of all too weak account
For earth with heavy griefs so overplussed.
    Ah! is Thy love indeed
A weed, albeit an amaranthine weed,
Suffering no flowers except its own to mount?
    Ah! must—
    Designer infinite!—
Ah! must Thou char the wood ere Thou canst limn with it?
My freshness spent its wavering shower i' the dust;
And now my heart is as a broken fount,
Wherein tear-drippings stagnate, spilt down ever
    From the dank thoughts that shiver
Upon the sighful branches of my mind.
    Such is; what is to be?
The pulp so bitter, how shall taste the rind?
I dimly guess what Time in mists confounds;
Yet ever and anon a trumpet sounds
From the hid battlements of Eternity;
Those shaken mists a space unsettle, then
Round the half-glimpsèd turrets slowly wash again.
    But not ere him who summoneth
    I first have seen, enwound
With glooming robes purpureal, cypress-crowned;
His name I know, and what his trumpet saith.
Whether man's heart or life it be which yields
    Thee harvest, must Thy harvest-fields
    Be dunged with rotten death?
      Now of that long pursuit
      Comes at hand the bruit;

That Voice is round me like a bursting sea:
　"And is thy earth so marred,
　　Shattered in shard on shard?
　Lo, all things fly thee, for thou fliest Me!
　　Strange, piteous, futile thing!
Wherefore should any set thee love apart?
Seeing none but I make much of naught" (He said),
"And human love needs human meriting:
　How hast thou merited—
Of all man's clotted clay the dingiest clot?
　　Alack, thou knowest not
How little worthy of any love thou art!
Whom wilt thou find to love ignoble thee
　　Save Me, save only Me?
All which I took from thee I did but take,
　　Not for thy harms,
But just that thou might'st seek it in My arms.
　　All which thy child's mistake
Fancies as lost, I have stored for thee at home:
　Rise, clasp My hand, and come!"
　Halts by me that footfall:
　Is my gloom, after all,
Shade of His hand, outstretched caressingly?
　"Ah, fondest, blindest, weakest,
　I am He Whom thou seekest!
Thou dravest love from thee, who dravest Me."

FRANCIS THOMPSON

THE PILLAR OF THE CLOUD

Lead, Kindly Light, amid the
　encircling gloom,
　Lead Thou me on!
The night is dark, and I am far
　from home—
　Lead Thou me on!
Keep Thou my feet; I do not ask
　to see
The distant scene,—one step
　enough for me.

I was not ever thus, nor pray'd
　that Thou
　Shouldst lead me on.
I loved to choose and see my
　path; but now
　Lead Thou me on!
I loved the garish day, and, spite
　of fears,
Pride ruled my will: remember
　not past years.

So long Thy power hath blest me,
      sure it still
   Will lead me on,
O'er moor and fen, o'er crag and
      torrent, till
   The night is gone;

And with the morn those angel
      faces smile
Which I have loved long since,
      and lost awhile.

JOHN HENRY CARDINAL NEWMAN

GOOD-BYE

Good-bye, proud world! I'm going
   home:
Thou art not my friend, and I'm
   not thine.
Long through thy weary crowds I
   roam;
A river-ark on the ocean brine,
Long I've been tossed like the
   driven foam;
But now, proud world! I'm going
   home.

Good-bye to Flattery's fawning face;
To Grandeur with his wise grimace;
To upstart Wealth's averted eye;
To supple Office, low and high;
To crowded halls, to court and street;
To frozen hearts and hasting feet;
To those who go, and those who
   come;
Good-bye, proud world! I'm going
   home.

I am going to my own hearthstone,
Bosomed in yon green hills alone,—

A secret nook in a pleasant land,
Whose groves the frolic fairies
   planned;
Where arches green, the livelong
   day,
Echo the blackbird's roundelay,
And vulgar feet have never trod
A spot that is sacred to thought
   and God.

O, when I am safe in my sylvan
   home,
I tread on the pride of Greece
   and Rome;
And when I am stretched beneath
   the pines,
Where the evening star so holy shines,
I laugh at the lore and the pride
   of man,
At the sophist schools and the
   learned clan;
For what are they all, in their
   high conceit,
When man in the bush with God
   may meet?

RALPH WALDO EMERSON

RECESSIONAL

God of our fathers, known of old,
  Lord of our far-flung battle-line,
Beneath whose awful Hand we
    hold
  Dominion over palm and pine—
Lord God of Hosts, be with us yet,
Lest we forget—lest we forget!

The tumult and the shouting dies;
  The captains and the kings depart:
Still stands Thine ancient sacrifice,
  An humble and a contrite heart.
Lord God of Hosts, be with us yet,
Lest we forget—lest we forget!

Far-called, our navies melt away;
  On dune and headland sinks
    the fire:
Lo, all our pomp of yesterday
  Is one with Nineveh and Tyre!
Judge of the Nations, spare us yet,
Lest we forget—lest we forget!

If, drunk with sight of power, we
    loose
  Wild tongues that have not
    Thee in awe,
Such boastings as the Gentiles use,
  Or lesser breeds without the
    Law—
Lord God of Hosts, be with us yet,
Lest we forget—lest we forget!

For heathen heart that puts her
    trust
  In reeking tube and iron shard,
All valiant dust that builds on
    dust,
  And guarding, calls not Thee to
    guard,
For frantic boast and foolish
    word—
Thy Mercy on Thy People, Lord!
                              Amen.
                    RUDYARD KIPLING

ROCK OF AGES

Rock of Ages, cleft for me,
Let me hide myself in Thee!
Let the water and the blood
From Thy riven side which flowed,
Be of sin the double cure,
Save from guilt and make me pure.

Could my tears forever flow;
Could my zeal no languor know;
These for sin could not atone,

Thou must save, and Thou alone.
Rock of Ages, cleft for me,
Let me hide myself in Thee.

Not the labors of my hands
Can fulfill Thy law's demands;
Could my zeal no respite know,
Could my tears forever flow,
All for sin could not atone;
Thou must save and Thou alone.

Nothing in my hand I bring;
Simply to Thy cross I cling,
Naked, come to Thee for dress,
Helpless, look to Thee for grace.
Foul, I to the Fountain fly,
Wash me, Saviour, or I die.

While I draw this fleeting breath,
When mine eyes shall close in death,
When I rise to worlds unknown,
See Thee on Thy judgment throne—
Rock of Ages, cleft for me,
Let me hide myself in Thee.

AUGUST M. TOPLADY

CROSSING THE BAR

Sunset and evening star,
  And one clear call for me!
And may there be no moaning of the bar,
  When I put out to sea,

But such a tide as moving seems asleep,
  Too full for sound and foam,
When that which drew from out the boundless deep
  Turns again home.

Twilight and evening bell,
  And after that the dark!
And may there be no sadness of farewell,
  When I embark;

For tho' from out our bourne of Time and Place
  The flood may bear me far,
I hope to see my Pilot face to face
  When I have crost the bar.

ALFRED, LORD TENNYSON

JOURNEY OF THE MAGI

"A cold coming we had of it,
Just the worst time of the year
For a journey, and such a long journey:
The ways deep and the weather sharp,
The very dead of winter."
And the camels galled, sore-footed, refractory,
Lying down in the melting snow.
There were times we regretted
The summer palaces on slopes, the terraces,
And the silken girls bringing sherbet.
Then the camel men cursing and grumbling
And running away, and wanting their liquor and women,
And the night-fires going out, and the lack of shelters,
And the cities hostile and the towns unfriendly
And the villages dirty and charging high prices:
A hard time we had of it.
At the end we preferred to travel all night,
Sleeping in snatches,
With the voices singing in our ears, saying
That this was all folly.

Then at dawn we came down to a temperate valley,
Wet, below the snow line, smelling of vegetation;
With a running stream and a water-mill beating the darkness,
And three trees on the low sky,
And an old white horse galloped away in the meadow.
Then we came to a tavern with vine-leaves over the lintel,
Six hands at an open door dicing for pieces of silver,
And feet kicking the empty wine-skins.
But there was no information, and so we continued
And arrived at evening, not a moment too soon
Finding the place; it was (you may say) satisfactory.

All this was a long time ago, I remember,
And I would do it again, but set down
This set down

This: were we led all that way for
Birth or Death? There was a Birth, certainly,
We had evidence and no doubt. I had seen birth and death,
But had thought they were different; this Birth was
Hard and bitter agony for us, like Death, our death.
We returned to our places, these Kingdoms,
But no longer at ease here, in the old dispensation,
With an alien people clutching their gods.
I should be glad of another death.

T. S. ELIOT

THE CHAMBERED NAUTILUS

This is the ship of pearl, which, poets feign,
   Sails the unshadowed main,—
   The venturous bark that flings
On the sweet summer wind its purpled wings
In gulfs enchanted, where the Siren sings,
   And coral reefs lie bare,
Where the cold sea-maids rise to sun their streaming hair.

Its webs of living gauze no more unfurl;
   Wrecked is the ship of pearl!
   And every chambered cell,
Where its dim dreaming life was wont to dwell,
As the frail tenant shaped his growing shell,
   Before thee lies revealed,—
Its irised ceiling rent, its sunless crypt unsealed!

Year after year beheld the silent toil
   That spread his lustrous coil;
   Still, as the spiral grew,
He left the past year's dwelling for the new,
Stole with soft step its shining archway through,
   Built up its idle door,
Stretched in his last-found home, and knew the old no more.

Thanks for the heavenly message brought by thee,
   Child of the wandering sea,
   Cast from her lap, forlorn!

From thy dead lips a clearer note is born
Than ever Triton blew from wreathèd horn!
    While on mine ear it rings,
Through the deep caves of thought I hear a voice that sings:—

Build thee more stately mansions, O my soul,
    As the swift seasons roll!
    Leave thy low-vaulted past!
Let each new temple, nobler than the last,
Shut thee from heaven with a dome more vast,
    Till thou at length art free,
Leaving thine outgrown shell by life's unresting sea!

OLIVER WENDELL HOLMES

NOT ONLY AROUND OUR INFANCY

Not only around our infancy
Doth heaven with all its splendors
    lie;
Daily, with souls that cringe and
    plot,
We Sinais climb and know it not.

Over our manhood bend the
    skies;
    Against our fallen and traitor
    lives
The great winds utter prophecies;
    With our faint hearts the
    mountain strives;
Its arms outstretched, the druid
    wood
    Waits with its benedicite;
And to our age's drowsy blood
    Still shouts the inspiring sea.

Earth gets its price for what Earth
    gives us;
    The beggar is taxed for a
    corner to die in,
The priest hath his fee who comes
    and shrives us,
    We bargain for the graves we lie in;
At the Devil's booth are all things
    sold,
Each ounce of dross costs its
    ounce of gold;
    For a cap and bells our lives we
    pay,
Bubbles we buy with a whole
    soul's tasking:
    'Tis heaven alone that is given
    away,
'Tis only God may be had for the
    asking.

JAMES RUSSELL LOWELL

NEARER, MY GOD, TO THEE

Nearer, my God, to Thee,
Nearer to Thee!
E'en though it be a cross
That raiseth me;
Still all my song shall be,
Nearer, my God, to Thee,
Nearer to Thee!

Though like the wanderer,
The sun gone down,
Darkness be over me,
My rest a stone;
Yet in my dreams I'd be
Nearer, my God, to Thee,
Nearer to Thee!

There let the way appear
Steps unto Heaven,
All that Thou send'st me
In mercy given;

Angels to beckon me
Nearer, my God, to Thee,
Nearer to Thee!

Then, with my waking thoughts
Bright with Thy praise,
Out of my stony griefs,
Bethel I'll raise;
So by my woes to be
Nearer, my God, to Thee,
Nearer to Thee!

Or if, on joyful wing,
Cleaving the sky,
Sun, moon and stars forgot,
Upward I fly,
Still all my song shall be,
Nearer, my God to Thee,
Nearer to Thee!

SARAH FLOWER ADAMS

ONWARD, CHRISTIAN SOLDIERS

Onward, Christian soldiers,
    Marching as to war,
With the Cross of Jesus
    Going on before.
Christ the Royal Master
    Leads against the foe;
Forward into battle,
    See, His banners go!
        Onward, Christian soldiers,
            Marching as to war,

With the Cross of Jesus
    Going on before.

At the sign of triumph
    Satan's host doth flee;
On then, Christian soldiers,
    On to victory.
Hell's foundations quiver
    At the shouts of praise;
Brothers, lift your voices,

Loud your anthems raise.
  Onward, etc.

Like a mighty army
  Moves the Church of God;
Brothers, we are treading
  Where the Saints have trod;
We are not divided,
  All one body we,
One in hope and doctrine,
  One in charity.
    Onward, etc.

Crowns and thrones may perish,
  Kingdoms rise and wane,
But the Church of Jesus
  Constant will remain;
Gates of hell can never

'Gainst that Church prevail;
We have Christ's own promise,
  And that cannot fail.
    Onward, etc.

Onward, then, ye people,
  Join our happy throng,
Blend with ours your voices
  In the triumph song;
Glory, laud, and honor
  Unto Christ the King,
This through countless ages
  Men and angels sing.
    Onward, Christian soldiers,
      Marching as to war,
    With the Cross of Jesus
      Going on before.
        SABINE BARING-GOULD

BOOK XV

THE CHILDREN'S HOUR

THE CHILDREN'S HOUR

Between the dark and the
    daylight,
  When the light is beginning to
    lower,
Comes a pause in the day's
    occupations
  That is known as the Children's
    Hour.

I hear in the chamber above me
  The patter of little feet,
The sound of a door that is
    opened,
  And voices soft and sweet.

From my study I see in the
    lamplight,
  Descending the broad hall stair,
Grave Alice and laughing Allegra,
  And Edith with golden hair.

A whisper, and then a silence;
  Yet I know by their merry eyes,
They are plotting and planning
    together
  To take me by surprise.

A sudden rush from the stairway,
  A sudden raid from the hall!
By three doors left unguarded
  They enter my castle wall!

They climb up into my turret,
  O'er the arms and back of my
    chair;
If I try to escape, they surround me;
  They seem to be everywhere.

They almost devour me with kisses,
  Their arms about me entwine,
Till I think of the Bishop of
    Bingen
  In his Mouse-Tower on the
    Rhine.

Do you think, O blue-eyed
    banditti,
  Because you have scaled the
    wall,
Such an old mustache as I am
  Is not a match for you all?

I have you fast in my fortress,
  And will not let you depart,
But put you down into the
    dungeon
  In the round-tower of my heart.

And there will I keep you forever,
  Yes, forever and a day,
Till the wall shall crumble to
    ruin,
  And moulder in dust away.

HENRY WADSWORTH LONGFELLOW

WHERE DID YOU COME FROM?

Where did you come from, Baby dear?
Out of the everywhere into the here.

Where did you get your eyes so blue?
Out of the sky as I came through.

What makes the light in them
    sparkle and spin?
Some of the starry spikes left in.

Where did you get that little tear?
I found it waiting when I got here.

What makes your forehead so
    smooth and high?
A soft hand stroked it as I went by.

What makes your cheek like a
    warm white rose?
I saw something better than
    anyone knows.

Whence that three-corner'd smile
    of bliss?
Three angels gave me at once a kiss.

Where did you get this pearly ear?
God spoke, and it came out to hear.

Where did you get those arms and
    hands?
Love made itself into hooks and bands.

Feet, whence did you come, you
    darling things?
From the same box as the
    cherubs' wings.

How did they all come just to be you?
God thought of me, and so I grew.

But how did you come to us, you dear?
God thought of you, and so I am here.

GEORGE MACDONALD

THE SWING

How do you like to go up in a
    swing,
    Up in the air so blue?
Oh, I do think it the pleasantest
    thing
    Ever a child can do!

Up in the air and over the wall,
    Till I can see so wide,

Rivers and trees and cattle and all
    Over the countryside—

Till I look down on the garden
    green,
    Down on the roof so brown—
Up in the air I go flying again,
    Up in the air and down!

ROBERT LOUIS STEVENSON

KEEP THE GLAD FLAG FLYING

When you get hard knocks and
    buffets—
  As in life you're bound to do—
Don't give in, nor whine and murmur,
  But determine to win through.

Strip your coat off, roll your sleeves up,
  Set to work and be sincere!
You'll win through a heap of trouble
  If you smile and persevere.

'Tis the one who's full of sunshine,
  And who genuinely tries,
Who will clear the clouds of trouble
  From his own and others' skies.

Deeds of honest loving-kindness
  Give a fallen fellow heart,
And upon his uphill journey,
  Help him play a manly part.

ANONYMOUS

THE LAMPLIGHTER

My tea is nearly ready and the sun has left the sky;
It's time to take the window to see Leerie going by;
For every night at teatime and before you take your seat,
With lantern and with ladder he comes posting up the street.

Now Tom would be a driver and Maria go to sea,
And my papa's a banker and as rich as he can be;
But I, when I am stronger and can choose what I'm to do,
O Leerie, I'll go round at night and light the lamps with you!

For we are very lucky, with a lamp before the door,
And Leerie stops to light it as he lights so many more;
And O, before you hurry by with ladder and with light,
O Leerie, see a little child and nod to him to-night!

ROBERT LOUIS STEVENSON

WYNKEN, BLYNKEN, AND NOD

Wynken, Blynken, and Nod one
    night
  Sailed off in a wooden shoe,—
Sailed on a river of crystal light
  Into a sea of dew.
"Where are you going, and what
    do you wish?"
  The old moon asked the three.
"We have come to fish for the
    herring fish
  That live in this beautiful sea;
  Nets of silver and gold have
    we!"
        Said Wynken,
        Blynken,
        And Nod.

The old moon laughed and sang
    a song,
  As they rocked in the wooden
    shoe;
And the wind that sped them all
    night long
  Ruffled the waves of dew.
The little stars were the herring
    fish
  That lived in that beautiful
    sea—
"Now cast your nets wherever you
    wish,—
  Never afeared are we!"
So cried the stars to the
    fishermen three,
        Wynken,
        Blynken,
        And Nod.

All night long their nets they
    threw
  To the stars in the twinkling
    foam,—
Then down from the skies came
    the wooden shoe,
  Bringing the fishermen home:
'Twas all so pretty a sail, it
    seemed
  As if it could not be;
And some folk thought 'twas a
    dream they'd dreamed
  Of sailing that beautiful sea;
But I shall name you the
    fishermen three:
        Wynken,
        Blynken,
        And Nod.

Wynken and Blynken are two
    little eyes,
  And Nod is a little head,
And the wooden shoe that sailed
    the skies
  Is a wee one's trundle-bed;
So shut your eyes while Mother
    sings
  Of wonderful sights that be,
And you shall see the beautiful
    things
  As you rock in the misty sea
Where the old shoe rocked the
    fishermen three:—
        Wynken,
        Blynken,
        And Nod.

EUGENE FIELD

THE DAY IS DONE

The day is done, and the darkness
  Falls from the wings of Night,
As a feather is wafted downward
  From an eagle in his flight.

I see the lights of the village
  Gleam through the rain and
    the mist,
And a feeling of sadness comes
    o'er me
That my soul cannot resist:

A feeling of sadness and longing,
  That is not akin to pain,
And resembles sorrow only
  As the mist resembles the rain.

Come, read to me some poem,
  Some simple and heartfelt lay,
That shall soothe this restless feeling,
  And banish the thoughts of day.

Not from the grand old masters,
  Not from the bards sublime,
Whose distant footsteps echo
  Through the corridors of Time.

For, like strains of martial music,
  Their mighty thoughts suggest
Life's endless toil and endeavor;
  And to-night I long for rest.

Read from some humbler poet,
  Whose songs gushed from his
    heart,
As showers from the clouds of
    summer,
  Or tears from the eyelids start;

Who, through long days of labor,
  And nights devoid of ease,
Still heard in his soul the music
  Of wonderful melodies.

Such songs have power to quiet
  The restless pulse of care,
And come like the benediction
  That follows after prayer.

Then read from the treasured
    volume
  The poem of thy choice,
And lend to the rhyme of the
    poet
  The beauty of thy voice.

And the night shall be filled with
    music,
  And the cares, that infest the
    day,
Shall fold their tents, like the
    Arabs,
  And as silently steal away.

HENRY WADSWORTH LONGFELLOW

THE SUGAR-PLUM TREE

Have you ever heard of the Sugar-Plum Tree?
'Tis a marvel of great renown!
It blooms on the shore of the Lollypop Sea
In the garden of Shut-Eye Town;
The fruit that it bears is so wondrously sweet
(As those who have tasted it say)
That good little children have only to eat
Of that fruit to be happy next day.

When you've got to the tree, you would have a hard time
To capture the fruit which I sing;
The tree is so tall that no person could climb
To the boughs where the sugar-plums swing!
But up in that tree sits a chocolate cat,
And a gingerbread dog prowls below—
And this is the way you contrive to get at
Those sugar-plums tempting you so:

You say but the word to that gingerbread dog
And he barks with such a terrible zest
That the chocolate cat is at once all agog,
As her swelling proportions attest.
And the chocolate cat goes cavorting around
From this leafy limb unto that,
And the sugar-plums tumble, of course, to the ground—
Hurrah for that chocolate cat!

There are marshmallows, gumdrops, and peppermint canes
With stripings of scarlet and gold,
And you carry away of the treasure that rains,
As much as your apron can hold!
So come, little child, cuddle closer to me
In your dainty white nightcap and gown,
And I'll rock you away to that Sugar-Plum Tree
In the garden of Shut-Eye Town.

EUGENE FIELD

IN THE GLOAMING

In the gloaming, oh, my darling,
When the lights are dim and low,
And the quiet shadows falling,
Softly come, and softly go;
When the winds are sobbing
    faintly,
With a gentle, unknown woe;
Will you think of me and love
    me?
As you did once long ago?

In the gloaming, oh, my darling,
Think not bitterly of me.
Tho' I passed away in silence,
Left you lonely, set you free;
For my heart was crushed with
    longing,
What had been could never be;
It was best to leave you thus, dear,
Best for you and best for me.
It was best to leave you thus,
Best for you and best for me.

                              META ORRED

LITTLE BOY BLUE

The little toy dog is covered with
    dust,
    But sturdy and staunch he stands;
The little toy soldier is red with
    rust,
    And his musket molds in his
    hands.
Time was when the little toy dog
    was new,
    And the soldier was passing fair;
And that was the time when our
    Little Boy Blue
    Kissed them and put them there.

"Now don't you go till I come,"
    he said,
    "And don't you make any noise!"
So, toddling off to his trundle bed,
    He dreamt of the pretty toys;

And, as he was dreaming, an
    angel song
    Awakened our Little Boy Blue—
Oh! the years are many, the years
    are long,
    But the little toy friends are true!

Ay, faithful to Little Boy Blue
    they stand,
    Each in the same old place,
Awaiting the touch of a little hand,
    The smile of a little face;
And they wonder, as waiting the
    long years through
    In the dust of that little chair,
What has become of our Little
    Boy Blue,
    Since he kissed them and put
    them there.

                              EUGENE FIELD

THE LAND OF COUNTERPANE

When I was sick and lay a-bed,
I had two pillows at my head,
And all my toys beside me lay
To keep me happy all the day.

And sometimes for an hour or so
I watched my leaden soldiers go,
With different uniforms and drills,
Among the bed-clothes, through
     the hills.

And sometimes sent my ships in fleets
All up and down among the sheets;
Or brought my trees and houses out,
And planted cities all about.

I was the giant great and still
That sits upon the pillow-hill,
And sees before him, dale and plain
The pleasant Land of Counterpane.

ROBERT LOUIS STEVENSON

THE STAR

Twinkle, twinkle, little star,
How I wonder what you are!
Up above the world so high,
Like a diamond in the sky.

When the blazing sun is set,
When the grass with dew is wet,
Then you show your little light,
Twinkle, twinkle, all the night.

Then the traveler in the dark,
Thanks you for your tiny spark;

He could not see which way to go
If you did not twinkle so.

In the dark blue sky you keep,
And often through my curtains peep,
For you never shut your eye
Till the sun is in the sky.

As your bright and shiny spark,
Lights the traveler in the dark,
Though I know not what you are,
Twinkle, twinkle, little star.

JANE TAYLOR

WILLIE WINKIE

Wee Willie Winkie rins through the town,
Up-stairs and doon-stairs, in his nicht-gown,
Tirlin' at the window, cryin' at the lock,
"Are the weans in their bed?—for it's noo ten o'clock."

Hey, Willie Winkie! are ye comin' ben?
The cat's singin' gay thrums to the sleepin' hen,
The doug's speldered on the floor, and disna gie a cheep;
But here 's a waukrife laddie that winna fa' asleep.

Ony thing but sleep, ye rogue! glow'rin' like the moon,
Rattlin' in an airn jug wi' an airn spoon,
Rumblin' tumblin' roun' about, crowin' like a cock,
Skirlin' like a kenna-what—wauknin' sleepin' folk.

Hey, Willie Winkie! the wean's in a creel!
Waumblin' aff a body's knee like a vera eel,
Ruggin' at the cat's lug, and ravellin' a' her thrums,—
Hey, Willie Winkie!—See, there he comes!

Wearie is the mither that has a storie wean,
A wee stumpie stoussie that canna rin his lane,
That has a battle aye wi' sleep before he'll close an ee;
But a kiss frae aff his rosy lips gies strength anew.

WILLIAM MILLER

THERE WAS A LITTLE GIRL

There was a little girl, she had a little curl
  Right in the middle of her forehead;
And when she was good, she was very, very good,
  And when she was bad, she was horrid.

HENRY WADSWORTH LONGFELLOW

LITTLE ORPHANT ANNIE

INSCRIBED

WITH ALL FAITH AND AFFECTION

To all the little children:—The happy ones; and sad ones;
The sober and the silent ones; the boisterous and glad ones;
The good ones—Yes, the good ones, too; and all the lovely bad ones.

Little Orphant Annie's come to our house to stay,
An' wash the cups an' saucers up, an' brush the crumbs away,
An' shoo the chickens off the porch, an' dust the hearth, an' sweep,
An' make the fire, an' bake the bread, an' earn her board-an'-keep;
An' all us other childern, when the supper-things is done,
We set around the kitchen fire an' has the mostest fun
A-list'nin' to the witch-tales 'at Annie tells about,
An' the Gobble-uns 'at gits you
          Ef you
             Don't
                Watch
                  Out!

Wunst they wuz a little boy wouldn't say his prayers,—
An' when he went to bed at night, away up-stairs,
His Mammy heerd him holler, an' his Daddy heerd him bawl,
An' when they turn't the kivvers down, he wuzn't there at all!
An' they seeked him in the rafter-room, an' cubby-hole, an' press,
An' seeked him up the chimbly-flue, an' ever'-wheres, I guess;
But all they ever found wuz thist his pants an' roundabout:—
An' the Gobble-uns 'll git you
          Ef you
             Don't
                Watch
                  Out!

An' one time a little girl 'ud allus laugh an' grin,
An' make fun of ever' one, an' all her blood-an'-kin;
An' wunst, when they was "company," an' ole folks wuz there,
She mocked 'em an' shocked 'em, an' said she didn't care!

An' thist as she kicked her heels, an' turn't to run an' hide,
They wuz two great big Black Things a-standin' by her side,
An' they snatched her through the ceilin' 'fore she knowed what she's
   about!
An' the Gobble-uns 'll git you
         Ef you
            Don't
               Watch
                  Out!

An' little Orphant Annie says, when the blaze is blue,
An' the lamp-wick sputters, an' the wind goes *woo-oo!*
An' you hear the crickets quit, an' the moon is gray,
An' the lightnin'-bugs in dew is all squenched away,—
You better mind yer parunts, an' yer teachurs fond an' dear,
An' churish them 'at loves you, an' dry the orphant's tear,
An' he'p the pore an' needy ones 'at clusters all about,
Er the Gobble-uns 'll git you
         Ef you
            Don't
               Watch
                  Out!

                      JAMES WHITCOMB RILEY

GOOD AND BAD CHILDREN

Children, you are very little,
And your bones are very brittle;
If you would grow great and stately,
You must try to walk sedately.

You must still be bright and quiet,
And content with simple diet;
And remain, through all
   bewild'ring,
Innocent and honest children.

Happy hearts and happy faces,
Happy play in grassy places—

That was how, in ancient ages,
Children grew to kings and sages.

But the unkind and the unruly,
And the sort who eat unduly,
They must never hope for glory—
Theirs is quite a different story!

Cruel children, crying babies,
All grow up as geese and gabies,
Hated, as their age increases,
By their nephews and their nieces.

   ROBERT LOUIS STEVENSON

THE OWL AND THE PUSSY-CAT

The Owl and the Pussy-Cat went to sea
    In a beautiful pea-green boat;
They took some honey, and plenty of money
    Wrapped up in a five-pound note.
The Owl looked up to the stars above,
    And sang to a small guitar,
"O lovely Pussy! O Pussy, my love!
    What a beautiful Pussy you are,—
        You are, you are!
    What a beautiful Pussy you are!"

Pussy said to the Owl, "You elegant fowl!
    How charmingly sweet you sing!
Oh, let us be married,—too long we have tarried,—
    But what shall we do for a ring?"
They sailed away for a year and a day
    To the land where the Bong-tree grows,
And there in a wood a Piggy-wig stood
    With a ring at the end of his nose,—
        His nose, his nose,
    With a ring at the end of his nose.

"Dear Pig, are you willing to sell for one shilling
    Your ring?" Said the Piggy, "I will."
So they took it away, and were married next day
    By the Turkey who lives on the hill.

They dined upon mince and slices of quince,
Which they ate with a runcible spoon,
And hand in hand on the edge of the sand
They danced by the light of the moon,—
The moon, the moon,
They danced by the light of the moon.

EDWARD LEAR

FABLE

The mountain and the squirrel
Had a quarrel,
And the former called the latter
"Little Prig";
Bun replied,
'You are doubtless very big;
But all sorts of things and
weather
Must be taken in together,
To make up a year
And a sphere.

And I think it no disgrace
To occupy my place.
If I'm not so large as you,
You are not so small as I,
And not half so spry.
I'll not deny you make
A very pretty squirrel track;
Talents differ; all is well and
wisely put;
If I cannot carry forests on my back,
Neither can you crack a nut."

RALPH WALDO EMERSON

THE DUEL

The gingham dog and the calico cat
Side by side on the table sat;
'Twas half-past twelve, and (what do you think!)
Nor one nor t' other had slept a wink!
The old Dutch clock and the Chinese plate
Appeared to know as sure as fate
There was going to be a terrible spat.

*(I wasn't there; I simply state
What was told to me by the Chinese plate!)*

The gingham dog went "bow-wow-wow!"
And the calico cat replied "mee-ow!"
The air was littered, an hour or so,
With bits of gingham and calico,

While the old Dutch clock in the chimney-place
Up with its hands before its face,
For it always dreaded a family row!

(*Never mind: I'm only telling you*
What the old Dutch clock declares is true!)

The Chinese plate looked very blue,
And wailed, "Oh, dear! what shall we do!"
But the gingham dog and the calico cat
Wallowed this way and tumbled that,
Employing every tooth and claw
In the awfullest way you ever saw—
And, oh! how the gingham and calico flew!

(*Don't fancy I exaggerate—*
I got my news from the Chinese plate!)

Next morning where the two had sat
They found no trace of dog or cat;
And some folks think unto this day
That burglars stole that pair away!
But the truth about the cat and pup
Is this: they ate each other up!
Now what do you really think of that!

(*The old Dutch clock it told me so,*
And that is how I came to know.)

EUGENE FIELD

THE MOO-COW-MOO

My Pa held me up to the
  moo-cow-moo
So close I could almost touch:
An' I fed him a couple of times
  or two
An' I wasn't a 'fraid-cat much.

But, ef my Pa goes into the house
An' ef my Mamma goes too,
I jest keep still like a little mouse
'Cause the moo-cow-moo might moo!

The moo-cow-moo has a tail like a rope,
An' it's ravelled down where it grows,
An' it's jest like feelin' a piece of
  soap
All over the moo-cow's nose.

The moo-cow-moo has lots of fun
Jest swingin' its tail about,
But ef he opens his mouth, I run
'Cause that's where the moo comes
  out.

The moo-cow-moo has deers on its
   head
An' his eyes bog out of their place:
An' the nose of the moo-cow-moo
   is spread
All over the end of his face.

An' his feet is nothing but finger-nails
An' his momma don't keep them cut

An' he gives folks milk in
   water-pails
Ef he don't keep his handles shut.

'Cause ef you or me pulls them
   handles, why
The moo-cow-moo says it hurts,
But our hired man he sets close by
An' squirts an' squirts an' squirts.

                EDMUND VANCE COOKE

A BUTCHER'S DOZEN OF CHILDREN'S RHYMES

I

I asked my mother for fifty cents
To see the elephant jump the fence.
He jumped so high he reached the sky,
And didn't get back till the Fourth
   of July.

II

Said the monkey to the donkey,
"What'll you have to drink?"
Said the donkey to the monkey,
"I'd like a swig of ink."

III

I'm a little Hindoo.
I do all I kindoo.
Where my pants and shirt don't
   meet
I make my little skindoo.

IV

I'd like a little
Of that nourishing victual,
But I'll take a lot
From the candy pot.

V

My father owns the butcher shop,
My mother cuts the meat,
And I'm the little hot dog
That runs around the street.

VI

I stood on the bridge at midnight,
When the clock was striking in
    town;
I stood on the bridge at midnight—
Because I couldn't sit down.

VII

Sam, Sam, the butcher man,
Washed his face in a frying pan,
Combed his hair with a wagon wheel,
And died with a toothache in his heel.

VIII

A horse and a flea and three blind mice
Sat on a curbstone shooting dice.

The horse he slipped and fell
    on the flea.
The flea said, "Whoops, there's
    a horse on me."

IX

I like coffee, I like tea,
I like the boys and the boys like me.
Tell your mother to hold her
    tongue,
For she did the same when she was
    young.
Tell your father to do the same,
For he was the one who changed
    her name.

X

Charlie Chaplin went to France
To teach the ladies how to dance.
Heel, toe, and around we go;
Salute to the captain,
Bow to the queen,
Turn your back
On the old submarine.

XI

You're a poet.
You don't know it,
But your feet show it—
LONGFELLOW!

ANONYMOUS

THE MOON'S THE NORTH WIND'S COOKY

(What the Little Girl Said)

The Moon's the North Wind's
    cooky.
He bites it, day by day,
Until there's but a rim of scraps
That crumble all away.

The South Wind is a baker.
He kneads clouds in his den,
And bakes a crisp new moon that
    . . . greedy
North . . . Wind . . . eats . . . again!

VACHEL LINDSAY

THE WALRUS AND THE CARPENTER

The sun was shining on the sea,
  Shining with all his might:
He did his very best to make
  The billows smooth and bright—
And this was odd, because it was
  The middle of the night.

The moon was shining sulkily,
  Because she thought the sun
Had got no business to be there
  After the day was done—
"It's very rude of him," she said,
  "To come and spoil the fun!"

The sea was wet as wet could be,
  The sands were dry as dry.
You could not see a cloud, because
  No cloud was in the sky:
No birds were flying overhead—
  There were no birds to fly.

The Walrus and the Carpenter
  Were walking close at hand:
They wept like anything to see
  Such quantities of sand.
"If this were only cleared away,"
  They said, "it *would* be grand!"

"If seven maids with seven mops
  Swept it for half a year,
Do you suppose," the Walrus said,
  "That they could get it clear?"
"I doubt it," said the Carpenter,
  And shed a bitter tear.

"O Oysters, come and walk with us!"
  The Walrus did beseech.
"A pleasant walk, a pleasant talk,
  Along the briny beach:
We cannot do with more than four,
  To give a hand to each."

The eldest Oyster looked at him,
  But never a word he said:
The eldest Oyster winked his eye,
  And shook his heavy head—
Meaning to say he did not choose
  To leave the oyster-bed.

But four young Oysters hurried up,
  All eager for the treat:
Their coats were brushed, their
    faces washed,
  Their shoes were clean and neat—
And this was odd, because, you know,
  They hadn't any feet.

Four other Oysters followed them,
  And yet another four;
And thick and fast they came at
    last,
  And more, and more, and more—
All hopping through the frothy
    waves,
  And scrambling to the shore.

The Walrus and the Carpenter
  Walked on a mile or so,
And then they rested on a rock
  Conveniently low:
And all the little Oysters stood
  And waited in a row.

"The time has come," the Walrus
    said,
  "To talk of many things:
Of shoes—and ships—and
    sealing-wax—
  Of cabbages—and kings—
And why the sea is boiling hot—
  And whether pigs have wings."

"But wait a bit," the Oysters cried,
  "Before we have our chat;
For some of us are out of breath,
  And all of us are fat!"
"No hurry!" said the Carpenter.
  They thanked him much for
    that.

"A loaf of bread," the Walrus said,
  "Is what we chiefly need:
Pepper and vinegar besides
  Are very good indeed—
Now, if you're ready, Oysters dear,
  We can begin to feed."

"But not on us!" the Oysters cried,
  Turning a little blue.
"After such kindness, that would
    be
  A dismal thing to do!"
"The night is fine," the Walrus
    said,
  "Do you admire the view?

"It was so kind of you to come!
  And you are very nice!"
The Carpenter said nothing but
  "Cut us another slice.
I wish you were not quite so deaf—
  I've had to ask you twice!"

"It seems a shame," the Walrus
    said,
  "To play them such a trick,
After we've brought them out so
    far,
  And made them trot so quick!"
The Carpenter said nothing but
  "The butter's spread too thick!"

"I weep for you," the Walrus
    said:
  "I deeply sympathize."
With sobs and tears he sorted out
  Those of the largest size,
Holding his pocket-handkerchief
  Before his streaming eyes.

"O Oysters," said the Carpenter,
  "You've had a pleasant run!
Shall we be trotting home again?"
  But answer came there none—
And this was scarcely odd, because
  They'd eaten every one.

LEWIS CARROLL

I WISH I WERE

I wish I were a
Elephantiaphus
And could pick off the coconuts
  with my nose.
But, oh! I am not,
 (Alas! I cannot be)
An Elephanti—
Elephantiaphus.
But I'm a cockroach
And I'm a water-bug,
I can crawl around and hide
  behind the sink.

I wish I were a
Rhinoscerèeacus
And could wear an ivory
  toothpick in my nose.
But, oh! I am not,
 (Alas! I cannot be)
A Rhinoscōri—

Rhinoscerèeacus—
But I'm a beetle
And I'm a pumpkin-bug,
I can buzz and bang my head
  against the wall.

I wish I were a
Hippopōpotamus
And could swim the Tigris and
  the broad Gangès.
But, oh! I am not,
 (Alas! I cannot be)
A hippopōpo—
Hippopōpotamus—
But I'm a grasshopper
And I'm a katydid,
I can play the fiddle with my left
  hind-leg.
                    ANONYMOUS

"I HAD A LITTLE HUSBAND"

I HAD a little husband
  No bigger than my thumb;
I put him in a pint pot,
  And there I bade him drum.

I bought a little horse,
  That galloped up and down;

I bridled him and saddled him,
  And sent him out of town.

I gave him some garters,
  To garter up his hose,
And a little handkerchief,
  To wipe his pretty nose.
                    ANONYMOUS

SWEETES' LI'L' FELLER

Sweetes' li'l' feller—
　Everybody knows;
Dunno what ter call 'im,
　But he mighty lak' a rose!

Lookin' at his mammy
　Wid eyes so shiny-blue,
Mek' you think dat heaven
　Is comin' clost ter you!

W'en he's dar a-sleepin'
　In his li'l' place,

Think I see de angels
　Lookin' thoo' de lace.

W'en de dark is fallin'—
　W'en de shadders creep,
Den dey comes on tip-toe
　Ter kiss 'im in his sleep.

Sweetes' li'l' feller—
　Everybody knows;
Dunno what ter call 'im,
　But he mighty lak' a rose!

FRANK L. STANTON

UP THE AIRY MOUNTAIN

Up the airy mountain,
　Down the rushy glen,
We daren't go a-hunting
　For fear of little men;
Wee folk, good folk,
　Trooping all together;
Green jacket, red cap,
　And white owl's feather.

They stole little Bridget
　For seven years long;
When she came down again
　Her friends were all gone.
They took her lightly back,
　Between the night and morrow;
They thought that she was fast
　　asleep,
But she was dead with sorrow. . . .

By the craggy hillside,
　Through the mosses bare,
They have planted thorn-trees
　For pleasure here and there.
Is any man so daring
　As dig one up in spite?
He shall find the sharpest thorn
　In his bed at night.

Up the airy mountain,
　Down the rushy glen,
We daren't go a-hunting
　For fear of little men;
Wee folk, good folk,
　Trooping all together;
Green jacket, red cap,
　And white owl's feather.

WILLIAM ALLINGHAM

MARY'S LAMB

Mary had a little lamb,
  Its fleece was white as snow,
And every where that Mary went
  The lamb was sure to go;
He followed her to school one
    day—
  That was against the rule,
It made the children laugh and
    play,
  To see a lamb at school.

And so the Teacher turned him
    out,
  But still he lingered near,
And waited patiently about,
  Till Mary did appear;

And then he ran to her, and laid
  His head upon her arm,
As if he said—"I'm not afraid—
  You'll keep me from all harm."

"What makes the lamb love Mary
    so?"
  The eager children cry—
"O, Mary loves the lamb, you
    know,"
  The Teacher did reply:—
"And you each gentle animal
  In confidence may bind,
And make them follow at your
    call,
  If you are always *kind*."

SARAH JOSEPHA HALE

JACK AND JILL

JACK and Jill went up the hill,
  To fetch a pail of water;
Jack fell down and broke his
    crown
  And Jill came tumbling after.

Up Jack got and home did trot
  As fast as he could caper,
And went to bed to mend his
    head
  With vinegar and brown paper.

ANONYMOUS

A GARLAND FROM MOTHER GOOSE

I

MISTRESS MARY, quite contrary,
How does your garden grow?
With cockle-shells, and silver bells,
And pretty maids all in a row.

II

THERE was an old woman who
   lived in a shoe,
She had so many children she didn't
   know what to do;
She gave them some broth without
   any bread;
Then whipped them all soundly
   and put them to bed.

III

PETER, Peter, pumpkin eater,
Had a wife and couldn't keep her;
He put her in a pumpkin shell
And there he kept her very well.

IV

HICKORY, dickory, dock,
The mouse ran up the clock;
   The clock struck one,
   The mouse ran down,
Hickory, dickory, dock.

V

A DILLER, a dollar,
A ten o'clock scholar,
What makes you come so soon?
You used to come at ten o'clock
But now you come at noon.

VI

   THERE was a little man,
   And he had a little gun,
And his bullets were made of lead,
   lead, lead;

He shot Johnny Sprig
   Through the middle of his wig,
And knocked it right off his head,
   head, head.

VII

IF I had as much money as I could
   spend,
I never would cry old chairs to
   mend;
Old chairs to mend, old chairs to
   mend;
I never would cry old chairs to
   mend.

If I had as much money as I could
   tell,
I never would cry old clothes to
   sell;
Old clothes to sell, old clothes to
   sell;
I never would cry old clothes to sell.

VIII

IF all the world were apple-pie,
And all the sea were ink,
And all the trees were bread and
   cheese,
What should we have to drink?

IX

PEASE-PUDDING hot.
   Pease-pudding cold,
Pease-pudding in the pot,
   Nine days old.
Some like it hot,
   Some like it cold,
Some like it in the pot,
   Nine days old.

X

Hey, diddle, diddle,
The cat and the fiddle,
The cow jumped over the moon;
The little dog laughed
To see such sport,
And the dish ran away with the
spoon.

XI

Little Jack Horner sat in the
corner
Eating a Christmas pie;
He put in his thumb, and pulled
out a plum,
And said, "What a good boy
am I!"

XII

Little Miss Muffet,
Sat on a tuffet,
Eating of curds and whey;
There came a great spider
That sat down beside her,
And frightened Miss Muffet away.

XIII

There was a crooked man, and he
went a crooked mile
He found a crooked sixpence
against a crooked stile:
He bought a crooked cat, which
caught a crooked mouse,
And they all lived together in a
little crooked house.

XIV

Little Boy Blue, come blow your
horn,
The sheep's in the meadow, the
cow's in the corn;

But where is the boy that looks
after the sheep?
He's under a hay-cock, fast asleep.
Will you awake him? No, not I;
For if I do, he'll be sure to cry.

XV

There was man of our town,
And he was wondrous wise,
He jumped into a bramble bush,
And scratched out both his eyes:

But when he saw his eyes were out.
With all his might and main,
He jumped into another bush,
And scratched 'em in again.

XVI

Three wise men of Gotham
Went to sea in a bowl;
If the bowl had been stronger,
My song had been longer.

XVII

Pussy-cat, pussy-cat, where have
you been?
I've been to London to look at the
Queen.
Pussy-cat, pussy-cat, what did you
there?
I frightened a little mouse under
the chair.

XVIII

Baa, baa, black sheep, have you any
wool?
Yes, sir; yes, sir, three bags full.
One for my master, one for my
dame,
And one for the little boy that lives
in the lane.

XIX

OLD King Cole was a merry old
soul,
And a merry old soul was he;
He called for his pipe, and he
called for his bowl,
And he called for his fiddlers three.
Every fiddler, he had a fiddle, and
a very fine fiddle had he;
Twee tweedle dee, tweedle dee,
went the fiddlers.
Oh, there's none so rare, as can
compare
With King Cole and his fiddlers
three!

XX

RIDE a cock-horse to Banbury
Cross,
To see a fine lady ride on a white
horse,
Rings on her fingers, and bells on
her toes,
She shall have music wherever she
goes.

XXI

PETER PIPER picked a peck of
pickled peppers;
A peck of pickled peppers Peter
Piper picked;
If Peter Piper picked a peck of
pickled peppers,
Where's the peck of pickled
peppers Peter Piper picked?

XXII

JACK SPRAT could eat no fat,
His wife could eat no lean,
And so, betwixt them both, you see,
They licked the platter clean.

XXIII

ROCK-A-BYE, baby, thy cradle is
green;
Father's a nobleman, mother's a
queen;
And Betty's a lady, and wears a
gold ring;
And Johnny's a drummer, and
drums for the King.

Hush-a-bye, baby, on the tree-top,
When the wind blows the cradle
will rock;
When the bough breaks, the cradle
will fall,
Down will come baby, bough,
cradle, and all.

XXIV

To market, to market, to buy a fat
pig,
Home again, home again, jiggety-
jig;
To market, to market, to buy a fat
hog,
Home again, home again, jiggety-
jog;
To market, to market, to buy a
plum bun,
Home again, home again, market is
done.

MOTHER GOOSE

WARNING TO CHILDREN

Children, if you dare to think
Of the greatness, rareness,
    muchness,
Fewness of this precious only
Endless world in which you say
You live, you think of things like
    this:
Blocks of slate enclosing dappled
Red and green, enclosing tawny
Yellow nets, enclosing white
And black acres of dominoes,
Where a neat brown paper parcel
Tempts you to untie the string.
In the parcel a small island,
On the island a large tree,
On the tree a husky fruit.
Strip the husk and cut the rind off:
In the center you will see
Blocks of slate enclosed by
    dappled
Red and green, enclosed by tawny
Yellow nets, enclosed by white

And black acres of dominoes,
Where the same brown paper
    parcel—
Children, leave the string untied!
For who dares undo the parcel
Finds himself at once inside it,
On the island, in the fruit,
Blocks of slate about his head,
Finds himself enclosed by dappled
Green and red, enclosed by yellow
Tawny nets, enclosed by black
And white acres of dominoes
But the same brown paper parcel
Still untied upon his knee.
And, if he then should dare to
    think
Of the fewness, muchness,
    rareness,
Greatness of this endless only
Precious world in which he says
He lives—he then unties the
    string.

ROBERT GRAVES

BOOK XVI

CHRISTMAS AND THE NEW YEAR

PEACE ON EARTH

It came upon the midnight clear,
　That glorious song of old,
From angels bending near the earth
　To touch their harps of gold:
"Peace on the earth, good-will to
　　men,
　From heaven's all-gracious King!"
The world in solemn stillness lay
　To hear the angels sing.

Still through the cloven skies they
　　come,
　With peaceful wings unfurled;
And still their heavenly music floats
　O'er all the weary world:
Above its sad and lowly plains
　They bend on hovering wing,
And ever o'er its Babel-sounds
　The blessed angels sing.

Yet with the woes of sin and strife
　The world has suffered long;
Beneath the angels' strain have
　　rolled
　Two thousand years of wrong;
And man, at war with man, hears
　　not
　The love-song which they bring:
O hush the noise, ye men of strife,
　And hear the angels sing!

For lo, the days are hastening on,
　By prophet-bards foretold,
When with the ever-circling years
　Comes round the age of gold,
When Peace shall over all the earth
　Its ancient splendors fling,
And the whole world give back the song
　Which now the angels sing!

EDMUND H. SEARS

JINGLE BELLS

Dashing thro' the snow in a one-horse open sleigh,
O'er the fields we go, laughing all the way;
Bells on bob-tail ring, making spirits bright;
What fun it is to ride and sing a sleighing song tonight!

Chorus:
　Jingle bells! Jingle bells! Jingle all the way!
　Oh! what fun it is to ride in a one-horse open sleigh!

A day or two ago I thought I'd take a ride,
And soon Miss Fanny Bright was seated by my side;
The horse was lean and lank, misfortunes seemed his lot,
He got into a drifted bank, and we, got upsot. (*Chorus.*)

Now the ground is white, go it while you're young,
Take the girls tonight, and sing this sleighing song;
Just get a bob-tailed nag, two-forty for his speed,
Then hitch him to an open sleigh, and crack! you'll take the lead.

(Chorus.)

J. Pierpont

A VISIT FROM ST. NICHOLAS

'Twas the night before Christmas, when all through the house
Not a creature was stirring, not even a mouse;
The stockings were hung by the chimney with care,
In hopes that St. Nicholas soon would be there;
The children were nestled all snug in their beds,
While visions of sugar-plums danced in their heads;
And mamma in her kerchief, and I in my cap,
Had just settled our brains for a long winter's nap,—
When out on the lawn there arose such a clatter,
I sprang from my bed to see what was the matter.
Away to the window I flew like a flash,
Tore open the shutters and threw up the sash.
The moon on the breast of the new-fallen snow
Gave a lustre of midday to objects below;
When, what to my wondering eyes should appear,
But a miniature sleigh and eight tiny reindeer,
With a little old driver, so lively and quick
I knew in a moment it must be St. Nick.

More rapid than eagles his coursers they came,
And he whistled and shouted, and called them by name:
"Now, Dasher! now, Dancer! now, Prancer and Vixen!
On, Comet! on, Cupid! on, Donder and Blitzen!
To the top of the porch, to the top of the wall!
Now dash away, dash away, dash away all!"
As dry leaves that before the wild hurricane fly,
When they meet with an obstacle, mount to the sky,
So up to the house-top the coursers they flew,
With the sleigh full of toys,—and St. Nicholas too.
And then in a twinkling I heard on the roof
The prancing and pawing of each little hoof.
As I drew in my head, and was turning around,
Down the chimney St. Nicholas came with a bound.
He was dressed all in fur from his head to his foot,
And his clothes were all tarnished with ashes and soot;
A bundle of toys he had flung on his back,
And he looked like a peddler just opening his pack.
His eyes how they twinkled! his dimples how merry!
His cheeks were like roses, his nose like a cherry;
His droll little mouth was drawn up like a bow,
And the beard on his chin was as white as the snow.
The stump of a pipe he held tight in his teeth,
And the smoke it encircled his head like a wreath.
He had a broad face and a little round belly
That shook, when he laughed, like a bowl full of jelly.
He was chubby and plump,—a right jolly old elf,
And I laughed, when I saw him, in spite of myself.
A wink of his eye and a twist of his head
Soon gave me to know I had nothing to dread.
He spoke not a word, but went straight to his work,
And filled all the stockings; then turned with a jerk,
And laying his finger aside of his nose,
And giving a nod, up the chimney he rose.
He sprang to his sleigh, to his team gave a whistle,
And away they all flew like the down of a thistle;
But I heard him exclaim, ere he drove out of sight,
"Happy Christmas to all, and to all a good-night!"

CLEMENT C. MOORE

JEST 'FORE CHRISTMAS

Father calls me William, sister calls me Will,
Mother calls me Willie, but the fellers call me Bill!
Mighty glad I ain't a girl—ruther be a boy,
Without them sashes, curls, an' things that's worn by Fauntleroy!
Love to chawnk green apples an' go swimmin' in the lake—
Hate to take the castor-ile they give for belly-ache!
'Most all the time, the whole year round, there ain't no flies on me,
But just 'fore Christmas I'm as good as I kin be!

Got a yeller dog named Sport, sick him on the cat;
First thing she knows she doesn't know where she is at!
Got a clipper sled, an' when us kids goes out to slide,
'Long comes the grocery cart, an' we all hook a ride!
But sometimes when the grocery man is worrited an' cross,
He reaches at us with his whip, an' larrups up his hoss,
An' then I laff and holler, "Oh, ye never teched *me!*"
But just 'fore Christmas I'm as good as I kin be!

Gran'ma says she hopes that when I git to be a man,
I'll be a missionarer like her oldest brother, Dan,
As was et up by the cannibuls that lives in Ceylon's Isle,
Where every prospeck pleases, an' only man is vile!
But gran'ma she has never been to see a Wild West show,
Nor read the Life of Daniel Boone, or else I guess she'd know
That Buff'lo Bill an' cowboys is good enough for me!
Excep' jest 'fore Christmas when I'm as good as I kin be!

And then old Sport he hangs around, so solemn-like an' still
His eyes they keep a-sayin': "What's the matter, little Bill?"
The old cat sneaks down off her perch an' wonders what's become
Of them two enemies of hern that used to make things hum!

But I am so perlite an' tend so earnestly to biz,
That mother says to father: "How improved our Willie is!"
But father, havin' been a boy hisself, suspicions me
When, jest 'fore Christmas I'm as good as I kin be!

For Christmas, with its lots an' lots of candies, cakes, an' toys,
Was made, they say, for proper kids an' not for naughty boys;
So wash yer face an' bresh yer hair, an' mind yer p's an' q's,
An' don't bust out yer pantaloons, an' don't wear out yer shoes;
Say "Yessum" to the ladies, and "Yessur" to the men,
An' when they's company, don't pass yer plate for pie again;
But, thinkin' of the things yer'd like to see upon that tree,
Jest 'fore Christmas be as good as yer kin be!

EUGENE FIELD

O COME ALL YE FAITHFUL

O come, all ye faithful, joyful and triumphant;
O come ye, O come ye to Bethlehem.
Come and behold Him, born the King of angels;
O come, let us adore Him, O come, let us adore Him,
O come, let us adore Him, Christ the Lord.

Sing, choirs of angels, sing in exultation,
Sing, all ye citizens of heav'n above:
Glory to God, in the highest:
        O come, etc.

Yea, Lord, we greet Thee, born this happy morning,
Jesus, to Thee be glory giv'n;
Word of the Father, now in flesh appearing:
        O come, etc.

In Latin
Adeste fideles, laeti triumphantes;
Venite, venite in Bethlehem;
Natum videte, Regem angelorum;
Venite adoremus, Venite adoremus,
Venite adoremus, Dominum.

ANONYMOUS

CHRISTMAS BELLS

I heard the bells on Christmas
    Day
Their old, familiar carols play,
    And wild and sweet
    The words repeat
Of peace on earth, good-will to men!

And thought how, as the day had
    come,
The belfries of all Christendom
    Had rolled along
    The unbroken song
Of peace on earth, good-will to men!

Till, ringing, singing on its way,
The world revolved from night
    to day,
    A voice, a chime,
    A chant sublime
Of peace on earth, good-will to men!

Then from each black, accursed
    mouth
The cannon thundered in the South,

And with the sound
    The carols drowned
Of peace on earth, good-will to men!

It was as if an earthquake rent
The hearth-stones of a continent,
    And made forlorn
    The households born
Of peace on earth, good-will to men!

And in despair I bowed my head;
"There is no peace on earth," I said,
    "For hate is strong,
    And mocks the song
Of peace on earth, good-will to men!"

Then pealed the bells more loud
    and deep:
"God is not dead, nor doth He
    sleep!
    The Wrong shall fail,
    The Right prevail,
With peace on earth, good-will to men!"

HENRY WADSWORTH LONGFELLOW

SILENT NIGHT

Silent Night! Holy Night!
All is calm, all is bright.
Round yon virgin mother and
    child!
Holy infant so tender and mild,
Sleep in heavenly peace, sleep in
    heavenly peace.

Silent Night! Holy Night!
Shepherds quake at the sight!
Glories stream from heaven afar,
Heav'nly hosts sing Alleluia,
Christ, the Saviour, is born!
    Christ, the Saviour, is born!

JOSEPH MOHR

GOD REST YOU MERRY, GENTLEMEN

God rest you merry, gentlemen,
  Let nothing you dismay,
For Jesus Christ, our Saviour,
  Was born upon this day,
To save us all from Satan's power
  When we were gone astray.
      O tidings of comfort and joy!
      For Jesus Christ, our Saviour,
      Was born on Christmas Day.

In Bethlehem, in Jewry,
  This blessèd babe was born,
And laid within a manger,
  Upon this blessèd morn;
The which His mother, Mary,
  Nothing did take in scorn.

From God our Heavenly Father,
  A blessèd angel came;
And unto certain shepherds
  Brought tidings of the same:
How that in Bethlehem was born
  The Son of God by name.

"Fear not," then said the angel,
  "Let nothing you affright,
This day is born a Saviour
  Of virtue, power, and might,

So frequently to vanquish all
  The friends of Satan quite."

The shepherds at these tidings
  Rejoicèd much in mind,
And left their flock a-feeding
  In tempest, storm, and wind,
And went to Bethlehem
    straightway,
  This blessèd babe to find.

But when to Bethlehem they came,
  Whereat this infant lay,
They found Him in a manger,
  Where oxen feed on hay,
His mother Mary kneeling,
  Unto the Lord did pray.

Now to the Lord sing praises,
  All you within this place,
And with true love and
    brotherhood
  Each other now embrace;
This holy tide of Christmas
  All others doth deface.
      O tidings of comfort and joy!
      For Jesus Christ, our Saviour,
      Was born on Christmas Day.

ANONYMOUS

A CHRISTMAS CAROL

The Christ-child lay on Mary's lap,
  His hair was like a light.
(O weary, weary were the world,
  But here is all aright.)

The Christ-child lay on Mary's breast,
  His hair was like a star.
(O stern and cunning are the kings,
  But here the true hearts are.)

The Christ-child lay on Mary's heart,
  His hair was like a fire.
(O weary, weary is the world,
  But here the world's desire.)

The Christ-child stood at Mary's knee,
  His hair was like a crown,
And all the flowers looked up at Him,
And all the stars looked down.

G. K. CHESTERTON

CHRISTMAS EVERYWHERE

Everywhere, everywhere, Christmas tonight!
Christmas in lands of the fir-tree and pine,
Christmas in lands of the palm-tree and vine,
Christmas where snow peaks stand solemn and white,
Christmas where cornfields stand sunny and bright.
Christmas where children are hopeful and gay,
Christmas where old men are patient and gray,
Christmas where peace, like a dove in his flight,
Broods o'er brave men in the thick of the fight;
Everywhere, everywhere, Christmas tonight!
For the Christ-child who comes is the Master of all;
No palace too great, no cottage too small.

PHILLIPS BROOKS

O LITTLE TOWN OF BETHLEHEM

O little town of Bethlehem,
How still we see thee lie!
Above thy deep and dreamless sleep
The silent stars go by:
Yet in thy dark streets shineth
The everlasting Light;
The hopes and fears of all the years
Are met in thee tonight.

For Christ is born of Mary;
And gathered all above,
While mortals sleep, the angels
   keep
Their watch of wondering love.
O morning stars together
Proclaim thy holy birth;
And praises sing to God the King,
And peace to men on earth.

How silently, how silently,
The wondrous Gift is given!
So God imparts to human hearts
The blessing of His heaven.
No ear may hear His coming,
But in this world of sin,
Where meek souls will receive
   Him still,
The dear Christ enters in.

O holy Child of Bethlehem,
Descend to us, we pray;
Cast out our sins, and enter in,
Be born in us today.
We hear the Christmas angels
The great glad tidings tell;
O come to us, abide with us,
Our Lord Emmanuel.

PHILLIPS BROOKS

THE TWELVE DAYS OF CHRISTMAS

The first day of Christmas,
My true love sent to me
A partridge in a pear tree.

The second day of Christmas,
My true love sent to me
Two turtle doves, and
A partridge in a pear tree.

The third day of Christmas,
My true love sent to me
Three French hens,
Two turtle doves, and
A partridge in a pear tree.

The fourth day of Christmas,
My true love sent to me
Four colly birds,
Three French hens,
Two turtle doves, and
A partridge in a pear tree.

The fifth day of Christmas,
My true love sent to me
Five gold rings,
Four colly birds,
Three French hens,
Two turtle doves, and
A partridge in a pear tree.

The sixth day of Christmas,
My true love sent to me
Six geese a-laying,
Five gold rings,
Four colly birds,
Three French hens,
Two turtle doves, and
A partridge in a pear tree.

The seventh day of Christmas,
My true love sent to me
Seven swans a-swimming,
Six geese a-laying,
Five gold rings,
Four colly birds,
Three French hens,
Two turtle doves, and
A partridge in a pear tree.

The eighth day of Christmas,
My true love sent to me
Eight maids a-milking,
Seven swans a-swimming,
Six geese a-laying,
Five gold rings,
Four colly birds,
Three French hens,
Two turtle doves, and
A partridge in a pear tree.

The ninth day of Christmas,
My true love sent to me
Nine drummers drumming,
Eight maids a-milking,
Seven swans a-swimming,
Six geese a-laying,
Five gold rings,
Four colly birds,
Three French hens,
Two turtle doves, and
A partridge in a pear tree.

The tenth day of Christmas,
My true love sent to me
Ten pipers piping,
Nine drummers drumming,
Eight maids a-milking,
Seven swans a-swimming,
Six geese a-laying,
Five gold rings,
Four colly birds,
Three French hens,
Two turtle doves, and
A partridge in a pear tree.

The eleventh day of Christmas,
My true love sent to me
Eleven ladies dancing,
Ten pipers piping,
Nine drummers drumming,
Eight maids a-milking,
Seven swans a-swimming,
Six geese a-laying,
Five gold rings,
Four colly birds,
Three French hens,
Two turtle doves, and
A partridge in a pear tree.

The twelfth day of Christmas,
My true love sent to me
Twelve lords a-leaping,
Eleven ladies dancing,
Ten pipers piping,
Nine drummers drumming,
Eight maids a-milking,
Seven swans a-swimming,
Six geese a-laying,
Five gold rings,
Four colly birds,
Three French hens,
Two turtle doves, and
A partridge in a pear tree.

ANONYMOUS

THE END OF THE PLAY

The play is done; the curtain
    drops,
  Slow falling to the prompter's
    bell:
A moment yet the actor stops,
  And looks around, to say farewell.
It is an irksome word and task;
  And when he's laughed and
    said his say,
He shows, as he removes the mask,
  A face that's anything but gay.

One word, ere yet the evening
    ends,
  Let's close it with a parting
    rhyme,
And pledge a hand to all young
    friends,
  As fits the merry Christmas
    time.
On life's wide scene you, too,
    have parts,
  That Fate ere long shall bid
    you play;
Good night! with honest gentle
    hearts
  A kindly greeting go alway!

Good night!—I'd say, the griefs,
    the joys,
  Just hinted in this mimic page,
The triumphs and defeats of boys,
  Are but repeated in our age.

I'd say, your woes were not less
    keen,
  Your hopes more vain than
    those of men;
Your pangs or pleasures of fifteen
  At forty-five played o'er again.

I'd say, we suffer and we strive,
  Not less nor more as men than
    boys;
With grizzled beards at forty-five,
  As erst at twelve in corduroys.
And if, in time of sacred youth,
  We learned at home to love
    and pray,
Pray Heaven that early Love and
    Truth
  May never wholly pass away.

And in the world, as in the
    school,
  I'd say, how fate may change
    and shift;
The prize be sometimes with the
    fool,
  The race not always to the
    swift.
The strong may yield, the good
    may fall,
  The great man be a vulgar
    clown,
The knave be lifted over all,
  The kind cast pitilessly down.

Who knows the inscrutable design?
　Blessed be He who took and gave!
Why should your mother, Charles,
　　not mine,
　Be weeping at her darling's grave?
We bow to Heaven that will'd it so,
　That darkly rules the fate of all,
That sends the respite or the
　　blow,
　That's free to give, or to recall.

This crowns his feast with wine
　　and wit:
　Who brought him to that mirth
　　and state?
His betters, see, below him sit,
　Or hunger hopeless at the gate.
Who bade the mud from Dives'
　　wheel
　To spurn the rags of Lazarus?
Come, brother, in that dust we'll
　　kneel,
　Confessing Heaven that ruled it
　　thus.

So each shall mourn, in life's
　　advance,
　Dear hopes, dear friends,
　　untimely killed;
Shall grieve for many a forfeit
　　chance,
　And longing passion unfulfilled.
Amen! whatever fate be sent,
　Pray God the heart may kindly
　　glow,
Although the head with cares be
　　bent,
　And whitened with the winter
　　snow.

Come wealth or want, come good
　　or ill,
　Let young and old accept their
　　part,
And bow before the Awful Will,
　And bear it with an honest
　　heart,
Who misses or who wins the prize,
　Go, lose or conquer as you can;
But if you fail, or if you rise,
　Be each, pray God, a gentleman.

A gentleman, or old or young!
　(Bear kindly with my humble
　　lays;)
The sacred chorus first was sung
　Upon the first of Christmas
　　days:
The shepherds heard it
　　overhead—
　The joyful angels raised it
　　then:
Glory to Heaven on high, it said,
　And peace on earth to gentle
　　men.

My song, save this, is little worth;
　I lay the weary pen aside,
And wish you health, and love,
　　and mirth,
　As fits the solemn
　　Christmas-tide.
As fits the holy Christmas birth,
　Be this, good friends, our carol
　　still—
Be peace on earth, be peace on
　　earth,
　To men of gentle will.

WILLIAM MAKEPEACE THACKERAY

RING OUT, WILD BELLS

Ring out, wild bells, to the wild
  sky,
  The flying cloud, the frosty
    light:
  The year is dying in the night;
Ring out, wild bells, and let him
    die.

Ring out the old, ring in the new,
  Ring, happy bells, across the
    snow:
  The year is going, let him go;
Ring out the false, ring in the
    true.

Ring out the grief that saps the
    mind,
  For those that here we see no
    more;
  Ring out the feud of rich and
    poor,
Ring in redress to all mankind.

Ring out a slowly dying cause,
  And ancient forms of party
    strife;
  Ring in the nobler modes of
    life,
With sweeter manners, purer laws.

Ring out the want, the care, the
    sin,
  The faithless coldness of the
    times;
  Ring out, ring out my
    mournful rhymes,
But ring the fuller minstrel in.

Ring out false pride in place and
    blood,
  The civic slander and the spite;
  Ring in the love of truth and
    right,
Ring in the common love of good.

Ring out old shapes of foul
    disease,
  Ring out the narrowing lust of
    gold;
  Ring out the thousand wars of
    old,
Ring in the thousand years of peace.

Ring in the valiant man and free,
  The larger heart, the kindlier
    hand;
  Ring out the darkness of the
    land,
Ring in the Christ that is to be.

ALFRED, LORD TENNYSON

INDEX OF AUTHORS

INDEX OF FIRST LINES

A barefoot boy, I mark him at his play, 137
A bit of color against the blue, 288
A bunch of the boys were whooping it up in the Malamute saloon, 382
"A cold coming we had of it, 478
A decrepit old gasman, named Peter, 220
A diller, a dollar, 505
A Friend of mine was married to a scold, 211
A handsome young airman lay dying, 217
A horse and a flea and three blind mice, 499
A little learning is a dang'rous thing, 99
A man of words and not of deeds, 274
A narrow fellow in the grass, 233
A promise made, 215
A raven sat upon a tree, 201
A scientist living at Staines, 218
A thing of beauty is a joy for ever, 264
A village maid was leaving home, with tears her eyes were wet, 215
A wise old owl sat on an oak, 213
Abide with me: fast falls the eventide, 443
Abou Ben Adhem (may his tribe increase), 6
About suffering they were never wrong, 64
Ae fond kiss, and then we sever, 122
Afoot and light-hearted I take to the open road, 249
Ah, what avails the sceptred race, 115
All I could see from where I stood, 95
"All quiet along the Potomac," they say, 187
All the world's a stage, 151
All are architects of Fate, 8
And what is so rare as a day in June, 238
Apostles of the hidden sun, 466
As a beauty, I'm not a great star, 222
As a rule, man is a fool, 220
As I walked out in the streets of Laredo, 337
As I was a-gwine down the road, 439
As I was going up the stair, 217
Ask me no more where Jove bestows, 107
Awake, my soul, and with the sun, 455
Ay, tear her tattered ensign down, 189

Baa, baa, black sheep, have you any wool, 507
Backward, turn backward, O Time in your flight, 171
Bang Street—, 218
Batter my heart, three personal God; for you, 468
Be strong, 23
Be with me, Beauty, for the fire is dying, 149
Before the beginning of the years, 82
Behind him lay the gray Azores, 298
Believe me, if all those endearing young charms, 103
Better never trouble, Trouble, 206
Better than grandeur, better than Gold, 9
Between the dark and the daylight, 484
Billy, in one of his nice new sashes, 214
Blessings on the hand of women, 135
Blow, blow, thou winter wind, 257
Bowed by the weight of centuries he leans, 269
Breathes there the man with soul so dead, 286
Busy, curious, thirsty fly, 153
By the rude bridge that arched the flood, 188
Candy is dandy, 209
Carry me back to old Virginny, 444
Charlie Chaplin went to France, 499
Children, if you dare to think, 508
Children, you are very little, 494
Cold in the earth—and the deep snow piled above thee, 457
Come live with me and be my love, 122
Comrades, leave me here a little, while as yet 'tis early morn, 56
Dark hills at evening in the west, 196
Darling, I am growing old, 427
Dashing thro' the snow in a one-horse open sleigh, 510
Death be not proud, though some have called thee, 36
Do all the good you can, 29
Do not go gentle into that good night, 40
"Don't care" is no friend of mine, 16
Don't you remember sweet Alice, Ben Bolt, 342
Down in the valley, 435
Drink to me only with thine eyes, 424

INDEX OF TITLES